CONFEDERATE RAGE, YANKEE WRATH

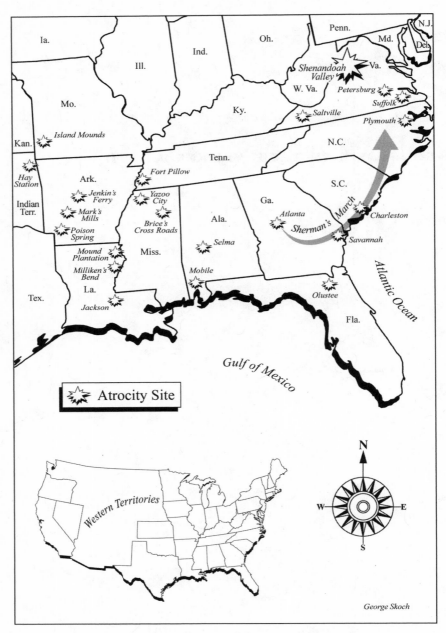

Atrocity sites shown here represent places east and west where Confederates and Yankees executed captured or defeated enemies.

Confederate Rage, Yankee Wrath

NO QUARTER IN THE CIVIL WAR

GEORGE S. BURKHARDT

Southern Illinois University Press
Carbondale

10 09 08 07   4 3 2 1

Library of Congress Cataloging-in-Publication Data
Burkhardt, George S., 1927–
  Confederate rage, Yankee wrath : no quarter in the
Civil War / George S. Burkhardt.
      p. cm.
  Includes bibliographical references and index.
  ISBN-13: 978-0-8093-2743-0 (cloth : alk. paper)
  ISBN-10: 0-8093-2743-0 (cloth : alk. paper)
  1. United States—History—Civil War, 1861–1865—
Atrocities. 2. Murder—United States—History—
19th century. 3. Murder—Confederate States
of America—History. 4. United States—Race
relations—History—19th century. 5. United
States—History—Civil War, 1861–1865—Prisoners
and prisons. 6. United States—History—Civil War,
1861–1865—Campaigns. I. Title.

E468.9.B89 2007
973.7—dc22   2006025663

Printed on recycled paper. ♻

The paper used in this publication meets the minimum requirements of American National Standard
for Information Sciences—Permanence of Paper for
Printed Library Materials, ANSI z39.48-1992. ♾

In memory of
   my sister, Rozalia, always so supportive
and
   for Qiao Hua, Christine, and Cynthia

CONTENTS

ILLUSTRATIONS

Plates

ACKNOWLEDGMENTS

Without the aid of many strangers, I could not have gathered the material for this work. A few became personally known—mainly, the wonderful interlibrary loan workers at California State University, Long Beach, and the Long Beach Public Library. For years, they answered endless requests for difficult-to-find books. Without their assistance, my research would have faltered.

Staffers at the major government repositories were unfailingly helpful. Special thanks are due Richard J. Sommers, Louise A. Arnold-Friend, John A. Slonaker, and Michael J. Winey at the United States Military History Institute, and DeAnne Blanton, Michael P. Musick, and Michael F. Knight at the National Archives. David Wigdor and James H. Hutson always helped at the Library of Congress, while National Park Service staffers David Barna and Wayne McLaughlin settled questions about their agency's count of black soldiers. Most recently, Park Ranger Tracy Chernault, Petersburg National Battlefield, quickly responded to requests for help. At the Naval Historical Center, H. A. Vadnais answered questions about era warships, and Claudie L. Pennington found photographs at the Naval Audiovisual Center. U.S. Naval Observatory experts provided twilight, sunrise, and sunset times for various dates and places during the Civil War years.

Many individuals lent their expertise, including Johanna Herring, Wabash College archivist; Albert Castel, Civil War historian; and Robert C. Mainfort Jr., Tennessee State archaeologist, and Dick Baumbach, Tennessee Department of Correction, who described Fort Pillow's current usage. John H. Thweatt, Tennessee State Library and Archives, guided me to letters and diaries concerning Fort Pillow. Bob Knecht, Kansas State Historical Society, steered me to a paper by Ethan Earle on Poison Spring, held by the New England Historic Genealogical Society. Vonnie

Shelton, McCracken County Public Library, Paducah, Kentucky, found references to smallpox during Forrest's raid, Ed Friedlander, M.D., "The Pathology Guy," explained North Carolina's clay eaters, and Professor Ingrid Wollank, Long Beach Community College, graciously translated letters in difficult nineteenth-century German script. Dave Zullo, Olde Soldier Books, Gaithersburg, Maryland, and William Scott Proudfoot, a college systems librarian in Saratoga, California, generously allowed quotes from letters in their possession.

Curators at university libraries invariably proved very helpful. Among them were Special Collections staffers at the Universities of Florida, Michigan, and North Carolina as well as Duke, Emory, and Tulane universities. At the University of Texas at Austin, Ralph L. Elder particularly assisted with the dating of an important letter.

Manuscript curators at museums and public libraries also aided my research, including John H. Rhodehamel, Huntington Library; Giuseppe Bisaccia, Boston Public Library curator; Jim Baggett, Birmingham Public Library; Patricia M. LaPointe, Memphis–Shelby County Public Library; and Charles E. Thompson, Detroit Public Library. My thanks also to Edie Jeter of the Valentine Museum, Cathy Carlson at the Museum of the Confederacy, both in Richmond, Virginia, and Laurie Risch of the Behringer-Crawford Museum in Covington, Kentucky. Mark Cave, the Historic New Orleans Collection, was most kind, as were staff at the Douglas County Library, Roseburg, Oregon. New York City librarians went out of their way to help.

Various state libraries, commissions, and archives yielded valuable documents. Historical societies, large and small, hold a treasure trove of documents from the Civil War. In no particular order, many thanks go to New Hampshire Historical Society's Elizabeth Hamlin-Morin, Atlanta's Anne C. Price, Florida's Marilyn Potts, Virginia's Robert A. McInness, and Rhode Island's Marta Martinez. Also very obliging were Barney Bloom at the Vermont Historical Society, Gary J. Arnold and John E. Haas at Ohio's, and Cory Seeman at Chicago's. Paul Brockman of the Indiana Historical Society helped considerably, as did Stephen T. Seames of Maine's historical society and Minnesota's Steve Nielsen and Hampton Smith.

Most crucial was the guidance, counsel, and wise encouragement offered by Sylvia Frank Rodrigue, executive editor, Southern Illinois University Press. Based in Baton Rouge, Louisiana, she not only weathered hurricanes but also my many queries and missteps.

For support and encouragement over the years, I am grateful to my wife, Qiao Hua; my daughter, Cynthia Dewey; and old friends Hendrik de Kanter, Lydia Lautenbach, and Patrick Loughran. If I have overlooked any who helped during the years, I apologize for the oversight.

Introduction

DURING THE CIVIL WAR'S last two years, Confederate soldiers massacred black and white Federals in every theater of the conflict. Historians have known about most such incidents but treated them as discrete and random affairs. But they were not distinct, unconnected events. Instead, they formed a pervasive pattern and stemmed from Southerners' common desire to defend and protect their heritage and society.

Southern soldiers first killed wounded, surrendered, or trapped black Federals as a matter of course, although that practice never became the Confederacy's declared official policy. However, it became a de facto policy by default because it was condoned, never punished, and always denied. When Confederates began murdering certain classes of white Federal soldiers in mid-1864, this also enjoyed Richmond's tacit approval, and high-ranking officers either admitted ordering such atrocities or did nothing to stop them.

Mark Grimsley asserts in his *Hard Hand of War* that Lincoln's emancipation edict was the touchstone of that hard war, the evolving effort to turn the North's destructive might against civilian targets that sustained the Confederate war effort. But emancipation and Lincoln's concurrent enlistment of black soldiers also created the conditions that prompted Confederate atrocities against black civilians and soldiers, and the resulting hard war set the stage for Southerners to refuse quarter or mercy to white Federal troops.[1]

Confederates resorted to such ruthless conduct because they perceived the two measures as a dire threat to their way of life, to home and hearth, kith and kin, honor and manhood. Southerners of every station firmly believed that slave emancipation and a black soldiery directly menaced their society as a whole and their individual status within that society. To them, the Emancipation Proclamation aimed to incite bloody slave revolts, a fearsome specter of murder, rape, and mindless destruction by rampaging black savages while armed and uniformed blacks challenged the very foundations of their slave economy and social structure. When the North inaugurated full-fledged hard war in 1864, making civilian goods and property targets for confiscation or destruction, that doubled the threat. Many Southern soldiers knew by then that they fought a losing fight and that made them desperate. So they turned to executing white soldiers who carried out certain hard war policies.

Meanwhile, in response to Confederates' merciless ways, black Federal soldiers retaliated in kind, committing atrocities of their own. In reprisal, they slew defenseless prisoners or refused quarter to those who surrendered. However, despite their best efforts to achieve parity, they lagged far behind the much more proficient enemy.

Lincoln and his generals took no concrete action to stop the slaughter of their black soldiers. As the saying goes, they talked a good fight—but did nothing. When Frederick Douglass, the former slave and prominent black leader, urged Lincoln to adopt an effective reprisal policy for black soldiers, the president replied, "Once begun, I do not know where such a measure would stop." He knew exactly where it would end, and that is why he declined to protect his black troops. If he ordered white Southerners executed for murdering black soldiers, Confederates would respond, not just by executing blacks but also by shooting whites. Lincoln knew the people would never stand for the sacrifice of whites for blacks when a virulent racial prejudice reigned in the North. Keeping the nation whole and winning the war was his enduring aim, and he could not afford to jeopardize that goal by alienating voters and losing support for the war. So, nonintervention became the Federal government's de facto policy on atrocities against black soldiers.[2]

However, when Confederates murdered white Federals, no such constraints applied. Early on, individual Federal commanders had usually acted swiftly and decisively in seeking retribution. Often, their retaliation far exceeded an eye-for-eye riposte. They not only hung or shot likely suspects randomly rounded up but also burned houses and villages in the neighborhood and destroyed or seized crops, livestock, farm implements, and every slave or contraband in the area. And when Confederates began executing some white soldiers in 1864, high Federal leaders, including Stanton, Sheridan, and Sherman, ordered life-for-life retaliation.[3]

As noted, many Civil War historians have long known about some atrocities. In the 1930s and 1940s, assessments varied. J. G. Randall, in his *The Civil War and Reconstruction*, wrote that "hundreds of Negroes were slain" at Fort Pillow, the war's most infamous atrocity. Still, he thought Confederate denials merited consideration and, in any event, believed that Southern no-quarter vows were merely threats. Noted historian Bell Irvin Wiley decided they were more than threats but did not delve into it, while Southern writer John L. Jordan in a 1947 article vehemently rejected any massacre at Fort Pillow and called the very idea an insult to the Southern Confederacy.[4]

By the 1950s and 1960s, historians realized that Fort Pillow was not the war's only such atrocity. Benjamin Quarles, in his *The Negro in the Civil War*, wrote, "Doubtless, too, there were other instances in which Negro troops were slain." Dudley T. Cornish, who wrote a benchmark work about black Federal soldiers in 1956, listed other atrocity sites besides Fort Pillow. In 1965 and 1967, respected historian James M. McPherson acknowledged that both black and white Federals were murdered at Fort Pillow but added that "for the most part the South did *not* officially execute white officers or black soldiers" (emphasis in original). The key word here is *officially*. In his 1967 work, *From Slavery to Freedom*, John Hope Franklin rather disagreed. He concluded that the high mortality rate for black troops resulted from several causes, including "The no quarter policy with which Confederates fought them."[5]

As the twentieth century closed, a spate of Civil War studies dealt with or devoted some space to the role of black Americans in the conflict.

That was in sharp contrast to the situation at the turn of that century, when black soldiers had disappeared from works by such eminent authors as Ida Tarbell, an early investigative journalist, and Woodrow Wilson, Princeton University professor and the twenty-eighth president. Phillip Shaw Paludan, in his A People's Contest, viewed such incidents as "sporadic atrocities" and erred again when he wrote that after Fort Pillow the North showed an "increased willingness to punish Dixie" for murdering black soldiers. Then Reid Mitchell, in Civil War Soldiers, described the lethal frustration building in Confederates as they struggled in a contest bringing increasing devastation to the South.[6]

During this later period, two studies of black soldiers appeared. In 1990, Joseph T. Glatthaar wrote Forged in Battle, followed in 1998 by Noah A. Trudeau's Like Men of War. Both reported many more incidents than had been noted earlier. Glatthaar decided that atrocities against black troops were "commonplace, as Confederates first hoped to discourage blacks from enlisting and later sought revenge." He also thought the atrocities escalated as Confederates became increasingly frustrated. Trudeau, very thorough in his battle accounts, noted even more atrocities. Yet he concluded, "The actual practice of Confederate forces . . . was considerably less extreme than advocated by the directives spilling out of Richmond."[7]

Glatthaar had joined Dudley T. Cornish in assigning the motive to an effort to deter black enlistments and to demoralize those already in Northern ranks. However, little evidence exists for such relatively subtle thinking by Southern troops. In reality, outrage and fury drove the ordinary soldier, and from the beginning Confederates consistently showed no quarter to black Federals. Glatthaar's "escalation" occurred only as the number of Colored Troops rapidly expanded and they took part in more battles, which therefore gave Confederates even more opportunities to kill. Trudeau is fractionally correct when he argues that Southern soldiers were less extreme than Richmond's directives ordered. They did not hang all white officers caught leading black troops; instead, they killed only a dozen or so after capture, although an unknown number were summarily dispatched on the spot. But Confederate soldiers were markedly more extreme in that they executed hundreds of black soldiers without the slightest pretense of form or legality.[8]

In 2002 and 2004, two excellent black soldier anthologies appeared. John D. Smith edited Black Soldiers in Blue, and Gregory J. W. Urwin edited Black Flag over Dixie. Smith sought to embrace the whole black soldier experience, though several essays touch upon Confederate atrocities; Urwin's collection concentrates upon the slaughter of blacks but mentions the execution of white Federals during Sherman's march to the sea and through the Carolinas, citing yet another work by Joseph T. Glatthaar. As anthologies, neither could easily provide a cohesive view of the Confederate de facto no-quarter policy and practice for black soldiers and, later, some white Federals.[9]

However, in 1988, Randall C. Jimerson noted that pervasive pattern in his *The Private Civil War.* In a chapter titled "Black Soldiers," he offered an analysis of cause and effect that merits review. Former slaves, Jimerson observed, were fighting against their masters, and "Southerners were outraged by presence of black troops in armies invading their sacred soil." Further, he said that Confederates felt it a "humiliation" to have to fight members of a degraded, inferior species; that most Southerners saw the use of black troops as the ultimate betrayal by former slaves, as a Yankee effort to stir servile insurrection; and that it all plucked at a raw nerve in the Southern psyche. Jimerson concluded, "The fury of these responses portended doom for blacks captured in battle."[10]

Some historians disagree, concluding that hatred caused the deadly reaction. Several authors in *Black Flag over Dixie* ascribe the slaughter to "racial hatred." Elsewhere, Reid Mitchell termed it a "virulent hatred," and Noah A. Trudeau said it was "fanatical." Bell Irvin Wiley had it both ways, in the same paragraph, in his *The Life of Johnny Reb.* He wrote, "Antipathy toward ordinary Yankees was deep and pervasive, but it was mild in comparison with the hatred which most Rebs felt for Negroes who wore the blue." Then, two sentences later, Wiley added, "The mere thought of a Negro in uniform was enough to arouse the ire of the average Reb." Probably hatred motivated some Confederates, but for most the emotion was an almost-feral rage. They directed that fierce anger at blacks who defied the taboos and social order and who threatened their manhood. Slaves, it must be kept in mind, were chattels, movable property like livestock, albeit capable of more complex tasks than a horse or mule. They were at best subhuman, otherwise just a lick above an ape. Still, Southerners and slaves often report affection between master and "servant," as whites often termed their thralls. At the same time, violence or its threat maintained slavery. One ex-slave declared, "Sure they would kill a nigger; he's no more'n a wolf." Only in a few postwar memoirs do white Southerners speak of hatred toward black soldiers as an explanation or excuse for wartime conduct.[11]

Conflicting views as well as consensus obtained with other issues. Historians largely agree that most Northerners opposed the Emancipation Proclamation and a black soldiery. Whether civilian or soldier, the goal was to preserve the Union, and slavery's abolition was no part of that aim, except as a weapon to suppress the rebellion. Still, Dudley T. Cornish, in his *The Sable Arm*, and Paludan wrongly argued that the proclamation either transformed the war into an antislavery crusade or made abolition coequal with preserving the Union.[12]

In general, historians also support the idea that a major reason for the eventual acceptance of black troops came from the realization that they would serve admirably as cannon fodder, sparing whites. But in *Embattled Courage*, Gerald F. Linderman argued that white soldiers viewed blacks less as substitute bodies for the meat grinder "than as others who would share their fate." Contemporary letters and diaries overwhelmingly support the first interpretation.[13]

Some dispute the existence of Confederate nationalism, which includes the South's well-defined class society founded on slavery. Recent works have reaffirmed and argued convincingly that Southerners embraced a rising nationalism. Southern letter, diary, and journal writers consistently refer to their country rather than to a state or section. One very original affirmation came from a dispirited Confederate infantryman in late 1864, when he despaired of the "one-horse confederacy." Their unity of purpose and conviction helps explain their lethal anger toward black Federals who they believed betrayed them and their country and then added insolence to injury by fighting against them.[14]

Confederate Vice President Alexander Stephens famously declared that slavery was the "corner-stone" of the new nation. That was true, although at the very end leaders and led were willing to let slavery expire rather than forfeit independence. Archer Jones, in his 1992 work *Civil War Command and Strategy*, wrote, "Language, religion, and history . . . differed little between the sections [North and South]. Slavery had provided the principal distinction." But that distinction had so radically transformed Southern character, culture, social structure, and economy that commonalities had sharply eroded during more than 250 years of slavery. One major difference was the lively culture of violence that flourished in the South. Scholars may argue about the origins and causes of a violent South, but few contest the fact. That penchant, that ready tendency to uninhibited lethal action, made it much easier for Confederates to vent their fury by shooting offending black or white Federals without any hesitation.[15]

Almost no attention has focused on the summary executions of captive white Federals during the war's last year, although the killings stemmed from the same perceived threat to order, society, honor, family, and home that generated the atrocities against black soldiers. Several things may account for this void. Most important, perhaps, was the absence of any large massacres with attendant publicity. The killings were small-scale events, involving individuals or small groups, although the cumulative total numbered in the hundreds. However, these incidents did not go entirely unnoticed at the time or in recent years. In the summer of 1864, for instance, a *New York Times* war correspondent in Virginia's Shenandoah Valley called one such affair a "massacre," and recently, as already noted, historians Joseph T. Glatthaar and Gregory J. W. Urwin mentioned the summary executions that occurred during Sherman's marches. However, these numerous killings were not recognized as a drastic shift in Confederate attitudes and practice or as part of a bloody pattern.[16]

An understanding of this dark part of the Civil War requires a comprehensive study, embracing all aspects and events, to provide cohesion and clarity. Another advantage of such a study is that given the indisputable pattern of atrocities, discrepancies or questions about a particular event diminish in importance if the incident fits solidly into the pattern. Often discrepancies arise because the best testimony comes from those who took part in any event. Still, as any soldier can confirm, the individual's knowledge of the action is often extremely restricted. What one hears or sees, the other does not; even if both see or hear the same thing, each may retain a different impression. This study attempts to pull it all together with analyses of cause and motivation leading to the Confederate no-quarter actions against black and white Federal soldiers.

Many Americans do not want to hear about such things. We view ourselves as fair and square, a people who fight their just conflicts in aboveboard, compassionate fashion while resolutely and bravely marching toward well-deserved victory. We consider the Civil War and World War II as good wars, though we would just as soon not learn that Americans killed helpless prisoners in either conflict. However, Americans understand and accept that the war in the Pacific was a vicious, take-no-prisoners fight because the Japanese initiated that deadly spiral. The Civil War, our first good big war, holds a special place in our minds and hearts. We think of it as a very civil affair, conducted according to all the rules, even though some are now regarded as quaint. For instance, soldiers then thought it wrong to fight on the Sabbath and regarded land mines as unchivalrous "infernal machines."[17]

Both sides burned and pillaged homes and fields, although Confederates never came close to matching Federal arson and plundering. Both committed atrocities, although Confederate war crimes far exceeded those of the Federals by every measure. With the exception of black soldier reprisals, Yankee violations usually resulted as a consequence of individual acts, rather from group disposition. Further, Northern soldiers harbored a mean prejudice against blacks and strongly opposed the Emancipation Proclamation and a black soldiery. Southerners sought independence to preserve their social structure, including a semifeudal way of life and slavery, which they managed with a paternalistic racism and maintained by physical force.

Many wonder how Confederates could so passionately profess a love of freedom when they kept millions of slaves in bondage. Lincoln scoffed, "The *perfect* liberty they sigh for [is] the liberty of making slaves of other people." Therefore, historian James M. McPherson was certainly in good company when he called that a paradox in his *What They Fought For, 1861—1865*. But there is no paradox, no contradiction, hypocrisy, double-talk, or inconsistency about the Southern cry for liberty, nor is there any fanfaronade or theatrics in their endlessly repeated pledges to fight to the death for that liberty. Thousands upon thousands fell or yielded body parts in that cause. Critical here is Lincoln's word *people*. To Southerners, slave owners or not, the African chattels were not people. They were animate property, nothing more.[18]

It is both troubling and difficult to try to comprehend those beliefs. Yet the only way to grasp these long-ago events is to try to understand them in the context of the times, according to the standards and values of those days. It is neither fair nor reasonable to judge events of the 1860s by today's codes and mores. It is also difficult because we filter those times through current experience and culture and even word usage. Even then, a word had different connotations for different people, and, screened through the prism of time, a word may have quite another definition today. For example, when Confederates said they were "perfectly exasperated" by encountering black Federals, that was not to say they were rather annoyed. It meant that they were absolutely enraged.[19]

That exasperation ensnared white Federal soldiers when they began burning and pillaging Southern homes while terrorizing the women, children, and elderly men left behind. Most able-bodied men were gone, serving in the army or already in a soldier's grave. Moving through the South as a prisoner of war, a Federal chaplain noted, "I saw hardly a man that was not a soldier." So there was no one left to protect soldiers' families when Yankee marauders came calling. Furious Confederates then began to give no quarter to those they found torching or looting Southern homes.[20]

While the twin concepts of war crimes and war criminals were not then clearly formulated, Confederates had violated existing rules of war and society by killing wounded, surrendering, and captive Federals. Yet the South refused to admit the wrongs, and a victorious North never prosecuted any Confederate leaders involved in the slaughters. Speculative thoughts subsequently arise about these events. For one thing, it is doubtful that either government had the power to stop the killing, no matter how fierce the Federal retaliation or how stern the Confederate high command's orders to cease and desist. After centuries of slavery, Southerners' attitudes, biases, fears, and other emotions were too deeply embedded for abrupt and radical change. Both governments might have had some success in halting the killing of white Federals, but that, too, is problematic. Confederates were desperate and Federals were determined.

Soldiers of both sides said that the war approached a no-quarter tipping point in the last year. How correct they were is uncertain. It is plain, however, that Confederates more and more often refused quarter to Federals and that the Yankees were ever more willing to retaliate for killings and mutilations. It is also quite clear that reprisals did not work and often only escalated the terrible cycle. For example, prompt and summary executions of guerrillas had no effect on their activity. So while it is ghastly to contemplate, Americans could have descended into the same kind of cruel warfare that characterized the fighting in the Pacific Theater or on the Russian front during World War II.

Less speculative is the question of why so many Confederate soldiers continued to fight when they knew full well that they had lost. As sensible men, they could desert, go home to protect their families or to survive. Thousands did just that; so why did so many stay? Max Hastings, in his *Armageddon: the Battle for Germany, 1944–1945*, implicitly asks that question about German troops who knew defeat loomed. Though the situations were not exactly parallel, duty, discipline, and comrades kept men in the trenches and up front. Then, for many German and Confederate soldiers, there was the atavistic compulsion to stop the barbarians from overrunning their homelands.[21]

Today, we castigate the Japanese for refusing to admit the full extent of their barbaric conduct during World War II, and we praise the Germans for accepting responsibility for their offenses and making reparations. Recognizing American Civil War atrocities will not resurrect the dead, erase racism, eliminate political expediency, or end war crimes. However, fairly and squarely confronting our blemished history will at least set the record straight and generate a more realistic understanding of the conflict, and it may induce a reluctance to repeat shameful actions.

Methodology

This study has relied upon primary sources or personal firsthand accounts to document developments and events. First preference went to letters, diaries, and journals written at the time, then to postwar memoirs, recollections, essays, and regimental histories, all in conjunction with the 128-volume *Official Records*. Accepted wisdom has it that the further removed in time from the actual event, the less reliable it is. Unless buttressed by reference to diaries or journals written during the war years, that may hold true for numbers, dates, and other details. But no matter how many years have elapsed, Civil War veterans often accurately recalled the temper and mood of that era, so vivid and indelible were their impressions. So, even when written thirty-five or forty years later, memoirs can still provide valuable information.

Many useful primary documents are now available in digitized form on the Web, many placed there by universities and historical societies. Some were used and cited in this work, but a cautionary note is in order: institutional sites are relatively stable, but private sites can and do disappear overnight. In the few instances when that happened herein, the document is tagged in its endnote citation as no longer accessible.

The reason for this reliance upon primary sources is, I hope, self-evident: the writers were there and speak with an authority later authors lack. Their spelling and punctuation are retained, unless perplexing to the reader.

This is not to say that these firsthand sources are always reliable, for they are not. Self-interest; self-aggrandizement; loyalty to a cause, comrades, or ideal; honest error; limited vision; and other impediments to perfect portrayals arise. Aware of these pitfalls, I have sought as many witnesses as possible for each of the tangible and intangible actions, the concrete and the abstract. That has proved possible in almost every instance. Given a general concurrence among the men and women who lived during those days, the event or point is rather well established.

I often consulted secondary sources, the studies by later writers. They provide insight, analysis, interpretations, guidance and conclusions, identification of primary sources, and new information. For instance, recourse to works on the South's culture of violence, Confederate nationalism, and slave laws pertain to the underlying causes for Confederate atrocities, while studies of the slaughters led to new interpretations and to undiscovered primary papers.

This study is organized so that chapters 1 and 2 explain and analyze the positions of North and South concerning emancipation and black soldiers. Succeeding chapters describe consequent atrocities experienced by black soldiers and their efforts to respond in kind. Chapters 15 to 18 describe and analyze Confederates' turn to summary executions of captured white Federals and the drift toward no-quarter warfare. Shifts in the narrative action from one geographical area to another within the same time frame are noted with a line space and a short heading.

1

Emancipation and Black Soldiers

MIDWAY IN THE CIVIL WAR, President Abraham Lincoln interjected two new and contentious elements: he issued the Emancipation Proclamation and he authorized the enlistment of blacks as soldiers. These two moves synergistically created the conditions for Southern atrocities; amplified Northern prejudices, which precluded effective retaliation; and generated much disaffection in the North. That said, Lincoln was not responsible for the massacres that resulted from his edicts. He considered many possible consequences, including Northern discontent and antipathy and the possibility of a murderous Southern reaction. But he decided, as he felt he must, on the preservation of the Union.

When the war began, slavery and its ramifications, the conflict's root cause, mattered little to most Northerners. Some opposed the institution, but only the abolitionists and their sympathizers actively agitated for slavery's end and demanded some equality for all black Americans. However, even the most dedicated abolitionists largely thought social equality unnecessary and unwanted.

From start to finish, people in the North focused on suppressing the rebellion and keeping the Union intact. Lincoln held to that abiding goal and made his position unmistakably clear in a famous letter to *New York Tribune* editor Horace Greeley. On August 22, 1862, Lincoln wrote, "My paramount object in this struggle *is* to save the Union, and is *not* either to save or to destroy slavery. If I could save the Union without freeing *any* slave, I would do it, and if I could save it by freeing *all* the slaves I would do it; and if I could save it by freeing some and leaving others alone I would also do that. What I do about slavery, and the colored race, I do because I believe it helps to save the Union; and what I forbear, I forbear because I do *not* believe it would help to save the Union." He added that it was his personal wish that all men might be free, but he would not allow that to interfere with his duty as he perceived it.[1]

Ulysses S. Grant had earlier expressed similar sentiments. In November 1861, then a junior brigadier general, Grant wrote to his father, "My inclination is to whip the rebellion into submission, preserving all constitutional rights. If it cannot be whipped in any other way than through a war against slavery, let it come to that legitimately. If it is necessary that slavery should fall that the Republic may continue its existence, let slavery go." Eight months later, in the summer of 1862, Grant again explained, "I am sure that I have but one desire in this war, and that is to put down the rebellion. I have no hobby of my own with regard to the negro, either to effect his freedom or to continue his bondage."[2]

Citizens and soldiers alike overwhelmingly agreed. Typical were the sentiments of an Indiana infantry officer in July 1862. He declared, "I have no sympathy for or against slavery in the states. My mission is to assist in saving the country, and let slavery take care of itself." But those who opposed slavery, who also were often anti-Negro, decried the government's indifference. Calling it a "vile stain" upon the country, a Massachusetts soldier complained that Lincoln "don't talk nigger enough, but its no use mincing the matter. Nigger has got to be talked, and thoroughly talked to and I think niggers will come out of this scrape free."[3]

Soon, the far-reaching and unpredictable war assumed a life and will of its own, altering or influencing policies, goals, and men as it progressed.

Two bold and ambitious generals acted on their own to change the status of black Americans, an exceedingly sensitive matter politically and socially. Major General John C. Fremont, the Republican presidential candidate in 1856, was the first to overreach. On August 30, 1861, just a month after he took command in Missouri, Fremont declared slaves free within his domain. When he refused to cancel his emancipation decree, Lincoln quickly revoked it, saying that the slavery issue was a political matter.[4]

Major General David Hunter was next to presume too much. Ordered to the Department of the South, his new command embraced South Carolina, Georgia, and Florida but comprised only a few coastal enclaves. Nevertheless, on May 9, 1862, shortly after his arrival, Hunter declared all slaves free in those states. Since Federal forces controlled only the small beachheads, his proclamation had little effect. Still, anger and dismay greeted his decree. Hearing the order, the 8th Michigan's colonel railed that he fought to save the Union, not to abolish slavery. Offshore, Rear Admiral Samuel F. Du Pont wrote, "I laughed outright when I first saw it—then I felt as if it was no laughing matter." Lincoln also took the order quite seriously, immediately vacating it. He pointedly added that whether he himself had the power to emancipate slaves or if he should exercise that power were "questions which under my responsibility I reserve to myself."[5]

Undaunted, Hunter decided to raise a fifty-thousand-man black army, a proposal contrary to both civil and military policies. Black men had fought in the Revolutionary War and the War of 1812, but the rules had changed by 1846 when the war with Mexico began. By 1861, when the Civil War started, the army rejected black applicants but the navy enlisted many in lower ranks, though a sometimes vicious prejudice existed against former slaves who came aboard. The army's exclusionary policy derived from the Federal Militia Acts of 1792 and 1795, which called for a citizen force of every free able-bodied white male. Congress did not specifically prohibit black enlistments, but the army narrowly interpreted legislators' intent. Army regulations banned all African Americans by rules effective in 1821. Federal and state civil authorities also construed the Militia Acts' "free white" wording as restrictive. But the Second Confiscation Act of 1862 allowed the president to use blacks in any way he judged best, and the Militia Act, passed at the same time, authorized him to accept blacks into service as laborers or for any military or naval duty. This act also provided for freeing slaves accepted for service, if their owners were in rebellion against the national government.[6]

Prodded by a concerned Congress, Secretary of War Edwin M. Stanton inquired about Hunter's recruiting effort and received a flippant reply. When Hunter sought authority to mobilize former slaves, approval, and pay for his one black regiment, Stanton raised the issue at a cabinet meeting on July 21. Discussion continued the next day, but Lincoln balked at arming African Americans, even though Congress had empowered him to do so. At most, he would allow commanders to arm slaves for strictly defensive purposes. Though the administration took no action against Hunter's regiment, none was necessary. Without Washington's approval, Hunter could not pay the men.[7]

Where Hunter failed, a subordinate succeeded. Rufus Saxton, promoted overnight from captain to brigadier general, supervised freed slaves on coastal plantations. Finding the plantations helpless against enemy raiders, he asked to mobilize up to five thousand former slaves for protection. He stipulated that white officers would lead his armed and uniformed force and, most important, he emphasized the defensive role they would play. Although Lincoln had rejected enlisting blacks as soldiers, he would allow freedmen to defend themselves. Stanton quickly authorized Saxton to arm, outfit, and pay as many as five thousand black volunteers. Saxton resurrected the 1st South Carolina, and the unit was mustered into service on January 31, 1863. It was the first officially sanctioned African American regiment, though it was fifth in order of mustering into the army.[8]

Also more successful than Hunter were Benjamin F. Butler, appointed general for political reasons, who governed occupied New Orleans, and Senator James H. Lane of Kansas, also another political general. Butler said he needed additional troops to defend the city from attack, and so he mobilized a brigade of free black men organized during Confederate rule. Without official approval, by November 24, 1862 he had inducted the 1st, 2nd, and 3rd Louisiana Native Guard regiments and their many black officers, thus adding about three thousand men to his strength.[9]

Far from bustling New Orleans, Lane scoured the prairie for black recruits. A fervent abolitionist, Lane was admired by his friends and called a "nigger-stealer" by his enemies. However, Lincoln favored Lane and authorized him to organize several regiments, unaware that Lane planned to recruit blacks as well as whites. Presently, Lane reported

that he would soon have enough men for four regiments of whites and
two of blacks. Secretary of War Stanton told Lane that the president
had not authorized him to raise black troops and warned, "Such regiments cannot be accepted into the service." Resistance to the idea also
mounted in Kansas. James M. Williams, one of Lane's recruiters, said
objections came from Southern sympathizers; from those prejudiced
against blacks; from loyal citizens who cited War Department opposition; and, finally, from "a large class who believed that the negro
race did not possess necessary qualifications to make efficient soldiers,
and consequently the experiment would result in defeat and disaster."
Civil authorities arrested and jailed recruiters and indicted Williams for
unlawfully depriving people of their liberty. Williams argued that he
operated under proper military authority. He referred to Lane, who was
defying the president, the highest authority, as he successfully organized
the 1st Kansas Colored Infantry.[10]

Lincoln, meanwhile, had slowly worked his way through the slavery
briar patch. He moved haltingly and cautiously, trying to decide whether
emancipation would help or hinder suppression of the rebellion and
restoration of the Union, his primary concerns. Much depended upon
his decision and he considered the matter for many months. Freeing
the slaves would seize the moral high ground, making it more difficult
for Europe to recognize and aid the Confederacy. It also would strip the
South of essential labor and weaken the slavery oligarchy's wealth and
power, thus loosening its feudal grip on the South. Although a minor
consideration, ending slavery would quiet the noisy abolitionists.

Yet such a move posed great risks. Jeopardy came just as much from
an adverse reception in the North as from a predictably negative reaction in the South. No matter how narrow or broad his edict, Lincoln
apprehended great opposition from Northern citizens and soldiers. Pro-
slavery and Peace Democrats would gain strength from such an unpopular measure. Ordinary citizens would see and dread a black tidal wave
rolling northward, fearing their incomprehensible ways and cheap labor.
Lincoln understood the common prejudices and surely shared some as
a man of his times and people. He easily grasped the anti-Negro fervor,
the rejection of equality with blacks. He knew, too, that many would
construe emancipation as transforming the struggle to save the Union
into a "nigger war," an abolition war. Moreover, freeing the slaves by
fiat was an unindemnified taking of private property, though he could
worry about that later.[11]

Lincoln finally decided that the benefits would exceed the losses. He wrote a decree, freeing slaves within any state then still in rebellion and submitted the first draft to his cabinet on July 22, 1862. Postmaster General Montgomery Blair objected, arguing, "There is . . . no public sentiment at the North, even among extreme men which now demands the measure." He warned that it would turn voters against the administration and the Republican Party in the fall elections. Secretary of State William H. Seward supported the edict but suggested delaying it until the Union won a military victory, thus giving it some weight and credibility. Other cabinet officers favored the measure but with reservations. Although Blair might prove correct in his gloomy prediction, Lincoln decided to go ahead, heeding only Seward's advice to wait until the war situation improved.[12]

That moment was slow to come because the war news brought little cheer. Lincoln had to wait two months for a season when the outlook improved or, at least, appeared to take a turn for the better. That occurred when Federal troops stopped General Robert E. Lee on September 17 in a bloody battle at Antietam, Maryland. While it was not the best of times, it would do. Accordingly, Lincoln released the Preliminary Proclamation on September 22, 1862, declaring it effective January 1, 1863.[13]

Northern governors rallied around Lincoln, but their support availed little. Postmaster General Blair's gloomy prophecy came true: the Preliminary Proclamation was a political disaster. Angry voters turned against the administration from east to west. Combined with the detested draft, battle reverses, Lincoln's suspension of habeas corpus, and public unhappiness with the war's overall progress, the proclamation contributed mightily to Democratic Party victories in the fall elections of 1862. From Kentucky, a Federal general wrote, "Nearly all the citizens of this state . . . have left the Union cause on account of Uncle Abe's Proclamation on the negro." Senator John Sherman, of Ohio, reported the proclamation "very injurious" in his state, and a general's wife said the same of Southern Illinois. Governor Oliver P. Morton, of Indiana, argued that the proclamation was a war strategy, but voters turned a deaf ear and Democrats triumphed. Lincoln lost in his own state of Illinois, and Pennsylvania voters sent a Democratic delegation to Congress. In New York, the administration's candidate lost to Democrat Horatio Seymour, who promptly became a sharp thorn in Lincoln's side.[14]

Strong misgivings had immediately beset Northerners. A New York woman believed Lincoln should have waited until the North had the power to enforce the decree. In Washington, Montgomery Blair's sister, Elizabeth Blair Lee, wrote that "it is a mistake . . . it is really felt to be a paper pronunciamento & of no practical result. It may be to get the Abolitionists to enlist but that is not their style & it will only organize a strong party against the Administration." Scornfully, a New York soldier insisted that freedom meant that "they [slaves] will starve without lifting a hand to save themselves." Others believed the edict strengthened the South's resolve and would serve only to prolong the war.[15]

A tiny minority lauded Lincoln's declaration. Albert G. Riddle, an abolitionist Ohio congressman, was giddy with delight. He called it "the greatest human utterance." Sergeant George Fowle, 39th Massachusetts Infantry, thought it only right and proper because "the fight is freedom or slavery . . . freedom to all men, white or black." In Virginia, a Unionist woman hailed the proclamation, although she owned many slaves. But spite may have spiced her cheers, as most of her slaves had already run away. In England, people approved but carped that the proclamation did not go far enough. Others wondered whether slave uprisings and savage massacres would follow, as Southern sympathizers predicted.[16]

Lincoln created confusion when he suggested another course of action. In his annual message to Congress, on December 1, 1862, he proposed gradual, compensated emancipation and pushed again for colonization or voluntary deportation of blacks. Gideon Welles, secretary of the navy, later insisted that both were integral to Lincoln's thinking. Jointly, the proposals appealed to large elements in the North. Many thought it unjust to deprive owners of their chattel property without payment, although the plan would have extended slavery to 1900. Many more favored isolating blacks and supported deportation or any other measure to achieve that end.[17]

Some thought the Preliminary Proclamation but a tentative announcement, a trial balloon. Rumors circulated that Lincoln might backtrack, but he issued the final proclamation on January 1, 1863. This version, with a new proviso for enlisting black soldiers, caused turmoil anew, sparking discord everywhere and mutinous unrest among Union troops. Congressman Riddle recalled that he and fellow abolitionists resisted gradual emancipation and wanted "a speedier and cheaper end of the cause of war." But the proclamation yielded neither. More than two years elapsed before slavery ended, and the war's cost during that period probably exceeded the cost of compensated emancipation. Just a relatively small number of slaves gained instant freedom. Those in the loyal, slaveholding Border

States were exempt from the decree, and only force of arms could free the four million slaves in the South.[18]

Expediency and self-interest obviously motivated some of the instant true believers in the proclamation. Most officials and military leaders either said that they approved or kept quiet. John Hay, one of Lincoln's private secretaries, reported that government insiders gleefully called one another abolitionists after the proclamation and "seemed to enjoy . . . appropriating that horrible name." Attorney General Edward Bates commented, "Abolition seems to be the strongest rallying point, and men who don't care a fig about it are suddenly very zealous in its cause." Still, while George B. McClellan, Army of the Potomac commander, opposed emancipation, William T. Sherman, who later led the Western armies, refused to have black soldiers and candidly admitted, "I would prefer to have this a white man's war." Grant, good soldier that he was, told Lincoln, "I have given . . . arming the negro my hearty support. This, with the emancipation . . . is the heavyest blow yet given the Confederacy."[19]

Other future presidents also supported the twin measures, though not always with great enthusiasm. Colonel Rutherford B. Hayes, the nineteenth U.S. president, was initially uncertain but warily agreed, "Desperate diseases require desperate remedies." Brigadier General James A. Garfield, the twentieth U.S. president, wrote, "I want to help in carrying out the Proclamation . . . Strange that a second rate Illinois lawyer should be the instrument . . . [of] one of the sublimest works of any age." Colonel Benjamin Harrison, twenty-third president, had joined to crush the rebellion but defended emancipation with the patently false argument that it reflected the will of the people.[20]

In truth, an overwhelming majority opposed freeing the slaves and enlisting black soldiers. The Emancipation Proclamation mainly reflected Lincoln's will and the hopes of abolitionists, Northern blacks, and antislavery people. Even so, some dedicated abolitionists complained that the proclamation was defective in one way or another. Frederick Douglass, ex-slave and black leader, criticized the edict as "marked by discriminations and reservations" and "inspired by the low motive of military necessity." One black soldier, a peacetime preacher in Chicago, first declaimed, "Abraham Lincoln . . . by one simple act of justice to the slave links his memory with immortality." Then, almost immediately, corrosive second thoughts caused him to rail against Lincoln's deportation agenda and his "pro-slavery ideas." Soon, however, Douglass and others decided that the proclamation was indeed a watershed event.[21]

Pragmatists, who wanted victory, and progressives, who took a long-term view, also embraced emancipation. Lincoln urged the pragmatic argument, telling a gathering, "I issued the proclamation on purpose to aid you in saving the Union." A Western cavalry officer argued, "Our Government did not use the war as a measure for destroying slavery, but they used slavery as a means of destroying the rebellion." Progressives concluded that for the nation to be whole, slavery must go. Major General John M. Schofield, who soldiered for forty-six years, wrote that "slavery was the great cause of the rebellion, and the only obstacle in the way of a perfect Union." John C. Ropes, a Boston lawyer and historian, postulated that "[to] be a united people it is necessary that we be a homogeneous people in the character of our labor and institutions . . . I have not gone in for waging the war for the emancipation of the slaves, but I have made up my mind that the slaves must be emancipated in order that we may again be a united nation."[22]

The ambivalent or undecided were uncommon. Prominent among the publicly irresolute was Charles Russell Lowell, poet and Boston Brahmin who endured biting criticism for his wavering. Others privately equivocated, like the soldier who wrote, "It may be the cause of some good and may not." Echoing that stance, a New Yorker admitted, "it may be one of the greatest and best acts that man ever done and it may not but I will not sit in judgment." In his diary, an Illinois youth confessed that he "was . . . at a loss to divine its effects."[23]

Most knew exactly where they stood and why they decried the measures. Some objected with thoughtful arguments against emancipation, focusing on its necessity, legality, and consequences. Ignoring the proclamation's favorable impact abroad and concentrating on its disruptive effect at home, some argued that slavery was doomed in any event and therefore the edict was unnecessary. Major General Fitz-John Porter contended, "Leave the whole thing alone, and as our armies advance, slavery must go under." Others thought it an unconstitutional use of war powers. This aspect so troubled one officer that after first accepting the proclamation as a military necessity, he later reversed himself. He explained, "Slavery is recognized in the Constitution, and altho' I believed Slavery to be wrong . . . both morally and politically, yet as long as our laws recognize it, we must submit." Many believed the decree would only lengthen the war, strengthening Southern determination and inspiring the South to fight harder. They agreed with the Pennsylvania minister who lamented, "I think it will do more harm than good." As proof, a Michigan soldier in Kentucky reported that the proclamation had greatly increased recruiting—but for Confederates.[24]

By far, the citizen-soldiers reacted with the greatest anger, bitterness, and resentment. Quickly an acute sense of betrayal pervaded the army, because most had volunteered to suppress the rebellion and restore the Union. In their view, Lincoln had breached that good-faith contract by changing the terms. He had turned their grand struggle into a shameful abolitionist campaign to slay the slavery dragon. That perception generated serious disaffection among the volunteers, the body and soul of the Union army. They felt tricked into risking life and limb for an unworthy cause. A New York infantry officer reported, "I find officers and men are much dissatisfied . . . and say it has turned into a 'nigger war' and are all anxious to return to their homes for it was to preserve the Union that they volunteered for."[25]

As the author of their discontent, wrathful soldiers heaped abuse upon Lincoln. One ranking officer called him a "great, big, damned jackass, a miserable imbecile." Sorely aggrieved, a Michigan soldier contended that "since his nigger proclamation . . . he will be remembered among the Vilest of the Vile. God . . . has turned on him . . . the union will be lost, if it is not all ready lost." A New Jersey soldier confirmed, "The men do nothing [but] curse the president now." However, a disenchanted Iowan went too far when he loudly announced he would like to shoot Lincoln, the "black abolitionist." His tirade offended superiors and he soon wore a twenty-pound ball and chain.[26]

The soldiers' complaints sounded a common theme, endlessly repeated. "I am the Boy that can fight for my Country, But not for the Negroes," wrote an Illinois infantryman, who later died for his country. A 39th Massachusetts soldier declared, "We dont care much witch way it gose sens we found out we are fiting for nigers." An Indiana soldier protested that the war had become a drive "to Free the nigars . . . and I do not propose to fight anymore in such a cause." Fuming, a Minnesota officer wrote, "This . . . is a prodigious humbug, and I want to get out of it . . . I begin to think that abolitionism is twin brother to the devil, and I should think the North would be tired of the Nigger." Although a War Democrat, Colonel Marcus M. Spiegel, 67th Ohio, announced, "I do not . . . want to fight for Lincoln's negro proclamation one day longer than I can help."[27]

However, General-in-Chief Henry W. Halleck warned that all officers were duty bound to carry out the twin measures. Colonel Edward H.

Ripley, 9th Vermont, asserted, "[The] Government will not tolerate a particle of opposition to their views." Thus, officers who incautiously cited the proclamation as the reason for resigning might well receive a dishonorable discharge, much to their surprise and dismay. Enlisted men, the bulk of the army, could not resign but could desert, and many protested by doing just that. Figures for absences prompted by the proclamation are impossible to determine. Anecdotal accounts, however, confirm that many quit the army at least temporarily. In the West, a British observer with Confederate troops saw forty or fifty deserters from Grant's army and asked their motive. They replied, "We enlisted to fight for the Union, and not to liberate slaves." In West Virginia, the 116th Ohio's commander wondered why guerrillas had captured so many of his men. He eventually learned they had surrendered to be paroled and then go home, and that his men traded coffee and sugar for presigned paroles held by Southern sympathizers. He said that "it was simply another way of deserting."[28]

Lincoln's decision to enlist black soldiers independently stirred fierce debate and generated largely negative reactions, although the idea was scarcely a bolt from the blue. As early as November 1861, a Union general had publicly urged it. Vice President Hannibal Hamlin, cabinet members, and ordinary citizen-soldiers had followed suit. Months before Lincoln acted, an Indiana artillery lieutenant thought it would be grand to have blacks do the scut work, and a Vermont soldier wrote, "I wish they would arm all the slaves there is in the south. . . . [T]hey are ready to go at the rebels like a mess of blood hounds." Hunter, Saxton, Butler, and Lane had organized black regiments, although many people may not have known about their efforts.[29]

Lincoln galvanized the great dormant opposition when he blessed the black soldier notion. Colonel John Eaton, who supervised contraband affairs in the Mississippi Valley, observed, "The undertaking was . . . most unpopular in many quarters, especially in the army." Torturing reality, Colonel Joseph Holt, the army's humorless judge advocate general, charged that the uproar over black soldiers resulted from the evil machinations of Southern sympathizers and that the opposition was "necessarily in the interests of treason." Were that true, Holt necessarily had millions of traitors on his hands. Rather, pride and prejudice, coupled with a profound unease about the ability and reliability of a black soldiery, fueled the outcry.[30]

White pride suffered because people strongly believed the conflict was the white man's burden, their exclusive and rightful business. Brigadier General Augustus L. Chetlain, who organized black regiments in Tennessee and Kentucky, recalled, "The argument was that this was a white man's war and should be fought out by white men." Major General William T. Sherman so argued, and a staff officer in Virginia almost plaintively asked, "Can we not fight our own battles, without calling upon these humble hewers of wood and drawers of water, to be bayonetted by the unsparing Southerners?" A wrathful citizen in Indiana protested to his congressman, "We of the west surely think this most degrading and miserably humiliating."[31]

Prejudice made men think about some odious consequences should the scheme become a reality. As one officer recalled, "Large numbers in the Federal army then believed that the plantation slave, in the scheme of evolution, was only a few steps from the anthropoid ape." So the idea of black equality in any form caused whites to recoil in anger. A troubled Indiana soldier worried, "Supposing them Brave and ferocious, They . . . help us restore our union. Then of course they would consider and justly too that they were entitled to the fellowship of the american people and equalize themselves with us & that will never do—" Bluntly, a soldier in Virginia wrote, "We don't want to fight side by side with the nigger. We think we are too superior a race for that." For a German officer with the 12th Missouri, terrible thoughts came with the stunning realization that bullets were colorblind. He shuddered at the possibility that he might "be wounded by the same ball that first traffics with a Negro and then pays me a visit."[32]

More rational was the widespread belief that former slaves lacked the essential qualities required for soldiering. Many thought forced servitude had crushed their spirit, and people seriously doubted whether they could or would fight their former masters. One New England officer recalled, "There was . . . a fear amounting to conviction they would flinch in an emergency." Voicing those doubts, an Indiana infantryman confided, "I believe if the whole black population of the united States were together . . . one Bomb shell would Disperse the whole of them. I may be mistaken." Shortly before authorizing black troops, Lincoln himself had openly doubted their worth and reliability. He said that he was not sure much could be done with freed slaves. Specifically, he added, "If we were to arm them, I fear that in a few weeks the arms would be in the hands of the rebels." Although he continued to harbor private misgivings,

Lincoln publicly insisted, "The bare sight of fifty thousand armed, and drilled black soldiers on the banks of the Mississippi, would end the rebellion at once."[33]

Presidential hyperbole may have reassured some civilians, but soldiers remained unconvinced. Even officers leading black troops feared their charges might not fight. All were aware of the possibilities should untried black soldiers falter or flee when attacking or attacked. That would endanger nearby white units and invite defeat. Sherman quickly made his position clear. He wrote, "Time may change this but I cannot bring myself to trust negroes with arms in positions of danger and trust." Time worked no change—he was ever unwilling to use black soldiers. Lieutenant Colonel Theodore Lyman, an Army of the Potomac staff officer, voiced the pervasive wariness, saying, "We dare not trust them in line of battle. Ah, you make speeches at home, but here, where it is life or death, we dare not risk it."[34]

Yet slowly, then with a rush, there began a great conversion on both issues. Citizens and soldiers calculated gains and losses and decided that the benefits of emancipation and a black soldiery outweighed the objections. "There are *two kinds* of Abolitionists just now," a Washington patent examiner wrote. He explained, "One kind perhaps make the abolition of Slavery the prime object and care more for that than they do for the Union. The *other* kind care much less about *Slavery*, in fact consider it but an incidental question compared with the Union, and are willing to *abolish* it, if that will *abolish* the rebellion." With such second thoughts, many Northerners adjusted their views. Now they saw freeing the slaves as strictly a war measure designed to weaken the Confederacy and to strengthen the Union. Impatiently, an Ohio soldier wrote, "Never mind what the copperheads and butternuts say about our fighting for the nigger. If they [cannot] . . . see the difference between the means employed, and the end in view, let them remain blind." So emerged the "practical abolitionist," though those who took that mantle always carefully distinguished themselves from the scorned true abolitionists.[35]

Practical abolitionists soon predominated in the army. Early or late, willingly or reluctantly, soldiers adopted the pragmatic view. Grudgingly, a Massachusetts youth admitted that his comrades favored it, but only because they were heartily sick of the war and approved any measures that would end it. Soon, like many others, a Pennsylvania soldier decided that "there is no other cause for this war but slavery and the sooner it is done the better for us." However, such sentiments distressed idealists and purists. Junius H. Browne, *New York Tribune* war correspondent, rejoiced that people finally grasped slavery's role in the war. But he lamented, "Hence they have grown Abolitionists; not so much, I am sorry to say, out of their sympathy with the negroes, as out of a cold and calm consideration."[36]

A similar shift changed the thinking about black soldiers. By June of 1863, a soldier in Louisiana had decided, "It is a grand idea—this raising a great army of Colored men to fight for their freedom & the Union." Others, however, had more selfish reasons for welcoming black troops. Ambitious Federals saw opportunity as only white men would officer the new regiments. Qualified enlisted men could gain higher status and better pay while officers might win quick promotion. Almost every soldier saluted the "better them than us" credo, agreeing it was far better for blacks to serve as cannon fodder than for whites. Sergeant Cyrus B. Boyd, 15th Iowa Infantry, clearly annunciated the idea: "If any African will stand between me and a rebel bullet, he is welcome to the honor and the bullet too." That thought or hope was often expressed unabashedly and crassly, and not confined to those in harm's way. For example, Iowa Governor Samuel J. Kirkwood declared, "When this war is over & we have summed up the entire loss of life . . . I shall not have any regrets if it is found that a part of the dead are niggers and that all are not white men—" The only disagreement with Kirkwood's vision came from the multitude who thought it better yet that black soldiers provide the lion's share of the dead. Bluntly, a Pennsylvania infantryman said, "The more nigers they get, the better I will be suited for I would rather see a nigers head blowed off than a white mans." Colonel Edward H. Ripley, the 9th Vermont's leader, was more succinct, declaring that it was "better to sacrifice niggers than white men."[37]

That view gained momentum with the appearance of the popular "Sambo's Right to Be Kilt," a humorous ditty. Charles G. Halpine, an Irish immigrant and staff officer, wrote it under the pseudonym of Private Miles O'Reilly. It began, "Some tell us 'tis a burnin shame / to make the naygers fight," but it quickly stipulated that it was perfectly acceptable if "Sambo's body should stop a ball / that was coming for me direct." Halpine's poem concluded, "The right to be kilt we'll divide wid him / and give him the largest half!" As the war wore on and casualty lists lengthened, that position solidified. When Confederates attacked nearby black troops in late 1864, a Maine infantryman commented, "Some of these colored individuals received a sudden discharge from the war as a result. I am not able to say that I feel quite as badly about this as if the same number of white men had succumbed." In the war's waning days, a black division's commander confided, "I shall feel less regret over the slain than if my troops were white."[38]

After the initial uproar over emancipation and black soldiers, most people did not believe the war had transformed into a crusade for black freedom or equality. They perceived both measures as means to win the war. For most people who lived and struggled during those years, for leaders and led, the enduring goal was to keep the nation whole by crushing the rebellion. Slavery's demise or survival was incidental.

2

The Southern Perspective

PERCEPTION BECAME REALITY for Southerners
when Lincoln signed the Emancipation Proclamation and called for
black soldiers. Months before, a Texas officer had voiced the common
conviction that "the subjugation of the South & the extinction of slavery
was the prime object in view with Abe Lincoln & every other abolition
leader in the north." They saw the North's true aims now admitted
and revealed, which immediately energized deep-seated fears and excited great anger. Always, Southerners lived with the dreadful specter
of a slave revolt, shaped by the inherited memories of earlier uprisings.
They firmly believed Lincoln meant to incite slave rebellion with the
proclamation, endangering the lives of defenseless home folks and the
honor of their women. Moreover, black soldiers were but uniformed
insurrectionists. Patently, the twin measures threatened social order and
structure, culture, and mores, their very existence as a free people. So

the war became ever more a personal affair as the Southerners defended themselves and their homeland against the "negro equalizing abolitionists of the north."[1]

Southerners initially scoffed at the emancipation edict because they knew it freed only a few slaves while millions remained firmly in bondage. Confident that the Yankees would never penetrate very far into the Confederacy, they worried little about losing their chattels. So everywhere people derided Lincoln's proclamation. On a Louisiana plantation, young Sarah Morgan acidly commented, "He has only proved himself a fool, without injuring us." Thomas Cooper DeLeon, a journalist in Richmond, recalled, "It was . . . looked upon as a vaunt as idle as if he had declared the throne of England vacant." Some called it "as ridiculous as the Pope's bull against the comet" and an educated South Carolina planter called it a "Brutum fulmen," Latin for a meaningless, futile threat. In the manor house on a three-thousand-acre plantation in Tidewater Virginia, the thinking was that Lincoln had only caused "dissentions among his own followers." In Mississippi, editors of the Natchez *Courier* relied upon satire to settle the matter when they printed a tart limerick:

> Abraham Lincoln, the wily wretch,
> Freed the slaves he couldn't catch.[2]

Second thoughts quickly banished the derisive smiles. Southerners soon decided the proclamation was a malignant, evil Yankee plot to foment slave revolts or "servile insurrection," as they termed it, while most able-bodied white men were away in the army. In terrible visions, they conjured rampaging black hordes—bent upon plunder, arson, murder, and rape—falling upon defenseless old men, women, and children. They remembered with a shudder the outbreak led by Nat Turner in 1831. Even more horrific, though more remote, was the embedded memory of the bloody and successful slave uprising in the Caribbean's Santo Domingo in 1801. Given the temper of the times and the remembrance of those earlier events, it was neither irrational nor absurd for Southerners to apprehend the worst. Northern Peace Democrats reinforced those fears when they also contended that the administration meant to spark slave revolts. Through force, fear, and ignorance, Southerners had kept their slaves docile and obedient, but that was absent Yankee subversion.[3]

One well-traveled gentleman warned that Southerners must fight Yankees in front while guarding against slave plots in the rear. Worried, an army nurse wrote, "We none of us know when we are safe." After Lincoln issued his decree, a young South Carolina woman called it infamous, and an artillery officer in Savannah termed it diabolical. He added, "I look upon it as a direct bid for insurrection, as a most infamous attempt to incite flight, murder, and rapine [by] . . . our slave population." In Louisiana, Sarah Morgan trembled when she thought about the "butchery of unreasoning animals who would stop at no cruelty." Years later, ex-Confederates remained convinced that Lincoln "deliberately intended not only to beggar a whole people" but also to promote the wholesale butchery of defenseless whites.[4]

Insurrection fears and rumors unnerved people throughout the war, but their worries proved groundless. For several reasons, a general insurrection was unlikely, and isolated uprisings had no chance of success. In any event, no confirmed instances of revolt occurred during the war. However, that was small solace to the slaves caught up in the insurrection hysteria. Those who aroused any suspicion that they challenged white control usually went straightaway to the hangman.[5]

Though the proclamation ignited no revolts, it pushed Southerners further into the collective schizophrenia caused by slavery. Shackled to rigid beliefs—and propped by the Bible, rationalizations, fictions, and myths—they struggled with conflicting but ineluctable realities. No one could reconcile the contradictions, but almost none would abandon hallowed creeds or accept unpalatable alternatives. Without thinking about it too much, they believed Africans enjoyed their highest, happiest place as slaves under the benevolent paternalism of their masters. But they also knew or suspected that many of their chattels felt the opposite, that slavery was "hell without fires," as one former slave put it. For years, chattels had run away to the North, and the proclamation would only exacerbate the problem. Still, Mary Boykin Chestnut, a South Carolina aristocrat, wondered, "Now if slavery is [so] disagreeable . . . why don't they all march over the border." Sometimes doubt arose as when Constance Cary, a wellborn young Virginia woman, wrote, "All my observations of the colored folk . . . kept me wondering if they could be happier free." That was a puzzle, a persistent conundrum for everyone. Late in the war, a Georgia soldier still thought that his family's slaves "have better sense than to leave . . . to follow Yanks. If they have, I guess they will wish they were back before long."[6]

Another paradoxical convention portrayed slaves as ever loyal but always treacherous. Mary Chestnut, who opposed slavery while surrounded by her own, appreciated the contradictions. Once she decided,

"We ought to be grateful that any one of us is alive. But nobody is afraid
of their own negroes." On another day, she thought that they "will not
rise and cut our throats in the rear. They are not really enemies of their
masters—and yet I believe they are all spies for the other side. Inconsistent?" But most did not acknowledge the dichotomy, and the faithful
slave icon retained a cherished niche in Southern lore, while accounts of
betrayal received only anecdotal treatment. Unquestionably, some slaves,
particularly body servants, remained steadfastly loyal to their masters.
However, great numbers aided Federals, and most fled to them given
the slightest opportunity. Before leaving, though, they frequently looted
their owners' homes and stables. Whites often noted defections with an
air of surprise, as did a South Carolina woman who reported, "Papa's
house was sacked by his own negroes." After her household slaves stole
money and ran away, a Maryland woman lamented, "Their gratitude is
so shameful." To explain the inexplicable, Southerners frequently blamed
Northern deceits or mysterious agitators for subverting deluded slaves.
Sallie Putnam, a Richmond matron, applauded the "simple and child-
like" slaves, so trustworthy, and then, in the same breath, accused some
"underground agency" of turning them to treachery, theft, and flight.[7]

Although they might have distrusted slaves as a whole, whites often
felt genuine affection for their own retainers. When soldiers wrote home,
they often included a "howdy" for the slaves or "servants," a common
euphemism for the black chattels. Profound grief could envelope them
when a slave died. Far from home, an aristocratic soldier expressed his
sorrow when his manservant "Poor Dick" died, despite his untiring efforts to nurse him back to health. In Texas, a soldier's wife mourned the
death of Isaac, "the best negro I ever knew." And, in close relationships,
slaves returned the affection. As one former body servant recalled, "I
loved young Marster John, and he loved me."[8]

Trusted or not, slaves and slavery were the mainstay of the section's
agricultural economy. Only with such an abundant supply of unpaid
workers could Southern planters engage in large-scale production of
labor-intensive crops and thrive as they did. Cotton, sugarcane, tobacco,
rice, and other commodities required many hands and bent backs in that
era of almost no farm mechanization. Slave workers filled the need. A
Mississippi cavalry officer could not envision defeat because he believed
it would mean yielding the land to "freed negroes and the wild beasts."
He declared, "I own no slaves . . . [but] I know that this country without
slave labor would be wholly worthless. . . . We can only live & exist by

this species of labor." Colonel Charles H. Olmstead, 1st Georgia Infantry, wrote that his people believed any interference with the institution
would destroy the economy. Major General John B. Magruder, a Virginian commanding in Texas, declared the proclamation a terrible threat.
He warned citizens that if they lost their chattels, "your lands become
comparatively worthless, while your homes will become the abodes of
your slaves."[9]

While the black thralls produced wealth from the land, each also had
an intrinsic value. They represented many millions of dollars in chattel
property, readily converted to cash. If freed by fiat, without compensa-
tion, many millions of dollars in slave equity would vanish overnight.
When chattels fled, owners bewailed the monetary loss. Just before the
final proclamation, a Virginia woman cried, "Four negroes gone to the
Yankies . . . that is six thousand dollars gone." That was peanuts to
Georgia's governor, Joe E. Brown, who railed about a slave loss of "four
thousand millions of dollars." To protect their investments, owners moved
slaves away from approaching Federals and resisted slave impressments
for defense work, fearing that injury, illness, or death would damage or
destroy their valuable property. Basil Duke, a Kentucky cavalry officer,
explained, "If a mule valued at $150 was worth caring for, there was a
similar and stronger inducement to care for a slave worth from $800 to
$1,000, and some pains would be taken to keep him in good health and
serviceable condition."[10]

An inordinate or unseemly concern about slave property angered
some people, and they denounced the unpatriotic avarice they perceived
among the slaveholding magnates. Richmond newspaper editor Edward
A. Pollard charged that "a greedy, vulgar, insolent aristocracy" saw the
war solely as a struggle to protect their slave assets. Congressman Warren
Akin, of Georgia, lamented, "They give up their sons, husbands, brothers
& friends, often without murmuring, to the army; but let one of their
negroes be taken, and what a houl you will hear." Ruefully, a Louisiana
regiment's Catholic chaplain wrote, "Money & their negroes appeared to
be their gods." And in Alabama, a wealthy planter declared, "West of the
Savannah River it is property first, life next, honor last." Unquestionably,
many large slaveholders felt that way but certainly not all of them.[11]

Aside from their intrinsic worth as capital investments with a very
low peacetime depreciation rate, slaves also yielded a cash crop simply
by procreating. That was another reason for slave owners, large or small,
to value the institution. Sometimes, as a doctor's wife in Virginia said,

"the stock [young slaves] . . . is the only thing profitable" on the farm. Many owners practiced selective breeding to improve their slave stock, thus increasing sale prices. They contracted for stud services or saved stud fees by impregnating slave women themselves. Accepted wisdom and the marketplace taught that an infusion of white blood markedly increased slave values. Northern soldiers, new to Southern ways, were surprised to see white or near-white slaves. Marching through Virginia, an Indiana officer dryly observed that "slaves . . . are fast becoming white washed."[12]

Even as Southerners defended the institution and decried the proclamation, slave values tumbled. Chattels fetched less and less in the marketplace when prices were adjusted for the horrendous wartime inflation. Several causes contributed to the relentless decline. Mainly, people lost confidence in the institution's viability as a consequence of the war. By mid-1863, a Yankee who had turned Confederate wrote, "I believe this war will be the downfall of slavery." A year later, a Tennessee planter decided, "Negro slavery is about played out under Yankee influence." Scathingly, a North Carolina congressman's wife wrote, "I dont think we will have many slaves after Jef and Abe get done fighting to free them." Sharing that view were those who believed the institution had outlived its usefulness or saw slavery as a blight as well as those who had always opposed it.[13]

Emancipation's social impact would match or surpass the economic disruption. The four million slaves enriched and empowered the landed aristocracy but also assured lower-class whites of acceptable status. Describing the South's social structure as a "stately feudal regime," a Georgia woman asserted that it "was framed in the interest of a ruling class." She added, "Never was there an aristocracy so compact, so united, so powerful." Contesting her assessment is very difficult. In the prewar South's white population of six million, about one-third belonged to slave-holding families, but just 1,700 had 100 or more slaves. These figures show that a very few held almost half the South's four million slaves. They were indeed a compact and powerful group, producing much of the region's wealth in cotton, rice, tobacco, and sugar on huge factory plantations. While the oligarchy was not always united on politics, members presented a cohesive front on most social and economic matters. They achieved consensus without conventions, votes, or decrees because they shared a core of similar interests and a unifying heritage.[14]

Just three or four social classes existed. A thoughtful Confederate soldier counted three, namely "landowners and slaveholders, middle class able to hire slaves and the poorer class despised by all, caste strictly observed." An analytical Northerner who had traveled extensively in the South identified four classes, although the bottom two differed only slightly. Another observer, Federal Major General John A. Logan, of Illinois, concluded, "The practical division of the whites was into the upper and lower classes. The upper [classes] rode the lower with boots and spur and the under dog mounted the 'nigger' whip in hand." No appreciable middle class had emerged. Blaming the institution for that void, a Federal chaplain said that slavery "allows no middle estate." But as Logan observed, a small middle class had appeared in a few cities where some industry and commerce had developed. Effectively, large slaveholders and landowners reigned, small farmers or yeomen formed the next level, and poor whites occupied the bottom of the squat pyramid. Some upward mobility was possible for earnest young white men, often with the aid of the powerful, so it was not an absolutely rigid hierarchy.[15]

Class distinctions remained largely intact during the war, though common men shed more blood and their families suffered more than the upper echelons. But a wellborn woman's sensibilities still suffered acutely when she had to deal with wounded soldiers "who had lived by the sweat of their brow." The scion of a wealthy Texas family advised his sister "*at all hazards*" to rebuff soldiers "who are your inferiors in education & social position." Give them something to eat, he urged, but keep them out of the parlor. Equally class conscious was the Virginia artillery officer who decided to hold daily lessons in reading, writing, and "a little ciphering" for his men. He explained that they belonged to the peasant class, nearly one-half were illiterate, and serving their country might deprive them of rudimentary learning. Defensively, he added that he was "no advocate for education, specially for the masses."[16]

The distinctions generated some resentment among those masses. Even as they patriotically gave and endured, they often held the aristocracy responsible for starting the war in the first place. For example, a Texas soldier grumbled that "nearly all the men who was conserned in bringing on this war is not in it now. The leaders and the negro holders are the men who can get out of the service." Ordinary soldiers and their families began to feel that they suffered while the wealthy prospered ever more, untouched by the cruel conflict. Soon many agreed with the disgruntled and disaffected North Carolina soldier who wrote, "this is a Rich mans Woar But the poor man has to doo the fiting."[17]

To many, the "15-nigger" or "20-nigger" laws substantiated that complaint. Confederate legislators enacted the laws to exempt men from the army if they were needed to oversee at least fifteen or twenty slaves. Usually, only the affluent qualified for this exemption, which became a festering aggravation for the plain folk. Private Alexander F. Fewell, 17th South Carolina, was not affluent but he was clever. Fewell, forty-two years old and the son of an up-country planter, claimed responsibility for more than one hundred slaves, won exemption, and returned for a while to his wife and six children. Hardscrabble farmer Peter Deckle, 29th Georgia, could only wish. Wistfully, he wrote, "I wosh mah had some forty or fifty negroes so she could have me taken out of service to attend to them for her and then I would be safe but as it is I have to grunt and indure it."[18]

Slaves formed the lowest caste, white Southerners knew, because God and the Bible ordained it and the historical record upheld it. That was so because their two-legged chattels obviously belonged to an inferior species of some sort. Often they speculated as to blacks' precise place among sentient beings. Wealthy Georgia planter John A. Cobb decided that "the negro affiliates with the monkey race." Uncertain, a Maryland doctor still knew for sure they were "servile and degraded" and "a debased creature, hardly human." An upper-class South Carolina woman decided, "The negro is the most inferior of the human race, far beneath the Indian or Hindu." Whatever the exact classification, black inferiority was an irrefutable verity for Southern people.[19]

Slavery itself reinforced that conviction. Whites bought and sold blacks, not the other way around. Although a circular argument, to Southerners it was additional proof. Supremacy resided with the buyers and sellers, the owners and the masters, those who controlled a slave's existence. Indians and free blacks also owned slaves, but such aberrations did not affect the basic premise. In any event, nonwhites were but a tiny fraction of slave owners. Mostly, it was whites who bought and sold Africans like cattle or mules; bred them to increase their workforce or as a cash crop; used the women as sexual outlets or to improve the offspring; leased, rented, traded, stole, inherited, or gave them away; paid taxes on them; and sold or killed the contumacious or vicious ones, just as they would sheepdogs gone bad. Duke, the Kentucky gentleman and slave owner, explained, "The Negro . . . from every social and political standpoint, was regarded simply as a chattel." One of those chattels drily agreed, saying, "In slavery, niggers and mules was white folks' living." He and millions like him were movable property like any other farm animal. Generally, they were more valuable than a horse or mule because slaves could undertake a variety of moderately complicated tasks. But they were counted and taxed in the same way as other livestock. To illustrate this viewpoint, a Federal related that a Louisiana woman was "blessed with forty slaves, or to use the euphonious language of the South, 'forty head of niggers.'"[20]

Southerners, like many Northerners, also feared that emancipation meant forced equality, which would drastically alter the social balance. If slaves were equal, the great mass of whites would be superior to no one. They would join blacks at the bottom of the heap, losing the status that sustained them in their semifeudal society. Recoiling from that unacceptable possibility, a 4th Georgia captain warned that "not only will the negroes be free but . . . we will all be on one common level." That possibility caused great dismay, turning people livid with rage. A Virginia infantry officer exclaimed, "To make the highest type of Anglo-Saxon subject to the African! Ye gods!" Men railed against the blasphemy, and soldiers often referred to Federal troops as an abolitionist army fighting to impose equality on a rightfully resisting South. An angry General John B. Hood once told Sherman, "You . . . desire to place over us an inferior race, which we have raised from barbarism to its present position, which is the highest ever attained by that race, in any country, in all time." Ending such discussion, a Georgia infantry sergeant declared, "A man who believes the negro is equal to himself is the best judge of the matter."[21]

Anxiety about freed slaves pushed terrible apprehensions to the surface. In that era of Victorian constraints, frankness about sex was unknown. But those inhibitions did not prevent Southerners from believing that animalistic male blacks lusted for white women. Secessionist firebrands earlier had played upon such repressed fears. South Carolina's John D. Ashmore, a prewar member of Congress, warned his constituents that the Federal government would unloose hordes of free blacks on them. He felt sure, however, that they would resist because they knew that "the honor of . . . wife and daughter would hardly be safe an hour" if those liberated slaves descended upon them. Like most Southerners, they needed little convincing that black men, seen as always in rut, posed a great danger if liberated from slavery's controls. After considering the matter,

Captain Elias Davis, 8th Alabama, announced, "I am willing to fight forever rather than submit to freeing negroes among us." Unthinkable as it was, that nightmare vision never waned. Artillery Captain Thomas J. Key, formerly an Arkansas newspaper editor, thought it no wonder that Confederates fought so fiercely. All knew, he asserted, that "sister, wife, and mother are to be given up to the embraces of their present 'dusky male servitors'" if the Yankees won.[22]

Yet even in that slave-based society, some aristocrats, both men and women, accepted the prospect of a slaveless South. Toward the end, the son of a Virginia plantation family decided "slavery is dead, and I say let the negroes go to the winds." Upper-class women particularly considered slavery a burden and wished it gone. Long before the proclamation, Mary Chestnut declared, "Slavery has to go. . . . All that has been gained by it goes to the North and to negroes. . . . I hate slavery." Susan Dabney Smedes, reared on a four-thousand-acre Mississippi cotton plantation with hundreds of slaves, asserted, "Very many slave-owners looked on slavery as an incubus, and longed to be rid of it." Free of her human chattels, a Louisiana matron confided, "I am happier & should be ten years younger . . . had there never been such a thing as *slaves*."[23]

No matter what their station, most Confederates contended that they did not fight to defend or expand slavery. To substantiate this, they constructed an alluring but fallacious syllogism: only slave ownership conveyed an interest in slavery; most soldiers did not own any slaves; therefore, they fought not to keep slavery but for far nobler motives. Major General John B. Gordon, a peacetime lawyer, wrote, "As for the South . . . perhaps eighty per cent. of her armies were neither slave-holders, nor had the remotest interest in the institution." This sophistry appeared mainly in postwar writings. However, Mary Chestnut used the argument in mid-1861 to deny that the war came about over Southern ambitions to extend slavery. But the truth was that every Southerner had a direct and vital interest in the institution, because slavery fashioned the region's social, cultural, political, and economic fabric. As noted previously, from poorest white to wealthiest aristocrat, slavery strongly influenced mores, defined the class structure, and drove the economy. All feared emancipation would disrupt all three, turning upside down their ordered world. Few wanted that to happen.[24]

For all the differences, it was a remarkably homogenous society. Southerners shared a common culture that included Protestant Christianity with an unwavering belief in the hereafter, a heritage of independence and self-reliance, hard work, patriotism, a strong penchant for violence, and a vibrant sense of superiority as warriors and as a people. Most savored a scorn of the moneygrubbing abolitionist Yankees or the strange foreigners. Somehow they maintained a presumption of equality among whites so that yeomen conversed on familiar terms with lordly plantation owners, though never invited to enter the grand manor.

Boston lawyer John C. Ropes tried to explain this after he interviewed Confederate prisoners in the fall of 1863. He wrote, "I must say the privates we talked with were far superior to the average of our privates. In manners they were exceedingly affable, and had the ease of manner which in the North we never see except among the upper classes. It is in short the difference between North and South, and is not attributable to the influence of Slavery, except very indirectly, as most of these men probably never owned a slave. I imagine it to result . . . from the greater equality of the white race produced by the laboring class being a distinct caste."[25]

The Southern character derived from a complex heritage, and slavery played a recognizable role in molding it. Notable among the traits was that propensity for direct physical force. In an understatement, Kentucky cavalier Basil Duke described the population as "generally pugnacious." That tendency stemmed from a synergistic mixture of causes, including finely honed notions of personal and family honor, the Scots-Irish border heritage, and the individualism and self-reliance fostered in the thinly populated rural South. Slavery, dependent upon force for its maintenance and control, contributed to that culture of violence. Social acceptance of force as normal or required, often for inconsequential matters, conferred a legitimacy that it lacked in the North.[26]

An observant traveler in the prewar South noted, "If a young man feels offended with another . . . he is impelled straightaway to strike him down with the readiest deadly weapon at hand." In a bizarre incident in a Nashville theater during the war, a besotted Texas soldier took offense when an actor struck an actress. Outraged, the soldier fired his pistol at the actor. In the melee that followed, the soldier's comrades fought to save him from arrest, killing two police officers and wounding another. When a Confederate naval officer returned home in 1864 after a lengthy voyage, he saw two men on the wharf who "became involved in a difficulty and, according to the custom of the country, drew their revolvers and began to shoot. One of them fell and floundered around on the planks like a chicken with its neck half wrung." That sight inspired a fellow officer to exclaim, "My own, my native land! Now I am sure that I am home again!"[27]

Slavery reinforced the propensity for violence inasmuch as force or its omnipresent threat was required to sustain it. As one Southerner carefully explained, "He [the slave] was regarded then as a piece of property, and when he did wrong was treated [as] . . . a refractory horse. . . . He must be brought into subjection." For the slave, that most often meant physical punishment, ranging from caning or flogging to hanging. Excesses occurred, as when owners ignored chattel value and community disapproval. Bitterly, a former slave said, "Sure they would kill a nigger; he's no more'n a wolf." However, ordinary violence, short of killing, usually served to maintain order.[28]

Since war, by definition, is a triumph of violence, for many Southerners the conflict was a more concentrated, intense version of peacetime activities. Though battles served up mounds of dead, Confederates continued to kill one another. Officers usually met on the field of honor to duel while enlisted men simply became involved in "personal difficulties," a euphemism for deadly encounters. Generals starred in notable affrays, and one of the less formal matches involved Nathan B. Forrest, the South's premier cavalry raider. In June 1863, a lieutenant felt slighted by Forrest and wounded the general with a pistol shot, whereupon Forrest fatally knifed his assailant in a hand-to-hand fight. Given their limited supply of men, it was plainly self-defeating for Confederates to allow their soldiers to shoot one another. But the code of honor prevailed, depriving the army of some good men but creating promotional opportunities for others. Surviving contestants suffered no punishment, though Southern laws prohibited duels. In contrast, by then Northerners shunned the practice, although a few lethal contests occurred.[29]

In keeping with their customs, Confederate commanders freely employed harsh measures to maintain discipline and to punish violations of military law. They branded miscreants with white-hot irons or flogged them and shot deserters wholesale. Jefferson Davis reportedly once said that "the poorest use . . . of a soldier was to shoot him." Nevertheless, his army shot scarce soldiers at a great rate. Exaggerating somewhat, a Texas cavalry sergeant complained that military authorities "think no more of shooting a man than we used to do of taking a drink." With an army less than half the size, Confederates probably executed as many men as the Federals. U. S. Army records show 267 men executed for assorted offenses, although the list is incomplete. Comparable Confederate records, if any existed, failed to survive the war. While providing less than precise evidence, Southern letters, diaries, and memoirs support the conclusion that military executions equaled or exceeded those carried out by the North.[30]

More than numbers distinguished disciplinary practices in the two citizen-soldier armies. Inspired by societal differences, Confederates exercised much harsher military justice. Colonel Charles H. Olmstead, 1st Georgia, vividly remembered an army corps commander telling him, "if you want anybody shot just wink your eye." Pondering Confederate practices, a Federal staff officer wistfully reflected, "I fancy their discipline on essential points is more severe than our own—that is, I fancy they shoot a man when he ought to be shot, and we do not." Indeed, Confederates unhesitatingly tried, condemned, and hanged or shot soldiers, even as they marched to battle. Further, they escorted officers before firing squads while Federal authorities merely cashiered or, rarely, imprisoned them.[31]

Confederate leaders also resorted to instant justice. As a Federal officer said, they were known for their "summary manner . . . of disposing of men on some occasions." In short, if a soldier misbehaved, an officer might shoot him on the spot. Federal officers dispensed summary justice now and then but apparently considerably less often. Although an extreme example, one Confederate colonel killed a sentry with a sword thrust when the soldier twice failed to salute him. Cavalryman Forrest, noted for mighty rages and snap judgments, once emptied a double-barrel shotgun into a crowd of recalcitrant soldiers. Ordinarily, however, it was the junior officers who maintained order in that irreversible manner.[32]

That inclination to violence, strengthened by frustrated rage, gave a deadly edge to Confederates' animus toward black Federal soldiers. While the proclamation infuriated Southerners, that anger paled beside the fury triggered by the thought of armed blacks fighting them. Emancipation was bad, but that thought was worse and the immediate, palpable devilment. The very idea incensed men and women of every class and station. Eloquent in her anger, a South Carolina woman exclaimed, "Just think how infamous it is that our *gentlemen* should have to go out and fight niggers, and that every nigger they shoot is a thousand dollars out of their own pockets! Was there ever anything more outrageous?" An untutored infantryman expressed the Southern male's more visceral reaction. He admitted that he wearied of the war but "the thought of having to fite negroes it will make the Blud boil in eney good southern man." Clearly, they believed the Yankees had set "a servile race armed against their masters."[33]

Any black who confronted, defied, or attacked whites broke an iron taboo, and violators risked severe punishment or death. Even a display of sauciness or insolence could abruptly end a black man's life. While all were full of ire at the notion of blacks fighting their masters, none were more so than Confederate soldiers. Such effrontery represented an immediate personal challenge to their pride, manhood, and honor. They reacted with quiet fury and murderous resolve, although they rarely verbalized that determination, at least in letters home. There was no need to do so, for most citizens and soldiers felt the same way. Speaking for them, the Richmond *Enquirer* predicted that if the Yankees sent black troops into battle that "none will be taken prisoners—our troops know what to do in such cases."[34]

Indeed, most knew exactly what they would do. Jerome B. Yates, a twenty-one-year-old 16th Mississippi sergeant, told his mother the Richmond papers predicted that they would soon fight black troops. Yates said that news pleased his comrades but that was not how he felt. He confessed, "I hope I may never meet a negro soldier or I cannot be . . . a Christian soldier." Similar sentiments came from 1st Lieutenant James A. Graham, 27th North Carolina, son of a prominent family. He wrote, "I have never yet met any of the negro soldiers and hope I never may." Regretfully, Captain Robert E. Park, 12th Alabama Infantry, prophesied, "The enemy . . . force our poor deluded, ignorant slaves into their ranks. They will prove nothing but 'food for our bullets.'" Lieutenant General Jubal A. Early declared that "those [blacks] that had voluntarily entered the enemy's service had justly forfeited their lives." Unmistakably, government, leaders, and society gave explicit or tacit approval to any measures adopted by the troops, already fiercely motivated to deal harshly with black Federals. Consequently, Confederate soldiers usually showed no mercy to captured or wounded black Yankees, striving instead to destroy the dangerously wayward property.[35]

Months before Lincoln authorized black troops, President Davis had acted to make the Confederacy's position unequivocally clear. In August of 1862, he had branded Hunter an outlaw for organizing and arming slaves. While Senator James Lane and his 1st Kansas Colored somehow escaped notice, Davis paid special attention to the reviled and detested Butler. In a Christmas season proclamation, he declared him a "common enemy of mankind" for a host of sins and transgressions. Among the listed "repeated atrocities and outrages" committed by Butler, Davis stressed the arming of slaves for a servile war. He pronounced Butler and his officers as no more than "robbers and criminals deserving death" and ordered Butler hanged immediately upon capture. Hunter and all officers who led black troops also faced execution as felons inciting or aiding servile insurrection. Davis and practically every other Southerner regarded black men bearing arms against their former masters as insurrectionists. Davis ordered those former slaves turned over to civil authorities in their home states, where slave rebellion, whether suspected, plotted, or actively pursued, was uniformly a hanging offense.[36]

On the opposite edge of the Confederate States of America, an Arkansas newspaper editor said amen to Richmond's stance. Elaborating on the black Yankee threat, he provided a cogent rationale for the stern reception of those captured. He wrote, "It follows irresistably that we *cannot* treat negroes taken in arms as prisoners of war without a destruction of the social system for which we contend. In this we must be firm, uncompromising, and unfaltering. We *must* claim the full control of all negroes who may fall into our hands, to punish with death, or any other penalty, or remand to their owners. If the enemy retaliate, we must do likewise, and if the *black flag* follows, the blood be upon their heads." But many Confederate soldiers were way ahead of the editor. Captain James C. Bates, 9th Texas Cavalry, in early September 1863 wrote that "The only course . . . is to take every Negro found in arms, and every man connected with them, into some thicket or swamp and hang them as soon as captured. This course we have heretofore pursued and our men *will continue to do so.*"[37]

Many believed that arming the slaves presaged a genocidal war against Southern whites, sparing none. In such a situation they saw but one solution, and Lieutenant General Theophilus H. Holmes, a West Point graduate from North Carolina, spelled it out. In October 1862, while commanding the Trans-Mississippi Department, he wrote his Federal counterpart that giving weapons to slaves enabled them to slaughter their masters. Holmes warned, "It cannot . . . be expected that we will remain passive, quietly acquiescing in a war of extermination against us, without waging a similar war in return."[38]

In summary, Lincoln's Emancipation Proclamation and approval of black soldiers increased Confederate soldiers' personal stake in the war. Both caused Southerners to fight harder and longer, in part because of the fear and the menace of slave insurrection. Further, enraged Confederates felt the very existence of black soldiers a deadly challenge and an immediate affront to manhood and honor. An angry Virginian swore that "after Lincoln's proclamation, any man that would not fight to the last ought to be hung as high as Haman." To a Kentucky Confederate, however, it was a wonderful gift from Lincoln. He thought that it was "worth three hundred thousand soldiers to our government at least."[39]

3

First Encounters

FROM THE START, a nagging question about black soldiers troubled many Northerners, although Southerners declared they already knew the answer. As an officer of the 1st Kansas Colored Infantry said, it was "the often mooted question of 'will they fight.'" Many white officers leading black troops always asked that when their men first faced the enemy. Yet a few insisted, as did one Yankee, "There is no disputing that . . . negroes make good soldiers, however much *some* may cavil about it." Southerners, on the other hand, confidently pronounced their former slaves innately incapable of standing up to their white masters. A second question centered on the conduct of Confederate troops when opposed by blacks and their white officers. Optimists among those officers believed the enemy would treat them properly; pessimists, or maybe the realists, said "our fate is sealed" if captured; Confederates knew exactly how they would deal with the black ingrates and their white leaders, so only occasionally recorded their views. But clear answers to these questions emerged only after a half dozen or so clashes over a course of several months.[1]

Black soldiers first fought Confederates in late October 1862, about a month after Lincoln had issued his preliminary emancipation decree but two months before he authorized black regiments. This was just after Southern armies had initially met success in northward advances until Federal forces stopped them east and west. The blacks' baptism of fire came when some 1st Kansas Colored troops met a stronger enemy force near Island Mound, Missouri. Few knew or heard about the minor incident on what was then the frontier. Yet the clash marked the beginning of African American combat operations and the opening skirmish in a private war between Southern troops and their former slaves. There the black soldiers learned about the "peculiar disadvantages" under which they would fight, and there they first experienced that special fury that Confederates reserved for them and their white officers.[2]

Skirmishing began soon after the 230 Federals crossed the Osage River on October 27 and bumped into 500 or so well-mounted Confederate cavalrymen. At midday on the October 29, more than one hundred enemy horsemen pounced upon an isolated group of three officers and twenty black soldiers. Lieutenant Elkanah Huddleston recalled, "Although our little band was ready to receive them, it was impossible to withstand the shock. . . . It was a hand to hand conflict in which guns, pistols, sabers and bayonets were used. No quarters were asked or given." Others offered equally dramatic descriptions, with one asserting that the struggle "raged with demonical fury."[3]

Lieutenant Joseph Gardner was among the first to fall, taking buckshot in the thigh and knee. One Confederate dismounted and approached Gardner, jeering that he would finish the "damned son of a bitch." With that, he put his revolver to Gardner's head and fired. As sometimes happened with the low-powered firearms used then, the bullet did not penetrate the bone mass but circled the skull and exited from the other side. Gardner survived his serious wounds and other battles only to die of chronic diarrhea not quite two years later. Captain A. J. Crew dueled with three Confederates and lost, falling dead with bullets to his heart, abdomen, and groin.[4]

Reinforcements arrived in time to save the small band from annihilation. As it was, seven black soldiers were killed and at least nine were severely wounded. Huddleston reported, "Of the loss of the enemy but little is known as they held the field long enough to get off their dead and wounded and also to strip our dead and carry off the clothes." Captain James M. Williams, soon to become the regiment's colonel, did not arrive on the scene until the next day. Still, he declared that they had defeated the rebels and inflicted severe losses. A congressional committee much later reported that the black soldiers had killed eighteen to thirty Confederates and had wounded another thirty to sixty, a very suspect set of statistics.[5]

Half the Continent Away

Soon some 1st South Carolina soldiers also had their first skirmish with the enemy. Resurrected and thriving in a South Carolina enclave, the regiment now had official sanction. It also enjoyed good coverage by war correspondents and the support of Northern friends and influential officers. Reorganized around Company A, forgotten on St. Simon's Island, the regiment drilled and filled its ranks in the fall of 1862. Brigadier General Rufus Saxton, who led the rejuvenation effort, in early November decided that the time was right to generate some favorable publicity and "to prove the fighting qualities of the negroes which some have doubted."[6]

Saxton ordered a seaborne raid along the Georgia and Florida coasts to destroy saltworks, to attack picket stations, and to carry off slaves. He sent sixty-two black soldiers on a small steamer with a little gunboat as their escort. During the week of November 3–10, 1862, they skirmished often, reportedly killing nine Confederates and capturing three. They also smashed saltworks and destroyed an estimated $20,000 worth of property. Moreover, they carried away ninety-four recruits, instantly enlisted by thrusting a musket into their hands.

Lieutenant Colonel Oliver T. Beard, 48th New York, the expedition's leader, lionized the black soldiers, declaring, "The colored men fought with astonishing coolness and bravery." Saxton surpassed Beard in lavish praise, soaring to splendiferous heights. He told Secretary of War Stanton the raid was one of the war's most important events, one that would "carry terror to the hearts of the rebels." He added, "Rarely in the progress of this war has so much mischief been done by so small a force in so short a space of time." Then he proposed assembling a fleet of small shallow draft steamers, each carrying one hundred black soldiers, and sending them raiding up the rivers and inlets along the coast. "In this way," he assured Stanton, "we could very soon have complete occupation of the whole country." Whatever Washington thought of Saxton's exuberant claims is unknown, but it ignored his plea for a swarm of river raiders.[7]

By themselves, the pinprick raids merely annoyed Confederates. But that armed blacks had confronted them was infuriating and provoked an early official directive regarding them. In early November, Confederates had raided Federal-held St. Catherine's Island off Georgia's coast, where they encountered six black soldiers. In a brief fight, the raiders killed two and captured the other four. Brigadier General Hugh W. Mercer, the district commander, asked for instructions about the prisoners. In his opinion, they should face swift and terrible punishment because they were "slaves taken with arms in hand against their masters and wearing the abolition uniform." Quickly the question went to Secretary of War James A. Seddon and President Jefferson Davis. Both agreed with Mercer. On November 30, 1862, Seddon wrote, "Slaves in flagrant rebellion are subject to death by the laws of every slave-holding State. . . . They cannot be recognized in anyway as soldiers subject to the rules of war and to trial by military courts; yet for example, and to repress any spirit of insubordination, it is deemed essential that any slaves in armed insurrection should meet condign punishment. Summary execution must therefore be inflicted on those taken." He added that the power to order executions must rest with area commanders to avoid abuse or temper overzealous subordinates. Barring very extenuating circumstances, however, death was the proper punishment for those slaves and "any others captured in like circumstances."

A copy of Seddon's letter went to Major General John H. Forney, commanding the District of the Gulf. One of Forney's subordinates, the 29th Alabama's colonel, had ordered his men to shoot "wherever & whenever captured, all negroes found armed & acting in concert with the abolition troops." Forney countermanded that order. He directed the colonel not to shoot them. Instead, he should hang them.[8]

This directive was the Confederate administration's first official statement on the treatment of former slaves captured while bearing arms and in Federal uniform. A few months earlier, Davis had labeled Hunter and Butler as felons, to be held for execution if captured, because they had organized and armed slaves for Federal military service. But in this new order, the black soldiers would also suffer death sentences. Though Davis and Seddon would allow such captives to be transferred to civilian courts for trial, if convenient and if done without delay, the same result would follow. As they noted, rebellious slaves were subject to the death penalty in every slave state. Their order came before Lincoln added the black soldier proviso to his proclamation and before tens of thousands of newly freed slaves swelled Federal ranks. That development obviously increased manyfold the probability that large numbers of delinquent slaves would fall into Confederate hands, thus creating new challenges. While this first order had limited circulation among Confederate officers in the area, apparently Federal authorities knew nothing about it at the time.[9]

A second directive, a proclamation by Davis, issued less than a month later, modified the previous order. Now, instead of summary executions, the rebellious armed slaves should be turned over to state courts for trial and hanging. In this Christmas-season announcement, Davis declared Butler an outlaw and a "common enemy of mankind" for a host of sins and transgressions. Among the "repeated atrocities and outrages" committed by Butler, Davis stressed the arming of slaves for a servile war. He pronounced Butler and his officers as no more than "robbers and criminals deserving death" and ordered Butler hanged immediately upon capture. As for black soldiers, they were nothing but insurrectionists, but they should be tried and punished in their home states. Their white officers also deserved death for inciting, aiding, or leading servile insurrections.[10]

Probably prudence and caution moved Davis to change the thrust of the first directive. His Christmas proclamation would have wider circulation, including readership in the North and in Europe. An order for summary execution of all captured black Federals would invite retaliation from the North and opprobrium from Europe. But few could object if those captives were hanged according to the laws of all the Southern states—or so they thought. Davis would not alter the terms for home consumption as most Southerners were "fearfully savage," as Sherman said, about turning their slaves into soldiers. In the words of Confederate Lieutenant General Jubal A. Early, "those [blacks] that had voluntarily entered the enemy's service had justly forfeited their lives."[11]

All along, however, Federals suspected that captured blacks might get short shrift from enraged Confederates. Colonel Thomas W. Higginson, a prominent Massachusetts abolitionist, reformer, and minister, had assumed command of the fully organized 1st South Carolina and led a raid up the St. Mary's River, the boundary stream between Georgia and Florida. With 462 officers and men, Higginson scouted between January 23 and February 1, 1863 but found few recruits. After losing slaves to Federals, owners learned to move them away when raiders neared. At

Township, Florida, Higginson ordered a surprise attack on a nearby Confederate camp. Instead, on their midnight march the enemy surprised them, killing one and wounding seven. Higginson reported Confederates lost twelve killed and many wounded, which figures he based on hearsay. However, that enabled him to claim a victory. Although he did not officially report any missing, Confederates apparently captured three of his men. Higginson privately vowed that if the rebels hanged them, he would hang two of theirs for every one of his. What happened to the captured men is now unknown.[12]

As Higginson conceded, the raids were trifling affairs. Yet he was pleased to say, "Hereafter it was of small importance what nonsense might be talked or written about colored troops. So long as mine did not flinch, it made no difference to me."

South to Florida

The next mission, to seize and hold Jacksonville, Florida, was a more significant affair, promising recognition and much publicity. Although Union forces previously had twice occupied the place, its capture by black troops would overflow with symbolism for both sides, yielding a political and psychological significance that exceeded its military importance. But Higginson said his chief aim was to get his men into action while keeping secret their plan. Generals Hunter and Saxton had other ideas. In no time at all, reports reached New York newspapers about the pending venture. Readers learned that "five thousand negroes . . . a liberating host" would bring about servile insurrection in Florida. No less fanciful, however, was Saxton's order to seize as much of Florida as possible. With only 900 men, including Colonel James Montgomery's skeleton 2nd South Carolina of 120 raw recruits, Higginson could occupy no more than Jacksonville itself.[13]

Still, he and his officers had high hopes of collecting a large number of black recruits. Acting on that belief, Higginson carried along piles of extra arms and uniforms. The enlistment process was exceedingly simple. Federals regarded every male, except the very young or old, as an eager volunteer, and each received a new blue soldier suit, which most happily donned. Though medical officers might later reject many and some walked away before mustering, they kept their spanking-new clothes from Uncle Sam. Probably many were unaware that Confederates regarded wearing Union blue as a mark of servile insurrection and that could make their shiny new suit a death warrant.[14]

Catching Confederates by surprise, Higginson landed unopposed at Jacksonville on March 10. Higginson's men found few able-bodied black men, perhaps five hundred resigned white inhabitants and some enemy troops hovering on the outskirts. Skirmishing enlivened succeeding days, and occasionally Confederates fired a railroad cannon, killing and wounding some Federals. Montgomery went jayhawking upriver and brought back prisoners, cotton, and many slaves. Meanwhile, Higginson worried that Confederates might fire the town or suddenly overwhelm him with a superior force. After ten anxious days, two white New England regiments unexpectedly arrived as reinforcements. Higginson learned to his wonderment that it was widely reported in the North that Confederates had captured and shot them all, and later he read his own obituary in a Northern newspaper. An even greater surprise came on March 28, when Hunter ordered the troops to abandon Jacksonville. Higginson suspected proslavery people had whispered Iago fashion in Hunter's ear and persuaded him to "to cut short the career of the colored troops and stop their recruiting." More likely was the official explanation that their force was too small for the task.[15]

On departure day, March 29, some Federals fired what was left of the town. It was an exciting spectacle, remembered long after by all who saw it. For many black soldiers, the scene reportedly replicated their image of Judgment Day, given the billowing smoke and the roaring flames. Others regretted the destruction and regarded the fiery scene as a reflection upon Federal arms. Watching from a transport, a *New York Tribune* correspondent wondered whether they had not descended to vindictive European standards in waging war. But he also reported that black troops had no part in the arson. Higginson thought it fortunate for his regiment's reputation that the *Tribune* and other newspapers absolved black soldiers. He also knew that much more was at stake than his regiment's good name. They were symbols and often held to a higher standard of conduct than white troops, even though deemed incapable of it because they belonged to an inferior race.[16]

During the Federal occupation, Jacksonville's apprehensive inhabitants knew they were at the mercy of their former slaves. Captain James S. Rogers, 1st South Carolina, wrote. "These people fear us with our black troops infinitely more than they do the white soldiers." From Fernandina, Florida, Private Orra B. Bailey, 7th Connecticut, wrote home, "Nothing has yet been done that stirs up the rebels like setting niggers to fighting them." Despite the wanton burning of Jacksonville, Northern people appreciated the dramatic irony of black soldiers occupying a Southern town, an unusual event. Lincoln watched and wrote Hunter, "I am glad to see the accounts of your colored force at Jacksonville, Fla. . . . It is important to the enemy that such a force shall not take shape and grow and thrive in the South, and in precisely the same proportion it is important to us that it *shall*."[17]

Southerners were well aware of the political, social, psychological, military, and economic implications of the successful forays by black troops, General Pierre G. T. Beauregard, the Confederate commander in the area, formally denounced the Federal penchant for arson. Torching Jacksonville and other places, he charged, was but "vindictive and illegitimate hostility." He attributed these violations to the "species of persons," the black soldiers, used on the several expeditions. Sharply critical, he castigated Federal officers for ignoring "the atrocious consequences which have ever resulted from the employment of a merciless, servile race as soldiers."[18]

Mayhem in Missouri

The 1st Kansas Colored men again could testify to the fury stirred in Southerners by black soldiers. After camping at Baxter Springs in southeastern Kansas, on May 18, 1863, twenty-five black soldiers and twenty white artillerymen went foraging near Sherwood, Missouri. There they soon reeled under a Confederate surprise attack. They lost sixteen killed and five captured, or almost 50 percent of the mixed force. But just three white artillerymen were among the dead and three became prisoners. In contrast, Confederates reported no casualties. Major Thomas R. Livingston, the Confederate leader, said he attacked with only sixty-seven mounted men and reported, "The enemy's loss in killed was, negroes, 23, and 7 white men." While their numbers conflict, both Livingston and Colonel James M. Williams, 1st Kansas commander, may have written truthful reports. Possibly, the additional men reported killed by Livingston were civilian teamsters or men not yet mustered into the 1st Kansas.

That there were no black wounded, that so many were killed, and that their casualties were so disproportionate to the white Federal losses strongly suggests that Confederates concentrated on the blacks. Williams' account supports that view. He reported, "I visited the scene . . . and then I beheld for the first time the horrible evidence of the demoniacal spirits of these rebel fiends in the treatment of our dead and wounded. Men of my command were found with their brains beaten out with clubs, the bloody weapon being left beside them, and their bodies horribly mutilated."

Livingston offered a prisoner trade, telling Williams, "I hev five of you solgers prisoners three Whight and two Black men. The whight men I propose Exchainging with you . . . as for the Negrows I cannot reccognise Them as Solgers and In consiquence I will hev to hold them as contrib-ands of ware." Williams reluctantly agreed because he did not feel that white troops should suffer because they served with black soldiers. But he warned Livingston that he would hold a like number of his men until there was an accounting for the black soldiers. He added, "And you can safely trust that I will visit a retributive justice upon them for any injury done them [black soldiers]." Then Williams learned that Confederates had killed a captured 1st Kansas Colored soldier. He demanded that Liv-ingston hand over the murderer. Angrily, he added, "You need not excuse the murder of the colored man by claiming that it was beyond your power to prevent it. If you are fit to command, you can control your men."

Livingston thumbed his nose at Williams. He replied that he indeed had no control over the guilty man and, anyway, "said offenders where-abouts is to me unknown." Williams wasted no more words or time and immediately ordered up a firing squad. Within thirty minutes, one pris-oner was a corpse. Aware that civilians had joined the attack on the forag-ing party, Williams decided that also required retribution. He ordered the countryside devastated within a five-mile radius of the attack. So his men burned Sherwood and every structure in the proscribed area.

Swiftly and decisively, Williams had exacted eye-for-an-eye retribu-tion. He was the first and apparently the only Federal commander to retaliate immediately and directly for a black soldier's execution. Many, including Lincoln, would threaten, bluster, and promise but never act; some would retaliate but only for the murder of white Federals. Wil-liams believed his prompt action was the only effective response. He noted, "This ended the barbarous practice of killing prisoners so far as Livingston was concerned, and this result, I think, fully justified my action in this case." However, Confederates soon realized there was an easy way to avoid trouble or retribution. It was simplicity itself—take no black prisoners in the first place.[19]

Native Guards Attack in Louisiana

Meanwhile, Butler's three Native Guards regiments and their black of-ficers had entered Federal service and joined in the effort to clear the

Mississippi River. Confederates still held Vicksburg, Mississippi, and Port Hudson, Louisiana, enabling the South to move supplies and troops from the Trans-Mississippi to the East. On April 29, 1863, Grant launched his final drive to capture Vicksburg. Initial planning had called for a joint operation between Grant and Major General Nathaniel P. Banks, Butler's successor. But Banks said he lacked the transport to move his 19th Army Corps to Vicksburg and instead proposed mounting his own attack against Port Hudson, about 150 miles upriver from New Orleans.[20]

Unfortunately for his troops and for the Union, Banks was an ambitious but grossly incompetent general. One of Lincoln's political appointments, he possessed little education and no ascertainable military skills. He was, however, an able and crafty Massachusetts politician who could attract money, men, and support to the cause. His political value was lost on the thousands who suffered wounds, maiming, and death because of his folly, and most of his soldiers felt only contempt for him.

Banks arrived before Port Hudson on May 23 with fifteen thousand troops and soon encircled the place and Major General Franklin Gardner's eight thousand Confederates. On the evening of May 26, Banks announced he had decided on an immediate assault upon the strongly entrenched enemy holding the high ground. He had already assured Grant that Confederates were panic stricken and that Port Hudson's fall "will be *instant and certain*." His battle plan, if it deserves that name, was so flawed as to invite disaster. Lieutenant Colonel Richard B. Irwin, 19th Army Corps adjutant, reported, "No time was fixed for the assault . . . nor any provision made to render the several attacks simultaneous." Overriding all objections, Banks ordered the attack for the next morning.[21]

On the extreme right of the Federal lines were 430 men of the 1st and 650 of the 3rd Native Guards, all commanded by Colonel John A. Nelson. Opposite them were about 550 men of the 39th Mississippi under Colonel William B. Shelby, some soldiers of a small battalion, and a few artillerymen. Supported by light and heavy artillery, they were dug in on a steep bluff overlooking the low ground in front. Before them a creek meandered and, between creek and bluff, river backwater formed another barrier before their positions. Given more experience, the black soldiers might have balked at advancing an inch against such a well-entrenched, almost invisible foe.[22]

Brigadier General William Dwight, who commanded that sector, was also unconcerned. He had taken it upon himself "to test the negro question." He wrote home, "The negro will have the fate of his race on his conduct." So he ordered the impossible attack shortly after 7 A.M. on May 27. The Native Guards met a hail of rifle fire and cyclones of cannister from Southern artillery, but a few of them managed to splash across the water barriers before they all fell back to the shelter of some trees. Their assault, like all that morning, was a costly failure.[23]

Casualty figures are suspect. Banks listed 44 killed, 133 wounded, and 3 missing for the 1st and 3rd Native Guards for the entire siege, with no breakdown for assaults. For the black 1st Engineers, he reported fifty-three casualties, including nineteen missing. Others gave much higher figures. The highest tally came from a 3rd Native Guards diarist who listed a staggering 371 killed and 150 wounded. A Confederate engineer officer wrote that "Two hundred of their dead, mostly negroes, were found upon the field the next day." Colonel Shelby, the 39th Mississippi's leader, said it was a "terrible slaughter" but that "Not one single man was killed or even wounded of my command."[24]

Black losses will never be known. No body count took place because Banks let the dead rot where they fell and the badly wounded lie between the lines until they died. Truces enabled white troops to recover their dead and rescue their wounded, but there were no such truces arranged on the Native Guards front. A Federal colonel recalled, "For reasons I could never learn, no flag of truce was ever sent to bury the colored soldiers who fell on that day." The black regiments had added recruits while on the march and in the area and many or most had not yet appeared on the muster rolls. If they died, they were forgotten men. It is also possible that some officers worked the substitution gambit, the ploy of assigning the names of dead or missing men to live replacements, as described by Joseph T. Wilson, a 2nd Native Guards soldier.[25]

Their attack immediately became freighted with political and social overtones. As one Confederate noted, "It was a battle between white and negro troops, and the first engagement of this war of any magnitude between the white man and the negro." In general, Confederates denigrated their conduct; Federals were favorably impressed, although some became irritated by the exaggerated accounts and sketches in Northern journals. George B. Sanders, a hospital steward with the 3rd Native Guards, matched the creative reporters and artists with a tale about the stoic black soldier with a leg shot off who pulled himself up on a log "with his leg a swinging and bleeding and fierd thirty rounds." In the short term, the hyperbole may have increased support for black troops in the North, but the exaggerations raised unsustainable expectations in the long term.[26]

After losing two thousand men on May 27, the troops expected to settle down to a sensible siege. They underestimated Banks's incompetence. He ordered another attack on June 14, even though prisoners and deserters reported the garrison had exhausted medical and food stocks, forcing them to eat mules and rats and to use tree bark for medicine. However weak and hungry, Confederates easily repulsed the uncoordinated assault, inflicting eighteen hundred casualties. On this doleful occasion, Native Guards had only a supporting role, so got off lightly.[27]

Port Hudson's garrison capitulated on July 9 after Vicksburg yielded on July 4, making its own position untenable as starvation neared. In Washington, this was treated as a great victory for the Union, a triumph won under Banks's adroit generalship. For that he received the Thanks of Congress, one of only fifteen officers so honored during the war.[28]

Even while occupied with the siege, Banks found time to manipulate the black soldier program to his advantage. He formed what he grandly called the Corps d'Afrique by appropriating the work of others, including Butler's Native Guards and five regiments organized by Brigadier General Daniel Ullmann, who was assigned that task by Lincoln. Of the corps' first ten regiments, Banks raised just one, the 1st Louisiana Engineers. While he wanted all the black troops under his command, he did not want any black officers and forced them out. He insisted that they were detrimental to the service, a constant embarrassment and annoyance while their presence "demoralizes both the white troops and the negroes." Doubtless some were incompetent and an embarrassment but assuredly no more so than Banks himself. However, it was true that the very existence of black officers angered many white soldiers.[29]

Black soldiers had much more to worry about than Banks's petty machinations. They knew Southern soldiers felt terribly vindictive toward blacks wearing Union blue. As a New York officer reported, "The rebs . . . fire on the negroes on all occasions." In one instance, he heard a Confederate call out to a white Federal standing by a black working party, "Hello, Yank. Get down there. I want to shoot that damn nigger!" That sort of behavior, widely known, inclined Federal troops to believe the rumors and campfire tales of atrocities committed by the rebels against captured or wounded black soldiers. For instance, citing one horrific story, Private Henry T. Johns, 49th Massachusetts, wrote, "I credit the assertions that the rebels . . . inhumanly murdered their [black] wounded and prisoners, piled them up on the parapet, and nailed them alive to the trees where their comrades could witness their dying struggles."[30]

Such atrocity stories circulated during the siege and persisted, taking on a life of their own. Although some black soldiers and a white officer went missing, their fates remain unknown. No corroborative firsthand testimony or evidence has emerged to support the atrocity allegations. Spurred by the grim tales, a war correspondent investigated and learned that no black prisoners were found in Port Hudson after it fell. He noted that "rumors are afloat, borne out . . . by facts, that our colored soldiers who have fallen into the hands of the rebels have not received the treatment recognized by civilized nations. In other words, we could find no negro prisoners in Port Hudson, and there were none in the hospital. The simple question is, Where are they?" Then an officer wrote a New York newspaper that "a white officer of colored troops and twenty men (colored) . . . were hanged within twenty-four hours after their capture." Ethan A. Hitchcock, the Federal commissioner of prisoner exchanges, became interested enough to inquire officially. Months later, a reply came from Port Hudson's new commanding officer, Brigadier General George L. Andrews, Banks's former chief of staff. Andrews wrote, "The letter from an officer at this post . . . was unauthorized and the statements . . . were unsupported by any evidence." He said he knew nothing of murders during the siege.[31]

Andrews liked to put the best face on unpleasant matters, especially those that might reflect upon him in any way. Apparently he spent no time investigating the question and quickly dismissed the allegations. Nevertheless, black troops who fought at Port Hudson firmly believed that murder was done there. They acted on that conviction more than a year later during a fight in Florida. A 2nd Maine Cavalry soldier wrote, "it did not make eny differance to them about the Rebs surrendering they would shoot them down the officers had hard work to stop them from killing all the prisoners when one of them would beg for his life the niggers would say rember port hudson."[32]

4

Milliken's Bend

AFTER JEFFERSON DAVIS'S PROCLAMATION
on Butler and after the first clashes between blacks and whites, Northerners felt uneasy. They sensed that the black soldiers and their officers
might face double jeopardy. Families worried about sons and brothers;
some soldiers shrugged it off while others fretted; a few denied reality.
One of the last was Captain William M. Parkinson, 8th Louisiana Infantry, African Descent. On May 20, 1863, he related how Confederates
overran one of their picket posts, left with some black prisoners, then
sent a man back to dispatch the seriously wounded white officer. Yet a
few days later he wrote home, "I hear that Jeff Davis has issued an order
to hang all officers of negro Reg if caught; Is it true."[1]

In that spring of 1863, it was not quite clear yet how Confederates would
comport themselves when fighting black Federals. Some indications

existed, as when they murdered and mutilated 1st Kansas Colored men or concentrated their fire upon black soldiers at Port Hudson. But possibly those were aberrations, flukes, or the work of fanatics, and Federals remained unsure. Confederates always knew what they would do about that particular challenge to the social order, but they had little need to express themselves on the subject and only a few spoke up.[2]

Port Hudson notwithstanding, Northerners continued to doubt that black troops would ever contribute much to the struggle. Some thought they might prove effective in quick, savage assaults, though determined resistance would just as likely cause them to turn and flee. Conversely, many believed that they would crumple instantly when attacked by Confederates. Oddly enough, some Southerners held a contrary opinion. Though they firmly believed their former slaves were mainly worthless as soldiers, they thought blacks might "against their tendencies . . . fight desperately" if cornered, just as would other of nature's creatures. More clashes in the spring and summer clarified Confederate practices and policy when dealing with black soldiers, and both sides learned something about their fighting ability.[3]

The first lessons came soon after Richmond ordered Lieutenant General Edmund Kirby Smith, Trans-Mississippi commander, to help lift the siege of Vicksburg, the fortified city vital to control of the river. In response, Smith sent Major General John G. Walker's Texas infantry division to Major General Richard Taylor in Louisiana. Smith told Taylor to use Walker's troops in some attempt to relieve and resupply Vicksburg. Taylor considered the strategy misdirected and futile. He recalled, "The problem was to withdraw the [Vicksburg] garrison, not to reinforce it. Remonstrances were of no avail. I was informed that . . . public opinion would condemn us if we did not try to do something." Indeed, Jefferson Davis said Vicksburg was the "nailhead" binding the Confederacy's two parts, and Lincoln, who ardently wanted it captured, called it the "key." Then their respective constituents agreed with that view. Now, however, some scholars say the city retained great political significance but little military value when the siege began. But that was true only after about mid-1862, when Federal gunboats ruled the river above and below the city. That domination stopped movement of supplies and Texas, Louisiana, and Arkansas troops from crossing the river and stranded there those already in the East.

Like it or not, Taylor made an effort to disrupt the Federal campaign. First, he ordered Walker to attack rear-area posts on the Louisiana side of the Mississippi above Vicksburg. Walker selected Brigadier General Henry E. McCulloch's brigade to take Milliken's Bend and Brigadier General James M. Hawes's brigade to capture Young's Point. They stepped off the night of June 6, to avoid the scorching sun and to spring early-morning surprise attacks.[4]

With fifteen hundred men in four regiments, McCulloch arrived within a mile and a half of Milliken's Bend at about 2:30 A.M. on June 7. However, a forewarned Colonel Herman Lieb, Milliken's commander, had already asked for help from Young's Point and had received 105 men of the 23rd Iowa and the gunboat *Choctaw*. Besides the Iowa men, Lieb had 941 raw recruits in several embryonic black regiments. But no black soldier had more than sixteen days' service, and some had served just a day or two. Lieb said that many were "unaccustomed to the use of muskets." In fact, many did not know how to load, aim, or fire one.[5]

Soon the Texans launched a full scale attack and charged the primary defense line, the river levee, McCulloch reported, "This charge was resisted by the negro portion of the enemy's force with considerable obstinacy, while the white or true Yankee portion ran like whipped curs." He failed to mention that his men charged while yelling "No quarter." One Federal officer insisted that they also carried a black flag, signifying they would neither give nor expect mercy, but this is a doubtful claim. Spurred to desperate resistance or frantic flight, almost half of Lieb's small force chose flight. First to flee were the Iowans. Agreeing with McCulloch, Lieb reported, "The 23rd . . . left the field soon after the enemy got possession of the levee, headed by their colonel, and were seen no more." Lieutenant Colonel Cyrus Sears, 11th Louisiana, suggested that the white troops decamped because they feared the Texans would murder them for fighting with their former slaves. Although Sears stayed, next to go was the 11th Louisiana, Lieb's strongest unit, with 395 men. They also followed the lead of their colonel, who rowed himself to safety aboard a gunboat.[6]

Hand-to-hand combat ensued when the Texans swarmed over the levee. Private Joseph P. Blessington, 16th Texas Infantry, wrote, "They made a stubborn fight. When our troops got into close quarters with them (the troops of the enemy were composed principally of negroes), bayonets were crossed, and muskets clubbed, and the struggle indeed became a close and deadly one." Lieutenant David Cornwell ordered his 9th Louisiana men to hold their fire and "not shoot a man if he could bayonet him and not to pull off his gun until the muzzle was against a rebel." One burly black soldier went forward "like a rocket" and savagely swung his rifle butt, "smashing in every head he could reach." Cornwell heard Confederates yelling, "Shoot that big nigger, shoot that big nigger!" In an instant, a bullet to the head stopped the rampaging Federal. Captain L. J. Hissong, also 9th Louisiana recalled, "Colored soldiers with their officers mixed up with the Rebels, clubbing with muskets, stabbing with bayonets and swords, shooting with pistol and musket." In Hissong's view, the melee had no parallel for ferocity during the war.[7]

Abruptly, Cornwell's luck ran out. He recalled, "I saw a johnny come in sight and told the darkey near me to plug him. He was too slow and the fellow plugged me. The ball shattered the bone of my right arm at the shoulder." He decided it could have been worse: "An inch to the right or left would have been my finish." In shock and pain, Cornwell still managed to make his way to the riverbank after yielding the levee to the Texans. There they had cover and concealment and there the gunboats *Choctaw* and *Lexington* had better fields of fire, though some Federals said the gunboats killed and wounded as many black soldiers as Texans.[8]

By this time, about midmorning or later, only about a third of Lieb's original force remained. But now he held a strong position on the riverbank, and the floating artillery platforms, the gunboats, could render effective aid. Confederates casualties were lighter, but they balked at exposing themselves to fire from the gunboats and they were exhausted from the long march, the fight, the heat, and the lack of water. Walker then decided it would be foolish to persist in an attack "which could only result in a fearful sacrifice of life." He ordered McCulloch to give it up. By then, his men had taken 184 casualties: 44 killed, 130 wounded, and 10 missing. In withdrawing, the Texans carried off their wounded and seventy to eighty prisoners, including a couple of officers.[9]

Although the Texans had attacked and ordinarily would have sustained more casualties than the defenders, the reverse was true. Lieb reported 652 casualties, including the 242 missing from the 11th Louisiana, but not the 23rd Iowa losses or any sustained by the many unmustered recruits or contrabands. Sears explained that contrabands would seize guns and join the fight. He noted, "Many such were killed, many wounded." He conceded it would be strange indeed "if the counts were not mixed, especially considering the very short acquaintance of the officers with their men." Another factor, which Sears seldom mentioned, was that all blacks looked alike to many Northern officers, making it difficult to fully determine losses.

Even so, unexplained anomalies marked the report submitted by Lieb, who was known as a straightforward, honest officer. For his own 9th Louisiana, he counted 66 officers and men killed on the spot, 108 wounded, and 22 missing, for a total casualty rate of 68 percent. Colonel William F. Fox, a respected Civil War statistician, listed the regiment's toll as 128 killed and mortally wounded, for a staggering 45 percent mortality rate. That meant that almost three times as many died as were wounded, although the usual ratio was four or five wounded for every man killed during the war. The 941 black soldiers at Milliken's Bend counted about 460 in killed, wounded, missing, or captured, or almost a 49 percent loss rate. These figures exclude the 11th Louisiana men who ran away, many of whom probably returned in a few days.

When Federals retreated to the riverbank, the Texans shot or bayoneted wounded black soldiers left behind. Sears said his men told him they had seen their comrades murdered, and Colonel Thomas K. Smith, there on detached duty, flatly said it was a butchery and that Confederates showed no quarter. Rear Admiral Porter said the same thing. From a nearby army hospital, Corporal Frank McGregor, 83rd Ohio, wrote home about the bloodthirsty Texans and their victims. He added, "I saw one poor darky who had six bayonet thrusts after having fallen by a shot. Many were killed thus by the enemy." The news spread quickly. Newspaper correspondents, separately writing from places distant from Milliken's Bend, heard and repeated it.[10]

With others, the Texans had also captured an entire company of forty-nine men and two officers. Immediately, those and other prisoners became a bother for all concerned. They brought embarrassment to Mc-Culloch, Walker, and Taylor; annoyance to Richmond; travail to Grant; and grim reality to officers and men of the black regiments. Initially, McCulloch felt his men had done well in recapturing Southern property, praised the young soldier who had tricked the company into captivity, and proposed rewarding the youth and a couple of other men with black prisoners as slaves. However, McCulloch's superiors were anything but pleased and were unwilling to reward anyone for such a faux pas. Both Walker and Major General Richard Taylor called it "unfortunate" that they had captured black soldiers. After confessing the error, Taylor asked his superiors for instructions.[11]

Lieutenant General Edmund Kirby Smith, Trans-Mississippi commander, was furious. He did not wait for official reports to reach him before he acted. He told Taylor, "I have been unofficially informed that some of your troops have captured negroes in arms. I hope this may not be so, and that your subordinates . . . may have recognized the propriety of giving no quarter to armed negroes and their officers. In this way we may be relieved from a disagreeable dilemma." That unpleasant situation would result if they openly executed black prisoners, possibly provoking Federal retaliation. Yet if they did not execute them, then they violated a basic Southern position on servile insurrection. He spelled it out again: "No quarter should be shown them." If, by mischance, they took black Federals prisoners, Smith ordered them turned over to state officials for trial and execution. In his view, such a course placed any onus upon civil authorities, relieved the army of responsibility, and Northern authorities could then take no exception.

A month after Smith issued his no-quarter orders, Secretary of War James A. Seddon weighed in with yet another modification. He advised, "Considering the negroes as deluded victims, they should be received and treated with mercy and returned to their owners." He added, "A few examples might perhaps be made, but to refuse them quarter would only make them, against their tendencies, fight desperately."

Earlier and later, Seddon advocated turning such prisoners over to civil authorities for trial and execution. But now the professed policy was to return them to their former owners, however impractical or impossible that was. Confederates always maintained that policy and practice were one and the same, no matter that the cumulative evidence proved that false. In practice, sometimes they tried to return former slaves to the owners; a few were tried in state courts, but mostly the no-quarter rule prevailed, no matter what Seddon said. In articulating the administration's position, he made several points. First, "negroes . . . captured in arms" were not soldiers—they were "deluded victims" innately incapable of fighting except as cornered animals. Second, they were recaptured property and their captors should spare them, offer merciful treatment, and return them to their owners. Third, Seddon approved executing a few to teach the others a lesson but advised that a blanket no-quarter policy was nonproductive. Notably, he omitted any instructions about white officers caught leading armed blacks. President Davis had already marked them as felons subject to execution.[12]

Meanwhile, tales of murder reached Federal authorities. Grant heard and acted upon the information. On June 22, about two weeks after the fight at Milliken's Bend and presumably after Taylor received the no-quarter order from Smith, Grant wrote a carefully phrased letter to Taylor: I feel no inclination to retaliate for the offenses of irresponsible persons, but if it is the policy of any general entrusted with the command of any troops to show 'no quarter' or to punish with death prisoners taken in battle, I will accept the issue. It may be you propose a different line of policy toward black troops and officers commanding them, to that practiced toward white troops. If so, I can assure you that these colored troops are regularly mustered into the service of the United States. The government and all officers serving under the government are bound to give the same protection to these troops that they do to any other troops.

Further, he hoped it was an erroneous report or that the executions occurred without official sanction. If the last, Grant urged that the guilty men suffer proper punishment. As a sharp reminder that he had the power and the means to retaliate, he noted that Federals had taken prisoners at Milliken's Bend and had treated them well, even though they were captured while "fighting under the black flag of no quarter."[13]

Colonel Thomas K. Smith, the officer on detached duty at Milliken's Bend, rode through the lines to deliver the letter. In reply, Taylor denied all. Writing before the receipt of Seddon's latest instructions, he advised Grant, "As regards negroes captured in arms, the officers of the Confederate States Army are required . . . to turn over all such to the civil authorities, to be dealt with according to the laws of the state wherein they were captured." Grant chose to accept the denial, either from conviction or for expediency's sake. He answered Taylor on July 4, 1863, the day Vicksburg fell, so likely he was also in an expansive mood. He wrote, "I could not credit the story, though told so straight, and I am now truly glad to hear your denial." Grant skirted the prisoner issue, merely noting, "I do not feel authorized to say what the Government may demand."[14]

No matter what Taylor said or what Grant wanted to believe, Confederates had executed two officers taken at Milliken's Bend. One was Captain Corydon Heath, formerly a sergeant of Battery G, 2nd Illinois Light Artillery. Heath was Lieutenant Cornwell's company commander in the 9th Louisiana, and Cornwell had seen him cut off and captured. The other was a Lieutenant Conn, 11th Louisiana. Confederates reportedly hanged Heath, but Conn's mode of execution is uncertain. Terse entries in the *Official Register* for volunteer officers note only that Heath and Conn were murdered after capture.[15]

Confederates captured up to eighty blacks at Milliken's Bend. Once taken alive, black soldiers usually could expect some safety in numbers, though there were no individual guarantees. As unfolding experience would show, Confederates often dispatched a few from a group of prisoners shortly after capture. That served to teach them a lesson, to establish control, or to exact vengeance. Probably an unlucky few Milliken's Bend captives became object lessons, but not all were hanged or shot. Their captors forcibly returned many to slavery and they wound up in Texas, where they "worked for the Confederacy," as Sears put it. He explained, "More or less of the men captured on picket [the forty-nine men] came scattering back until near Mar. 22, 1866, when the regiment was mustered out." The fate of the other thirty men is unknown.[16]

Milliken's Bend surprised and shocked Southerners who thought that they knew their chattels. It was a revelation: blacks would fight. With an air of wonder, Confederates admitted their former slaves had fought stubbornly and desperately. Sometimes they injected face-saving qualifications, as when one Texan reported that they "fought bravely for a little while" and then ran. Confederates invariably dismissed blacks as soldiers, and this was one of the rare occasions when they acknowledged either their courage or their fighting ability. Such startling news traveled swiftly. In Texas, a soldier's wife wrote that she had heard Confederates were "whiped" at Milliken's Bend. On a nearby Louisiana plantation, a young woman rejected the report: "It is said the Negro regiments there fought like mad demons, but we cannot believe that. We know from long experience they are cowards."[17]

Confederate attacks and raids continued in the area, leaving a swath of destruction. They burned plantations managed by Yankees on a free labor system and seized their ex–slave laborers. Black troops often guarded these enterprises, and Confederates fell upon them with a vengeance. Three days before the fight at Milliken's Bend, about sixty Southern cavalrymen attacked ninety black soldiers camped at Lake St. Joseph. Confederates reported, "Killed the captain (white), 12 negroes, and captured the remainder." There were no Federal wounded and no Confederate casualties, both in sharp contrast to normal battle experience, which strongly suggests that Confederates executed wounded men and perhaps their officer.[18]

In another clash above Milliken's Bend, black soldiers inflicted more casualties than they incurred, an uncommon result, but still lost the fight. On June 24, Confederates surrounded a Federal outpost at Mound Plantation, about ten miles below Lake Providence. Assistant Surgeon E. P. Becton, 16th Texas Cavalry, reported that "our cavalry attacked some negro warriors forted up on a high mound." Those warriors were 113 soldiers and 3 white officers of the 1st Arkansas Infantry, African Descent, and they held trenches dug atop an Indian burial mound. With a clear view, they fired with great accuracy, killing 4 and wounding 18 Confederates. That unexpected and effective resistance rankled the Southerners. For the life of them, literally, they could not allow their former slaves to best them. Indifferent to the cost, they would set matters straight. One soldier explained, "I think those with uniforms and arms should share the fate ordered by Col. [William H.] Parsons when he told the boys to charge them . . . kill them take none with uniforms on."

Reinforced and ready to assault, Parsons again demanded surrender. He and his men knew an attack would cost them dearly. Still, they felt confident that their superior ability would prevail, provided success came before Federal relief troops arrived. Such trial by fire proved unnecessary. The three Federal officers knew their fate if overwhelmed and decided glory's price was too high. So they voted to save themselves by sacrificing their men. Offering to yield if they were treated as prisoners of war, they stipulated they would surrender their men unconditionally. Parsons grudgingly accepted those terms.[19]

Confederates also rounded up black civilians in the vicinity, "some 800 in number—big, little, old, and young . . . all that tried to escape were shot." Indeed, bodies littered the area, as Federals afterward confirmed. Then they herded the recaptured slaves and the black soldiers toward Delhi, Louisiana. But during that brief march, more than 10 percent of the mound's defenders inexplicably expired. Writing from Delhi, one of Walker's infantrymen tersely noted, "Some 12 or 15 of the Negroes died before we got here with them." *Died* was likely his euphemism for killing. Those that survived the trek returned to slavery, assigned "to *garrison* the plantations," as an army surgeon joked. Further, possibly two of the three officers who ingloriously sought to save their own skins at the expense of their men may have failed in their purpose. Sometime later, citizens of the area gave sworn statements that a Confederate staff officer ordered the pair shot and buried in woods near Monroe, Louisiana. However, this cannot be confirmed and remains an open question.[20]

The Mounds Plantation affair was another embarrassment for Walker. Again, he had to apologize for taking black prisoners. He straightforwardly declared, "I consider it an unfortunate circumstance that any armed negroes were captured, but . . ." Then he explained that their fort was very strong, that an assault would have cost lives and time, and that the best thing to do was to accept the proffered conditions. Still, he could report that they had recaptured about two thousand strayed slaves and returned them to their masters. Surgeon Becton found the affair distinctly unsatisfactory. He complained, "These little negro skirmishes do not amount to anything . . . when the history of this was is written we will be 'left out in the wet.'"[21]

Moreover, those little skirmishes could never compensate for the twin blows of July 4, 1863, the day that Vicksburg surrendered and Lee retreated from Gettysburg. Of the two, Vicksburg's loss caused the greater immediate injury. Surrender of that city and Port Hudson a few days later returned the Mississippi to the Union, splitting the Confederacy into two unequal parts. Soon the Federals had fleets of gunboats patrolling the waterway, blocking any substantial Confederate movement on or across the river. Most Southerners knew the sundering of the Confederacy was a grave and irreparable strategic reversal, though many were uncertain about Gettysburg's significance.[22]

So it was that the war's third summer turned into a bleak time for disheartened Southerners. After his capture at Vicksburg, a 2nd Missouri corporal lamented, "The region from which the fighting material was drawn, was being rapidly circumscribed, and the military resources of the country . . . were almost exhausted." Across the river, a Texas cavalryman in Louisiana told his family, "This has caused deep gloom. . . . We are gone up I fear." After retreating from Gettysburg, a dispirited North Carolina soldier told his wife, "I can say to you that I got out of heart as sone as we got in Pensilvania to see the men they have thare that never bin in the war . . . more men that never bin in the war then we Ever had in the war and so I can't see no use in fiteing they would better setil it some way for I Believe in my heart that we are whiped . . . the yankees got half of the confedersy now and stil a giting more."[23]

Those at home, both high and low, also felt the tug of doubt and the first pulse of desperation. A Georgia woman thought that "things have never appeared so dark." Reportedly even Vice President Alexander H. Stephens privately lost hope after the double reverses. Yet, though despondent, most remained determined to see it through, ever hopeful of some decisive victory, European intervention, or an election triumph for peace advocates in the North. Many, in fact, summoned a new resolve.[24]

Summary Disposals at Jackson, Louisiana

Now the animus toward black Federals only increased and Confederates soon provided another demonstration of their seething anger. About

325 Federals, including 250 black soldiers, marched from Port Hudson, Louisiana, to nearby Jackson to collect black recruits. Led by an inept lieutenant, they worked undisturbed and had rounded up fifty candidates by early afternoon of August 3. Then they began to hear whispers about Confederate cavalry riding toward them. One townswoman thought that "if everybody knew it, even children, there was little chance of its being a surprise to the Yankees." But it was, at least to their leader. He thought it all too vague and sent scouts to find out for sure. None returned—they were killed, captured, or cut off. Soon Confederates verified the reports for him. They fell upon the town about 5 P.M., striking with five hundred mounted men under Colonel John L. Logan, 11th Arkansas Infantry.[25]

Brisk street fighting took place as the Federals retreated through the town. Some holed up in a brick college building and fired from the windows. Confederates ended that resistance when they brought up a mountain howitzer and lobbed shells inside. One eyewitness was thirteen-year-old Celine Fremaux, whose family lived in town. She recalled, "The booming of cannon mixed with the lighter shot and a sort of roar like many voices and trampling of feet and hooves. The fighting came nearer and nearer. We could see the fire and the dim forms." Pushed through town, the Federals kept right on going. In their haste, they missed the Port Hudson road and took a path that soon became impassable for artillery and wagons. They quickly abandoned all, losing guns, caissons, wagons, and forty horses and mules, leaving the animals in their traces as they fled.

Brigadier General George L. Andrews, Port Hudson's new commander, put the best face possible on the dismal affair. He reported, "After a conflict of some length, finding the enemy in greatly superior numbers, the detachment retreated with no great loss at first." Unlike Andrews, Colonel Logan was there, and his account more closely matched reality. He reported, "I met the enemy at Jackson, whipping him handsomely. The enemy fled in the greatest confusion, leaving his dead and wounded behind him. It was a complete rout." Logan lost twelve killed and wounded, or about 2 percent of his force. Andrews's initial and incomplete casualty list showed his men lost at least a quarter of their strength, including four officers and forty-five men from the black units. They probably lost more than that, not counting the fifty recruits they had corralled. W. H. Pascoe, one of Logan's cavalrymen, recalled, "The negroes in camp broke and ran, but not before a large number had been killed, while the military ardor of those that escaped was cooled."[26]

Black soldiers left behind were as good as dead. While daylight remained, Confederates killed the wounded, shot prisoners, and hanged
any stragglers they caught. At first light the next morning, Logan's men
began hunting down those who had escaped the previous evening's
slaughter. When found, many were dispatched on the spot. Spared at
first, twenty-two black Federals and a white officer were marched away
from Jackson and then shot in a group on the road. A few avoided capture and returned safely to Port Hudson to give eyewitness accounts of
the atrocities.

Celine Fremaux remembered it all vividly and confirmed their reports. She recalled, "After the little battle in Jackson quite a number of
niggers had become separated from their commands. They knew the
law: All slaves taken armed against the whites were hung or shot. So they
wandered about the woods for some days. Some . . . were caught by the
soldiers and summarily executed. I knew this was done but of course I
never saw an execution." Nevertheless, she stumbled upon some grisly
evidence. At dusk one day, she walked through a pine thicket. She recalled, "I saw something moving and nearly lost my strength! Just before
me, a little to one side, two niggers were hung to a tree limb, their feet
just clear of the ground."[27]

Andrews responded to the reports by writing Logan on August 5,
offering him face-saving excuses for the murders before threatening retaliation. Logan denied everything and vowed counterretaliation. Meanwhile, the day before, he had asked superiors what to do with his black
captives. While the timing is uncertain, right about then Logan had no
such prisoners to worry about. Perhaps he was unaware of that, though
his men knew. He must have learned the truth shortly, however, because
it did not take long for the story to reach the department commander,
General Joseph E. Johnston. He ordered his cavalry leader, Major General Stephen D. Lee, to investigate a report that "twenty-three prisoners
(one white officer and twenty-two colored and negro privates) were put
to death in cold blood and without form of law, and, if it is true, to bring
the culprits to trial."[28]

Again the pesky business returned to plague Logan. He demanded full
reports in writing and without delay from Colonel Frank P. Powers, his
cavalry chief, and Colonel John Griffith, who led an Arkansas mounted
infantry regiment. They had marched the prisoners off on the wrong
road after leaving Jackson. In almost identical language, both said their
prisoners tried to escape and so were shot and killed in the attempt. Both

pointedly noted that no other Federals were present, which meant there were no hostile witnesses. Logan sent their responses to Lee, along with his own candid comment. He wrote, "My own opinion is that the negroes were summarily disposed of; by whom I cannot say, as all deny [involvement]." Lee sent the correspondence to Johnston and advised that he did not consider it in the army's best interest to pursue the matter.

Johnston, a Virginian, West Point graduate, and fourth ranking full general in the Confederate army, deplored the killing if the prisoners "were put to death in cold blood and without form of law." Plainly, he had no argument with the result. Yet he wanted executions done according to the rules, unlike Lieutenant General Smith, who just wanted it done. Johnston's legalistic position never had a chance. Confederate soldiers preferred direct and summary action.[29]

5

Fort Wagner

VICKSBURG'S FALL AND LEE'S RETREAT from Gettysburg in July 1863, the war's third summer, buoyed the North, although discontent, war weariness, and racism still simmered in a volatile stew. That mix boiled over in mid-July, when mobs ran wild during the New York City draft riots. Rebelling against conscription, the protesters hunted down and lynched blacks, burned a black orphanage, trashed draft offices, set fires, and looted stores. As the antidraft and anti-Negro rampage ebbed, Confederate defenders shredded the 54th Massachusetts Infantry (Colored) at Fort Wagner, Charleston, South Carolina.

Union land and sea forces had hammered at the city's gates for months. Although Charleston was an important port, its "symbolic significance was greater than its strategic importance," as a leading Civil War historian noted. As it was close to eastern population centers, the clash of

arms drew many war correspondents, although often they had little to
report. However, in early June 1863, newsmen had something to tell
their readers when that regiment of free Northern blacks, the 54th Massachusetts, arrived to take part in operations against the city where the
war had begun.[1]

During the ensuing fighting, Confederates killed some black prisoners, but almost a hundred became live captives, though a score or more
soon died of mortal wounds. Those who survived endured an experience
as strange and scarifying as it was unique. The publicity attendant upon
their capture limited Confederate options and revealed how seriously
they feared Yankee retaliation, a needless concern, and how much they
worried about an adverse European reaction if they summarily disposed
of those prisoners, a valid consideration. Hard-line civil authorities and
pragmatic military leaders clashed over their disposition, and both pres-
sured the judiciary when the matter went to civil courts. Finally, all
agreed that the prisoners were unwelcome "embarrassments" and created
an impossible dilemma, thus precluding any action. But only the unusual
glare of publicity caused the contretemps; without it, the results would
have been much different.

Twenty-six-year-old Colonel Robert G. Shaw, a volunteer officer and
son of a prominent Massachusetts abolitionist family, led the 54th. On
June 11, the regiment took part in a coastal raid. Led by Colonel James
Montgomery, the Kansas "bush-whacker," as Shaw termed him, the 54th
and part of Montgomery's 2nd South Carolina sailed up the Altamaha
River to the small town of Darien, Georgia. Undefended and nearly
deserted, the little settlement stirred Montgomery's old Border warfare
instincts. He ordered the place plundered and the black soldiers cheerfully obeyed. They stole everything in sight, useful or not, from shops
and homes. Then Montgomery ordered Darien put to the torch. Shaw
objected but Montgomery insisted that Southerners must learn that it
was real war and that the hand of God would sweep them away "like
the Jews of old." Referring to Confederate sanctions against black troops,
he added, "We are outlawed, and therefore not bound by the rules of
regular warfare." Such questionable logic left Shaw unpersuaded, but
Montgomery cheerfully assumed all responsibility. So the town went
up in smoke, and one of Shaw's soldiers reported, "The town of Darien
is no more."[2]

Shaw contemptuously referred to Darien as "this dirty piece of business . . . this barbarous sort of warfare." He declared there was no justifi-

cation for torching Darien and feared that it would harm the reputation of black troops and their officers. His fears were realized as the news about Darien circulated. Some Northern newspapers denounced it, and soldiers looked askance at Montgomery's zealotry and the plundering. For Southerners, it only reinforced deep-seated convictions about Yankee vandalism and African savagery. Marching toward Gettysburg, a Confederate officer picked up a scrap of windblown newspaper and read about Darien. Angry and indignant, he complained that his noble men had saved a Yankee town from flames while black Federals torched the Georgia village.[3]

Determined "to prove that a negro can be made a good soldier," Shaw wanted an active combat role and equal pay for his men. Under the rules, black troops received just $10 a month, minus a monthly deduction of $3 for clothing. That meant that all black soldiers, whether private or sergeant-major, received $7 a month, about half the white private's $13. That differential had mollified the great many Northerners who strongly opposed any semblance of equality for blacks. In effect, the North treated them as second-class soldiers and the South did not consider them soldiers at all. Black troops strongly resented the discrimination, often refusing to take the half pay, and some deserted while others became mutinous. Shaw's men were among those who renounced the inequitable pay, and thus went eighteen months without a penny. Finally persuaded that fairness required equal pay for all soldiers, Congress adopted a uniform scale on June 15, 1864, and eventually made it partially retroactive. But it was not until September of 1864 that the 54th Massachusetts men got their soldiers' mite, and the resentment lingered for many years.[4]

However, Shaw soon got his wish to show his men fit for more than "mere guerrilla warfare" and to fight with white troops. Major General Quincy A. Gillmore, a West Point graduate who had replaced Hunter, probably had minimal interest in validating the black soldier program. But he needed more troops for an attack on Morris Island, which controlled the water approaches to Fort Sumter, key to the harbor. White troops took most of the island on July 10 but waited until the next day to launch a weak attack against the strong point on the northern tip. That redoubt, which Confederates always called "Battery Wagner" and Federals "Fort Wagner," easily repelled the assault. Meanwhile, Gillmore moved the 54th to James Island.[5]

On James Island, Shaw strolled about and decided nothing much would happen there. But several days later, early on July 16, about fourteen

hundred Confederates slammed into his picket line of five officers and
two hundred men, overwhelming the thin line of black soldiers. At times,
some men found themselves cut off and fighting front and rear. While
attempting to escape, a few hid and some fled to a creek, where several
drowned. Others, with a clear line of retreat, backpedaled slowly, firing
as they went. That delaying action allowed the white 10th Connecticut
pickets on the left to withdraw safely. Praising the black soldiers, a Connecticut officer said they had prevented the enemy from surrounding his
regiment. After the Federals fell back on their main line, Confederates
abandoned the attack. Shaw's men then returned and reoccupied their
old picket line.[6]

During the brief affray, 25 percent of the pickets became casualties.
Captain Luis F. Emilio counted eleven killed or mortally wounded, twenty-five wounded, and thirteen captured, for a loss total of forty-nine. Nevertheless, officers and men were pleased that the regiment had behaved well
in its baptism of fire. One exuberant soldier declared, "The rebels yelled
and hooted, but they could not drive us." Shaw was particularly gratified
with the praise from his commanding general and from officers and men
of white regiments. He was ever alive to what others thought of his black
soldiers and, in their reflected shame or glory, how he appeared.[7]

Confederates, who derided black soldiers' conduct in the fight, reported capturing fourteen. One Southern soldier reported, "The prisoners believe they are to be hung, and gave as a reason for fighting as
well as they did, that they would rather die of bullet than rope." The
black soldiers had cause for concern. While some soldiers had survived
capture, others had not. Emilio related, "It was told by some of those
who lay concealed, that where the Confederate officers were, the colored
soldiers had been protected; but that in other cases short shrift was given,
and three men had been shot and others bayonetted." Confirming the
battlefield executions, a Confederate artilleryman wrote, "They were
surprised by our troops and literally shot down while on their knees
begging for quarters and mercy." The soldier who told of the prisoners'
fear of hanging also described one black soldier's attempt to surrender:
"But unfortunately somebody's gun went off about the same time, and
the fellow was killed."[8]

Told that Confederates shot some of his wounded men, Shaw believed
none of it. Tethered to a romantic vision of the war, he rejected cruel
reality. Shaw declared, "It is very common for frightened men to tell
fearful stories of what they have seen." While denying that unpleasant

truth, he willingly accepted the prospect of his own death in the pending attack against Fort Wagner.[9]

Shaw and his men were to spearhead the attack. Brigadier General Truman Seymour, the assault force leader, said they chose the 54th because it was a strong regiment with good officers. Colonel Norwood P. Hallowell, formerly the 54th's second in command, offered a more cynical reason. He wrote, "A characteristic of veteran troops is that they cannot always be made to attempt the seemingly impossible." His point was that the inexperienced black soldiers would attack because they did not know any better. A New York newspaper correspondent said the real reason was that the generals regarded the black soldiers as expendable. While that possibly figured in their thinking, probably it was not the sole consideration. In any event, Shaw eagerly welcomed the perilous assignment, despite the acute exhaustion and hunger of his men.[10]

About 7:45 P.M. on July 18, the regiment led the attack with 620 officers and men. Sheets of flame flared on the ramparts, and a storm of lead scythed through the advancing ranks. "They mowed us down," one black soldier said, and no one on either side would ever contradict him. Bent over, as if pushing through a fierce gale, the Federals pushed onward. Sergeant Major Lewis Douglass related, "Men fell all around me. A shell would explode and clear a space of twenty feet. Our men would close up again but it was no use." Lieutenant John W. M. Appleton said he could hear canister tearing into the flesh of men near him. Many fell dead and wounded as they crossed a water-filled moat, then more crumpled as they climbed the fort's sharply inclined face. "We went at it," Private James H. Gooding recalled, "over the ditch and onto the parapet . . . but we could not get into the fort."[11]

Then, in the darkness, Federals in the second attack wave fired upon 54th soldiers from the rear. Still, a few entered Fort Wagner, where the close-quarter fighting was even deadlier. Men were shot once, twice, and three times before they fell. 1st Lieutenant James W. Grace related, "Such a tremendous fire right in our faces caused us to fall back." 1st Sergeant Stephen A. Swailes agreed, "It [was] madness to attempt anything farther." But extricating themselves proved almost as costly as attacking. Confederates rolled lit short-fused artillery shells down on men huddled at the slope's base and shot them as they withdrew.[12] Gillmore, the assault's author, finally admitted the attack had failed with heavy losses. Without hesitation, he quickly blamed the 54th for the debacle and declared that the "leading regiment was soon thrown into a state of

disorder, which reacted disadvantageously upon those which followed."
But his troops, mostly white, declared the attack was doomed from the
start and that it was a "useless Slaughter . . . of no benefit to the Country
or anyone."[13]

However, the 54th garnered very favorable coverage in the Northern
press; Sergeant William H. Carney won the Medal of Honor, the first
black recipient; and most white soldiers praised them, though a few
thought they got too much credit. But the 54th sustained more casualties than any other unit, losing about 45 percent of its assault strength.
Emilio, later the 54th's historian, tallied 79 men mortally wounded or
killed, including Shaw, and 281 casualties in all. At least seventy-eight
men became prisoners, but about twenty of them were mortally wounded.
All told, Federals listed more than fifteen hundred casualties, or about
34 percent of the attack force. Confederates reported just 174 killed,
wounded, and missing from the 1,200-man garrison during both the
artillery barrage and the assault.[14]

As usual, the appearance of black soldiers had enraged defending
Confederates. A North Carolina officer wrote, "This great slaughter
shows how desperately our men, maddened and infuriated at the sight
of negro troops, fought." Fifty years later, the 32nd Georgia's colonel was
still angry that the Yankees had used blacks against them at Wagner, or
anywhere else for that matter. Confederates also insisted that the 54th
soldiers had "fled in wild terror" and "rushed like a crowd of maniacs
back to the rear." Black prisoners, wounded or not, endured dire threats
and mistreatment. Knots of angry soldiers surrounded them and warned
that they would be hanged before sundown. Evacuated from Morris
Island to Charleston, one batch of wounded 54th men spent the night
lying untended on a wharf, when Confederates there refused to move
them to a hospital.[15]

To show their utter contempt for an aristocratic Yankee who betrayed
his race and class, they sought to punish and disgrace Shaw even in death.
First they stripped him down to his underwear, robbing the corpse of
clothing, arms, and valuables. Then they tipped him into a common
burial pit. An officer who supervised the work said, "I put that Yankee
colonel just where he deserved to be—in a hole with six of his niggers."
They let the outside world know about it and obviously gained some
satisfaction from Northern outrage. At the time it was taboo to bury
whites and blacks together, and it was a violation of military custom to
inter officers and enlisted men together. In reaction to Shaw's death and

rude burial, one of his men angrily wrote, "I still feel more Eagor for the struggle than I ever yet have, for now I wish to have Revenge for our galant Curnel and the spilt blood of our captin."[16]

Of more immediate interest to black soldiers was the fate of their captured comrades, a concern not shared by ranking Federal officers. During a parley for the exchange of wounded prisoners, Union Brigadier General Israel Vogdes carefully avoided mentioning wounded black soldiers. Doubtless he omitted them from the agenda because he feared it might jeopardize the return of wounded white soldiers. His Confederate counterpart, Brigadier General Johnson Hagood, also reported that neither Vogdes nor anyone in his entourage inquired about Shaw, though they had asked about other officers and requested and received the body of the 7th New Hampshire's colonel. Right after that meeting, Gillmore loudly complained that Confederates had failed to deliver wounded blacks and called it a breach of faith. General Pierre Gustave T. Beauregard, the Confederate commander, immediately and acidly replied that "You chose, sir, to ignore your negro ally."[17]

Again, black prisoners created an irksome, perplexing problem. On July 16, after the action on James Island, Hagood had asked, "Thirteen prisoners 54th Massachusetts, black. What shall I do with them?" Many more such prisoners resulted from the assault on Wagner and still no answer came. Since most were free men from Northern states, that placed them in some uncertain, debatable category. Beauregard was at a loss, so he asked Richmond, "Several . . . claim to be free, from Massachusetts. Shall they be turned over to the state authorities with the other negroes?" President Davis and Congress had already decreed that armed blacks and their white officers were insurrectionists, subject to execution. Yet tens of thousands of them were entering Federal service, promising endless difficulties. Most recruits came from the South's slave population, but others were from Northern slave states. Then there were two kinds of free blacks—the very few from the South and the many from the North.

White officers leading black troops clearly aided and promoted servile insurrection. Still, the administration hesitated to hold show trials and publicly hang them, although some had already met summary ends. Then there were other considerations: European opinion and Federal reaction. They still hoped for European recognition, and wholesale executions of captured black soldiers and their officers would not further that cause. Seddon and military leaders feared Federal retaliation, but politicians saw only the threat to social order, responding to fierce and raw emotions. Quite rapidly, the whole thing became a quagmire of unwelcome choices.

Beauregard repeated his request for guidance on July 21. Almost plaintively he asked, "What shall be done with the negro prisoners who say they are free? Please answer." Secretary of War James A. Seddon replied the next day, ordering, "They are to be handed over to the authorities of the State where captured to be dealt with according to the laws thereof." Beauregard then informed South Carolina Governor Milledge L. Bonham that the prisoners were all his. Civil authorities took them in mid-August and placed them in Charleston's city jail. There the new prisoners found four black sailors, held there since the end of January, when Confederates captured their gunboat, the USS *Isaac Smith*. Later, a few men from the 55th Massachusetts Infantry (Colored) joined the miserable group.[18]

Now it was Bonham's turn to flail around in the quicksand. Previously he had demanded that Beauregard turn over the captured blacks and their officers so he could try them forthwith for their capital offenses. Beauregard had stalled, citing "grave international questions," and forwarded the demand to Richmond. Then Bonham learned that Davis and Congress had issued conflicting instructions. Davis had directed that officers be turned over to the states for trial and likely execution and the black enlisted men treated as "unwilling instruments in . . . these crimes" and returned to slavery. Congress, filled with firebrand politicians, voted for sterner treatment. They decided military tribunals should try the officers while state courts deal with the men.[19]

Bonham requested clarification. He pointed out that "free negroes will be punishable . . . with death" under South Carolina laws, although he could commute sentences and Davis could do the same for officers under the resolution passed by Congress. He thought the several authorities should cooperate to achieve uniform punishment for the same crime. Still, he said he would immediately order trials for slaves and free Southern blacks but delay action on the free Northerners. Seddon quickly handed the letter to Davis, who, just as smartly, returned it, requesting his views. But Seddon had no firm answers. He offered a tentative solution, suggesting that purposeful delay might solve the problem. Seddon wrote:

> Under present circumstances the free negroes should be either promptly executed or the determination arrived at and announced not to execute them during the war. I do not think they should

be regarded as regular prisoners of war, but dealt with in some exceptional way to mark our stern reprobation of the barbarous employment of such inciters to insurrection with all its attendant horrors in our slave-holding states. This might perhaps be effectually done both to deter and to meet the requirements of our own people by holding them to hard labor during the war. I incline to advise the latter course.

Davis noted that Congress left him with no discretion concerning captured black Federals but that he had some latitude concerning their white officers. Still, the army needed to yield the black Federals to the states, though that created new difficulties. Referring to Bonham's concern about unequal punishments, Davis pointed out that cases would differ, and that Confederate tribunals would deal with one class while state courts, with varying laws, would handle another class. He saw no solution except to adopt Seddon's suggestion: bring no cases to trial. However, he was not sure how much discretion Bonham had. Either Bonham believed he had no discretion or he chose not to exercise it. In any event, he quickly ordered a trial for four 54th Massachusetts soldiers, allegedly former slaves, and appointed equally able prosecution and defense attorneys. The judges, however, felt severe pressure both for and against convictions. For example, Beauregard's chief of staff reminded everyone that any "retaliation would fall alone upon the military forces of the Confederacy." Proceedings ended when the judges escaped their predicament by declaring that they lacked jurisdiction.

Bonham then gave up on the Massachusetts prisoners. A year later, he told Seddon that like cases tried before similar courts had resulted in convictions and executions. Still, he said he "fully appreciated the embarrassments surrounding this question." In reply, Seddon admitted to difficulties in carrying out the wishes of Congress. States objected to receiving black Federals and, when accepted, they could not arrange trials. By that time, the latter half of 1864, Seddon worried even more about "the serious consequences which might ensue from the rigid enforcement of the act of Congress."[20]

Meanwhile, Lincoln had issued an executive order addressing the status of black Federals. Dated July 30, 1863, the order declared that the United States would protect all of its soldiers. He wrote, "The law of nations and the usages and customs of war . . . permit no distinctions as to color in the treatment of prisoners of war." Further, he promised eye-for-eye retaliation for violations. Lincoln pledged, "For every soldier of the United States killed in violation of the laws of war a rebel soldier shall be executed, and for everyone enslaved by the enemy or sold into slavery a rebel soldier shall be placed at hard labor on the public works."[21]

It was a fangless order, though pleasing to contemplate. Most Northerners would support the principle, at least in the abstract. Few, however, wanted it carried out, and it would always meet strong public and military resistance. Some Northerners had ethical objections, balking at a return to barbarism or lowering Federal conduct to the enemy's standards. Mainly, though, soldiers and civilians alike believed that eye-for-an eye retaliation worked both ways and would only result in more graves for white soldiers without benefiting blacks. Lincoln probably understood all this, but he believed he should make the gesture. However, neither he nor anyone else acted upon its provisions. Though it was a categorical directive, War Department officials ignored it, never adopting any rules to apply the order. Few troop commanders knew of it, and apparently none invoked it to punish and deter violations. Southern soldiers continued to kill wounded or captured blacks with impunity. They modified the practice of returning former slaves to private owners when their military labor needs had higher priority. But the men were still enslaved, with the army acting as their new masters.

As time passed, the respective positions hardened. Confederates resolutely refused to exchange black soldiers. They thought it preposterous even to suggest exchanging blacks for whites, when that clearly would bestow de facto equality upon their former slaves. Also taking a hard line, the North halted all prisoner trades unless blacks were included. Himself a captive, a Pennsylvania infantry officer explained, "It appeared no arrangements for a general exchange could be effected, for the rebels would not recognize the negro as a soldier and consent to his exchange; and our government would not discriminate against him. The prisoners generally supported the government in that position, though they had to suffer on account of it."[22]

For months the black prisoners languished in the Charleston city jail, the "nastiest, dirtiest, filthiest, lousiest place" most would ever experience. Ethan A. Hitchcock, the Union's commissioner for prisoner exchanges, admitted he could do nothing for them. Opposed to following the South's "savage example" of retaliation in kind, Hitchcock said that only force of arms and victory would achieve the desired results. But then Governor Bonham finally tired of the whole business and transferred the black captives back to military control on December 8, 1864. They were transferred to an army prisoner of war camp at Florence, South Carolina.[23]

That move proved fatal to more than a third of the prisoners in less than three months. After extensive investigation, Captain Emilio found that thirty-nine men went from Charleston to Florence. In February of 1865, as Sherman's troops approached, Confederates moved prisoners from Florence, shifting them from one place to another until they ran out of space and time. Finally, they wound up in woods between Wilmington and Goldsboro, North Carolina. There, between February 26 and March 4, harried Confederates paroled them, including the 54th Massachusetts soldiers. They were the survivors of starvation, disease, and shootings. In his final accounting, Emilio reported, "We have a record of twelve who died before, and two immediately after release—a fearful mortality in less than three months, and nearly four times as great as sustained in seventeen months at Charleston."[24]

6

Olustee

AS THE UNENDING WAR WORE ON, grim re-
solve had replaced the earlier exuberant enthusiasm. In mid-1863, a New
Hampshire soldier wrote that "the Rebs are mighty obstinate and fight
like the d——l" and soon a Confederate officer returned the left-handed
compliment by observing that "the yanks . . . are a persevering people."
The Yankees also persisted in mobilizing black men, and, by the fall of
1863, more than thirty-seven thousand served in fifty-eight regiments.
Judging the experiment a success, the administration had authorized
another twenty or thirty black regiments. As thousands of former slaves
began wearing Union blue, they took part in more expeditions, raids,
and battles. Increasingly, black and white Federal forces brought the war
home to Southern civilians, causing grief, fear, hardship, humiliation, loss
of property, imprisonment, and even death. All of this further inflamed

Confederate soldiers, honor bound to protect family and hearth and to punish intruders.[1]

Raids by black Federals terrified Southern civilians the most. Their forays undermined morale and demonstrated that the Confederacy could not always protect its own citizens. That the blacks wore uniforms made it worse, not better. Uniforms vested power and authority in the beings that Southerners considered feral and primitive. Consequently, women left alone trembled, fearing unspeakable horrors, when black troops approached. So a young Louisiana woman declared she would rather face a firing squad than the "unreasoning animals." Fear and frustration gnawed at Southern soldiers far from home when they heard appalling stories about Yankee arson, robbery, pillage, and brutality and dark tales of abuse by black troops. They felt an impotent rage when they could not be there to defend their families, a primary duty in their culture. Doing what he could from afar, one anxious soldier told his wife to keep a pistol with her if Federal troops occupied their area. If they approached their door, he instructed that she must "meet them *boldly*, pistol in hand." That might have proved risky advice for women during one of the first large-scale forays by black troops.[2]

Black Raiders Hit North Carolina

Brigadier General Edward A. Wild led his African Brigade on that incursion, leaving Norfolk, Virginia, on December 5, 1863. A physician who had studied in France and had served as a medical officer in the Turkish army, Wild was a fervent abolitionist and advocate of black equality. His seventeen-hundred-man column embarked on a month-long raid through eastern North Carolina's rich agricultural region. The object was to free slaves, find recruits, suppress guerrillas, and discomfit the enemy. When a supply ship failed to arrive, Wild decided to live off the countryside. A war correspondent reported, "The inhabitants being almost exclusively 'secesh,' the colored boys were allowed to forage at will along the road."

Wild said that he favored a rigorous style of warfare. That meant he burned homes and barns, killed livestock, and took hostages, both male and female. However, he swore, "All our prisoners had the benefit of a drumhead court-martial." Wild himself pulled the drop on a makeshift gallows prepared for one alleged guerrilla. Unfortunately for the condemned man, the fall proved too short to break his neck and he took long minutes to die by strangulation. Then Wild pinned a placard to the corpse on which he had written, "This guerrilla hanged by order of Brigadier-General Wild. Daniel Bright, of Pasquotank County." Besides strangling the hapless Bright, Wild succeeded in bringing off about twenty-five hundred slaves. But most were women and children, and he collected no more than one hundred able-bodied males for his African Brigade. In the process, he lost seven men killed, nine wounded, and one captured.

Tales of child murder, arson, and mistreatment of white women by Wild's black troops ignited Southern passions, causing a Confederate congressional committee to investigate. Major General George E. Pickett condemned Butler, then commanding the Department of Virginia and North Carolina, as the raid's instigator. Pickett declared, "Butler's plan, evidently, is to let loose his swarm of blacks upon our ladies and defenseless families, plunder and devastate the country." He wanted his men to "hang at once every one captured [from] . . . the expedition." The evidence, although mostly ex parte, indicates that Wild got carried away with his notions of righteous vengeance. At a time when society required gallant treatment of women, Wild crudely embarrassed and humiliated his female hostages. For instance, they were compelled to relieve themselves in the street while under the eye of a black soldier-guard. Some excesses caused even Butler to flinch. He revoked Wild's order to hang the women unless his captured men were returned unharmed.[3]

Although pillaging was widespread during the war, many commanders thought it particularly important to keep black soldiers in check. Colonel Samuel A. Duncan, who led a black brigade on a foray in Virginia, said that pillaging demoralized his men. He hoped that in the future they would "be employed in the more legitimate methods of warfare." Another colonel complained that the expedition had erased in one week the discipline instilled over many months. He ordered his officers to shoot any man who refused to stop plundering. When a disobedient black soldier was shot where he stood, the colonel thought that went far toward restoring discipline. Their superior, Brigadier General Isaac J. Wistar, wrote that the "demoralizing consequences of general license to plunder private property . . . are peculiarly applicable to colored troops, who, according to my observation, especially require to be held with a firm hand."[4]

Some of the anger and concern expressed by absent Confederate soldiers over raids by black troops cloaked a deeper, often unspoken anxiety about rape. Southerners heard usually false but lurid tales of black soldiers defiling white women, often retailed by Confederate officers. For instance, when Brigadier General St. John R. Liddell described a foray by black infantry in Alabama, he asserted, "They often ravished the women, who offered their concealed valuables without avail to these diabolical scoundrels for immunity from outrage." Alarmed and fearful women, often left alone, believed and trembled. In North Carolina, a plantation mistress heard that a foraging party of black soldiers had raped twenty-five white women. She wrote in her journal, "Many are dead & some with a far less happy fate live shrieking maniacs or sunk in hopeless misery." To them, rape by a black was a horrible indignity, a loss of honor never regained, a shame never erased.[5]

Yet Northerners regarded rape of a white woman by a black man the same way as did Southerners. Federal commanders had absolutely no tolerance for the offense. In the Shenandoah Valley, a Yankee officer reported, "A Negro who was attached [to an army unit] . . . attempted to rape a white woman and was seized and shot immediately." In Florida, a Northern woman doctor noted that white soldiers raped black women with impunity, but black soldiers who ravished white women drew the death penalty. She described the case of three young black soldiers charged with committing "an outrage on a white woman." They were arrested shortly after midnight, tried by a drumhead court-martial, and hanged the same day. In Virginia, Federal authorities staged a public hanging in full view of Confederate troops, allowing a civilian photographer to record the event. With proper ceremony, they led convicted rapist William Johnson, 23rd U.S. Colored Infantry, to the gallows on June 20, 1864.[6]

Yet the incidence of rape among all Civil War soldiers was extremely low. However, both the number of black Federals executed and those so punished for rape were greatly disproportionate to their numbers in the army. Possibly they committed capital crimes or rape more often than did white soldiers, or perhaps military authorities were quicker to believe the charges and impose death sentences, or perhaps both conditions obtained. At any rate, of the 56 black soldiers officially reported executed, 12 died for committing rape, but only 5 of 218 whites executed forfeited their lives for that crime.[7]

Southerners were willing to believe that Federal authorities dealt swiftly and harshly with blacks who attempted or committed rape. But they also believed that a blind animal lust afflicted black males, and they doubted their officers could always control them. So, while they dreaded

interior raids by black Yankees, Confederates relished their appearance
on the battlefield. There they could severely chastise their former slaves
for defying law and order.

Chastisement in Florida

Another such an opportunity came with a battle in Florida in early 1864,
one which should never have taken place. Olustee, or Ocean Pond, as
Confederates called it, was also the state's first and only major engagement.
About five thousand men took part on each side, although each thought
he faced two or three times his own side's number. They fought a stand-
up battle in open woods, unusual at that stage of the war when soldiers
automatically dug in. It was also unusual because it was the unintended
consequence of a misguided effort by Lincoln to gain political advantage.
And for the first time, black troops constituted a substantial portion of the
Federal strength in a significant action. Not so unusual, however, was the
Federals' defeat because of their leader's incompetence.[8]

In early December 1863, Lincoln decreed that a seceded state could
rejoin the Union when one-tenth of that state's voters affirmed their
loyalty and when the state satisfied some other conditions. Modern historian James M. McPherson wrote that "Lincoln hoped to set in motion
a snowballing defection from the Confederacy." With this ukase he had
returned Louisiana and Arkansas to the fold, which, in turn, would
strengthen his position for the presidential election later that year. But
there was no snowball effect. Acting on faulty information, Lincoln
directed Major General Quincy A. Gillmore, Department of the South
commander, to send an expedition to secure Florida. He also gave John
Hay, one of his private secretaries, a major's commission and a stack of
loyalty oath forms and told him to go along.

Gillmore ordered Brigadier General Truman Seymour, leader of the
failed attack on Fort Wagner, to take three brigades and sail for Jacksonville. Arriving on February 7, 1864, Seymour was soon assailed by grave
doubts about the entire operation. He wrote Gillmore that "the desire
of Florida to come back now is a delusion." Seymour also warned that
explaining a military defeat would be difficult. Officers already there
in fortified enclaves wondered whether it were a political or a military
expedition and suspected corruption. Misgivings beset Gillmore and the
freshly minted Major Hay, Lincoln's personal envoy. Hay soon realized
his mission was premature and his loyalty forms excess baggage. Citizens
refused to take the oath because they were not in the least repentant

and remained loyal to the Confederacy. For his part, Gillmore issued categorical written orders to Seymour, telling him to stay put and not to risk a repulse by marching inland.[9]

Then, out of the clear blue, Seymour advised that he had decided to push inland one hundred miles, despite Gillmore's objections and the worries of his own officers. They questioned not only the advance but also Seymour's erratic leadership. Major John W. M. Appleton, 54th Massachusetts (Colored), wrote in his journal, "We are under Gen. Seymour, a man we have no confidence in, and believe so prejudiced that he would as soon see us slaughtered as not." John Hay, Lincoln's personal envoy, observed, "Seymour has seemed very unsteady and queer since the beginning of this campaign. He has been subject to violent alternations of timidity & rashness." However, Seymour commanded and they had to obey and start marching.[10]

Seymour had three New York infantry regiments in one brigade, two from New England and the 8th U.S. Colored Infantry in a second, while the 54th Massachusetts and 1st North Carolina made up a black brigade commanded by James M. Montgomery, the Kansas jayhawker. Four artillery batteries provided the heavy firepower. At midafternoon on February 20, after marching about fifteen miles, leading elements unexpectedly encountered a strong enemy force near Olustee. Seymour's battle plan was a military textbook example of ensuring defeat in detail, the destruction in turn of each of the separated parts of a force. He fed unit after unit, one by one, into the maw of the Confederate grinder. Pushed piecemeal into the fight, the troops always faced a concentrated and stronger enemy. Describing the costly, incomprehensible blundering, a Massachusetts cavalryman commented, "The regiments came up singly, went in cheering, and stayed to be annihilated." Andrew F. Ely, 2nd Lieutenant with the 8th U.S. Colored Infantry, reported, "In my Company *sixty-two* went into the fight [and] we brought out *ten men* fit for duty."[11]

In the late afternoon, Seymour hurled his last troops against the unwavering Confederates. Into the caldron went the black brigade. White Federals cheered them, though they knew the day was already lost. Yet there was still time for the black soldiers to distend the casualty rolls. Quickly, the 1st North Carolina's leader fell mortally wounded, and its second-in-command, Major Archibald Bogle, was shot in the legs and abandoned on the battlefield. Another 228 men rapidly became statistics, including 77 men posted as missing. Then the 54th Massachusetts entered the fight with 495 men after a two-mile run from the rear, where

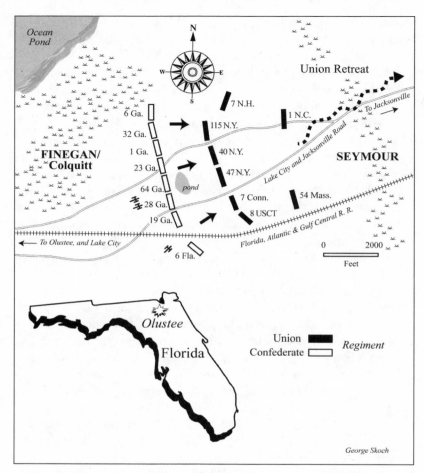

The battle of Olustee, fought by about five thousand troops on each side on February 20, 1864, ended with a decisive defeat for Federals led by the erratic Brigadier General Truman Seymour and with the slaughter of wounded and captured black Yankees.

Seymour had them guarding the wagon train. Somehow, they counted only eighty-seven casualties, including eight missing.[12]

When he ran out of fresh regiments, Seymour ordered a retreat after losing a third of his troops and artillery. He said his defeated troops withdrew in perfect order, and one of his staff officers embroidered upon that fiction by asserting that all stores were saved. Everyone else said a demoralized mass of men stumbled through an inchoate nightmare march of exhaustion, pain, and fear while frantically abandoning weapons, equipment, and supplies. By the next day, a semblance of order had returned. Stragglers caught up with their units and regiments reformed. Frightened locomotive crewmen earlier had built up too much steam pressure and the engine broke down. That stranded many wounded men huddled on flatcars. Seymour ordered the exhausted 54th Massachusetts men to march back four miles and hitch themselves to the crippled engine. Then the black soldiers pulled and pushed the train for mile after mile to Jacksonville. There, safe behind the trenches, one cocky young 54th lieutenant referred to Olustee as a mere "flurry." His men knew better. Orderly Sergeant A. S. Fisher wrote, "I am not A tall well at this time As I am cosid to Sufer Very much from A Hard forst march and A Hard fought Battle."[13]

Although he had earlier warned Gillmore that a defeat would be difficult to explain, Seymour had no difficulty in concocting a fanciful account blaming everything and everyone but himself for his overwhelming defeat. Seymour and an ever-loyal staff officer also maintained that they had left behind only a few badly wounded men, a statement that both knew was a falsehood. He had made no provision for either the removal or the treatment of hundreds of wounded. In his casualty report, Seymour shuffled figures to minimize losses. He reported 203 killed, 506 missing, and 1,152 wounded. Confederates reported 934 casualties and said they found 418 wounded Federals on the battlefield, captured 200, and buried about 400.[14]

Black soldiers wondered about the many wounded comrades left on the battlefield and feared for their well-being. Surgeon Charles P. Heichhold, 8th U.S. Colored Infantry, said, "How the rebels have disposed of the colored men who fell into their hands we have not heard yet; but we hope that the fear of retaliation, if not the dictates of humanity, will cause them to reconsider their threat of outlawry." But hope withered when Confederates named only a few black soldiers on a list of 449 prisoners they submitted. Even Seymour's flawed casualty return counted 157 black soldiers as missing. His successor observed, "The very small number of colored prisoners attracted immediate attention, as it was well known that the number left wounded on the field was large."[15]

Neither the dictates of humanity nor threat of retribution had restrained ordinary Confederates. Many went into the battle primed "to teach them a lesson." One old soldier recalled that the officer leading

2nd Florida cavalry troopers told his men that "negroes from Georgia and South Carolina . . . have come to steal, pillage, run over the state and murder, kill and rape our wives, daughters and sweethearts. . . . I shall not take any negro prisoners in this fight." Most needed no encouragement. Murder began even before the fight ended and flourished after the defeated Federals left the battleground.[16]

Shot in the ankle and left behind when Federal forces retreated, a 48th New York infantryman watched as Confederates scoured the battlefield they now controlled. He recalled:

> I could see the rebels come to our wounded, and take their money, watches, and whatever they found on their persons; while they stripped the dead altogether. The wounded negroes they bayoneted without mercy. Close beside me was a fine-looking negro, who was wounded in the leg; his name was Brown, an orderly sergeant in one of the companies of the 8th United States Regiment. A rebel officer happens to see him, and says, "Ah, you rascal, you will not remain here long!" and, dismounting from his horse, placed his revolver close to the negro's head, and blew his brains out.

Later, while a prisoner, the infantryman observed the harsh treatment accorded the wounded Major Bogle. His captors said hanging was too good and that he ought to be buried alive "with one of his negroes beneath him, and one above him."[17]

As dusk fell, William F. Penniman, 4th Georgia Cavalry, rode over the battleground and observed, "In passing over the field, and the road ran centering through it, my attention was first attracted to the bodies of the yankees, invariably stripped, shoes first and clothing next. Their white bodies looked ghastly enough, but I particularly noticed that firing seemed to be going on in every direction, until the reports sounded almost as frequent enough to resemble the work of skirmishers." Penniman asked a young officer for the cause of all the gunfire. The officer replied, "Shooting niggers, Sir. I have tried to make the boys desist but I can't control them." Penniman remarked that it "seemed horrible to kill the wounded devils" and the other agreed, even as the killing continued.

Early the next morning, Penniman again traversed the battlefield. He noted, "The results of the shooting of the previous night became quite apparent. Negroes, and plenty of them, whom I had seen lying all over the field wounded, and so far as I could see, many of them moving around from place to place, now without a motion, all were dead. If a negro had a shot in the shin, another was sure to be in the head." He found that few black prisoners were taken, and fewer still arrived at the prisoner of war pen. He recalled, "One ugly big black buck was interrogated as to how it happened that he had come back to fight his old master, and upon his giving some insolent reply, his interrogator drew back his musket, and with the butt, gave him a blow that killed him instantly." He observed that very few black wounded went on the surgeons' operating table, and when they did, "their legs fairly flew off, but whether they were at all seriously wounded I have always had my doubt."[18]

Some men reported the killing with unconcealed satisfaction, while others mentioned it only in passing, as incidental to the day's work. In letters home, however, none acknowledged taking part in the slaughter themselves. Always others, "the boys" and "our men," had dispatched the helpless blacks. Writing home that night, Henry Shackelford, 19th Georgia, related, "The yankees . . . pitched three negro regiments against us. . . . How our boys did walk into the niggers, they would beg and pray but it did no good." The next day, Orderly Sergeant James M. Jordan, 27th Georgia, wrote, "We met with a more stubborn resistance than was expected, although we met with 2 or 3 negro regts. . . . The negroes were badly cut up and killed. Our men killed some of them after they had fell in our hands wounded." In a fine script marked by imaginative spelling, Private Joab Roach, 17th Georgia, related that "the yankees Brought theare negro troops out to fight. We Cild and wounded a great meaney of them and after the Battle was over the Boys went over the Battlefield and knoct the most of the wounded negros in the head with lightwood knots."[19]

Some shuddered at the fight's carnage but thought killing black Federals fitting and just, though many conceded they had fought stubbornly if not as veterans. Captain Winston Stephens, 2nd Florida Cavalry, viewed the human detritus, then wrote that "Never in all my life have I seen such a distressing sight." Yet he thought it a useful object lesson and instructed his wife, "Tell the negroes if they could have seen how the negroes were treated I think it would cure them of all desire to go." Private Edwin D. Tuttle, 26th Virginia, saw some wounded Federals and confessed, "I deeply pityed the Whites but I am afraid I did not have the right spirit toward the Nigs." He added, "I tell you, our men slayed the Negrows & if it had not been for the officers, their would not one of them been spaired." According to some reports, camp slaves also dispatched black Federals. Captain Stephens, a dependable witness, related that one Federal made a friendly overture to a servant who, grossly offended by the gesture, promptly killed him. Less reliable was a hearsay report by Private Tuttle. He wrote, "Some of the Black Cooks in the Georgia Regts went on the Battle Field & knocked many of them, the wounded [black Federals], in the head with lightwood knots."[20]

Although Seymour listed 157 as missing from the black regiments, that figure did not include all of those left either on the field or on the retreat. In a preliminary report, Confederates said they held three unwounded and "many" wounded blacks. Brigadier General Joseph Finegan added that he also held "one major, of the First North Carolina (negro) Regiment." That was the badly wounded Archibald Bogle, left on the field and supposed dead by Federals. Then Confederate artillery officer Charles C. Jones, who missed the fight, wrote his wife on February 27 that he had seen "144 Federal prisoners, among them a few negroes captured in the recent battle of Olustee." Internal Confederate correspondence in late May revealed that at least seventy-one black soldiers captured in Florida still lived and that many had been slaves in North Carolina. But it is uncertain how many were captured at Olustee and how many at other places. Flawed Federal casualty returns and incomplete Confederate prisoner tallies preclude an accurate count. From sources on both sides, it is known that Confederates treated some black wounded and sent some to prison camps. It is also known that some died of wounds on the retreat and that Confederates dispatched others who fell by the wayside on the trek back to Jacksonville.[21]

Considering the imprecise and incomplete casualty figures available, as usual it is impossible to determine exactly how many wounded or surrendered black soldiers Confederates executed on the battleground or on the retreat road's waysides. But looking at the Southern no-quarter history as a whole, it is more accurate to assume a higher rather than a lower toll. In this instance, they probably slew seventy-five or more helpless blacks. Those who survived the methodical killing went to the open-air stockade at Andersonville, Georgia. There and at other Southern prison camps, black captives experienced a heavy mortality rate. "The negro soldiers suffered most," said Homer B. Sprague, a Connecticut officer and a prisoner himself. They succumbed to unattended wounds, malnutrition, illness, and vindictive mistreatment. For example, Corporal James H. Gooding, the very literate 54th Massachusetts correspondent for the New Bedford (Massachusetts) *Mercury*, took a bullet in his thigh but received little or no treatment for his wound at Andersonville and died there five months later.[22]

Major Archibald Bogle, the 1st North Carolina officer initially reported dead, stirred Southern fury when captured. In their wrath and contempt for white men who led black troops, Confederates shipped him to Andersonville, a prison stockade for enlisted men. Although twice wounded, prison officials denied Bogle medical attention. When he demanded officer status, he said they treated him worse than the lowest enlisted man. With the same punitive design in mind, Confederates later consigned another officer from Bogle's regiment to that dreaded place. Assistant Secretary of War John A. Campbell approved the transfer, mockingly writing, "He cannot complain of miscegenation."[23]

By itself, Olustee had no great military significance. As a Federal staff officer said, such affairs did not influence the war one way or another. Nevertheless, Confederates made the most of it and the good news spread quickly. Even a captive Confederate cavalry major heard the pleasing news, courtesy of Northern newspapers, while he was a prisoner at far off Johnson's Island, Ohio. From Mobile, Alabama, a Tennessee soldier happily reported that the army had "perfectly annihilated two colored regiments, killing every one save eight, who was afterward captured and killed." Secretary of War Seddon advised President Davis that Federals had suffered a great disaster "in the decisive battle of Olustee." While it was a disaster for Seymour's troops, it was a decisive reversal only for Lincoln's political aims in Florida. His hope of returning the state to the Union proved a chimera. People there overwhelmingly supported the Confederacy, and Lincoln had acted on bad information. Moreover, Federals could find only a few slaves to conscript; organizing a loyal white regiment, another hope, also proved a fantasy.[24]

After his defeat, Seymour behaved like an unhinged tyrant until he was relieved of command. He denied any responsibility for Olustee or for the equally disastrous assault at Fort Wagner, which he described as a "virtual success." He also denied that he was proslavery or a "habitual contemner" of black troops or their race. Although censured by Gillmore and roundly condemned by his men and in newspaper reports, Seymour suffered no consequences for his "utter imbecility" or "miserable mismanagement," as two of his men charged. Instead, he went to Virginia to lead a division in the 6th Army Corps.[25]

Brigadier General John P. Hatch, Seymour's replacement, exerted himself on behalf of the black soldiers slain at Olustee. Seven months passed before he amassed sufficient evidence, and then he wrote, "It is now known that the most of the wounded colored men were murdered on the field. These outrages were perpetrated so far as I can ascertain, by the Georgia Regulars and the Georgia volunteers in Colquitt's brigade." He added that apparently Florida troops had no hand in the slayings. Hatch told Major General Ethan A. Hitchcock, the prisoner exchange commissioner, that he held many Georgia troops as prisoners and wanted to pursue the matter. It was a waste of ink and energy. Washington might bemoan the atrocities, but it would not retaliate for the murder of black Federals, given the probable future cost to white soldiers and the certain public outcry that would follow.[26]

7

The Yazoo to Suffolk

INEXPERIENCED BLACK REGIMENTS often paid in blood before they could hold their own against a veteran enemy. That proved particularly true for the few black cavalry regiments. However, whatever their branch, whether infantry, artillery, or cavalry, and no matter where they served, black soldiers quickly understood that they were dead men if captured or left wounded on the field. No matter where the battlefield, no matter from what state they came, Southern soldiers killed wounded and captured black soldiers with the same diligence and ferocity. No significant regional differences existed in that lethal inclination. From the contemporary record, the only discernible distinction was that Texans were more addicted to public vaunt and bluster about refusing quarter to black Federals than were other Southern soldiers. Several actions east and west in early 1864 illustrate these conclusions.

In the beginning of the black soldier experiment, Lincoln valued black soldiers more as auxiliaries and as symbols than as fighters. He thought they could man backwater forts, thus freeing white soldiers for active service. Although unenthusiastic about the scheme, army leaders had concentrated on forming infantry units for use as garrison and labor service. They also organized more than a dozen black heavy artillery regiments, but they were artillery units mostly in name only, rarely having any cannon of any kind assigned to them. They avoided organizing functional artillery or cavalry units because both required teamwork and cavalry service needed responsible initiative and fast thinking. Federal leaders believed, as did most Americans of the time, that such requirements greatly exceeded the black man's ability.[1]

Two other considerations also influenced Northern officials. Simple prejudice made them dislike the idea of black soldiers riding while whites walked. Even under ordinary circumstances, white troops often complained that the blacks enjoyed too much favored treatment as it was. Then wartime imperatives created a practical obstacle. Already the war had taken a heavy toll of horses, and experienced, effective white cavalry units often found it difficult to secure an adequate number of good mounts. From a pragmatic standpoint, it was not wise to give scarce horses to untested black units.[2]

Still, by late 1863, the North had four black cavalry regiments. Then Massachusetts organized the 5th Massachusetts Cavalry (Colored) in May of 1864 and sent the regiment to Virginia, and the 5th U. S. Colored Cavalry became active in October while the 6th U.S. was still organizing. Troop commanders also occasionally mounted black infantrymen to gain mobility during a particular operation. Such temporary expedients aside, the seven cavalry regiments constituted only about 4 percent of the 166 black regiments organized during the war, a much lower proportion than that for white troops, and most functioned only fitfully as horse soldiers.[3]

Only the 3rd U.S. Colored Cavalry compiled a lengthy, continuous record as a mounted unit. Organized in October 1863 at Vicksburg as the 1st Mississippi Cavalry, African Descent, the regiment took part in many expeditions and engagements in the West. Service was hard, marked by defeats and murder, retaliation and counterretaliation. Like the 1st Kansas Colored soldiers, the unit took many casualties during its constant campaigning. Unlike the 54th Massachusetts (Colored) or a few other black units in the East, the 3rd's reverses and victories went largely unnoticed. Toward the war's end, the 3rd received high praise from a veteran white cavalryman. Sergeant Lucien P. Waters, 11th New York Cavalry, certified that the men of the 3rd distinguished themselves in fighting experienced enemy cavalry. He called them "dire avengers" and said that "right glad were they to square accounts with their old masters."[4]

Grief on the Yazoo

Still recruiting and mounted mostly on mules, 3rd Colored Cavalry scouts rode straight into serious trouble while on the Yazoo River expedition of January 31 to March 7, 1864. Soldiers and gunboats had gone on this diversionary foray to draw Confederate attention while Sherman sent a much larger force on a railroad-wrecking raid to Meridian, Mississippi. Colonel James H. Coates, 11th Illinois Infantry, led the Yazoo thrust with a modest force of about twelve hundred men, almost equally divided between white and black troops. Among the latter were 250 men of the 3rd Colored Cavalry, then known as the 1st Mississippi Cavalry, African Descent. At Yazoo City, a strongly pro-Southern town, Coates learned on February 28 that Confederates hovered nearby and had attacked his pickets. He told Colonel Embury D. Osband, the 3rd's commander, to scout a road leading eastward.[5]

Forty men, mostly on mules, and three officers trotted out and unexpectedly met a small group of enemy troopers who fled. Eagerly, the Federals pursued them until they found themselves racing almost into the camp of an entire Texas cavalry brigade. Then it was the black soldiers' turn to wheel and ride for their lives. But they had gone too far and turned back too late. Confederates, mounted on swifter horses, cut across fields to catch up with the fleeing Federals.

Major Edwin M. Main said it was a running fight all the way back to Yazoo City. Confederates said there was no fight about it. A 1st Texas Legion officer said that the "black rascals . . . run like wild animals trying to get back to Yazoo City." Describing the chase, a 9th Texas soldier related, "We would charge in amongst them and shoot them off . . . many would fall off and get on their knees with their hands uplifted and pray for mercy." He said that in response the "boys would . . . blow their brains out." Exaggerating a bit, the legion officer added, "There was about 60 of them and only six of them got back to the City. The rest bit the earth." Private Newton A. Keen, 6th Texas, declared, "It was fearful to see how they were slain: but war glorries in the destruction of human flesh."[6]

Brigadier General Lawrence S. Ross, the Texans' leader, reported that the six-mile stretch of road to town was strewn with black bodies, a bit of a stretch itself. Officially, the 3rd reported eight dead, ten missing, and four wounded, including a captain who took a load of buckshot in his hip. Coates listed nineteen missing. Afterward, his men found six bodies with "every appearance of having been brutally used," and Coates concluded that they had been murdered. In reality, all the missing were dead men, shot or sabered from their saddles or killed upon capture. It was another lopsided black soldier loss, showing nineteen, or almost 50 percent, killed and four wounded. Confederates reported no casualties.[7]

The Texans frankly said they followed a no-quarter policy with black Federals. Lieutenant Samuel B. Barron, 3rd Texas, said: "As for the negro troops—well, for some time the fighting was under the black flag—no quarter being asked or given." Many justified the killing by saying that the black troopers had murdered two 6th Texas cavalrymen a few weeks earlier. Sergeant Victor M. Rose, 3rd Texas, said the Texans' deaths had caused "an informal 'war to the knife,' which claimed many victims." Ross, however, blamed an entirely different Federal unit. Mainly, then, they slew the black cavalrymen because they were blacks who fought their erstwhile masters. For their part, 3rd Cavalry soldiers and their officers knew they fought a merciless enemy in a no-quarter war. They may not have liked it, but they accepted the conditions. Major Main recalled, "To the black troopers and their white officers, capture meant death, and as the Texans were known to take no 'nigger' prisoners, the black soldiers had to face the alternative, victory or death."[8]

Several days later, Ross demanded to know if Coates intended to treat prisoners properly or if he had decided upon the "cold-blooded and inhuman" policy of killing captives, as had happened to the two 6th Texas soldiers. Ross warned that if Coates had embraced a no-quarter policy, then he would regretfully accept the terms and take no prisoners. Replying immediately, Coates said he, too, deplored such mistreatment of prisoners and he regretted the murders of black soldiers during the recent skirmish outside Yazoo City. But to Ross and almost every other Confederate, a vital distinction obtained—the dead Federals were black; the murdered Texans, white. To Southerners, there was no equivalency of any kind, and to try to equate the deaths was preposterous and an insult. They belonged to the planet's highest order, while the blacks were but viciously wayward chattels, members of some lower order of sentient beings.[9]

As before a storm, an eerie quiet settled upon Yazoo City and its defenders. It did not last long. On the morning of March 5, Ross's Texans and a small brigade of mostly Tennessee cavalrymen attacked. After initial successes, Ross failed in repeated efforts to take the main redoubt. Although surrounded, 3rd Colored Cavalry and some 11th Illinois soldiers stubbornly repelled all attacks. Stymied by their determined resistance, Ross delivered an ultimatum demanding immediate and unconditional surrender. Quite frankly, he declared he would not recognize the black Federals as soldiers or promise them or their officers protection as such. He warned that unless they surrendered immediately, he would be unable to restrain his men when they stormed the redoubt. All defenders, black or white, would be put to the sword. One of his staff officers conveyed the warning to Major George C. McKee, commanding the redoubt. McKee said, "That means General Ross will murder the prisoners if he is successful." Ross's emissary, a young lieutenant, hesitated and then replied, "No, not exactly that; but you know how it will be."

McKee knew exactly. Angered, he refused to receive the oral communication and said he wanted such an ultimatum in writing. Given Ross's threat, McKee countered with his own. He declared that he would kill every man who fell into his hands should Ross be repulsed. Ross then submitted a written demand for surrender and stipulated that if they yielded, they would receive correct treatment. If he had to assault, Ross wrote, "I will try and have them protected if they surrender during the charge; but you may expect much bloodshed." Lieutenant Barron, 3rd Texas, said that "how they would have fared at the hands of an incensed brigade of Texas troops . . . was not pleasant to contemplate."[10]

The 3rd Colored Cavalry officers and men were acutely aware of those unpleasant consequences. Main knew that "no quarter could be expected." So he and fellow officers told McKee to exclude them from any surrender because they knew what would happen and they preferred to die fighting. However, McKee refused to surrender, and there was no assault and no test of Ross's resolve "to kill and spare not." Confederates decided an all-out attack was not worth the cost. Better, they thought, simply to declare victory and leave. So they did just that.[11]

Confederates counted just fifty-seven casualties—six killed and fifty-one wounded. Federal losses were probably more than twice that number. Main reported the 3rd Cavalry alone had seventeen killed and twenty-three wounded in the Yazoo City fight. Coates listed Federal casualties only for the expedition as a whole, a total of 183 killed, wounded, and missing. During the foray, the white 11th Illinois listed forty-seven casualties, or about 25 percent of the total. The 3rd Cavalry and the 8th Louisiana

Infantry, African Descent, constituting just a bit more than half the expedition's strength, listed 136 casualties, or 75 percent of the losses. Two factors usually accounted for such disparities: the black soldiers often lacked experience and Confederates concentrated fire upon them.[12]

Among those listed as captured or missing were sixteen men from the 11th Illinois. Ordinarily, they would survive capture. But Ross made that a shaky assumption. Despite his professed desire for civilized warfare, his own men questioned Ross's commitment to that principle. They heard that he planned to take no prisoners, white or black, and opposing Federals then had responded by saying that they would take no prisoners from his command. One of Ross's officers wrote, "This caused a great deal of dissatisfaction among our boys. [They] said they did not enlist to fight under the black Flag and this is no better and you would hear it in every camp damned if I dont leave if this prisoner killing is not stoped."[13]

Ross was not alone in his reported advocacy of taking no prisoners. From the beginning, some Southerners had urged hoisting the black flag. Though many Confederates felt no constraints about such a policy for black Federals, they opposed such a blanket no-quarter rule for white Yankees. They believed it was barbaric and repugnant to their sense of morality, ethics, and humanity. They also rejected the idea because they believed Federals would surely respond in kind. Most realized that the North had the edge in manpower, and they believed that practically the whole world had sent mercenaries to aid the Yankee enemy. Given those numbers and the threat of retaliation, logic and simple arithmetic argued that to adopt comprehensive no-quarter doctrine was a losing proposition. However, reason frequently deserted those convinced of Southern warrior superiority and invincibility.[14]

Just a month later, another 3rd Colored Cavalry detachment experienced a reprise of the first costly encounter with Ross's men. On March 31, as they rode out to protect loyal cotton growers, Ross's 3rd and 9th Texas also marched to break up plantations near Snyder's Bluff and Harris's Bluff, in Mississippi. Approaching from different directions, they arrived in sight of Roach's Plantation and the Federal post there at daylight. Meanwhile, the 3rd Colored Cavalry also neared, moving steadily towards the 3rd Texas Cavalry. Behind the black soldiers came the 6th Texas. At Roach's Plantation or Snyder's Bluff, different names for the same action, Confederates attacked front and rear. "A general slaughter ensued," wrote Lieutenant Griscom, 9th Texas, "*leaving 40 dead Negroes on the field &* ran the ballance into Their infantry fortifications and camps." Ross, more conservative, reported that his men killed thirty black soldiers. Federals officially reported half the deaths, listing sixteen killed and three wounded. A somewhat different version appeared in a monthly return when a Federal officer wrote that Confederates had captured the sixteen men and then executed them, "not excepting the wounded." However it came about, five were killed for one wounded, the direct reverse of normal loss experience but almost a standard for black troops.[15]

"Perfectly Exasperated" in Virginia

About the time the clash occurred in the streets of Yazoo City, the 2nd U.S. Colored Cavalry engaged in a similar fight at Suffolk, Virginia. To the repeated dismay of the town's inhabitants, Suffolk was important to the control of a contested area and endured battle, siege, and raid. Alternately and for varying periods, the opposing sides had occupied the place. Confederates left again in early March and the 2nd U.S. Colored Cavalry moved in, much to the residents' disgust. Their commander, Colonel George W. Cole, was experienced, but his regiment had formed at Fortress Monroe just two months earlier. On the morning of March 9, 1864, the regiment divided and began a reconnaissance. Not far from town, Cole's group met Brigadier General Matthew W. Ransom's infantry brigade and a regiment or two of Thomas L. Clingman's, all veteran North Carolina troops.[16]

Propelled by a bloodlust for the "infernals," as some termed the black soldiers, Ransom's men rushed forward. Sergeant Major Thomas R. Roulhac, 49th North Carolina, related, "The men were perfectly exasperated at the idea of negroes opposed to them & rushed at them like so many devils." In those days, it should be repeated, "perfectly exasperated" meant more than very annoyed; instead, it denoted extreme anger or rage. Outnumbered and outclassed, the 2nd Colored Cavalry troopers fled from the maddened Confederates. Private Gabriel P. Sherrill, another 49th soldier, wrote, "the negroes wont fite if they have eny chance to run but they will fite if they aire hemed sow that they cant run then they will fite for they know it is Deth eny ways if we got hold of them for we have now quarters for a negrow." That perception was reinforced when several blacks holed up in a small house and continued to resist. Although surrounded and isolated, they refused to surrender, killing two and wounding several of Ransom's veterans. Tiring of that, Confederates set the house ablaze. Those who ran from the house were immediately bayoneted; those that stayed inside died in the smoke and flames.[17]

As many Confederates said, they enthusiastically cleansed the town of black soldiers, killing as many as possible in the process. Perfect unanimity obtained: they wanted no black captives. "Ransom's brigade never takes any negro prisoners," declared one soldier. For emphasis, he repeated, "We did not take *any* prisoners." Georgia artillerymen with Ransom also said that they took no prisoners there but, on the other hand, added that they never intended to do so. That was not precisely true. Some black Federals fell into their hands but were quickly killed. Sergeant Major Roulhac explained that "several [were] taken prisoner & afterwards were bayoneted or burned."[18]

Suffolk was a minor affair with few casualties on either side. Cole's confusing report listed eight dead, six wounded, and two missing; Confederates counted two killed and three wounded. However, Suffolk helps illustrate the point that Confederate troops from every section and state harbored the same unforgiving rancor toward their former slaves in Yankee uniforms. It was ever so, as a black division's commander said, that "white soldiers . . . go into battle with none of the peculiar disadvantages to which my men will be subject." Moreover, Confederates extended that animosity to the dead. Instead of proper burial, as they would give whites, they left black soldiers to fester and decay where they fell. Exceptions to the rule usually occurred only when Southern troops occupied static defensive positions and decomposing bodies posed a threat to their health or olfactory comfort.[19]

Suffolk also illustrates two problems that hinder accurate reporting. First, the opposing sides often submitted accounts so at odds that, except for the same date and place, they might describe entirely different events. In this instance, Confederates said they routed the Yankees, an accurate statement. Cole's superior said the black cavalrymen beat the enemy in every charge they made and, in another amusing claim, reported that they lost "no prisoners or horses except those that were killed." Then there is the problem of misreported black casualties. Cole initially listed eleven men as missing, but, contrary to the usual experience, they returned to the regiment after hiding in a swamp. Ordinarily, however, most black soldiers listed as missing were dead men, either killed in action or dispatched upon capture. Yet their officers persisted in keeping them on the missing list, even when they later learned their men were dead. That practice has also contributed to the enduring uncertainty about the real numbers and losses for black troops.[20]

Black soldiers' exposure to risk greatly increased as the war's tempo intensified in the spring of 1864. Grant, promoted to lieutenant general and command of Union forces, planned large, coordinated offensives. In the West, Sherman would strike for Atlanta; in the East, Grant would direct a renewed effort to destroy Lee's Army of Northern Virginia and to capture Richmond. Confederate leaders, on the defensive, expected renewed attacks and sought to frustrate or cripple Federal offensives before they began. To balk Sherman, Lieutenant General Leonidas Polk in early March ordered cavalry leaders Stephen D. Lee and Nathan B. Forrest to strike at enemy rear areas. Polk thought damaging raids would draw off Federal troops, thus stymieing Sherman's effort to concentrate his forces.[21]

Forrest, then forty-three years old, already enjoyed considerable renown as a bold raider. Southerners viewed him as their paladin, a bright and shining sword for their cause. A gentleman-soldier from Mississippi wrote, "Our people think that old Forest is the greatest man of the age." Though they applauded Forrest's exploits, some preferred to admire him from a comfortable distance. In the class-conscious South, his prewar slave trading made him a social pariah. His wartime reputation was also that of a strict disciplinarian who would not tolerate insubordination, though he disobeyed superiors when he felt like it. Stories circulated North and South about Forrest's severity and violent temper. An Arkansas infantryman admitted that he so feared Forrest's storied rages that he once risked a sentry's bullet to avoid going near the general.[22]

In the North, the popular press made Forrest famous, casting him as a daring marauder. He became an almost legendary figure, an elusive, destructive raider apt to materialize anywhere in the West. Soldiers saw him as a constant menace, always ruthless. Generals regarded him as endless trouble, and Grant thought him probably the South's ablest cavalry leader. Sherman, who often had to contend with Forrest, called him a devil and warned, "There never will be peace in Tennessee till Forrest is dead."[23]

Forrest earned his reputation early in the war. In late 1862, his men overran a Federal field hospital and the surgeon cried out, "My God, the bottom of hell has dropped out and the dregs are upon us." Yet most white soldiers captured by Forrest said he treated them decently. Sherman himself volunteered that hundreds of men had told him just that. Forrest said he had captured thousands and declared, "I will leave it to any prisoner I have ever taken if I have not treated them well." But the key word was *taken*, and that was what worried commanders of black troops. They feared Forrest and his men might not take many black prisoners. When a rumor circulated that Forrest had offered $1,000 for the head of any black regiment's commander, one affected colonel readily credited the story. Further, some Federals doubted that Forrest's men always took white prisoners. During a fight near Okolona, Mississippi, 72nd Indiana mounted infantrymen reportedly saw Forrest's troops murdering wounded whites.[24]

Mortification in Kentucky

These assorted reports and rumors, true or not, added to Forrest's fearsome reputation, and he capitalized on it. In this way, he added intangible but effective weight to his limited strength. For the West Tennessee incursion, he had about five thousand cavalrymen, with some artillery and supply wagons. At Jackson, Tennessee, he ordered a small force northward to capture a Federal post at Union City. He selected it because he thought Colonel Isaac R. Hawkins, the commander there, would quickly surrender, just as he had on an earlier occasion. Sure enough, when Hawkins received a surrender-or-die ultimatum over Forrest's name on March 24, he meekly surrendered, much to the disgust of his officers and men. Captain Thomas P. Gray soon escaped and reported, "I heard the rebels say repeatedly that they intended to kill negro troops wherever they could find them. . . . And they said that they did not consider officers who commanded negro troops to be any better than the negroes themselves."[25]

Forrest led a larger column of two cavalry brigades north to Paducah, Kentucky, a key city on the Ohio River border with Illinois. He arrived there shortly after high noon on March 25 and entered a fervently pro-Southern city with a prewar population of forty-five hundred, including five hundred slaves. But the war had transformed the strategic river port, bringing Northern troops to man a strong fort and to protect an army general hospital, quartermaster warehouses, a marine way, and railroad yards. Learning of Forrest's approach, Federals had prepared for a fight while evacuating loyal citizens and hurriedly removing sick black soldiers from the army hospital. A ward nurse confided, "We knew should the Rascals come they would show them no mercy but kill every man of them."[26]

Colonel Stephen G. Hicks, the Federal commander, had 665 troops, including 274 men of the 1st Kentucky Heavy Artillery (Colored), to defend an earthen fort ringed by a deep moat and abatis. Offshore in the river, two gunboats, the *Peosta* and the *Paw Paw*, energetically shelled Paducah, pounding it with more than seven hundred artillery rounds in a few hours. The fort's six cannons also belabored the town. While Tennessee troops sacked stores and shops, a mostly Kentucky force attacked the fort. Soon they called a truce and sent in Forrest's trademark ultimatum: "Surrender or die." Hicks refused and repelled three attempts to overrun the fort. Battered and bleeding, Confederates pulled back for the night. In the morning, Forrest proposed a prisoner exchange, which Hicks also rejected. Mockingly, he noted that Forrest had easily captured his prisoners because almost all were hospital patients too feeble to reach safety in the fort. With that, Forrest abandoned the fight and rode away with his plunder.[27]

Forrest afterward said he prudently left Paducah because a smallpox epidemic raged there, although the hospital staff reported just one case. He asserted that he got the supplies and horses for which he rode 105 miles in 50 hours and that he never intended to take the fort. In official reports, he omitted the failed attacks and did not tell superiors where senior officers became casualties. Forrest combined losses for Union City and Paducah to produce an absurdly low figure of only twenty-five men killed and wounded at both places. His carefully crafted version of events portrayed the foray as a grand success. In distant Richmond, where they prized any positive news, officials were pleased. As the news circulated, distorted from inception, some believed Forrest had captured Paducah.[28]

The animals and stores Forrest confiscated largely belonged to private citizens, almost all Southern loyalists. His losses, while unknown, certainly greatly exceeded Forrest's minimal figure. When Forrest departed, Hubert Saunders, a gunboat sailor, walked through Paducah and scornfully wrote home that "by Forrest account to Jef Davis he did a big thing! In that account he only lost 25 men and we fifty, while we only lost 14 men while the way the rebel dead laid around in the town looks like a big 25 besides their losing a general." With the last, Saunders referred to Colonel Albert P. Thompson, the Kentucky brigade's leader, killed during the last assault on the fort. Northern newspapers also belittled the raid. One correspondent, present during the fighting, scathingly wrote, "One thing is certain—they came, they saw, and they got most terribly thrashed. They plundered dry-goods and shoe-stores extensively, and obtained a large number of horses; but merchandise and horses have seldom been bought at so dear a price."[29]

Black soldiers had helped exact that price when they defended the fort. In part, that is why Confederates doggedly insisted that they had never meant to take the fort. Denial allowed Forrest and his men to ignore the very visible role black Federals had played in repelling their attacks. For Forrest, the former slave trader, and for his troops, proud Southerners all, probably that aspect of their experience at Paducah was the most humiliating. Certainly a Northern war correspondent thought so and cheerfully pilloried Forrest on that score. He wrote, "One of the most mortifying things to Forrest, connected with his terrible defeat here, must be the reflection that his men were whipped in part by 'nigger' soldiers whom he had come to take and shoot, with their officers." However framed, the Paducah affair cast some doubt on Forrest's pronouncement that "negro soldiers cannot cope with Southerners."[30]

Meanwhile, Forrest carefully considered his next move. So far he had not accomplished much of anything. Union City was an unimportant antiguerrilla police post; Paducah was important, but there he had met a galling repulse. While he had annoyed the enemy, he had not disrupted their plans. Sherman understood the Confederate strategy and stubbornly refused to divert troops to counter the raiders. Forrest wanted a redeeming victory, a morale booster that would reverberate in Richmond. Doubtless he also wanted to prove that black Federals were no match for their former masters. So, looking westward, he decided to hit Fort Pillow, a post on the Mississippi River which he knew had a mixed garrison of white and black troops.

8

Fort Pillow

NEITHER FORREST NOR HIS MEN knew that Fort Pillow would become a cause célèbre, a bitter controversy reverberating for many years after their attack. Assuredly, they never dreamed that it would create a great propaganda coup for the North or a benchmark for Civil War atrocities, light the fuse for a private war or provide a chilling battle cry. While it was not the first, last, or largest, the massacre that ensued was the only one widely and almost immediately publicized by many different sources from both sides. Civilians, newspaper correspondents, and Federal sailors and soldiers arrived just after the last killings, and they repeated what they had seen and heard. There, also, Confederate officers conceded a slaughter had occurred but defended the bloodletting, and Forrest's men soon wrote home and to newspapers candidly describing the butchery of black and white Federals. In the days following the horrendous bloodbath, survivors told their detailed stories and Federal authorities quickly published those accounts in a widely distributed book, so that even Forrest had a copy by midsummer. In short, Fort Pillow speedily turned into a hollow victory for the Confederacy.[1]

From a military standpoint, Fort Pillow had no importance in 1864. Each side had at times occupied and abandoned the place. Confederates had built it and then left in June 1862. Federals ignored the empty fort for three months before sending troops to watch over the Mississippi River near the midpoint of Tennessee's river border with Arkansas. After that, nothing much happened at the isolated post with its small civilian population, trading store, and tiny hotel. Sherman eventually decided the post was unnecessary and ordered it vacated in early January 1864. Without his approval or knowledge, the area commander ordered black and white troops to return in early February. Major William F. Bradford's cavalry battalion of loyal Tennesseans arrived first and then a unit of thirty-four black artillerymen came shortly after. Major Lionel F. Booth's four companies of the 6th U.S. Colored Heavy Artillery were ordered there on March 28.[2]

Forrest led a two-brigade force of about fifteen hundred men, with Brigadier General James R. Chalmers in nominal command. One brigade had Mississippi, Missouri, and Texas troopers in seven regiments and an independent battalion, while the second brigade had three Tennessee regiments. After a long, exhausting ride in miserable wet weather, which caused sickness and short tempers, the first troops arrived about 5 A.M. on April 12, just as morning twilight brought dim visibility. They saw an earthwork with a perimeter of 320 feet. Shaped like an irregular, shallow bracket, it faced landward on a seventy-five- to one-hundred-foot bluff overlooking the Mississippi. Six-foot-thick walls shielded defenders, and a deep, wide moat ringed the works. However, a half dozen knobs on nearby hills enabled snipers to fire down into the fort, cabins near the south face could conceal riflemen, and ravines creasing the ground permitted the protected approach of assaulting troops. On the north side, a creek flowed into the river, and, near its mouth, a ravine turned southward, encircling the fort for almost half its length. Design flaws required defenders to expose their heads when firing and created blind spots near the earthwork.[3]

Major Booth, a twenty-six-year-old former Regular Army soldier, had 580 officers and men and 6 cannons to defend the fort. Considered experienced and competent, Booth had said he could hold the place against any force for forty-eight hours. In addition, he also had fire support from the gunboat *New Era*, commanded by James Marshall. When the shooting started, scores of black women, adolescents, and children, sick and well, fled from their quarters near the fort to the riverbank. But at least nine civilian volunteers joined the garrison, including a sutler, a black man, and a commercial photographer.[4]

Booth ably led the defense until about 9 A.M., when he fell with a bullet in his chest. His death deprived the garrison of the capable leadership needed against Forrest. Command then devolved upon Major Bradford, who proved weak and inept. Formerly a West Tennessee lawyer, Bradford had begun recruiting his battalion at Union City in December 1863. After shifting to Fort Pillow, he had recruited enough men to form a requisite fifth company, thus assuring him of title and rank. Neither side thought much of him, but Confederates held him in particular contempt, considering him a renegade who allied himself with the Yankees for personal gain rather than honorable conviction.[5]

Shortly after Booth's death, Forrest ordered his men to press forward. Soon he had the place closely invested, and his sharpshooters had killed or wounded almost a third of the garrison's twenty-one officers. But aside from the Federal officers, both sides had experienced only light losses. About 1:45 P.M., Forrest called a truce and demanded unconditional surrender. He warned that the garrison would suffer the consequences if he had to assault. Signing Booth's name, Bradford asked for an hour to consult with his and the gunboat's officers. Annoyed, Forrest said he had not asked for the gunboat's surrender and gave Federals twenty minutes to yield or to endure a bloodbath. Again signing Booth's name, Bradford wrote, "I will not surrender." 1st Lieutenant Mack J. Leaming carried that final answer to Forrest, ending the parley. The gunboat's log showed the truce flag as fluttering down at 3:15 P.M.[6]

During the truce, Confederates became incensed when Federals taunted them from behind the ramparts. "The negro troops were particularly offensive," recalled one Southerner. Another later declared that the men nurtured an "inveterate hatred" for the Federal Tennesseans and the black soldiers, but especially against the latter. A regimental commander added, "I verily believe that after the insults given them during the truce they would have taken the fort by storm anyway." Aware of Forrest's surrender-or-die ultimatums, his men took the threats at face value, though they later insisted that the dire warnings were meant only to frighten timid Federals into submission. If so, no evidence exists that Forrest ever explained this to his men.[7]

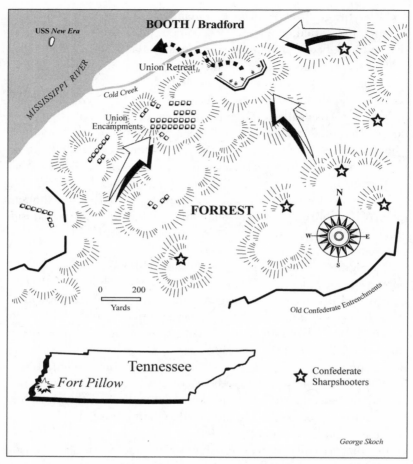

Fort Pillow, the war's most infamous massacre but not its largest, occurred April 12, 1864, when famed Confederate cavalry raider Nathan B. Forrest's men overran the isolated post's black and white garrison, and then went on a killing spree.

As soon as the truce ended, Forrest ordered his bugler to sound the charge. The swift, sudden onslaught stunned Lieutenant Leaming. Seemingly by nightmare magic, he saw enemy hordes leap forward as if rising from the earth within twenty yards of the fort. They swarmed into the dry moat, then up and onto the parapet. Some tumbled lifeless back into the ditch, but in a trice, hundreds were firing point-blank into the defenders' faces. When they burst into the fort, John Penwell, a civilian volunteer, had just fired his gun. He said, "I saw the rebels come running right up to us. I was just feeling for a cartridge. . . . I threw my musket down. A fellow . . . asked if I surrendered. I said, 'Yes.' He said, 'Die then, you damned Yankee son-of-a-bitch' and shot me and I fell." Luck favored Penwell that day—the bullet punched right through his chest, making a clean wound.[8]

Bradford fulfilled the bleak expectations of friend and foe. When Confederates swarmed into the fort, Bradford cried out, "Boys, save your lives!" With that, he ran and many of his men followed suit. Some Federals thought the blacks were the first to panic, but Henry F. Weaver, a white 1st sergeant of the black 6th Heavy Artillery, said, "They all appeared to go at the same time, as near as I could tell." In any event, after Confederates surged into the fort, many fled toward the riverbank. Offshore, aboard the *New Era*, Captain Marshall saw that the fort had fallen. Then Confederates trained one of its heavy cannons on the gunboat, and a shell whistled overhead. Marshall said he had to steam away because enemy gunners could sink him if he stayed within range. His ship's log showed that the fort's flag came down about then.[9]

Once inside the fort, Confederates began an indiscriminate massacre. That is exactly what took place, though for years defenders of Southern honor contested that assertion and Forrest's apologists sought to relieve him of any responsibility. Independent historians also questioned the massacre label, lacking some evidence that is now available. Now accessible are contemporary letters and diaries of Forrest's soldiers and historians have unearthed the timely newspaper accounts by his soldier-correspondents. Immediately published were the eyewitness statements of Federal survivors recorded by the congressional investigators. However, many people suspected their ex parte testimony, believing it either greatly exaggerated or fabricated. But such a conclusion is unsustainable, considering that private letters, Northern newspaper correspondents, and affidavits secured during the army's investigation basically confirm the accounts given to the congressional committee. It is also impossible to ignore Southern fury toward blacks as evinced before and after Fort Pillow and that same rage felt for Southerners who fought for the Union, as shown in later incidents.

Without question, a horrific slaughter ensued after Forrest's troops entered the fort. Without let or hindrance, they slew helpless, wounded, unarmed, or surrendered black and white Federals; hospital patients;

civilian men, women, young boys, and allegedly, black children. Some Confederates later tried to justify the killing with the contention that some black soldiers refused to surrender or continued to resist. At the time, though, most made no pretense that it was anything but a wholesale butchery impelled by remorseless fury. But they were skittish, even in private letters home, about the killing of white Federals. Sergeant Achilles V. Clark, 20th Tennessee, a slaveholder and former college student, told his sisters, "The slaughter was awful. Words cannot describe the scene. The poor deluded negroes would run up to our men fall upon their knees and with uplifted hands scream for mercy but they were ordered to their feet and then shot down. The white men fared but little better. Their fort turned out to be a great slaughter pen. Blood, human blood stood about in pools and brains could have been gathered up in any quantity."[10]

Surgeon Samuel H. Caldwell, 16th Tennessee Cavalry, told his wife that the carnage was terrible. He added, "It was decidedly the most horrible sight that I have ever witnessed." Others suggested that the killing resulted from a transitory frenzy that lifted after a short time. One soldier-correspondent reported, "For ten minutes death reigned in the fortification, and along the river bank. Our troops maddened by the excitement, shot down the retreating Yankees, and not until they . . . turned to beg for mercy did any prisoners fall into our hands—Thus the whites received quarter, but the negroes were shown no mercy."[11]

An early, brief dispatch by a soldier-correspondent reported Forrest's troops bravely entered the fort and then, "Indiscriminate slaughter followed—about a hundred prisoners were taken, the balance were slain. The fort ran with blood; many jumped into the river and drowned, or [were] shot." Almost four weeks later, an account in another newspaper was apparently the first to assert that some resistance continued after Confederates overran the defenders. This soldier-correspondent related that a bloodlust seized the men when they entered the fort. "Then the work of slaughter and death commenced," he reported. "The sight of negro soldiers stirred the bosoms of our soldiers with courageous madness. . . . Those that were hid or protected still kept firing upon and killing our brave boys; but our troops still rushed upon them, all the time fighting and killing. The sight was terrific—the slaughter sickening."[12]

Survivors said that initially Forrest's men killed every Federal in sight. Sergeant W. P. Walker, a white soldier, said, "They just shot us down without showing any quarter at all. They shot me, for one, after I had surrendered—they shot me in the arm and the shoulder and the neck and in the eye." Deciding that all was lost, Lieutenant Leaming tossed aside his sword, whereupon a nearby Confederate took careful aim and shot the unarmed Leaming through the body. Another white dropped his rifle and surrendered. He related, "I begged them not to shoot me and [one] . . . said, 'God damn you, you fought with the niggers and we will kill the last one of you.' Then they shot me." Francis A. Alexander, a white cavalryman, ran, but a marksman dropped him with a bullet to his leg. He then heard Confederates say that "they intended to kill us all for being there with their niggers." Alexander soon learned that some sought personal vengeance upon Unionist Tennesseans. "When our boys were taken prisoner," he said, "if anybody came up who knew them, they shot them down."[13]

Charles Robinson, a civilian photographer, thought that many of the fort's defenders, including himself, had hurried down the bluff to the riverbank after Confederates climbed over the ramparts. "Our men ran or rather tumbled down. . . . As soon as the rebels got to the top of the bank there commenced the most horrible slaughter that could possibly be conceived." Sensing disaster, several white soldiers earlier had abandoned their posts and hidden at the base of the bluff. One skulker recalled, "It was but a few minutes before the men came over the hill like sheep over a brush fence, when I saw whites and negroes getting shot down. I threw up my hands and said, 'Don't shoot me, I surrender.'" Instantly they fired and he fell; when he struggled to rise, they shot him again. Another skulker cowered behind a log and also tried to surrender. In response, he got a bullet in his buttocks. He remembered, "All I heard was, 'Shoot him, shoot him!' . . . 'Kill him, kill him!' That is about all I heard."

Robinson huddled with a white soldier near the river and watched as Forrest's men used pistols to dispatch unarmed Federals. He related, "One of them soon came to where I was laying with one of the Co. C boys. He pulled out his revolver and shot the soldier right in the head, scattering the blood and brains in my face and then putting his revolver right up against my breast, he said, 'You'll fight with the niggers again, will you? You damned Yankee!' and he snapped his revolver but she wouldn't go off as he had shot the last load out when he killed the soldier by my side." Saved by an empty pistol, he again escaped death when his captor told other Confederates not to shoot Robinson because he was his property. Two other civilians, a Vermont Yankee turned cotton planter and Dr. Charles Fitch, an army contract surgeon, also barely avoided summary execution. But the fort's civilian sutler was not so lucky—a vengeful Southerner shot him dead.[14]

Aware that murder was abroad, many soldiers and civilians did not pause at the riverbank. Perhaps with some exaggeration, one Confederate reported, "The number in the water was so great, that they resembled a drove of hogs swimming across the stream. But not a man escaped this way." In one of his inconsistent statements about civilian losses, Forrest said that more than one hundred male citizens fled to the river, jumped into the water, and drowned. Yet in another report, one that would embarrass Southern leaders, Forrest declared that "The river was dyed with the blood of the slaughtered for 200 yards."[15]

Whites fared better than black soldiers. One Confederate officer remarked that "when . . . the smoke cleared, there was not many of them left." Lieutenant Leaming said, "I know the colored troops had a great deal the worst of it. I saw several shot after they wounded them; as they were crawling around, the secesh would step up and blow their brains out." Even as the killing enveloped them, white Federals realized that blacks were the favorite targets. Wounded, one soldier hid behind a stump with two other whites. He recalled, "Some darkeys came there and we told them to go away. We saw the rebels were shooting them and we allowed if they were not with us, we might get clear." While he survived, few black soldiers got entirely clear.

Black soldiers sometimes learned why death came calling. Before shooting him, Confederates cursed Private Arthur Edwards, "God damn you, you are fighting against your master." Private George Shaw heard almost the same words before a bullet tore through his mouth and exited at the back of his head. Usually, however, Forrest's men simply gunned down any black they saw. When they ordered a former slave from Mississippi back up the bluff, he obeyed. Confronted by a man who leveled his gun at him, he grasped the barrel. Offended by that, the Confederate immediately shot him. He remembered, "I let go, and then another one shot me." Another black soldier, Private Emanuel Nichols, wounded earlier, became a stoic when they shot him again. He recalled, "A man shot me under the ear and I fell down and said to myself, 'If he don't shoot me any more this won't hurt me.'"

Officers of black units, detested as vile traitors to their race, society, and civilization, faced their greatest peril immediately after capture. When Forrest's men first caught Captain Delos Carson of the black

6th Heavy Artillery, they chatted amiably enough with him. One of his soldiers, a witness to the encounter, reported, "They talked with him a little time. . . . They asked him how he came to be there, and several other questions." Then came the fatal query: did he belong to a black regiment? Bravely or foolishly, Carson replied, "Yes." Without another word, an officer shot him dead.

Doctors and patients dispassionately described the hospital murders. Dr. Fitch, a contract surgeon, worked among the wounded at the field hospital when Confederates pounced. Referring to his patients, Dr. Fitch reported, "I think they were all killed except two, the most of them were chopped to pieces with Sabers." The two who escaped were white officers, although Confederates probably did not know they both belonged to the black 6th Artillery. Private Eli Carlton, a black soldier wounded before the surrender, had then gone to the field hospital at the bluff's base. He said, "I was in the hospital when they shot me a second time."[16]

During the attack and the insensate rampage that followed, women and youngsters were killed or wounded, and survivors charged that Confederates also slew black children. Little question exists about the adult female victims, both black and white. Army doctors treated wounded women, and burial parties later found a dead white women. These luckless females came from the contraband camp near the fort or were visiting soldier relatives. Witnesses also said that Forrest's men shot black youths who had worked on the fortifications or as officers' servants. Another story, the tale of a child's heartless murder, won wide acceptance in the North and later caused much trouble for Chalmers, Forrest's subordinate. According to one eyewitness, Chalmers ordered the execution of an eight-year-old boy. Possibly that murder occurred, but Chalmers was not the agent.[17]

Some Confederates tried to stop the killing, and a few still interceded to save the lives of individual white and black soldiers. Largely, however, cries to halt the slaughter went unheeded. Sergeant Clark, the former college student, related, "I with several others tried to stop the butchery and at one time had partially succeeded. . . . Finally our men became sick of blood and the firing ceased." Also, orders came to remove the fort's cannons and to collect government stores and men wanted to secure personal booty. Many fell to robbing the living and the dead, while others went to sacking the nearby settlement, including its general store. This last diversion proved a godsend for several white Federals when their captors took them to the store. That gave the Yankees a

chance to change into civilian clothing and escape. And in the confusion, Robinson, the civilian photographer, obtained a safe-conduct pass
from Confederate officers.[18]

Although anxious to leave the area, Confederates inexplicably expend-
ed the time and effort to bury the dead, white and black. Burial parties
correctly segregated the fallen, separating blacks and whites according
to the mores of the day, and officers apart from enlisted men, as military
etiquette dictated. But that work gave rise to another set of atrocity charges
when they buried some men alive. One who rose from an untimely grave
was Private Daniel Tyler, a former slave who undoubtedly looked more
dead than alive with two gunshot wounds and an eye gouged out. About
sundown, they tossed him into a hollow and pitched dirt over him. He
recalled, "They covered me up . . . all but one side of my head. I heard
them say they ought not to bury a man who was alive. . . . They dug
me out, and I was carried not far off to a fire." Not so fortunate was the
wounded man who was "breathing along right smart." The gravediggers
said that he would die anyhow and left him in the ground.[19]

Confederates blamed the victims. Forrest said the Federals were all
drunk, and his chief apologist declared that some were so "profoundly
stupefied by liquor" as to mimic death. Others, he explained, unreason-
ably feared receiving no quarter and simulated death so expertly as to
defy detection. Another version came from a soldier-correspondent who
wrote, "You have heard that our soldiers buried Negroes alive at Fort
Pillow. That is true. At first fire, after Forrest's men scaled the walls,
many of the Negroes threw down their arms and fell as if dead. They
perished in the pretence and could only be restored at the point of a
bayonet. To resuscitate some of them, more terrified than the rest, they
were rolled into the trenches made as receptacles for the fallen. Vitality
was not restored until breathing was obstructed and then the resurrec-
tion began."[20]

As dusk gathered and nightfall neared, Confederates tried to signal
the New Era to arrange for removal of Federal wounded. But the sailors
did not see the signals in the growing darkness. Meanwhile, some determined Confederates succeeded in shooting a few more wounded blacks,
although an officer ordered one of the shooters arrested. With darkness
upon them, Forrest delegated command to Chalmers and rode away to
camp for the night, never to return. A member of Forrest's escort troop
summed up the day's events when he wrote in his diary, "We arrived at
Fort Pillow and attacked the same early in the day. The fort was defended

by about 450 blacks and 250 whites. We captured about 40 blacks and 100 whites and killed the remainder."[21]

As the next day dawned, Confederates discovered that Major Bradford had escaped and saw gunboat No. 28, the *Silver Cloud*, steaming upriver and shelling even small groups of Confederates. Lieutenant Leaming, badly wounded but alert, recalled, "About this time a squad of rebels came . . . for the purpose of murdering what negroes they could find. They began to shoot the wounded negroes all around there." Survivors agreed that Forrest's men killed only blacks that second day. Sergeant Daniel Stamps said, "I saw them shoot some 20 or 25 negroes the next morning who had been wounded. . . . They did not attempt to hurt us white men the next morning." Another white soldier watched as Confederates prodded recumbent black soldiers to see if they were still alive. If so, they were shot.[22]

When Confederates heard the gunboat's cannons, they immediately began burning all buildings. As the arson squads worked, they usually warned occupants before applying the torch. However, some were careless or indifferent and very likely incinerated some dazed or badly wounded men. Private William J. Mays, a white Federal, said, "They came with a chunk of fire to burn the building where I was in with the dead. They looked in and said, 'these damned sons of bitches are all dead,' and went off." Mays, with only flesh wounds, got out safely, and others, including Lieutenant Leaming, also escaped from burning buildings. But the fires charred some corpses, making for an uncertain cause of death.[23]

Forrest heard the gunboat's cannons and told his adjutant, Captain Charles W. Anderson, to ride back and arrange a transfer of Federal casualties. William Ferguson, the *Silver Cloud's* captain, readily agreed to a daylong truce and the *New Era* returned to help. Soon the mail steamer *Platte Valley* arrived and, later, the hospital boat *Red Rover* appeared. Sailors, steamer passengers, and soldiers joined to move the wounded from shore to ship while naval details buried more of the dead. Many passengers, including women, toured the grisly battleground and saw the ravaged dead, some half-buried or unburied.

All those witnesses made Fort Pillow a unique event. Neither before nor after were there so many independent observers so soon present at such a major atrocity. Their presence caused wide and rapid dissemination of reports about the "Fort Pillow Massacre," including very questionable tales of crucifixions. Within a few days, the North knew about the slaughter on the faraway banks of the Mississippi. One correspondent wrote that the sights and smells so sickened him that he could write no more. But he summoned the strength to continue, "I have every evidence that instead of honorable warfare . . . the Confederates pursued that of indiscriminate butchery." In a dispatch to the *Illinois State Journal*, another writer on the mail steamer described the "fiendish barbarities perpetrated by the murderers of Fort Pillow." Ferguson, the *Silver Cloud's* captain, deplored the "furious and vindictive savageness . . . never equaled by the most merciless of the Indian tribes."[24]

As the truce neared an end, Federal and Confederate officers fraternized at the *Platte Valley's* bar. Southerners repeatedly said that neither black soldiers nor white Tennessee Unionists could expect mercy. Brigadier General Chalmers admitted that most black soldiers lost their lives after Confederates overran the fort. He said that "the men . . . had such a hatred toward the armed negro that they could not be restrained" from killing them after capture. Chalmers added that neither Forrest nor he had ordered the slaughter and that both had tried to stop it. One of his staff advised that "they did not recognize negroes as United States soldiers, but would . . . show them no quarter—neither the negroes nor their officers." Captain Anderson, Forrest's aide, explained that they considered black soldiers "as property, and as such, being used by [Federals] . . . had destroyed them."[25]

When Confederates rode away, they counted no more than one hundred casualties. Forrest listed twenty killed and sixty wounded, and others reported similar loss numbers. About a month later, Chalmers listed fourteen killed and eighty-six wounded. The discrepancy likely arose because Forrest had used early uncorrected returns. Yet even using Forrest's tally and his fifteen-hundred-strength figure, then he sustained a death rate of slightly more than 1 percent and total casualties of about 5.3 percent. With Chalmers's figures, deaths were less than 1 percent and overall casualties nudged 7 percent. No matter whose figures are used, Confederate losses were remarkably low after an assault against a fortified position.[26]

Federal losses approached 100 percent. Of the twenty-one officers, twenty became casualties. Ten were killed, three wounded, six became prisoners, and one lieutenant escaped by donning civilian clothes and walking away. However, the precise number of enlisted men in each loss category cannot be determined. Just before the attack, the garrison numbered 580 officers and men, but some men deserted after that report. On the other hand, probably present were some uncounted recruits, both black and white. As of April 8, Bradford's Battalion had 285 officers and men, and about 85 were killed while almost all the rest were either wounded or captured, adding up to a 97 percent loss. The two black artillery units had a strength of 292 officers and men, and 112 lived through the massacre. Survivors included a maximum of fifty-seven men taken prisoner, thirty-two wounded, two officers absent that day, and about twenty soldiers who escaped by hiding. Based on this survivor count, 180 black soldiers and their officers fell during the slaughter, but that toll rose to at least 200 when badly wounded men succumbed or died on the march southward as prisoners. By this tally, the black units had more than 68 percent killed and lost 93 percent of their strength.[27]

Yet Forrest's men and the sailors reported burying about 450 bodies, although duplications occurred. That tally does not include those who drowned or some overlooked by the burial parties. A large number of civilians and some uncounted recruits probably account for the extra graves. In Southern reports, the civilian mortality rate almost matched that of the garrison. Confederates blamed the citizens for the high toll, insisting that the foolish and fearful people had plunged lemminglike into the river to drown. Forrest also reported capturing "about 40 negro women and children," a statement later important when his apologists denied women and children were present. He advised President Davis, "It is safe to say that in troops, negroes, and citizens the killed, wounded and drowned will range from 450 to 500." Still, he was more correct when he later suggested that "the actual loss of life will perhaps never be known."[28]

9

The Camden Expedition

FORT PILLOW LAY ABANDONED AND SILENT, but the furies loosed there flew far and wide. Shocked and outraged Northerners called for bloody revenge, although some predicted it would prove a very counterproductive victory. Black soldiers used it as a touchstone when they retaliated in kind, and some white commanders stubbornly resisted attacks because they feared a replay of Fort Pillow. As a propaganda vehicle, the massacre motivated Northerners, enabled their government to claim moral superiority, both domestically and abroad, and put the Confederacy on the defensive. Yet Yankee outrage, foreign disapproval, or threat of retribution never stopped ordinary Confederates from repeating the atrocities when opportunity offered. With or without Fort Pillow, however, black troops would have taken matters into their own hands and, in reprisal, killed Confederate wounded and prisoners when they had the chance. In warfare, murder begets murder.

Before any reaction occurred north or south, the furies hastened to claim another life. Major William F. Bradford, it will be recalled, disappeared after he gave his captors his word of honor that he would not escape. They caught him as he trudged toward Memphis in civilian clothing and pushed him before a firing squad on the evening of April 14. Forrest declared, "I understand that he attempted to escape, and was shot." Other Confederates admitted that Bradford was executed but offered differing explanations for the action.[1]

Again, Lincoln wrestled with a Gordian knot. If he exacted Old Testament vengeance, Confederates would counterretaliate by executing white soldiers, and Northern people would never stand for that; if he ignored Southern crimes against black soldiers, he reneged on the government's obligation and duty to protect all soldiers. Months earlier he had directed that "for every soldier of the United States killed in violation of the rules of war, a rebel soldier shall be executed; and for everyone enslaved by the enemy or sold into slavery, a rebel soldier shall be placed at hard labor." But that was an edict largely ignored. Only a couple of generals specifically cited it, and none carried out its retaliatory provisions when Confederates executed black soldiers. Moreover, when Frederick Douglass, the prominent black leader, importuned him to order indiscriminate vengeance, Lincoln replied, "Once begun, I do not know where such a measure would stop."[2]

On April 18, less than a week after the massacre, Lincoln told a crowd in Baltimore, "There seems to be some anxiety in the public mind whether the government is doing its duty to the colored soldier, and to the service at this point." He declared that black soldiers deserved the same protection afforded any other soldier. Lincoln confessed that "the difficulty is not in stating the principle, but in practically applying it." Yet difficult or not, he promised redress. He declared that if it were true that Confederates had murdered thirty or three hundred black soldiers, then the government would do something about it. Solemnly, he vowed that "the retribution shall . . . surely come."

It was an empty promise. Like the protagonists in Greek or Shakespearean tragedies, Lincoln had to choose between two good options. Uncertain what to do but striving for some resolution, on May 3 he asked cabinet members to submit written opinions about the proper course.

They reconvened three days later when all urged caution and argued against indiscriminate retaliation. Secretary of the Interior John P. Usher apparently offered the decisive opinion. Referring to Grant's imminent spring offensive, Usher argued that "We are upon the eve of an impending battle. Until the result shall have been known it seems to me to be inexpedient to take any extreme action." Usher's argument prevailed and there the matter rested. In effect, Lincoln and his cabinet chose to do nothing. They considered an unimpaired, unified struggle to preserve the Union the greater good.[3]

Lincoln's private secretaries thought that neither he nor the cabinet ever again seriously considered the question. But Lincoln did, for it weighed upon him, even though Grant's offensive raised new and more pressing concerns, including huge casualty lists. On May 18, while waiting at the telegraph office for battle reports from Virginia, Lincoln wrote a lengthy order threatening mild, bloodless reprisals for Fort Pillow and for any future mistreatment of black soldiers. Then he put aside the unsigned order and apparently left it at the telegraph office. Years later, that forgotten directive turned up in the papers of the deceased military telegraph chief.[4]

Lincoln's generals added their voices to the chorus of outrage, excoriating the killing and recommending retribution. But they also offered dispassionate, even cynical assessments. Major General Cadwallader C. Washburn, commanding at Memphis, declared, "The Sioux Indians after this will be regarded as models of humanity." He promised his troops would not spare any Confederates involved in the massacre. Grant told Sherman, "If our men have been murdered after capture, retaliation must be resorted to promptly." But Sherman saw a default gain for the North. He wrote, "I know well the animus of the Southern soldiery, and the truth is they cannot be restrained. The effect will be of course to make the negroes desperate, and when in turn they commit horrid acts of retaliation we will be relieved of the responsibility." Like Sherman, Major General James B. McPherson, Army of the Tennessee commander, considered Fort Pillow a Pyrrhic victory for Southern arms. He concluded, "It is a deplorable affair, but will in the end I am certain be most damaging to the rebels."[5]

Northerners initially understood that Confederates had butchered only black soldiers. Charging that they had repeatedly murdered them with impunity, a black New York City resident urged the immediate mass execution of a matching number of Rebel prisoners as an object lesson.

Senator Reverdy Johnson, of Maryland, protested that not even cannibals would behave as had Forrest's men. An angry Ohio woman said that fiends had presided at Fort Pillow, and an army baker near Washington railed against the "horrible wholesale murders." *Harper's Weekly* editors regretfully advocated eye-for-eye retaliation. In Memphis, an officer of black troops went further, recommending hanging two captured rebels for every Federal slain. A Quaker officer in Nashville predicted, "The massacre at Fort Pillow will be avenged most terribly." Senator John Sherman, of Ohio, feared that the savagery marked a new and terrible stage in the war.[6]

Meanwhile, Senator Benjamin F. Wade and Representative Daniel W. Gooch, Radical Republican members of the watchdog Joint Committee on the Conduct of the War, promptly journeyed halfway across the country to the scene. There they groomed witnesses, asked leading questions, elevated the responses of illiterate men into statesmanlike prose, and returned with a devastating report. They pronounced Fort Pillow "a scene of cruelty and murder without a parallel in civilized warfare, which needed but the tomahawk and scalping-knife to exceed the worst atrocities ever committed by savages." Congress ordered their report published and distributed as a bound volume less than a month after the event. That served to sustain for a while the public's motivation and the clamor for revenge, which Secretary of the Navy Gideon Welles called a "popular noisy demand" for blood.[7]

As Sherman had predicted, black troops sought retribution on their own. A Vermont officer in the East said his black soldiers fully realized that if they straggled, were captured, or fell wounded, they could expect no mercy, "except such mercy as the bayonet or the bullet has to offer." Accordingly, after Fort Pillow most fought a private no-quarter war under a tacit compact with Confederates. Their battle cry became "Remember Fort Pillow," understood by all as a do-or-die challenge. In Tennessee, a black brigade's leader recalled, "After Fort Pillow, my command virtually fought under the black flag. We soon found that all our men that were captured and all wounded that we had to leave were promptly killed, and from that [time] on my officers and men never reported capturing any prisoners, and no questions were asked." At Grant's headquarters in Virginia, they also asked no questions. With tongue in cheek, a staff officer confided, "Don't know how it is—we have made no enquiry. . . . I suppose they have to kill their prisoners before they can take them."[8]

Even Forrest said black troops fought more stubbornly after Fort Pillow. He thought that foolish and charged that their officers cruelly indoctrinated them with the erroneous belief that they could expect no mercy from his men. Others, however, thought the blame or credit for the new resolve belonged to Forrest. He had provided the key incident and the black soldiers' rallying cry. An infantry major saw other positive results. He wrote that it would "create a hundredfold more sympathy in the army for the negro than ever existed before and will insure Forrest 'a strong rope and short shrift' if he ever falls into the hands of negro soldiers."[9]

Southerners privately endorsed the bloodshed but publicly denied the wanton slaughter. To them, it was not murder or a massacre but was something akin to exterminating good sheepdogs turned sheep killers. Posted near Richmond, an infantryman wrote, "General Forrest captured Fort Pillow and about Six hundred. Most of them was Negroes. He didn't [take] any of them prisoners, killed everyone of them. I think that was the best thing he ever done in his life." Similar sentiments came from a twenty-year-old East Tennessee woman. She exulted, "General Forrest . . . put most of the garrison out of harm's way, killed every officer there. Good for him. I think he did exactly right." In North Carolina, a plantation mistress heard the news and hoped it was true. She wrote, "If they will steal our slaves & lead them on to murder & rapine, they must take the consequences."[10]

Three vital concerns generated the public denials: the Confederacy's reputation abroad, possible Yankee retaliation, and a treasured self-image. Still hoping for European recognition, Southerners feared the atrocity reports would adversely influence opinion in France and England. Jefferson Davis fretted about the "misrepresentation of events . . . thrown upon the world." Secretary of War James A. Seddon energetically defended Forrest, castigated the North's report, and contradicted himself with a slip of the pen, all at the same time. In a waspish denunciation, he deeply deplored "the groundlessness of the misrepresentations so industriously circulated by our unscrupulous enemies respecting the merciless conduct of our troops on that occasion." Forrest submitted a revised report with the river no longer dyed red with the blood of the slaughtered. Indeed, all references to slaughter vanished. He recalculated Federal casualties and reduced them by half. During this creative exercise, Forrest emphasized the compassionate behavior of his men and his own efforts to succor the Federal wounded.[11]

Southern civil and military leaders knew the North had the advantage in men and matériel and so worried about retaliation. They worried needlessly, but they did not know that at the time. Then they heeded

Lincoln's vow of retribution and his generals' threats, and they knew that they themselves would strike back in an instant were the roles reversed. Later, Surgeon John A. Wyeth, Forrest's faithful apologist, turned the lack of retribution to advantage in a transparent sophistry. He argued that Federal officials had promised retaliation if Confederates had massacred the garrison but there was no retaliation; therefore, that proved no atrocity occurred.[12]

Preserving their self-image caused a difficult internal conflict in the hearts and minds of many Southerners. Federals had turned their slaves to lethal use against their owners, so they saluted the killing because that was the only way to handle insurrectionist chattels. But at the same time, they rejected the massacre charge because Northerners framed it as a reflection upon Southern honor, decency, humanity, chivalry, and lawfulness. Perhaps that was the reason Mary Chestnut, the able Southern chronicler of those years, privately refused to believe that it had occurred. "Tell that to the marines!" she sniffed. However, others rejected the notion that the slaughter besmirched the South. An artilleryman serving in Charleston's defenses belittled Northern outrage. He prayed that the South would furnish ever more bloody examples, and he hoped that "Fort Pillow with all its fancied horrors shall appear as insignificant as a schoolboy's tale."[13]

Atrocities Abound in Arkansas

That artilleryman's wish came true on April 18 in Arkansas. There, Confederate Indians scalped black soldiers while their white cohorts settled for shooting prisoners and the wounded. That massacre resulted from a scheme to enlarge Federal control of Arkansas and Louisiana and to seize part of Texas, with the incidental goal of showing the national flag as a caution to the French forces occupying Mexico. Stupendously incompetent Nathaniel P. Banks, the political general who had sent hundreds to pointless death at Port Hudson, led the main thrust, known as the Red River campaign. Accurately, that venture has been described as "a costly fiasco for the Union side . . . a huge land-and-water enterprise."

Major General Frederick Steele led a smaller force of about nine thousand men from Little Rock to join Banks in the Red River effort. In turn, Brigadier General John M. Thayer and his Frontier Division of 3,500 men, including the 1st and 2nd Kansas Colored Infantry regiments, marched from Fort Smith to join Steele's column. But both Steele and Thayer lagged far behind schedule and Steele's troops marched on half and quarter rations while Confederates constantly harassed them. One of the few light moments came on April 9, when Thayer's black regiments arrived. One of their officers recalled, "We . . . found scores of white soldiers on each side of the road, as eager to see the colored soldiers as children to see their first elephant."[14]

However, on that day, Banks's Red River drive had collapsed, and he began a long, tortuous retreat. At least two black regiments had gone on the expedition but served in support positions. Still, one of their officers wrote that "I have seen some of the toughest fighting that I ever saw. . . . We lost our Major and Adjt and Some few men the Major and Adjt were taken prisoner and Shot after being taken." Sherman called it an utter failure, a colonel on the bungled campaign said it was most disastrous, and Confederates hailed a victory. Still, it was not a total loss, as the fiasco enabled Lincoln to get rid of Banks.[15]

Steele knew nothing of Banks's reverses until he reached Camden after abruptly turning away from his Red River goal. He sought temporary sanctuary in the fortified town and there heard disquieting reports that Confederates had routed Banks. By then, food for man and beast had become a pressing problem for the thirteen thousand men and an equal number of horses and mules. Both Camden, a once flourishing town, and the surrounding countryside were almost bare of provisions. Confederate troops had lived off the land, and now, as Federals desperately went foraging, the enemy burned anything remaining. Not much remained in Camden because the hungry men had killed and devoured sheep, hogs, and cattle and raided family storerooms when they arrived. Those supplies gone, the men subsisted on half allowances of corn intended for the horses and mules.[16]

As their skimpy food supply dwindled, small detachments undertook risky scouts for food. Steele ordered a large foraging party to fetch a five-thousand-bushel cache of corn hidden about sixteen miles from Camden. That assignment went to Colonel James M. Williams and his 1st Kansas Colored. Besides his own 438 officers and men, Williams had 195 troopers from three Kansas cavalry regiments and a two-gun section of the 2nd Indiana Battery. All told, he would have about 665 men to guard his train of 198 wagons. Yet all knew the enemy gathered strength each day, and sixteen miles was a long, lonely march from Camden. The prospect made prudent men nervous. Captain Ethan Earle protested that their objective lay behind twelve thousand Confederates. He related, "A Strong remonstration was made by the officers against sending out

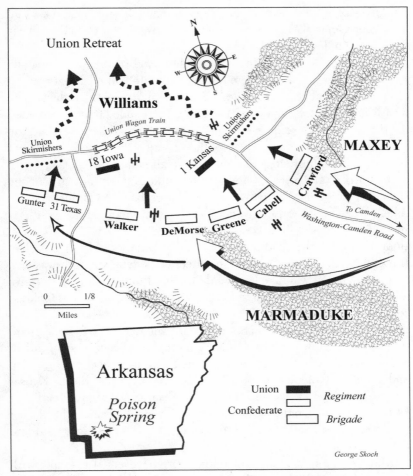

Poison Spring, where Confederates scalped and killed wounded and surrendered soldiers of Colonel James M. Williams's 1st Kansas Colored Infantry, was the first of several atrocities committed by both sides during the Arkansas campaign of March and April 1864.

so small a force with the certainty of being taken—any larger force was refused; the regiment went."[17]

Nothing disturbed their foraging and they filled their wagons, although Confederates had burned about half the five-thousand-bushel supply. But they had not gone unobserved. Brigadier General John S.

Marmaduke, a West Point graduate, gathered troops for an attack. Soon Brigadier General Samuel B. Maxey and his cavalry division of 1,335 Texans and Indians arrived, and Marmaduke's strength grew to 3,335 men. Colonel Tandy Walker, commanding 2nd Indian Brigade's 680 Choctaws and Chickasaws, said they were hungry and half-clothed and, he might have added, more than half wild. An artilleryman said the Indians were a garishly dressed, hard-looking lot, and Walker added that they thirsted for the blood of their despised enemy, the black soldiers. He said the blacks were seen as "the ravagers of their country, the despoilers of their homes, and the murderers of their women and children."

At sunrise on April 18, Confederates rode to the attack. About the same time, Colonel Williams started his train back to Camden. To his relief, 385 men of the 18th Iowa, 90 more cavalrymen, and 25 artillerymen with a two-gun howitzer section reinforced him. With these fresh troops, Williams then had 1,166 officers and men, while Marmaduke had three times that number. Actually, effective Federal strength was less. Cavalrymen had wandered off while the hard marching and excessive labor on short rations had disabled at least a hundred 1st Kansas Colored soldiers. Major Richard G. Ward said his black soldiers had spent sixty-three of the last seventy-eight hours on duty, and many had to stand guard during the remaining fifteen hours. Williams knew he headed toward an ambuscade, especially when a disoriented Confederate courier rode up and asked for Colonel Charles DeMorse. Williams and the 1st Kansas Colored had met DeMorse and his 29th Texas Cavalry a year earlier at Honey Springs when the black soldiers trounced the Texans. The courier exaggerated Confederate strength, telling Williams that eight thousand to ten thousand lay in wait.

Marmaduke's ambush formed an inverted, reversed L shape, with Confederates on the Federals' right flank on the L's long arm and across their front near a place called Poison Spring, site of a post office. In a moment, two batteries opened on the column and dismounted cavalrymen struck front and flank. Williams immediately realized that they would overwhelm his force but hoped that more reinforcements would arrive in time to save the day. He hoped in vain. Williams said his men fought stubbornly, although the need to protect the stalled wagon train limited their defensive tactics. Confederates' freedom of movement, greater numbers, and superior firepower soon proved decisive. By 2 P.M. nearly one-half of Williams's men were out of action and the remaining troops were out of ammunition. With no help in sight, he abandoned the train, telling the men to run. Organized resistance collapsed as the men fled to nearby woods, swamp, and canebrakes, where it was difficult for pursuing cavalry to follow.[18]

Fleeing Federals could see Confederates killing helpless black soldiers. Earle angrily reported, "All the colored men in our regiment, wounded and left in the field, were killed by the rebels!" Major Ward recalled, "We were obliged to bring our wounded away the best we could, as the rebels were seen shooting those that fell into their hands." An Arkansas cavalryman wrote that "if the negro was wounded our men would shoot him dead as they were passed and what negroes that was captured have from the best information that I can obtain have since been shot." He estimated that "there were 10 negroes killed to one white Fed." General Edmund Kirby Smith, the Confederate Trans-Mississippi commander, wrote his wife that they captured about "200 prisoners and left 600 reported dead . . . principally negroes who neither gave nor recd quarter." He added that he saw only two black prisoners, but they did not live long. Writing in his journal, Lieutenant William M. Stafford, a Texas artillery officer, said flatly that no blacks were taken prisoner. Feigning death when left behind on the battlefield, a black soldier watched the enemy finishing off the wounded and heard them exult, "Where is the First Nigger now?" Then came the answering cry, "All cut to pieces and gone to hell by bad management."[19]

Confederates excitedly told how the Indians, whooping and waving scalping knives, descended upon the black Federals. An observant sixteen-year-old soldier related, "I want to say right here that we had a hot time. Among their forces were about 300 Negroes. You ought to see Indians fight Negroes—kill and scalp them. Let me tell you, I never expected to see as many dead Negroes again. They were so thick you could walk on them and with white Yanks mixed with them." A youthful artilleryman recalled that "it was with the greatest difficulty that the Indians could be kept from killing every negro prisoner and scalping all the dead negroes." A sergeant, who had himself sworn never to take a Yankee prisoner, told his wife that five hundred black Federals had escorted the captured wagon train. He related that "the Choctaw Indians were turned loose on them and in a few minutes they had killed 480 negroes and scalped them, taking only two negroes prisoners. These only lived a short time."[20]

Many found grim satisfaction in the black death toll. "I have seen enough myself to know . . . our men is determined not to take negro prisoners and if all of the negroes could have seen what occurred that day they would stay at home," wrote one Confederate, believing that the massacre would serve as an object lesson to chattels. Lieutenant Colonel John M. Harrell, who led a battalion during the fight, recalled that Confederates cut blacks down right and left. Almost invariably, Southern black mortality counts were double or triple those reported by Federal officers. These contrasting tallies were not necessarily at odds. Often Confederates made no distinction between soldiers and black teamsters and laborers in their reports, which would explain much of the disparity in the numbers. For example, a Texas cavalryman wrote home that they "captured about 180 wagons loaded with supplies, besides . . . killing over 300 negroes." Then after the fight, Southern cavalrymen blocked an escape route and reported killing "at least 80 negroes." Many were most likely civilian teamsters fleeing to safety.[21]

Survivors stumbled into Camden for the next two or three days, and their stories quickly circulated. Battle-tested veterans shuddered when they learned that Confederates had scalped the wounded and the dead. Soldiers of the 2nd Kansas Colored reacted strongly when they heard that "no prisoners were taken from the colored troops, but all instantly killed." Colonel Samuel J. Crawford, their commander, had no doubt that "the wounded colored soldiers were murdered on the field, as directed by the President of the Confederacy." He called his officers together and they decided to take no more prisoners while the enemy continued to murder black soldiers. But they also decided that "no wounded Confederate should be harmed or injured in any way, but left where he fell." Somewhat ambiguously, Crawford later asserted, "This agreement was subsequently carried out, as far as possible in the heat of battle."[22]

The 1st Kansas Colored counted 117 dead and 65 wounded at Poison Spring. Mortally wounded men increased the death toll, but their number is unknown. As it stands, the regiment had 27 percent killed and a total loss of almost 42 percent. The entire 1,155-man force sustained 301 casualties, or about 26 percent. Again black soldiers had an inordinate share—60 percent of the total, and 82 percent of the dead.

Confederates celebrated a lopsided victory. Their initial reports listed 115 casualties: 17 killed, 88 wounded, and 10 missing. Samuel B. Maxey, the senior brigadier, thought units that had not yet reported would add no more than thirty casualties to the total. Using 145 as the final figure, then his attacking soldiers sustained a mere 4.4 percent casualty rate as compared with the Federals' 26 percent. Besides inflicting a painful defeat, they also captured 170 food-filled wagons, more than 1000 horses and mules, field artillery pieces, many rifles, and 100-odd white prisoners.[23]

Federal morale, already low, slipped further. His troops began to feel that Steele used men like sacrificial lambs, indifferent to any calamity that engulfed them. As if to confirm that view, a few days later he sent another wagon train through enemy territory to fetch supplies from Pine Bluff. Lieutenant Colonel Francis M. Drake, the train commander, counted 240 wagons and, to his dismay, between 50 and 75 other vehicles, including sutler wagons and 8 ambulances. Besides soldiers, teamsters, and at least seventy-five unarmed black recruits, many civilians assembled for the trek, including about three hundred contrabands. More runaways and refugees would join the column during the march. Steele believed an infantry brigade of twelve hundred men, four pieces of artillery, and four hundred cavalry would provide adequate protection. As a precaution, cavalry scouted part of the route beforehand. All was well—they saw no Confederates lurking in the bushes.[24]

Confederate scouts spotted the train the day after it left Camden and reported it to Brigadier General James F. Fagan, a cavalry division commander. With his four thousand troopers, including five hundred men of Brigadier General Joseph O. Shelby's brigade, they attacked the three-mile-long Federal train on April 25 at a place known as Marks' Mills. After more than five hours of fighting, a fierce struggle with many casualties, the contest ended in surrender and defeat for the Federals. Again, Steele had lost a train, but this time Confederates killed, wounded, or captured most of the escort troops.[25]

Frenzied killing continued long after the surrender. Targeted were the hundreds of slaves who had joined the column in an aborted flight to freedom. A Confederate officer recalled, "No orders, threats or commands could restrain the men from vengeance on the negroes and they were piled in great heaps about the wagons, in the tangled brushwood, and upon the muddy and trampled road." Captain R. H. Fleming, a prisoner, witnessed the carnage and related, "Large droves of contrabands . . . were shot down where captured. A rebel soldier took four contrabands to General Shelby, a rebel brigade commander, and asked what he should do with them. 'Shoot them' was the answer, and the soldier quietly sitting on his horse, shot them down, the same as so many pigs." Lieutenant Benjamin F. Pearson, also a prisoner, noted that "there was not an armed negro with us & they shot down our Colored servants & teamsters & others what were following to get from bondage, as they would shoot sheep dogs." Wounded and immobilized, Drake said his captors butchered a large number of blacks, including his personal servant.[26]

The wholesale slaughter of valuable slaves would seem self-defeating. Yet this occurred many times during the war and showed most cogently the fury Southerners felt when slaves defected to the Yankees or even attempted it. It was costly punishment, considering that each dead slave represented an average loss of $1,000. But those fugitives had violated a core taboo, that of defying their white masters. Moreover, many Southerners regarded such chattels as a loss in any event, judging them fatally tainted by contact with Yankees and infected with terminal defiance. No one counted the dead blacks, but probably at least two hundred or more were killed. One Southerner apparently included both whites and blacks when he counted 507 bodies. Incomplete Confederate returns showed 293 in killed, wounded, and missing, while Drake placed Federal casualties at 250 in killed and wounded. A postwar accounting listed 100 dead and 250 wounded for Federals, which is likely the more accurate figure. Some eleven hundred to twelve hundred became prisoners, but as many as three hundred, mostly cavalrymen, escaped to Pine Bluff or Camden. Some black men also evaded death by hiding in nearby swamps.[27]

Within hours, Federals in Camden had heard about the latest disaster. Steele called their situation perilous and none disagreed. Soon they would have no food or forage while their numbers had dribbled away in wagon train debacles. At a council of war, Steele and senior officers agreed they should leave while they could. They destroyed excess equipment the next day and abandoned mules and horses too weak to travel. That night, with wagon wheels muffled, they quietly left Camden for a 120-mile march to Little Rock.

Weary and glum, they reached the Saline River and a crossing point at Jenkins' Ferry on April 29. But the river was too deep to ford, and torrents of rain churned the bottom land into a porridge of mud. Engineers started throwing a pontoon bridge across the swollen river and, in a few hours, they had their floating span in place. Meanwhile, infantry prepared for the attack they knew would soon come.[28]

Pursuing Confederates neared the crossing in a drenching rain as a gloomy dawn broke on April 30 and quickly attacked on a narrow front. Colonel Crawford heard the firing swell to a roar while he and his 2nd Kansas Colored waited at the pontoon bridge. He decided the rear guard needed help, and he quick marched his tired men the mile and a half back to the firing line. Reporting to Brigadier General Samuel A. Rice,

Crawford asked where his 660 men should go. Rice responded, "Do you think you can take them in?" To Crawford, that meant that Rice wondered whether his black soldiers would really fight. Nettled, Crawford replied that his men would go anywhere any live regiment would go. Rice smiled and directed him to the right of the brigade line.[29]

There they stood and fought for the next two hours. Then the situation changed dramatically when a section of enemy artillery suddenly appeared and opened fire with canister, the giant shotgun blasts of metal. Crawford said he would either have to take the guns with a bayonet charge or fall back. Rice gave him permission to charge, giving the black soldiers their chance to exact vengeance for Poison Spring.[30]

When Crawford's men fixed bayonets and left cover, they became easy targets. But their own fire brought down thirty-odd artillery horses, effectively holding the guns in place, and then they sprang upon the gunners. Lieutenant Reuben F. Playford, acting adjutant, said the men killed with clubbed rifle butts and bayonet. Crawford declared that "one thing is certain . . . [we] took no prisoners on that field." That was not quite true—there was one. He was Lieutenant John O. Lockhart, who went to the wrong place with his guns. Luckily for him, an officer captured him, thus ensuring his survival. He complained that his men were killed after they had surrendered and that he lost half his thirty-two-man section in a few moments. Crawford told Lockhart that since Confederates had murdered black soldiers at Poison Spring, his men would take no prisoners. But, he added, they would spare Lockhart because he was wounded and unarmed. Other Confederates quickly heard that the black Yankees shouted "no quarter" when they charged and that the artillerymen were indiscriminately bayoneted. However, the black soldiers also took casualties—they counted fifteen killed, fifty-five wounded, and three missing.[31]

About noon, the firing died down, Confederates fell back from the battleground, and only the wounded remained. Then, like avenging ghosts, black soldiers began to prowl the somber field. Private Milton P. Chambers, 29th Iowa, explained to his brother that "the negroes want to kill every wounded reb they came to and will do it if we did not watch them . . . one of our boys seen a little negro pounding a wounded reb in the head with the but of his gun and asked him what he was doing: the negro replied he is not dead yet! I tel you they wont give them up as long as they can kick if they can just have their way about it. It looks hard but the rebs cannot blame the negroes for it when they are guilty of the same trick." Wounded in the leg, Private John H. Lewis, 18th Texas Infantry, sheltered behind a stump. He recalled, "Soon I looked around and saw some black negroes cutting our wounded boys' throats, and I thought my time would come next." That thought energized him, giving him the strength to limp safely away.[32]

Others were not so fortunate. Surgeon David S. Williams, 33rd Arkansas Infantry, related, "We found that many of our wounded had been mutilated in many ways. Some with ears cut off, throats cut, knife stabs, etc. My brother, A. J. Williams, acting sergeant major, had his throat cut through [the] windpipe and lived several days. I saw several who were treated in the same way." Junius N. Bragg, another 33rd Arkansas surgeon, told of caring for a soldier who "had his throat cut by a negro" while lying wounded, and a 28th Texas Cavalry doctor reported that they found wounded men with "their throats cut from ear to ear by the Negroes." Rather than fearing a knife at his throat, Private J. R. Jones, 14th Texas Infantry, feared a bullet. He recalled, "One of the negroes threw his gun on me to shoot, but I begged him out of it." Colonel Crawford denied his men murdered enemy wounded. Perhaps he was ignorant of the mayhem but, in any event, he obviously could not attest to the actions of each of his six-hundred-odd men.[33]

After successfully withdrawing across the Saline River, Steele boasted, "They [Confederates] did not capture a man except those whom I thought it necessary should be left on the battle-field." He said it was for the greater good to leave them, even though he regretted the necessity. Abandoned blacks regretted it even more, for they were marked for murder. Federals who stayed to care for their wounded reported that "a Texas soldier . . . killed, in the hospital, nine of the wounded men belonging to the 2d Kansas Colored Infantry." Surgeon William L. Nicholson, 29th Iowa, who also stayed when Steele withdrew, reported that Confederates soon rode up to his field hospital. He related, "One, dressed as an officer, drew his revolver and shot three wounded 'niggers' who lay in the yard." When he protested, calling it cowardly murder, some onlookers thought it might be a good idea to shoot him, too. Still a live prisoner two weeks later, Nicholson had six wounded black soldiers under his care. As they lay helpless, a lone Confederate appeared with a pistol in each hand and shot every black in the head, killing all. Outraged, Nicholson protested to the Confederate commander, who replied that the blacks had brought it upon themselves. Nicholson soon realized that position was not an aberration. In his journal he wrote, "In fact, all the bystanders considered it rather a meritorious action than otherwise."[34]

Both sides claimed victory at Jenkins' Ferry. A pragmatic appraisal came from a Confederate infantryman who concluded, "Hard to tell who got the best of it, but that ended the fighting in this part of Arkansas." Few would dispute that. Steele blamed Banks's defeat for his own, but his officers and men scornfully named him the culprit. Perhaps the sharpest cut of all came from a farm boy–soldier from Iowa who called Steele a whisky-bloated villain unfit to command a flatboat. An uncertain but surely derogatory meaning was evident in Colonel Crawford's charge that Steele was a "tenor singing dog fancier."[35]

Still, the sorry affair had a positive aspect for black soldiers. A 2nd Kansas Colored officer explained, "It was a question . . . whether the blacks would fight. The 30th of April settled the point with some of the rebels, as well as convinced the white soldiers of our army." Even German American soldiers of the 27th Wisconsin, often scornful of black Americans, agreed that they had done well at Jenkins' Ferry. Brigadier General Frederick Salomon, a division commander, said they had behaved with conspicuous gallantry. Steele was not quite so positive but conceded that "the African can be made as formidable in battle as a soldier of any other color." However, little publicity attended the Camden Expedition, as it was named. Excepting the troops involved, few knew about the Poison Spring slaughter or the Jenkins' Ferry reprisals, so those incidents generated neither outrage nor praise. Banks's Red River debacle garnered the headlines and the interest.[36]

As already argued, black soldiers did not need Fort Pillow to excite them to retaliation. Although Poison Spring and Jenkins' Ferry took place days and weeks after the Fort Pillow massacre, apparently the news had not reached the two black Kansas regiments. They had marched from Fort Smith before it happened and were cut off from the outside world while on the expedition. But immediately they realized that they fought a no-quarter war with Confederates, and the black soldiers responded in kind. Given the throat-cutting exercise at Jenkins' Ferry, their reprisals showed they could be just as savage and merciless as their former masters. This, of course, reinforced a circular argument by Confederates that blacks were innately a brutish species as proved by their barbaric reaction to just punishment for fighting their masters. A more logical thought, one that would increasingly occur to people on both sides, came from

Lieutenant William Blain, 40th Iowa Infantry. After returning from the useless expedition, he wrote, "The 'rebs' appear determined to show no quarter to Black troops or officers commanding them. It would not surprise me in the least if this war would ultimately be one of extermination. Its tendencies are in that direction now."[37]

DARK ARTILLERY; OR, HOW TO MAKE THE CONTRABANDS USEFUL.

Strongly prejudiced Northerners initially doubted that black men, scorned as alien inferiors, could or would help fight the war, and this satiric cartoon from the popular weekly *Frank Leslie's Illustrated* shows that skepticism. The caption reads, "Dark artillery, or, how to make the contrabands useful." Library of Congress.

Northern wartime propaganda photographs show this youth first as a slave
in rags and tatters, and then as a free, button-bright drummer boy in the
1st Kansas Colored, the regiment murdered and scalped at Poison Spring,
Arkansas. Massachusetts Commandery Military Order of the Loyal Legion and U.S. Army
Military History Institute.

Disabled by wounds or disease, soldiers like Private Nick Biddle transferred to the Veterans Reserve Corps, eventually about twenty thousand strong, where they wore kersey blue uniforms and served as guards, cooks, and hospital orderlies.
U.S. Army Military History Institute.

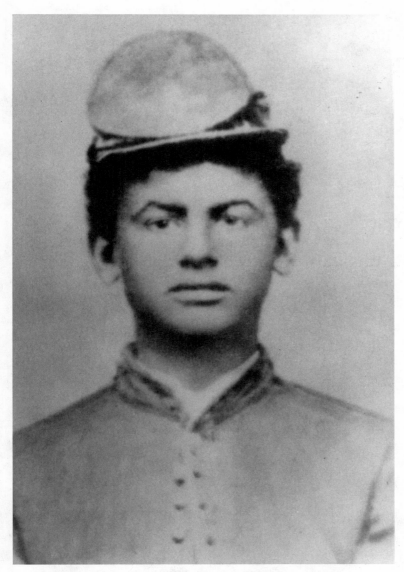

Youthful Charles S. Graffel, ranked as undercook, served with the white 2nd California Cavalry, a regiment that fought Indians and protected goldfields and bullion shipments far from the war's main battlegrounds.
U.S. Army Military History Institute.

1st Lieutenant Peter Vogelsang, who enlisted as a private in the 54th Massachusetts Infantry (Colored), late in the war overcame stubborn army bias to become one of a handful of black officers. Courtesy of the State Archives of Florida.

Sergeant Stephen Swailes, 54th Massachusetts, commended for valor
at Olustee, twice wounded, and strongly recommended for promotion,
had to wait until March 26, 1865, for his 2nd lieutenant's commission.
Courtesy of the State Archives of Florida.

Break time is welcome before an elegant windowed bombproof at Dutch Gap near Richmond, where black soldiers braved constant Confederate mortar fire while digging a bypass canal, one of Major General Benjamin F. Butler's failed schemes. Library of Congress.

Standing in formation for dress parade in November 1864, the 1st U.S. Colored Infantry had already fought at Wilson's Wharf and in the June attack upon Petersburg. Massachusetts Commandery Military Order of the Loyal Legion and U.S. Army Military History Institute.

roops, Nov. 16, 1864.

In a stiff wind, a 2nd U.S. Colored Light
Artillery gun crew drills undisturbed, but
Forrest obliterated one section at Fort Pillow,
and another had to spike and abandon its
guns at Brice's Cross Roads when attacked
by Forrest in June 1864. Courtesy of the Chicago
Historical Society.

Serving in a strictly segregated army,
wounded and sick black soldiers pose for the
camera while recovering at their own separate
convalescent hospital at Aiken's Landing,
Virginia. Library of Congress.

Punished more severely and more often than white soldiers, black Federals complained bitterly of unequal treatment, including long, increasingly uncomfortable rides on the wooden horse for minor offenses, as seen here. Massachusetts Commandery Military Order of the Loyal Legion and U.S. Army Military History Institute.

Disproportionately to their numbers in the army, black soldiers went to the gallows or before firing squads for mutiny or rape, and here Private William Johnson, 23rd U.S. Colored Infantry, dangles at rope's end after a rape conviction. Massachusetts Commandery Military Order of the Loyal Legion and U.S. Army Military History Institute.

A hard-bitten frontiersman, Daniel K. Harden transferred from the white 12th Kansas Infantry to become a 2nd lieutenant in the 2nd Kansas Colored Infantry, a regiment that vowed to take no prisoners after the Poison Spring massacre. Courtesy of the Kansas State Historical Society.

Major John W. M. Appleton, 54th Massachusetts Infantry (Colored), survived disastrous battles, though before the defeat at Olustee, Florida, an angry Southern woman warned him that if captured, he would "surely be hung because you command nigger troops." Courtesy of the State Archives of Florida.

Lieutenant General Nathan Bedford Forrest holds a flag bearing the words "No Quarter" as he shoots helpless Federals at Fort Pillow in this biting cartoon by Thomas Nast, part of an 1868 broadside. Library of Congress.

When Forrest assaulted the Federal fort at Paducah, Kentucky, on March 25, 1864, the USS *Peosta* fired 530 artillery shells into the Southern city, setting buildings ablaze, and then repeated the bombardment when Forrest's troops returned about two weeks later. U.S. Naval Historical Center.

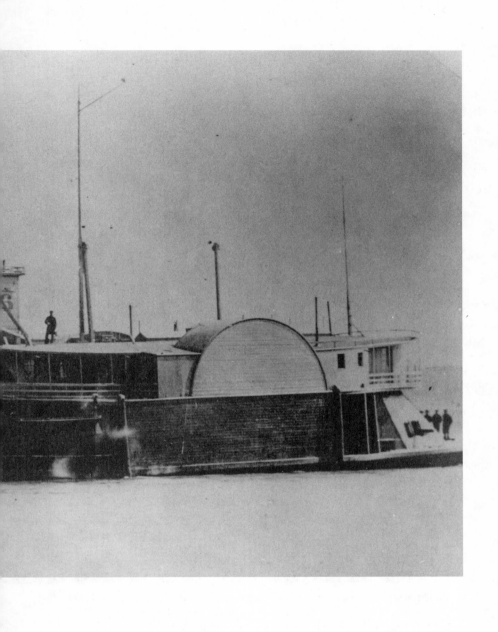

Northern artists, none present at the time, used their unrestrained imaginations for vivid portrayals of the Fort Pillow Massacre, as in this one by Kurz and Allison, originally a chromolithograph. Courtesy of the Chicago Historical Society.

Though worn by weather, the Crater's immensity is still apparent nine months after the explosion and the relentless massacre of black troops there on July 30, 1864. National Archives.

Brigadier General William Mahone, a Virginia Military Institute graduate, allegedly ordered his men to take no black prisoners at the battle of the Crater, though his troops surely needed no such orders to commit the war's single largest massacre of black Federals. Massachusetts Commandery Military Order of the Loyal Legion and U.S. Army Military History Institute.

Private Louis Martin, 29th U.S. Colored Infantry, perhaps ponders his future after barely surviving the battle of the Crater and the ensuing wholesale slaughter of black soldiers. National Archives.

Convicted of killing a wounded Federal officer in his hospital bed and murdering black soldiers at Saltville, Virginia, Champ Ferguson sits in a Nashville prison not long before he went to the gallows. Courtesy of the Filson Historical Society, Louisville, Kentucky.

Lieutenant General Wade Hampton ordered his cavalrymen to execute captured Federals, something not generally known at the time, though this 1868 cartoon by Thomas Nast shows that people soon understood he had hanged and shot Sherman's men. Library of Congress.

Sherman's men, here relaxing in Atlanta, quickly learned while marching through Georgia and the Carolinas that stragglers, couriers, and foragers risked summary execution if captured by Confederates. Library of Congress.

Gathered for burial near Fredericksburg, Virginia, these fallen Yankees are no different from the white Federals executed later by angry, desperate Confederates in the Shenandoah Valley or on Sherman's march through Georgia and the Carolinas.
Library of Congress.

Ordinary Confederate soldiers, like these three unbowed men captured at Gettysburg in 1863, would later refuse quarter to black and white Federals in the East and West. Library of Congress.

10

The Plymouth Pogrom

APRIL 1864 SET THE WAR'S RECORD when a third major atrocity took place within a few days of Fort Pillow and the Camden Expedition. On North Carolina's coast, half the continent away, Confederates again demonstrated their deadly intolerance for whites or blacks who defected to the North. This third massacre also provided more evidence, if any were needed, that this reaction was not a regional quirk but systemic. On April 20, Georgia, North Carolina, and Virginia troops overwhelmed the Federal enclave at Plymouth and then methodically killed black soldiers, white Unionists, and refugee contrabands. This last, the slaughter of runaway slaves, was a repetition of what had happened at Marks' Mills in Arkansas or Mounds Plantation in Louisiana and what would happen later at other places. But on this occasion, the North lacked a clear understanding of events, and

Southerners, quick learners, tried to suppress reports about the black victims. Again, Richmond denied all, and Washington noisily protested but quietly did nothing. Not until recently have historians pieced together a comprehensive account of that massacre, though as a self-contained incident rather than part of a whole. But that narrower approach can distort the study, as argued at the beginning of this work.[1]

Early in the war, Federal forces had seized beachheads on North Carolina's coast, including Plymouth, Washington, and New Bern, towns stretching in a slant line from north to south on Albemarle and Pimlico sounds. As elsewhere in North Carolina, many people along the coast held strong pro-Union sentiments, and much animosity existed between the factions. Soon these enclaves became havens for Unionist families, fugitive slaves, deserters, and men evading Confederate conscription. Federal authorities aided and sheltered "Buffaloes," men who actively resisted the Confederacy or who joined special regiments filled with turncoats and Unionists. Recruiting officers for black regiments vied with one another to enroll runaway slaves. These outposts affronted Southern pride, increased strife and dissension in the region, and, in time, became festering cankers. "Plymouth has been a thorn in our side & the garrison there a perpetual uneasiness to us," a planter's wife declared.[2]

On the eve of the Union's great 1864 spring offensives planned by "Grant the hammerer," Richmond decided to eradicate those irritants. Major General George E. Pickett, wrongly acclaimed for his role at Gettysburg, marched upon New Bern. He gave it up as a bad job on February 3 and withdrew, blaming others for his failures. But he did claim credit for capturing 297 Federal soldiers and 14 blacks. Among the prisoners were 2nd North Carolina Union Volunteers, most of whom had deserted the Confederate army. Southerners considered them turncoat traitors; Federals insisted they were loyal citizens, earlier forced to join in treasonous activity. The Southern view prevailed, and soon twenty-two Union Volunteers were tried and hanged. Major General John J. Peck, the Union commander, protested that the men were "duly enlisted" in Federal service. Pickett replied that they were also "duly executed" as deserters. Peck fumed and charged that "the blood of these unfortunates will rest upon you and your associates." He warned that his government would immediately act to redress their deaths, which, of course, was utter nonsense. For all of the righteous outcry in the North, both armies routinely executed turncoats, though only a few deserted Federal service for the South.[3]

Next, with Richmond's backing, the ambitious Brigadier General Robert F. Hoke planned an attack on Plymouth. General Pierre Gustave T. Beauregard, soon to command in North Carolina and Southern Virginia, opposed detaching troops for minor missions and thought that Federal leaders would not be diverted by sideshows in North Carolina. He was correct—Grant had already advised Chief of Staff Halleck to abandon the isolated posts. Though he realized that Lincoln would be reluctant to give them up and he worried about the effect on North Carolina Unionists, Grant persisted. He told Benjamin Butler, who presided over the enclaves, that it would be best to evacuate them. Butler, sitting in Virginia, saw no reason to worry. He refused to believe Confederates were building an ironclad warship to attack the enclaves, and he refused to send reinforcements.[4]

With six thousand men, including artillery and cavalry, Hoke began besieging Plymouth on April 17. At the same time, the ironclad CSS *Albemarle*, two years under construction, started down the Roanoke River. Hoke needed the *Albemarle* to dispose of four Federal gunboats patrolling offshore from Plymouth. With their firepower, the gunboats could interdict approaches to the waterfront town and block a land attack.[5]

Serene in the belief that no enemy was near, the garrison was surprised by the attack on that pleasant Sunday afternoon. Brigadier General Henry W. Wessells, Plymouth's commander, nominally had twenty-eight hundred troops but probably had no more than twenty-two hundred men available to man the defensive works that ringed the town in a two-and-a-half-mile perimeter. In addition to four infantry regiments with about 1,550 effectives, he also had 166 men of the 2nd North Carolina Union Volunteers, some armed refugees, and perhaps 200 black soldiers and recruits. Wessells, a Regular Army veteran of the Seminole and Mexican wars, also had to contend with the many panicky civilians, including Northern teachers, officers' wives, deserters, Unionist North Carolinians, and hundreds of contrabands. He sent a large number of white women and children, the sick and disabled, and some blacks to Roanoke Island aboard the army transport *Massasoit*. Departure of the ship, with its frightened cargo, stirred a sense of foreboding in some soldiers who watched.[6]

Although Hoke's artillery sank an armed steamer, the *Bombshell*, and captured one redoubt at great cost on April 18, the garrison had taken only a few casualties and had firmly held the main defenses. Everything changed in the early morning hours of April 19, when the *Albemarle* steamed out of the night. Gliding silently downstream like a nightmare specter, the ironclad avoided river obstructions and mines and shrugged off artillery fire. Quickly, the *Albemarle* rammed and sank the USS *South-field*, then drove away the other gunboats so essential to Plymouth's defense. Unscathed and triumphant, the ironclad waited in the darkness, and the garrison knew what that portended. Captain John Donaghy, 103rd Pennsylvania, recalled, "We felt our case was desperate, but there was a grim determination among the men to die hard if need be." However, the 2nd North Carolina Volunteers and other Unionists despaired, so Wessells told them to fend for themselves. His advice was unnecessary—many had already fled; some paddling away in canoes.[7]

At dawn the next day, April 20, Hoke launched his final onslaught, and soon Confederates overran all Federal positions except for Fort Williams, though they suffered heavy losses. Calling a truce, Hoke demanded unconditional surrender from Wessells and said that if he had to assault, he could not be responsible for the consequences. Lieutenant Colonel Henry T. Guion, 1st North Carolina Artillery, reported that Hoke also warned that waving a white flag would not necessarily save them. Lieutenant Alonzo Cooper, 12th New York Cavalry, wrote, "This Gen. Wessells construed as a threat of a repetition of the Fort Pillow massacre." Wessells refused and fighting resumed, but not for long. Under heavy fire from all sides, Federals soon yielded, whereupon Hoke chose not to carry out his no-quarter threat and Federals said they were "treated very kindly."[8]

After subduing last pockets of resistance, Hoke gave his men free rein to plunder, and they fell to sacking the place with a will, as if they looted a Yankee town. While busy pillaging, Confederates paid scant attention to their prisoners. That proved a blessing for some 2nd North Carolina soldiers. Knowing that they would be shot or hanged if identified, many quickly assumed the names of absent, sick, or dead Yankee soldiers. Captain Donaghy recalled, "One came up to me, his uniform was the same as ours, but his cap had no distinguishing letters on it, so I directed one of my men to trade caps with him, thus making him appear as a member of company F 103rd Pennsylvania Volunteers." He avoided detection only to die while a prisoner at Andersonville. Donaghy also told of a hospital steward, a deserter from forced Confederate service at New Orleans, who subsequently joined the Federal army. He escaped immediate discovery but was identified many miles away, and then presumably led to his death.[9]

Hoke soon lined up captives so citizens and soldiers could identify turncoats, deserters, Buffaloes, and black soldier recruiters for the hangman. One spotter was a townswoman personally acquainted with two Federal officers who were recruiters. One of them, 1st Lieutenant Oliver R. McNary, recalled, "She looked me straight in the eye for a few seconds . . . and then turned away . . . She did not betray me." Neither did she identify fellow recruiter Captain Hiram L. Marvin, assigned to the 37th U.S. Colored Infantry. From a Northern sympathizer, McNary had heard that he and Marvin were on the Confederates' wanted list, and Hoke had specifically asked Wessells about the pair. McNary went to an officers' prison camp. Marvin, formerly a sergeant with the 85th New York, melted back into his old regiment as an enlisted man. Another recruiter followed suit, rejoining the 12th New York Cavalry. That extricated him from one perilous position but deposited him in Andersonville, where he died three months later.[10]

That winnowing process continued during the march to a railhead to entrain for prison camp. Sergeant Major Kellogg recalled that "the ranks were searched for deserters from the rebel army, a number of whom were detected and taken away. We never knew their fate, but suppose them to have been shot." Warren L. Goss, a Massachusetts artilleryman, said he knew exactly what happened to some. He related, "On our way from Plymouth to Tarboro I saw several of our North Carolina men selected out . . . and, without even the ceremony of a drum-head court-martial, strung up to the limb of trees by the roadside." After one search for Buffaloes, Private Charles C. Mosher, 85th New York, noted, "Our little Smith is safe with us yet." He referred to a Unionist drummer boy who had assumed a dead soldier's name. At Tarboro, Confederates reportedly identified fifteen men as turncoats and hanged them. Though some Southerners thought the doomed men had trials, Federals said they went straightaway to the rope.[11]

No screenings were required to identify black Federals, and Confederates immediately began shooting them. But there is no way to determine how many were executed or, for that matter, the number of black soldiers and recruits present at the surrender. Wessells officially reported 244 unattached recruits, many of them blacks, and about 100 of them fought in Plymouth's defense. Several black regiments had recruiters working there, and one, the 10th U.S. Colored Infantry, apparently had sent a sizable detachment. Those men and their recruits may have added another one hundred men to the black soldier total. By one Confederate estimate, Federals had seven hundred uniformed blacks at Plymouth but considerably less than half that number is more likely the correct figure.

Recruiting practices peculiar to black regiments contributed significantly to the confusion about numbers. Major General John J. Peck, Federal district commander, complained that units deployed excessively large recruiting contingents and enlisted every black they could persuade, trick, or coerce into the army, without regard to physical or mental condition. Another irritant was the practice of issuing uniforms before a medical examination. When found unfit for duty, rejects kept the clothing and continued to wear whole or partial uniforms. Army laborers and camp idlers also often wore bits and pieces. But there and elsewhere, Confederates vowed to shoot any black man caught wearing Union blue. Chaplain Amos S. Billingsley reported that "as far as I know, they managed to redeem the promise." That was also the understanding of a North Carolina woman who reported that an acquaintance's slave "was shot, as all negroes were who were dressed in Yankee uniforms, *so I have heard.*" Orderly Sergeant Samuel Johnson, a black recruiter for the 2nd U.S. Colored Cavalry, said he saw that "all the negroes found in blue uniform, or with any outward marks of a Union soldier upon him, was killed." He quickly shed his uniform, pulled on civilian clothing, and safely merged with Plymouth's faceless black throngs.[12]

Federals said blacks, civilians and soldiers, died in a ruthless pogrom. A New York soldier charged that Hoke's men raised the black flag against black soldiers, and Captain Donaghy wrote, "They were shot down in cold blood after they had laid down their arms; some rushed to the river and tried to escape by swimming across, but few, if any, succeeded." Shunning haphazard killing, some Confederate officers turned to more efficient methods. They used firing squads to execute batches of black prisoners. Lieutenant Cooper reported, "The negro soldiers . . . were drawn up in a line at the breastwork, and shot down as they stood. This I plainly saw from where we were held under guard, not five hundred yards distance. . . . When the company of rebs fired, every negro dropped at once, as one man." Sergeant Johnson, the black recruiter, witnessed the same or a similar mass execution and artilleryman Goss related that men who had "surrendered in good faith . . . [were] shot down like dogs."[13]

By far the greatest slaughter occurred when hundreds of blacks, mostly civilians, and some Unionists suddenly rushed from Plymouth for the supposed safety of nearby wooded swamps. Confederates quickly pursued them, beginning a relentless butchery. Confederate Lieutenant William I. Clopton wrote home that "several hundred negroes . . . attempted to escape when the town fell but were pursued & all most the last one of them killed." Lieutenant Cooper, a prisoner, noted that "we could hear the crack, crack, crack of muskets, down in the swamp where the negroes had fled to escape capture, and were being hunted like squirrels or rabbits." The hunters had it all their way, for few, if any, of their quarry carried weapons. An 11th Virginia officer related that those "who took to the swamps, were pursued by Dearing's Cavalry and left in the swamp, dead or alive; none of them were taken prisoners, or brought out of the swamp." They tracked and killed members of a disorganized, defenseless rabble blindly thrashing through mire and swamp water in desperate flight. "It was a massacre," said a New York soldier.[14]

Confederates continued to scour the swamp for days. Chaplain Billingsley, who remained in Plymouth, reported, "For two days after the surrender, I heard very frequent firing in an adjoining swamp." From all accounts, most of the victims were black males, runaways from area farms and plantations. Estimates of the number killed in the murder spree vary wildly, ranging from three hundred to six hundred. Allowing for exaggeration and for minimizing, Confederates probably slew between three hundred and four hundred. Benjamin F. Blakeslee, a 2nd lieutenant with the 16th Connecticut, wrote that "three or four hundred negroes" were slain. Four days after the slaughter, a twelve-year-old boy and some friends inspected the killing ground. With the scene still vivid in memory, the boy said he had seen hundreds of unburied blacks.[15]

While Hoke's men efficiently killed hundreds, some escaped through the swamps and reached safety. Many in the large black population had not attempted to flee. Young and old men, women, and children had sought freedom in the enclave and then hoped only to survive the siege. Confederates viewed these compliant fugitive slaves as recovered property, and General Braxton Bragg, Davis's military adviser, asked North Carolina's governor to restore runaways to their proper owners. But he also urged him to keep that effort out of the newspapers. Bragg explained that was necessary "to avoid . . . complications with the military authorities of the United States in regard to the disposition which will be made of this class of prisoners." Apparently, Davis and Bragg thought many of the captured blacks were Federal soldiers, hence their unnecessary caution.[16]

Plymouth's fall delighted the South. President Davis congratulated Hoke and promoted him to major general; Congress passed a joint resolution of thanks to Hoke and the *Albemarle*'s captain. In all the rejoicing, the victory's high price somehow escaped critical scrutiny. Available reports indicate that Confederates had more than one thousand casualties, about seven times the likely Federal battle loss. Wessells thought his killed and wounded did not exceed 150, and later statistical studies support that figure. But his total loss was almost 100 percent because about 2,400 Federals became prisoners of war.[17]

Washington initially refused to credit word of Plymouth's fall or rumors of another massacre. But by April 26, six days later, Federal authorities had accepted the bad news, though little information reached them through official channels. Mainly, they had to rely upon newspaper reports compiled from refugee narratives. In this way, they learned that Confederates had slaughtered black refugees, shot black soldiers, and executed Union loyalists. Attorney General Edward Bates declared, "For the sake of humanity, I hope this is not true." He thought that the Plymouth killing spree, added to the Fort Pillow massacre, would introduce a brutal ferocity to the war. He concluded, "For such barbarity can hardly fail to produce a corresponding barbarity, in retaliation." He and others feared that no quarter would become the rule rather than the exception. Aside from humanitarian concerns, they also worried the carnage would increase opposition to the war and damage the administration's prospects in the fall elections.[18]

Ordinary citizens read chilling newspaper accounts under grim headlines, such as "North Carolina troops taken out and shot after surrendering" and "Negro Soldiers Butchered." In New York, the *Times* reported that most Unionists were executed and announced, "All the negroes found in uniform also shot." With Fort Pillow scarcely a week behind them, journalists had a ready comparison. The *Herald* labeled Plymouth's fall "The Fort Pillow Massacre Re-enacted." Their correspondent wrote that the Rebel plan "for the future disposition of the negroes is emancipation from, and not for, life." *Tribune* editors called for a condign response, asserting that the Plymouth affair "only proves that what was supposed to be an exceptional barbarity at Fort Pillow, has been adopted as the deliberate policy of the rebels. As the issue is to be made it must be met."[19]

As usual, the North declined to meet the issue. In tacit agreement, Congress, the army, the people, and the administration continued a firm policy of inaction when Confederates massacred blacks. However, when Southerners murdered white Federals from Northern states, retaliation could be swift and harsh. In any event, as usual, the South denied all. Robert Ould, Confederate prisoner exchange chief, called Sergeant

Johnson's sworn statement a villainous lie. With a touch of humor, Ould said if the North wanted the truth, then all it had to do was ask any of the captured officers, "always excepting the chaplains." In another indignant rebuttal, a Confederate officer asserted, "No armed prisoners of any color were killed at Plymouth." Since armed prisoners are rarities, his statement fell short of confuting the atrocity charges.[20]

It is well here to make a point that applies to any battle account of any era. Soldiers are not detached observers but active participants who know only what transpires within their limited reach of vision and activity. Moreover, men side by side may have different recollections of the same scene, while those in a similar situation on the opposing side may also have differing accounts of the identical incident. Many may later learn what happened elsewhere, out of sight and sound, but not necessarily, and what they hear secondhand afterward is not necessarily true. That is why it is so desirable to obtain as many contemporary firsthand accounts as possible of an event or even of moods and trends.

To illustrate, years later, support for Southern protestations of innocence emerged from an unlikely bloc: old Yankee soldiers, veterans of two white Pennsylvania regiments captured at Plymouth. They said they were well treated and their Confederate captors were gentlemen, thus incapable of murder. Eyewitness accounts of wanton killing, they said, came from men beset by stress and perfervid imaginations who erred. They also argued that Wessells would have known and protested unlawful killings, and since he did not, then there were none. Finally, the 101st Pennsylvania's historian recalled the flight of blacks and Unionists to the swamps and declared that "[they] would, no doubt, be hunted for as sport by many well meaning men." To clinch his argument, he asked, "Had the conditions been reversed, would not many Yankees [have] enjoyed the same kind of sport?"[21]

As usual, Confederates left dead blacks unburied when Hoke departed a noisome, plundered Plymouth to attack Washington and New Bern. Federals evacuated Washington without a fight, and Hoke then invested New Bern. Beauregard urged Hoke to issue a surrender-or-die demand and to mean it. Before he could issue that ultimatum, Richmond abruptly recalled Hoke and his troops to Virginia. Nerves were on edge there, for Grant advanced on the capital city, Butler moved toward Petersburg, Major General Franz Sigel moved on the Shenandoah Valley, and Lee needed every man.[22]

The Richmond-Petersburg Front

As Grant concentrated his forces for the spring offensive, he organized black regiments into brigades and divisions to add to his field armies. As the Army of the Potomac pushed southward toward Richmond in early May, the 9th Army Corps' black 4th Division guarded supply trains in the rear. Commanded by Brigadier General Edward Ferrero, a former New York dancing master, most of his men were as fresh and green as the springtime grass. They comprised nine regiments, most organized in the previous four or five months, and half still needed recruits to fill their ranks. As train guards, distant from the frontlines, they supposedly would have a quiet learning period.

But Confederate cavalry units also operated in the rear areas, looking for lightly defended wagon trains or weakly held posts. On May 7, a 9th Virginia Cavalry trooper noted, "Two Regts of negroes are reported at Brandy Station & many think we are on our way to capture them." They did not know that most black troops had marched away several days earlier from Germanna Ford and Brandy Station, the site of Federal supply depots. Only a small detachment and stragglers remained. Early the next day, the Virginians neared Germanna Ford. The trooper wrote, "Soon commenced to fall in with large numbers of stragglers who surrendered without resistance. [W]e captured then negro soldiers, the first we had seen they were taken out on the road side and shot, and their bodies left there—." Another 9th Cavalry soldier spared his sister the details when he wrote, "I have seen some few negro soldiers. Some few have been taken prisoners. It is needless for me to say what became of them." Colonel Bryan Grimes, of North Carolina, confirmed that whites were taken prisoner near Germanna Ford but no blacks.[23]

Just a week later, however, Confederates inexplicably spared black prisoners though given ample cause to shoot them. While undoubtedly a good faith account, the sole narrator may have received embellished or twisted reports from those involved, particularly concerning a brave or foolish sergeant. On Butler's Army of the James front, 5th U.S. Colored Infantry soldiers went foraging on May 16. Shortly, the twenty-man party walked into an ambush. Some escaped by plunging into nearby woods, but others stood and fought. Overwhelmed, nine were captured. Somehow a black sergeant seized a pistol and shot two guards, enabling two men to escape. In the confusion, two more successfully hid. That left five. Now their captors had the added and extreme provocation of the sergeant shooting his way out. Instead of killing the lot, Confederates shot just one wounded man and took the other four as prisoners. One slipped away the next day and that left three. They went to prisoner-of-war camps and survived almost a year in captivity, returning to Federal control in March 1865. Yet nearby on that same day, another black infantryman suffered the more customary treatment from the enemy. Private Robert G. Fitzgerald, 5th Massachusetts Cavalry (Colored), wrote in his diary, "I have seen one of their [black infantry] pickets that was killed this afternoon he was shot in the calf of the leg which disabled him. They then came up to him and broke his skull with the butt of their muskets. His brains are scattered over his face and head[—] can such men eventually triumph. God Forbid."[24]

About that time, a Pennsylvania soldier wrote home, "The rebs takes no prisoners of the colored troops." That was the general rule, but, as noted, exceptions occurred. However, Butler, now Army of the James commander, used that conviction in May when he assigned Brigadier General Edward A. Wild and his African Brigade to garrison Wilson's Wharf on the James River. Major General Fitzhugh Lee, Robert E. Lee's nephew, thought it his duty to eradicate those blacks from their strongly fortified post with the ironclad *Atlanta* supporting them offshore. Besides the formidable defenses, Lee ran up against what might be called "The Fort Pillow syndrome." When Lee rode up at midday on May 24, he sent a surrender-or-die ultimatum. Wild and his officers decided that "the language was interpreted by us to mean that their success and our failure meant another Fort Pillow massacre." Wild refused, and his black soldiers inflicted heavy losses when Lee vaingloriously and futilely assaulted.[25]

In the Southern view, Fitzhugh Lee's defeat was considered most humiliating because black troops had somehow defeated him. Northerners reveled in the Southern discomfort. Then Lee and his men became the butts of even more painful jibes from other Confederates. Shortly after the 1st Maryland Cavalry retreated before a superior Federal force, the regiment's adjutant encountered Lee. It was May 27, a few days after the Wilson's Wharf affair. Lee guyed them, "This is a pretty howdy-do for the Maryland cavalry—let the Yankees run you off the face of the earth." Booth shot back, "Well, General, one thing is certain, the people who have been after us were white men; we stayed long enough to find that out anyway." Although Lee managed to laugh, it was likely a trifle forced.[26]

Black soldiers triumphed again when Major General William F. (Baldy) Smith led his 18th Army Corps to Petersburg's gates on June 15, 1864. About 15,000 troops, including Brigadier General Edward W. Hinks's

3,750-man black division, rolled up the first defense lines. Then, for reasons never satisfactorily explained, Smith suspended operations, forfeiting a golden opportunity to capture Petersburg. Although the grand prize slipped through Smith's bumbling hands, his black soldiers won plaudits for their fighting. A Rhode Island infantry officer candidly admitted, "I have not been much in favor of colored soldiers, but yesterday's work convinced me that they will fight." Agreeing, an Ohio cavalryman wrote home, "All the soldiers give the Colored Troops much praise: they have done well—they took the first line of fortifycations." Even Confederate Brigadier General Edward P. Alexander, a professional soldier, conceded their successes. Positive accounts appeared in Northern newspapers and *Leslie's Weekly* depicted black soldiers hauling off a captured cannon.[27]

Though they endured confusion, exhaustion, and friendly fire and listed 507 killed and wounded, black soldiers were rightfully proud of the day's work. Sergeant Major Christian A. Fleetwood, 4th U.S. Colored Infantry, scribbled in his diary, "Went into action early charged out of woods. Cut up badly. Regt. broke and retreated. Fired into by 5th Mass. Lost Regt. Charged with 22d [U.S. Colored Infantry]. Took the Battery. Advanced upon works. . . . Lay under their fire balance of the day, advancing by degrees in line. About 7 p .m. final charge made. Seven guns taken by our Regt." A euphoric Chaplain William H. Hunter, 4th U.S. Colored Infantry, soared to premature heights when he declared, "The 15th of June, 1864 is a day long to be remembered by the entire colored race on this continent. It is the day when prejudice died in the entire Army of the U. S. of America."[28]

While prejudice did not expire, black soldiers could remember it as a day of retribution in their private no-quarter war. Private Robert G. Fitzgerald, 5th Massachusetts Cavalry (Colored), noted in his diary, "but few prisoners taken." If his regiment took some, other black units took none. When an officer intervened to stop them from killing captives, they vigorously protested that Southern soldiers "would kill us, and had killed us wherever they could find us, and we were going to change the game." Still not satisfied, they sought to dispatch prisoners taken by white units. A New York infantryman said nearby black soldiers rushed over to kill their captives. He related, "I didn't see but one killed. . . . A great bushy Nigger came up to him, knocked him down, and ran his bayonet through his heart. Our boys turned on the Niggers and kept them back." A Vermont soldier told how one of his officers rescued a wounded Confederate surrounded by black soldiers bent on murder. He wrote, "He drew his revolver and peremptorily ordered the negroes . . . to disperse and had the wounded rebel cared for."[29]

Most whites understood the reasons and motivation for the black soldiers' pitiless conduct. Charles F. Adams Jr., the Massachusetts patrician, wrote, "All admit . . . the darkies fought ferociously, and, as usual, the cruelty of Fort Pillow is reacting on the rebels, for now they dread the darkies more than the white troops; for they know that if they will fight the rebels cannot expect quarter. Of course, our black troops are not subject to any of the rules of civilized warfare. If they murder prisoners . . . it is to be lamented and stopped, but they can hardly be blamed." A New Jersey officer commented, "The Rebel prisoners are very fearful of being left to . . . colored troops as they fear their own acts of inhumanity will be repaid. The Nigs are all anxious to kill but not to take prisoners, and their cry is Ft. Pillow." He told about a prisoner who refused to go to the rear if escorted by black soldiers. "One of the guard," he related, "told him to move on; he refused again, when without further words the Nig ran him through with a bayonet killing him instantly."[30]

Southern soldiers had indeed realized that they could expect little mercy from black Federals. A New York officer related, "All seem to have a great fear of negro soldiers and the first Reb. we captured in the Wilderness was perfectly wild until we assured him that 'Burnside's niggers' were really harmless unless stirred up with a sharp stick." In late September, a 29th Connecticut Infantry (Colored) captain wrote home, "Deserters came in on our picket line the last two nights we were at the front & were quite terrified when they found they had thrown themselves into the hands of the avenging negro." Defending his black soldiers' murderous ways, another officer asserted, "We can bayonet the enemy to terms on this matter of treating colored soldiers as prisoners of war, far sooner than the authorities can bring him to it by negotiation. . . ." His optimism was misplaced. Neither negotiation nor bayonet could bring Southern soldiers to terms in that regard.[31]

11

Brice's Cross Roads

IN JUNE 1864, FORREST AND HIS MEN again slew black soldiers wholesale, but this time as something of a sporting event, similar to the hunt in the Plymouth swamps. While the black death toll was much higher than that at Fort Pillow, Brice's Cross Roads lacked the drama and sensational publicity. Area Federal commanders learned of the bloodshed, but Washington may have had only an inkling that another no-quarter incident had occurred. For Union leaders, the execution of captured or wounded blacks surely caused conflict and embarrassment. While they could ignore or did not know about the murders at Milliken's Bend, Olustee, Poison Spring, or other obscure places, they were acutely aware of the Fort Pillow and Plymouth atrocities. But Washington apparently preferred to regard these as random events rather than parts of a consistent murder pattern, thus lessening the need for a meaningful response.

Among other reasons for hesitation, Lincoln always argued that it was wrong to punish the innocent for the crimes of others. Yet even when Federal troops captured men from Confederate units known to have murdered black soldiers, neither investigation nor punishment followed. Further, even after the spring massacres, some highly placed Federal officers were openly skeptical that Confederates habitually killed wounded or captured black soldiers. Lieutenant Colonel Horace Porter, one of Grant's aides, dismissively commented, "The black boys . . . all had a notion that their lives would not be worth praying for if they fell into the hands of the enemy." And so these atrocities continued, one after the other.[1]

At the same time, doubts and contradictory sentiments about black soldiers still unsettled Northerners eighteen months after Lincoln authorized their use. Though they had adjusted to their presence, welcomed blacks as cannon fodder, and knew they had fought in battles east and west, many white soldiers remained unconvinced that they were reliable fighting men. Citizens and soldiers alike appreciated the utility of blacks intercepting bullets or shrapnel. Elizabeth Blair Lee, the young Washington matron, confided, "They are however the best population . . . to be food for gun powder if it saves better men it is something gained—" Asked why some generals refused blacks their right to be killed, a 10th Massachusetts officer replied, "I imagine that they do not amount to any certain sum in a fight and in such tough battles as we have it will not do often times to put in troops which you cannot depend upon." He added, "Another reason I presume is that the Rebels show them no mercy if captured and our government is too weak to protect them."[2]

Lincoln walked a shaky tightrope. To him and his adherents, saving the Union was the primary goal, the greater good. Were it a straightforward, purely military challenge, his task would have been easier. But politics intervened. To achieve the goal, he believed he must win reelection, and so he could not afford to alienate too many voters. No matter what his instincts or inclination, he could not protect blacks at the expense of white soldiers. Though they abided black assistance, Northerners retained their virulent prejudices. Resentments simmered, intensified by a perception that Lincoln favored blacks. A disgruntled Michigan soldier grumbled, "The soldiers are losing all confidence in the administration. . . . Lincoln wants the nigger on a level with the white man." Giving action to words, a New York regiment changed its collective mind about

voting for Lincoln in the fall presidential election. Explaining his reversal, one soldier announced, "I cannot go for a man who thinks more
of the niger than a white man." An angry Lemuel Jones, a Federal 6th
Kentucky soldier, wrote his brother that he hoped "old abe lincoln . . .
had to sleep with a negro every night as long as he lives and kiss ones ass
twice a day." Others muttered about the "eternal negro" and often their
antipathy knew no bounds. Lieutenant Charles H. Cox, 70th Indiana,
forthrightly confessed, "I do despise *them* and the more I see of them,
the more I am against the whole *black* crew." In Louisiana, an 89th U.S.
Colored Infantry officer growled that once out of the army "I shall feel
perfectly contented if I never set eyes on a darkey." Traveling to Washington from Virginia, an army chaplain noted, "The soldiers vented all
their spleen among the negroes. Nothing is heard on the cars, boats, etc.
etc. but imprecations on the 'wooly heads!'"[3]

Though black soldiers gained equal pay in June 1864, many complained about unequal treatment by prejudiced officers. They often suffered physical abuse, causing bitter resentment. From Virginia, a 43rd
U.S. Colored Infantry soldier wrote, "I do not think it right that soldiers
should be cuffed and knocked about by their officers. . . . There are men
in this regiment who were born free . . . and will not stand being punched
with swords and driven around like a dog." But they could do little in
protest without risking charges of mutiny and a firing squad.[4]

Yankee mistreatment of blacks offended Southerners whose bias took
a different form. In view of their willingness to exterminate any number of rebellious former slaves, their protective attitude toward obedient
blacks might appear an impossible contradiction. But it was not—they
simply distinguished between good and bad chattels, feeling affection
for some and seldom hating any. When Federal troops tramped through
her neighborhood in June of 1864, a Virginia woman protested, "They
talked dreadfully about the negroes." Even at the war's end, a refugee
girl complained, "The Yankees . . . have been behaving very rudely to
the negroes today, cutting at them with their swords, beating them and
tormenting them generally."[5]

By this time, severe and multiplying strains beset the Confederacy
and its people. Soldiers knew or sensed that the war went against them,
provoking disaffection and, most visibly, mounting desertions. On the
home front, people struggled as food shortages worsened, the currency
depreciated, inflation escalated, lawlessness increased, and Federal armies
penetrated Dixie. Many fled before the advancing Yankees, becoming

unhappy refugees in their own land. Yet still they hoped and believed, savoring each small victory, always hoping for a sudden triumph of Confederate arms; a negotiated peace with a war-weary North; European recognition; or, all else failing, divine intervention. Private J. T. Kern, 45th Mississippi, fervently hoped for the last when he wrote, "God surely will not suffer such inhuman monsters to torture us much longer, but will dash them to pieces in his wrath." Such undercurrents of apprehension began to permeate much of the Southern body politic, influencing thought, word, and deed.[6]

Southerners continued to fear a slave uprising while insisting they enjoyed unswerving loyalty from their thralls. In middle Georgia, the mistress of a plantation with two hundred slaves praised their unsurpassed fidelity. This amused a Virginia-born Federal officer who remarked, "They seem to believe firmly that their negroes are so much attached to them that they will not leave them on any terms." In reality, as he asserted, many slaves seized the first opportunity to flee. In Tennessee, a loyal Southern woman, sorely disillusioned, declared that "as to the idea of a *faithful servant, it is all a fiction.*" She thought that slave property was worse than useless, for slaves would not work, informed upon their owners, and brought Federal raiding parties down upon their heads, and, personally, she wished that she "had never seen *one.*" Yet it was also true that some slaves, particularly menservants or household help, remained steadfastly loyal to their masters. "Faithful slave" stories are legion and cannot be dismissed.[7]

Even in mid-1864, Southerners continued to feel betrayed and angry when slaves defected. Often they also pitied their chattels as led astray by the vile Yankee abolitionists. *Deluded* was by then the stock adjective used to describe those who decamped or who joined Federal forces. Deluded, misled, tricked or not, Southerners believed those who allied with the Northern enemy must pay the ultimate price, even as they blamed the Yankees for the consequent bloodshed. They sincerely regretted that they had to kill the "poor deluded wretches" who had become the witless victims of callous Northern manipulation.[8]

Mercy Alights in Florida

Exceptions to the no-quarter rule sometimes had no immediately discernible rhyme or reason to them. One such incident occurred in late May when Confederate cavalry sank the armed navy tugboat USS *Columbine* on upper St. Mark's River in Florida. Clogging the decks of the little steamer were more than sixty men of the 35th U.S. Colored Infantry, a regiment that had lost many men to battlefield executions at Olustee. But when Captain John J. Dickison and his men captured forty-seven black soldiers from the *Columbine*, they kept them alive. The federals probably survived because Dickison hoped to return as many as possible to their former owners and because he feared retaliation against his small and well-known band or against their families and property if they dispatched the prisoners. In any event, only their white officer suffered mistreatment. To punish him for his association with black troops, Confederate authorities sent him to Andersonville, the terrible stockade for enlisted prisoners.[9]

A fairly regular exception applied to black sailors. A few were executed upon capture, but most arrived safely in prison camps. Once there, they had a chance of being traded for Confederate sailors, even though the North had suspended the exchange cartel because the South would not include black soldiers in the process. Several reasons account for this anomaly in Southern conduct. Apparently, they viewed sailors, usually captured without arms, as much less of a threat to order, status, and honor, and they were relatively few in number. Their dark uniforms were seafaring working clothes, likely nonmilitary to the soldier's eye. As sailors, they labored at a calling followed by many blacks before the war. Mostly, however, naval personnel exchanges occurred because Federal Secretary of the Navy Gideon Welles and his counterpart in Richmond, Stephen R. Mallory, arranged their own private repatriation agreements.[10]

"Sport" in Mississippi

Black soldiers, however, received the usual treatment just a few weeks later in another clash with Forrest and his men. They belonged to the 55th and 59th U.S. Colored Infantry regiments and to a light artillery battery, forming Colonel Edward Bouton's Colored Brigade of about 1,350 officers and men. Stationed in Memphis, these men had heard about Fort Pillow, and, like other black troops in the area, they were vengeance bent, having vowed never to give quarter to the enemy. Confederates, in turn, had learned about their oath to take no prisoners and that made them yearn the more for another encounter with their former slaves.[11]

Bouton's brigade formed part of an eight-thousand-man force sent out from Memphis to intercept and eliminate a never-idle Forrest, who threatened Sherman's vulnerable railroad supply line. Sherman chose the undistinguished Brigadier General Samuel D. Sturgis, a fellow West

Pointer, to lead the challenging effort. It was immediately obvious that Sturgis was the wrong choice to lead anybody anywhere. His second-in-command was falling down drunk from the start, and Sturgis did his manful best to keep up with him. Then on June 10, Sturgis let the wily Forrest pick the battleground near Brice's Cross Roads, Mississippi. It was a site extremely favorable for the four thousand Confederates but most disadvantageous for the hapless Federals.[12]

To reach the battlefield, they had to traverse a narrow corduroy road across a swamp and then debouch in a tight semicircle. As a Confederate explained, the constrictive approach forced Federals into the battle unit by unit, rather than as a unified, effective whole. When Sturgis and his second-in-command, Colonel William L. McMillen, finally viewed the battleground Forrest had selected for them, it is unlikely either saw anything too clearly. Both had belted whiskey from the moment they awakened. As regiments successively entered the fight, they found themselves shredded front and flanks by Confederates' concentrated fire. Bouton and his black troops, last on the scene, stepped into a fight already lost. A 55th U.S. Colored Infantry lieutenant recalled, "Following out the plan of getting us licked in detail, our regiment was sent into action by companies." Federal cavalry slipped away and white troops began to withdraw, though 250 supply wagons blocked the corduroy road, the only passable route to the rear. Disgusted and angry, an Iowa cavalryman observed, "Nothing was left undone . . . to make the disaster complete."[13]

However badly mismanaged, Federal resistance had dismayed Confederates who feared they faced a repulse. Their spirits lifted when Federals began to retreat, and the adrenalin flowed when the black soldiers appeared. Lieutenant William Witherspoon, serving with Forrest's 7th Tennessee Cavalry, recalled, "We boys knew there were negroes somewhere. . . . We kept asking each other where were the damned negroes?" He said they had fought from 9 A.M. to 4 P.M. and were becoming exhausted when they heard someone cry, "Here are the damned negroes." With that discovery, Witherspoon said, new life and energy infused them and they made a mad rush for the sector where the long-awaited black Yankees had appeared.[14]

Confederates said the blacks quickly broke and ran under their fire, but white Federals, often slow to credit black soldiers, insisted they fought long and well. All agreed that Bouton's men believed their lives forfeit if cornered or captured and that they shouted their Fort Pillow battle cry. Southerners said black troops also wore white paper badges imprinted with the words "Remember Fort Pillow," which they considered another infuriating challenge. But no Federal mentioned the badges, which have all the earmarks of an instant fable. Captain John W. Morton, Forrest's artillery chief, said he heard the story but carefully noted that he could not recall seeing the symbols. Yet the tale, unlikely as it seems, circulated widely, and many Confederates believed it or said they did.[15]

When Bouton's men yelled their Fort Pillow battle cry, all understood that as a declaration of black-flag warfare, meaning no quarter would be asked for or given. One of Forrest's men grimly recalled, "They had sworn before they left Memphis never to take any of Forrest's men prisoners, and they kept their oath." Some Confederates also heard that Bouton's soldiers carried a black flag. Another Confederate remarked, "This incensed the Southern soldiers and they relentlessly shot them down."[16]

From the time Bouton's men appeared on the battlefield until the last straggler was picked off days later, Confederates concentrated their fire and ire upon them. One Federal officer reported, "Negro soldiers were shot down by the squads, after they had surrendered." Another Federal recalled, "Many of the men were never heard of after, although it is known that some were chased by the cavalry and by bloodhounds, and, as they were caught, promptly murdered." Colonel Bouton flatly declared that "all our men that were captured and all wounded that we had to leave behind were promptly killed." Major General C. C. Washburn, the area commander, later talked to black survivors who provided eyewitness accounts. He concluded that "the massacre of Fort Pillow had been reproduced . . . at Brice's Cross-Roads."[17]

As the black soldiers retreated, Forrest's men energetically pursued and tracked them down, agreeing that "it was fun—big sport." Some of them called it "a hunt for wild game" or a "rabbit hunt." An officer said that some "colored troops huddled in gangs and were shot down." A citizen in the area affirmed that Confederates relentlessly executed black Yankees. Although mistaken about their numbers in Sturgis's force, a member of Forrest's escort bragged about the black death toll when he wrote, "Here the Federal troops were mostly niggers and we killed the largest part of them." Another soldier frankly boasted, "We captured white prisoners all along but no negro prisoners were taken."[18]

But others said a few were captured, although they may not have lived long afterward. Sergeant Richard R. Hancock, 2nd Tennessee, reported that his search party found three black Federals. He recalled, "We did not kill them on the spot, as the poor misguided wretches had been made to believe." Instead, Hancock wrote, they treated them kindly and escorted them to a prisoner collection point. Although he did not say so explicitly, Lieutenant Witherspoon also left the impression that they took some black prisoners. Yet Bouton listed 160 of his men as missing, and Forrest's men admittedly captured but a handful. Based on experience, a black soldier-historian suspected the captivity of those few was brief and ended badly. He wrote, "The fate of the black soldiers taken . . . is unknown." White prisoners went to Andersonville and other prison camps, but there was no mention of blacks among them.[19]

During the long retreat, Captain James C. Foster led what was left of the 59th U.S. Colored Infantry. Foster struck due north and reached a road recently traversed by retreating Federals. Soon they caught up with a large group of white soldiers but received a hostile reception from their leader, Colonel Alexander Wilkin, 9th Minnesota. Foster related, "He expressed regret that [we] . . . had found him, as we could not hope to escape, Fort Pillow being fresh in his mind." Wilkin believed that consorting with black soldiers was dangerous and wished they would go away. Accordingly, Foster recalled, "I promptly offered to relieve him of our presence." But the colonel had second thoughts when he learned the black soldiers had guns and ammunition while his entire brigade boasted less than a hundred rifles. Wilkin then decided it would be advantageous to keep the black soldiers between his men and pursuing Confederates.[20]

Whites' efforts to disassociate themselves from black soldiers were commonplace in such desperate situations. They knew the animosity Confederates felt for black Federals. Cognizant of that murderous rage, they feared that they would suffer through mere proximity, whether voluntary or involuntary. With no faith in Southern discriminatory powers, whites either ordered blacks away or avoided them. This amused Forrest's men, who found comic relief in the spectacle of white and black Federals at odds. Witherspoon, the 7th Tennessee officer, recalled, "When found in mixed squads, Yanks and negroes, often they would be fighting, whites endeavoring to force the negroes away and the negroes equally determined on staying with the Yanks." Another Southerner, a Ripley resident, quipped, "The Yanks were afraid to be caught with the niggers, and the niggers were afraid to be caught without the Yanks."[21]

Bouton's brigade suffered inordinate losses, whether considered in comparison with white units or alone. Black casualties were not only excessive—60 percent were killed, wounded, or missing—but also greatly distorted in the number killed. The 1,350 officers and men, comprising about 16 percent of Sturgis's 8,300-man force, contributed 50 percent of the recorded killed and the same percentage of the wounded. In numbers, 110 blacks were killed of the listed 223 dead and 247 of the 506 wounded. But those raw figures are deceptive. Bouton listed only the 247 he said were severely wounded and added that another 300 were slightly wounded. Many of those severely wounded later died. Bouton also listed 160 men and 11 officers as missing. The missing men were almost certainly dead, as were some of their white officers. In effect, the two regiments likely counted four hundred dead. Using that figure, then the brigade experienced a wounded-to-killed ratio of about 1 to 1, in contrast to the war's average of 4.8 wounded to 1 killed.[22]

"It is certain a great many negroes were killed," said a youthful eyewitness, a Southern sympathizer. To explain that high toll, Confederates blamed the black soldiers, using the cornered-rat analogy. A Tennessee officer wrote, "As at Fort Pillow, the negroes acted with a dogged and reckless obstinacy having no relationship to courage, but partaking more of the nature of animals that were hemmed and refused to be caught." Others said that Federal officers had conditioned blacks to expect no mercy. "Impressed with this notion, and animated by the apprehension engendered, they perversely refused to halt and surrender," Sergeant Hancock argued. He said that explained "why so many [blacks] were killed and so few captured." In a letter to Washburn, Forrest charged that the fight "was far more bloody than it would otherwise have been but for the fact that your men evidently expected to be slaughtered when captured." He denied his men had murdered anyone and said such accusations were grossly insulting. And he repeated that he regarded captured blacks not as Federal soldiers but as recovered Southern property.[23]

One historian declared that Brice's Cross Roads was "the most humiliating Union defeat in the western theater." So it was that scorn, invective, censure, and even suggestions of treason engulfed Sturgis upon his return to Memphis. Henry M. Newhall, 4th Iowa Cavalry, related, "A great many officers and men think that the old General (Sturgis) sold us for they had a trap set for us and marched us rite into it." Sturgis not only had lost the battle, his artillery, his wagon train, and more than 2,200 of his men, or 27 percent of his force, but he also had forfeited what little respect and status he possessed. Sherman ordered a searching inquiry into the debacle and "especially whether it, in any measure, resulted from General Sturgis being in liquor." In his testimony, Sturgis blamed superiors for ordering him to embark upon an impracticable expedition and said an overwhelming force of twenty thousand veteran Confederates was the immediate cause of his crushing defeat. Sherman would have none of it, snorting, "It is all nonsense about Sturgis being attacked by 15,000 or 20,000. He was whipped by a force inferior to his own." Very quickly, Sturgis was relieved of his duties and told to await orders, which never came.[24]

The Black Flag Waves in South Carolina

Black Federals and Confederates just about tied in a no-quarter contest a few weeks later near Charleston, South Carolina. There Major General John G. Foster launched an amphibious assault on islands guarding harbor approaches. On July 1, 1864, about five thousand infantry with some cavalry and artillery embarked for the foray. Several black regiments joined the expedition, including the 26th U.S. Colored Infantry, led by Brigadier General Rufus Saxton, the black soldiers' longtime friend and advocate. His men and other troops landed on Johns Island, where they could threaten key Confederate positions, thus imperiling Charleston itself.

Two small Georgia infantry regiments responded to the threat and, almost immediately, black troops attacked them. William H. Andrews, a 1st Georgia sergeant, watched as the black soldiers charged part of his line. In an instant, they overwhelmed an isolated detachment and fourteen of twenty Confederates fell dead or wounded. He wrote, "We saw the Negroes when they mounted our works and saw them as they jumped down (horror of horrors) and put the bayonet to the wounded." Andrews added, "It certainly caused my blood to run cold. I had faced death on many hard-fought fields, but had never faced the black flag before, where quarter would not be asked for or given. It certainly was enough to cause the heart of the bravest to quake with fear."[25]

Reinforcements arrived in time to aid the hard-pressed Georgians and together they counterattacked. Then it was the Southerners' turn for ruthlessness. Finding wounded blacks lying on the field, they bayoneted them, though officers reportedly saved some. Andrews said that the black Federals became badly frightened and ran when they saw the summary executions. Yet one Federal almost killed Andrews with a bullet that whizzed through space he had vacated just an instant earlier. He next saw a comrade rapidly losing a hand-to-hand struggle until a friend shot the black soldier. Another black tried to surrender but ran when several Confederates urged everyone to shoot him. Many quickly did just that, and the Federal fell with six bullets in his body.[26]

While still on Johns Island, one 26th U.S. Colored Infantry officer was just as unfortunate. He was 2nd Lieutenant James C. Spry, who fell wounded and was captured. He either died of his wound or vengeful Confederates dispatched him. In any event, he was never heard from again.[27]

None of this appeared in the official reports. Federal officers wrote only that the black soldiers "behaved handsomely" while Confederates said they were "handsomely repulsed." Despite their rage, some Confederates felt a hesitant sympathy for wounded blacks left between the lines after the fight. During the night, they winced as they heard the plaintive cries of those men calling to their comrades for help that never came. But when the next day passed with only sporadic artillery exchanges, Andrews sniffed, "Guess Mr. Nig don't want to pay us a visit again." Still, he and other Southern soldiers had learned that the no-quarter model worked both ways.[28]

12

The Petersburg Mine

IN VIRGINIA, STALEMATE HELD the opposing armies in place on the Petersburg-Richmond front in the war's fourth summer. Grant had driven toward Richmond in the Union's coordinated 1864 spring offensives but at a horrendous cost in casualties. In a generally accepted analysis, a modern military historian wrote, "The northern public did not view the costly campaign . . . as the succession of glorious victories as painted by [Secretary of War] Stanton. Nor did many see the siege of Petersburg as more than a deadlock with no end in sight." So when offered a daring scheme to end the impasse and smash Lee's Army of Northern Virginia in one fell swoop, Grant embraced the idea.

However, bad management turned the brilliant plan into a bloody fiasco. As well, the war's most horrific slaughter of black soldiers occurred as a result. Though that aspect passed unnoticed in the North, many

Southerners knew that such a bloodbath had taken place at Petersburg on July 30, 1864. About five hundred black soldiers, wounded, surrendered, or trapped, fell in a no-quarter rampage by Confederates that day, making it the war's largest single massacre. While it was a modest affair compared to twentieth-century mass murders, black Federals killed that day were not disposed of with machine-gun efficiency. Confederates put them individually to the sword, sometimes literally. A seemingly inexhaustible supply of eyewitness accounts by numerous soldiers from many different Northern and Southern states and the casualty lists attested to the slaughter's scope and character. In a subsequent investigation, Federal authorities asked no questions about the inordinate number of black casualties, even as Confederates gloated. Most historians since then have skipped or only lightly touched upon the cost to the black troops. Although the Mine assault killings differed in the numbers involved and the great variety and number of witnesses, the massacre was simply another atrocity in a dismaying series.

Beginning in June, the armies had burrowed into the ground on a thirty-five-mile long front from Richmond south to Petersburg. Though attrition favored the stronger North over time, neither side could easily break the deadlock imposed by the complex defense systems on both sides of the front. But in the Federal 9th Army Corps sector, the Confederate line projected outward in a salient so that only about 135 yards separated the two trench lines. Directly opposite the salient, Lieutenant Colonel Henry Pleasants, a peacetime mining engineer, led the 48th Pennsylvania Infantry, a unit filled with many former coal miners. Pleasants proposed digging a tunnel to a point below the Confederate salient, packing the end with explosives and then blowing a huge gap in the enemy line. That would open the way for assaulting troops to sweep down into Petersburg, capture the city, split Lee's army, and render Richmond untenable.[1]

Major General Ambrose E. Burnside, 9th Corps commander, quickly approved Pleasants's plan and ordered tunneling to begin. But he initiated the far-reaching project without consulting his superior, Major General George G. Meade, Army of the Potomac commander. That riled Meade, adding to the bad blood already existing between the two. From first to last, Meade had little faith in what became known as "Burnside's mine" and willfully obstructed it at every turn. When Pleasants began digging the 510-foot tunnel on June 25, 1864, Meade refused him tools, materials, or assistance in any form. Most important, he rejected Pleasants's request for twelve thousand pounds of powder for the explosion. He insisted that he and his Regular Army engineers knew that eight thousand pounds would suffice. Burnside carefully explained that "the greater the explosion, the greater the crater radius." In short, the larger blast would make a wider hole with gently sloping sides, easily passable for assaulting troops. He said he spoke from practical experience and so did Pleasants. Meade said army manuals dictated otherwise and the rule book won.[2]

As the mine neared completion, Grant increasingly saw it as a splendid opportunity to break the stalemate. Burnside's 9th Corps of about fourteen thousand officers and men would spearhead the assault. Numerically, his black 4th Division was the strongest, with forty-three hundred men in nine regiments. Although untried in battle, they were fresh, brash, and enthusiastic, so Burnside chose them to lead the assault. He ordered Brigadier General Edward Ferrero, their leader, to plan and train for a rush to Cemetery Hill, the key to Petersburg.[3]

Meanwhile, Meade intensified his obstructionist efforts. Grant impatiently dismissed Meade's objections, and the assault was set for July 30. Grant then told Meade, "The details for the assault I leave to you to make out." That was a crucial error. On the morning of July 28, Meade and Burnside met to discuss the operation. As their conference ended, Meade abruptly ordered Burnside to substitute white troops for the black division as the lead element. Burnside vigorously protested the last-minute change and finally Meade agreed to submit the question to Grant. Yet not until the forenoon of July 29, only hours before the attack, did Burnside learn that Grant had upheld the switch. Meade later explained he merely wanted the best troops to spearhead an assault that he considered only a forlorn hope. But Grant reported, "General Meade said that if we put the colored troops in front . . . and it should prove a failure, it would then be said . . . that we were shoving those people ahead to get killed because we did not care anything about them." Still later, Grant admitted that Meade's interference had most likely fatally sabotaged the plan.[4]

That last-minute change caused a pernicious ripple effect. Black soldier morale plunged; white troops were not briefed about the operation; and Burnside, angry or petulant, abdicated major responsibilities. One 9th Corps veteran commented, "General Burnside . . . seemed on this occasion to lose command of himself as well as of his troops." His most egregious lapse occurred when he ordered the casting of lots to decide which white division would spearhead the assault. As if fated, the lot fell to Brigadier General James H. Ledlie and his 1st Division. Ledlie was the least capable divisional commander, and his soldiers had no confidence in him. They had good reasons—as Grant said, Ledlie was not only inefficient but, far worse, a coward. Further, he took refuge in the bottle when unnerved by battle. Grant forthrightly blamed himself for not doing anything about the bad choice.[5]

At exactly 4:44 A.M. on July 30, just about morning twilight time, the four tons of powder exploded. Watchers saw a volcanic eruption throw men, timber, guns, and debris high into the sky, followed by a deep rumbling sound or a heavy roar, depending upon the observer's location. In an instant, the blast obliterated much of the salient and killed or wounded about 350 Confederates. Some were entombed in underground bombproofs and survivors were stunned and disoriented by the shock.

After hesitating at least fifteen minutes, Ledlie's men finally advanced. Ledlie himself took shelter in a surgeon's bombproof fifty-five yards behind the front line and there sipped medicinal rum to soothe his nerves. His men halted at the crater's lip and gawked at a pit two hundred feet long, fifty feet wide and twenty-five to thirty feet deep. But Meade's insistence upon four tons of powder, rather than the six wanted by Pleasants, created a trap instead of a gap in the Confederate lines. One of Grant's staff explained that "its sides were so steep that it was almost impossible to climb out after once getting in." Nevertheless, Ledlie's ten regiments slipped, slid, and tumbled into the giant foxhole, instantly losing all unit cohesion. Officers shouted orders and threats, but nothing could pry the men from their sanctuary. There they stayed, mulishly immovable.[6]

Burnside's 2nd and 3rd divisions next crossed and began clearing enemy trenches to the right and left of the crater. But some units swerved and slid into the sheltering pit, swelling the disorganized mob milling about within its steep walls. With no designated commander present and unit cohesion gone, anarchy ruled. Although shocked by the explosion, Confederates began to recover. Shortly after 6 A.M., Lee ordered Brigadier General William Mahone to send two brigades from his division to contain the breach.

Mahone rode ahead to see Major General Bushrod R. Johnson, whose division held the endangered sector. An unpopular leader, Johnson was proof that the Union had no monopoly on mediocre generals. Mahone found an unworried and uninformed Johnson a mile from his shattered lines, comfortably composing himself for breakfast at about 8:30 A.M. General Beauregard, also present, told Johnson to turn over his spare troops to Mahone for a counterattack. Johnson readily agreed and returned to his breakfast table. After inspecting the broken line, Mahone ordered up a third brigade from his own division.[7]

Meanwhile, with the attack obviously stalled, Burnside ordered the black 4th Division to join the melee. Experienced officers thought that a great mistake. A black brigade's commander believed the situation had already deteriorated from forlorn hope to "forlorn hopelessness." Stubbornly, Burnside repeated the order. Colonel Joshua K. Sigfried's brigade went first. Freeman S. Bowley, an eighteen-year-old 1st lieutenant, crossing with the leading 30th U.S. Colored Infantry, saw an enemy cannon spout flame and recalled, "Then came the rushing, hurtling sound of grape-shot . . . and I heard a smashing sound, and a file of four men were swept away from my very side." Colonel Delavan Bates, commanding the 30th, and Colonel H. Seymour Hall, 43rd U.S. Colored Infantry, led their men to the right, away from the crater and along the Confederate trench line. But two regiments tumbled straight into the crater, and there they stayed, no more anxious to leave than white soldiers. Colonel Henry G. Thomas crossed next with his 2nd Brigade of five regiments. He skirted the crater, moving obliquely about eight hundred feet until he and his men reached the head of the 1st Brigade. In the open and exposed, the brigade lost heavily in officers and men. That caused three regiments to lose their initial enthusiasm and to lag behind. So it was a much-diminished brigade that assembled at 8:10 A.M. for the dash to Cemetery Hill.[8]

As Thomas's men organized, Sigfried's 30th and 43rd formed parallel to the Confederate trenches. Yelling wildly, they coiled for the charge and rushed forward, jumping into the enemy trench. A Confederate major ordered his men to "die but never surrender to niggers" and bolted for a bombproof. Black soldiers followed and bayoneted the major's men, enforcing his order. About two hundred other Confederates quickly surrendered, and a 43rd lieutenant saved some when he stopped his men from killing them where they stood. But Colonel Hall, the 43rd's leader, said that his soldiers slew many prisoners, despite officers' efforts to restrain them. Not all officers even exercised self-restraint. William Baird, a 1st lieutenant with the 23rd U.S. Colored Infantry, witnessed an incident that made him reflect that the war had greatly devalued life. His colonel ordered a captured Confederate officer to help carry a wounded black soldier. Baird recalled, "The Confederate with an oath said he would not help carry any negro . . . the colonel whipped out his revolver and shot him dead."[9]

While Sigfried's men fought through the maze of bays, traverses, and bombproofs in the trenches, Colonel Thomas' 2nd brigade started for Cemetery Hill. Heavy fire stopped them in their tracks. Soon after that failed effort, an order came from Ferrero's bombproof to take the crest immediately. Colonel Bates, advancing with about two hundred men, recalled, "How far we went I do not know, for a volley from our front and right disabled about one-half of our officers and one-third of the privates." On that "awful morning," as he termed it, Bates then fell with a bullet through his face.[10]

When they advanced, so did Mahone's Virginians. Lieutenant Bowley remembered, "Looking to the front I saw a splendid line of gray[.] . . . They were coming, and coming with a rush." To a watching 4th Rhode Island corporal, they looked fierce and feral. He recalled, "On they came . . . crouching like a tiger to spring upon its prey." In a trice, they slammed into Thomas's men. Observing from a distance, a black soldier wrote, "Col Div of 9th Corps charged or attempted broke and run!" Panic flashed through the black ranks and they faltered, then turned and fled. Yet it was hardly a monochrome flight—hundreds of white 10th and 18th corps troops also stampeded at the same time.[11]

Before Mahone's men charged, mine survivors told them that the black Yankees had attacked while shouting "Fort Pillow! No Quarter!" Some also heard that the blacks carried out the threat. Southerners repeatedly cited the battle cry when describing the ensuing unrestrained massacre, and some mentioned blacks' killing prisoners. One of Mahone's men, Private Henry V. L. Bird, 12th Virginia, told his wife, "The negro charging cry of 'no quarter' was met with the stern reply of 'amen." . . . [W]hat a horrible vengeance we took for the men so inhumanely butchered by the negros in the morning." Captain Henry A. Chambers wrote, "There was but little mercy shown them . . . they first cried 'no quarter' and our men acted on this principle." Southern newspapers also were pleased to report that the black Yankees had realized their no-quarter aspirations.[12]

However, most Confederates there that day had never personally heard the battle cry or had seen blacks murder prisoners. It was largely secondhand information and simply intensified their murderous anger. John C. Featherston, a 9th Alabama officer, explained the immediate affront, "This was the first time we had met negro troops, and the men were enraged at them for being there and at the whites for having them there." Edward P. Alexander, the artillery general, said the men felt very bitter about Northern use of blacks as soldiers and saw them as agents of

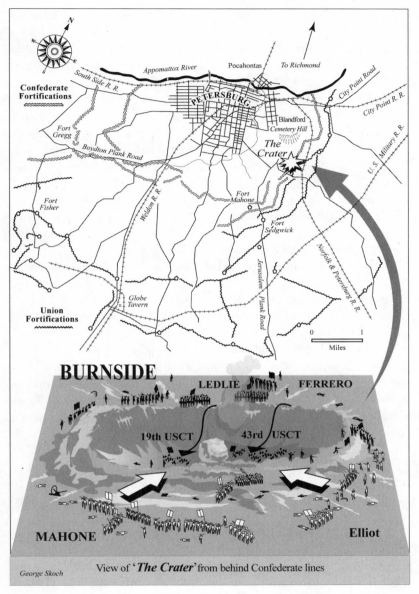

View of '***The Crater***' from behind Confederate lines

George Skoch

The battle of the Crater on July 30, 1864, held great promise for the North but turned into a disaster, resulting in the war's greatest massacre of black troops when many were trapped in the crater formed by the explosion of a Federal mine underneath Confederate lines.

servile insurrection and massacre. However explained, they had murder
in their hearts because the blacks defied the old order.[13]

A young Virginia officer described the results, telling his sister, "As
soon as we got upon them, they [blacks] threw down their arms to surrender, but were not allowed to do so." Wounded blacks also were not
allowed to live. Mahone's men made short work of them, killing with
bayonet or rifle butt. Then they reached the line seized by Federals, and
Major William H. Etheredge, commanding 41st Virginia, jumped into
a trench with one of his sergeants. They landed amid black and white
Yankees who instantly shot the sergeant, while another Confederate killed
a Federal on the verge of shooting Etheredge. Private George S. Bernard,
12th Virginia, was surprised to encounter a black soldier, the first he had
ever seen. In the main trench, Bernard saw another black pleading for
his life while one Confederate lashed him with a ramrod and another
tried to shoot him. With a second shot, the Federal fell dead.[14]

Mahone's men steadily pushed stubbornly resisting Federals toward
the crater. About 10 A.M., Wright's Georgia brigade joined the ferocious
close-quarter fighting. Men struggled in a perplexing maze in which
opponents often stood only a few feet apart while concealed in traverses
and bays. Sword in hand, a 61st Virginia lieutenant parried the bayonets of two burly black soldiers only to be impaled on the bayonet of a
Confederate who went to his aid. Misjudging a bayonet thrust, a black
soldier speared only his enemy's hat, giving his opponent an opening to
kill him. Sometimes prayers or luck played a role, as when a 17th South
Carolina soldier ducked into a hole or burrow in the trench wall for
rest and shade. When he again peered out, he saw that black Federals
filled the trench. Quickly he slipped back into his den and prayed they
would not discover his hiding place. They did not and he admitted, "I
was almost scared to death and prayed until the big drops of sweat ran
down my cheeks. I said, 'Lord have mercy on me and keep those damned
niggers from killing me.'"[15]

Mahone asked twenty-three-year-old Major John C. Haskell, an artillery officer, to move small, easily portable Coehorn mortars into the
trenches near the crater. Soon their high-trajectory shells, fired from just
fifty yards away, burst among the Federals crowding the crater. Haskell,
who had lost an arm in battle two years earlier, decided to scout for a better firing position. Warned that he might encounter the enemy anywhere,
he carried a borrowed revolver. At a turn in the trench, he met a Federal
officer and black soldiers. Both officers raised their pistols, but Haskell

fired first, scoring a head shot and conclusively winning the duel. He reported nearby Confederates "got" the fifteen or twenty black soldiers behind their fallen officer.

Excited and fascinated, a North Carolina youth watched as men scoured bombproofs to find and kill former slaves or cracked the skulls of those caught in the open. Another North Carolinian reported, "They piled them three or four deep in the ditches [trenches]." When they found a lieutenant and fourteen black soldiers huddled in a bombproof, the officer balked at surrendering. "He was evidently afraid of 'no quarter,'" one of Mahone's men recalled. Then a 41st Virginia captain, infuriated at the idea of fighting blacks, positioned himself to skewer the first one to emerge, a frightened man who fell to his knees and begged for mercy. His pleas touched a merciful chord and the cornered Federals won at least a temporary reprieve from death.[16]

Dorsey M. Binion, a 48th Georgia soldier, related, "When we got to the works it was filled with negros[.] . . . We did not show much quarter but slayed them some few negroes went to the rear as we could not kill them as fast as they [fled] us." Successful surrender was no guarantee of continued safety. Brigadier General Alexander reported, "Some of the Negro prisoners, who were originally allowed to surrender by some soldiers, were afterward shot by others." Colonel William J. Pegram, a twenty-three-year-old rising star in Lee's army, said that once scores of blacks rushed in with whites and so managed to surrender. Pegram added, "I think over two hundred negroes got into our lines[.] . . . I don't believe that much over half of these ever reached the rear. You could see them lying dead all along the route to the rear." Colonel Stephen M. Weld, 56th Massachusetts, witnessed both immediate and delayed executions. He had ducked into a bombproof with another officer and a black soldier. Obeying a surrender demand, they emerged. Weld recalled, "They yelled out, 'Shoot the nigger, but don't kill the white man' and the negro was promptly shot down by my side." Going to the rear, Weld particularly noticed one black soldier walking just ahead of him. He related, "Three rebels rushed up to him in succession and shot him through the body. He dropped dead finally at the third shot."[17]

Among the last driven from the trenches and into the pit were Lieutenant. Bowley and a dozen 30th U.S. Colored Infantry soldiers. They leaped into an inferno. Shells exploded in the crater, and bullets from traverse and trench openings thudded into the massed men. To stop the bullets, desperate soldiers plugged the openings with corpses, white and black, Federal and Confederate. Equally desperate 35th Massachusetts men began digging a trench back to Federal lines but found the claylike ground too hard. Men lined the crater's rim, rapidly loading and firing. Bowley recalled that they "were dropping thick and fast, most of them shot through the head. Every man that was shot rolled down the steep sides to the bottom, and in places there were piled up four and five deep." Adding to the misery, a scorching sun had raised the temperature to 105 degrees by midday. Most men knew that matters could only worsen, and some risked a dash across the lines. Confederate artillery and rifle fire swept that space and many fell while crossing.[18]

Mahone reportedly reminded his men that the black Yankees had cried "Remember Fort Pillow! No Quarter" and ordered them to take no black prisoners. Even if they heard that injunction, none needed prompting. Smelling blood and victory, Confederates rushed into the crater from all sides shortly after 1 P.M. Then began the truly manic killing. Major Haskell, thrust into the crater by pushing, maddened infantry, wrote, "Our men, who were always made wild by having negroes sent against them . . . were utterly frenzied with rage. Nothing in the war could have exceeded the horrors that followed. No quarter was given, and for what seemed a long time, fearful butchery was carried on." Captain Matthew N. Love, 25th North Carolina, declared that "such slaughter I have not witnessed upon any battlefield any where." On the crater's south side, John S. Wise, a seventeen-year-old serving with his father's Virginia brigade, said sight of the black Federals excited the troops to a frenzy. He added that "our men . . . disregarded the rules of warfare . . . and brained and butchered the blacks until the slaughter was sickening." Writing home, a North Carolina soldier related, "we went rite in . . . on them and Bayoneted them."[19]

"There was no volley and cheer to excite the men to the work of death . . . without firing a single shot we closed with them—they fought like bulldogs and died like soldiers," said a 12th Virginia soldier. Captain Frank Kenfield, 17th Vermont, recalled that "as the rebels charged in upon us I heard the order given 'save the white men but kill the damn niggers.' And I saw them run their bayonets through many a colored man showing him no mercy." Since the pit was so crowded, they had to rely on physical force and use of bayonets, rifle butts, and swords. Haskell watched berserk men thrust, slash, and club until exhausted, even as fresh soldiers arrived to join in the killing. He reported that they spared very few blacks. Tersely, a North Carolina youth, related, "They just piled them as they wold come."[20]

Adding to the horror, some Federals imitated enemy actions. A New York soldier explained, "It was believed among the whites that the enemy would give no quarter to negroes, or to the whites taken with them, and so to be shut up with the blacks in the crater was equal to a doom of death." Suiting action to fears, some whites murdered blacks to shield themselves from Confederate vengeance. While fratricide occurred, soldiers probably embellished its incidence. Major Haskell, however, provided a reliable firsthand account. Still in the crater, he heard a frantic cry for help. He related, "I saw my orderly about to shoot a rather good-looking Yankee, and stopped him. He told me that this man had caught up a musket, and shouting out that he would kill the 'damned niggers,' had dashed out the brains of a colored soldier." A nearby Federal said the man, an officer, had killed one of his own men. Haskell reported, "I heard of more than one other case, but this I saw. I told the man that I thought he well deserved the death to which the orderly at once put him."[21]

Blood sprayed everywhere as the crater quickly transformed into an open-air abattoir. Haskell said he took no direct part in the slaughter but recalled, "I was yet so covered with blood that I threw away my coat to get rid of the horror of its being soaked through." Men repeatedly said that blood ran in rivulets and collected in puddles. An Alabama soldier related, "Nearly all . . . negroes were killed, and actually their blood ran in a crevice made by the blow-up." Lieutenant Colonel William H. Stewart, commanding 61st Virginia, asserted that "human gore ran in streams that made the very earth mire." Most likely a 16th Mississippi officer exaggerated when he reported, "The carnage was so great that the Confederates stood in blood to their shoe-tops." Still, a 19th U.S. Colored Infantry officer reported that blood coated the ground between the lines and that the stench was almost unendurable.[22]

The dead rapidly accumulated in countless heaps. Sergeant Jerome Yates, a twenty-two-year-old 16th Mississippi soldier, told his sister, "Most of the Negros were killed after they surrendered. The ground was covered with dead Negros." Another Mississippian voiced regret, saying, "We felt sorry for the poor nig & looked upon him as a victim of the diseased sentiment of the North." The butchery ended only when Confederates physically wilted or ran out of prey. Private Bird, the 12th Virginia soldier, reported, "The only sounds which now broke the stillness was some poor

wounded wretch begging for water and quieted by a bayonet thrust." A
61st Virginia officer recalled, "Our bloody work was all done . . . and many
almost sank from exhaustion." Years later, the memory of the killing pit
still haunted Frank Kenfield, the 17th Vermont officer. He said, "I often
think of this scene and a cold shudder goes through me as I think of how
those poor colored men were butchered in cold blood."[23]

About 2 P.M., surviving Federals managed to surrender. Confederates
had mended the rupture in their lines and recaptured a gory pit that
shocked hardened veterans, men supposedly inured to ghastly battlefields.
Appalled by the scene, a North Carolina officer called it "the most horrible sight I ever witnessed." An 8th Alabama surgeon declared, "I have
never any where seen such a slaughter." He added, "Negroes and Yankees
. . . lay so thick that one could have walked over several acres of ground
stepping from one corpse or wounded wretch to another." Mixed with
the dead and wounded, he saw parts and pieces of bodies mangled and
blackened. Mahone reported taking 1,101 prisoners, including one-legged
Brigadier General William F. Bartlett. Though the bloodletting in the
crater had ended, friendly fire soon killed and wounded more Federals. When hundreds of prisoners moved en masse across an open area
behind Confederate lines, Federal artillery opened fire, thinking they
were Confederates.[24]

One of the last to leave the pit was Lieutenant Bowley. He thought no
severely wounded black soldiers were brought out, but he erred. A captured Federal surgeon, paroled to work in a Petersburg hospital, treated
some, and Major Haskell saw forty or fifty wounded blacks lying in the
open behind the lines. Haskell learned that a Federal surgeon had ejected
them from a hospital. He had the men carried back, attended to, and
secured a promise from the Union doctors to provide proper attention.
Haskell recalled, "However, I heard later that they got so little care that
all those who were at all badly hurt died."[25]

Confederates corralled the prisoners in an open field, mixing officers
with enlisted men, blacks with whites. Wounded white prisoners also
underwent compulsory integration. Francis J. D'Avignon, the paroled
Federal surgeon, was ordered to place one white patient, especially an
officer, between two blacks. He wrote, "I gave my attention to the Black
& to the white soldiers, uniformly alike, to the great annoyance & regret
of the Southerners." Often white captives bemoaned the involuntary
integration more than the lack of food, water, or care. As some realized,
it was psychological warfare. One motive for the forced intermingling

derived from the popular belief in the South that Northerners sought social equality for blacks. So convinced, they liked to rub Yankee noses in that equality.[26]

Officers of black regiments had more to worry about than the equality issue. They knew that Jefferson Davis had declared them criminals who abetted servile insurrection. Their apprehensions became acute when a Confederate staff officer appeared and assured them that "they were to swing instanter." Some removed their shoulder straps to conceal their rank, while others claimed that they belonged to white regiments. Despite their well-founded fears, Confederates took no serious punitive measures against them. In rejecting deception, one U.S. Colored Infantry lieutenant became a legend. When asked his name, rank, and regiment, he defiantly replied, "Lemuel D. Dobbs, Nineteenth Niggers, by God!" Bowley reported that he and another officer also boldly said they belonged to the 30th U.S. Colored Infantry and saw the words "Negro officer" written opposite their names.[27]

Early the next day, the unwilling captives starred in a combination circus parade and morality play. Lieutenant Bowley recalled, "It was Sunday, and our captors proposed to make a grand spectacle of us for the benefit of Petersburg citizens." Guards pushed them into line, placing alternating ranks of officers and black soldiers at the head of the column. Leading the parade was one-legged Brigadier General Bartlett, necessarily mounted. According to a 23rd U.S. Colored Infantry lieutenant, many officers of white units felt terribly humiliated, and he believed that they gladly would have seen officers of black troops hanged or shot if that would have spared them the parade. In any event, all drew jeers and abuse from the spectators, including an elderly woman who jibed, "Birds of a feather will flock together." But with a quick riposte, a 32nd Maine lieutenant retorted, "Yes, but we don't mix in the nest as you do down here."[28]

After the show parade, Confederates segregated the prisoners according to rank and color and separated them from their valuables and clothing. Ironically, at this juncture, the survival odds shifted to favor black soldiers. Shoulder-strap Federals went to officers' prison camps, where they would endure poor but bearable conditions. White enlisted men went to Andersonville or other prison camps, where hunger, disease, and high mortality rates awaited them. Black soldiers went to a holding pen in Petersburg, where their former owners could repossess them. John S. Wise, the youthful aide in his father's Virginia brigade, said the black Yankees much preferred reenslavement rather than mistreatment or death as prisoners. To illustrate, he told the story of a slightly wounded Confederate who had received a ten-day convalescent furlough. Penniless, he had no place to go. When he wandered near the black prisoner holding pen, a strange black captive offered to be his slave. The wounded soldier replied that he would instantly sell him. That suited the prisoner. Between them, they tricked the officer in charge. As promised, the soldier sold his newly acquired property and enjoyed a wonderful furlough with the proceeds while the Federal returned to servitude.[29]

When all was said and done, a brilliant plan had gone awry and thousands had died or suffered in vain. Men on both sides agreed upon that. Confederate John H. Chamberlayne accurately described the Federal effort when he wrote, "A month of mining, his whole force concentrated, & his own time & place selected enabled him to lose from 4500 to 5000 men & gain nothing." His estimate of casualties was also quite accurate, more so than the official Federal figures. Meade's final report listed 4,400 casualties, showing 458 officers and men killed in action, 1,982 wounded, and 1,960 missing. Probably the correct total was about five thousand. Even at the time it was obvious that Meade's death count was far too low. During a truce two days after the battle, Federals buried 650 to 700 of their own dead found between the lines in mass graves, and, after the war, workers exhumed 646 remains from those sites. Lee confirmed the burial numbers and reported that about five hundred Union dead lay in the crater and adjoining trenches, with many officers and blacks among them. Based on this evidence, the killed numbered at least twice Meade's tally of 458. Doubtless many dead were erroneously listed as missing.[30]

Once more, black mortality numbers elude a precise count but the death toll was probably almost quadruple the 239 officially reported. Again, the difference lies in the 658 listed as missing, most of whom were dead, and with the 728 wounded, many of whom soon died. Conservatively, between 900 and 950 black soldiers died that day. Of that number, Confederates massacred more than half, although black troops also suffered severely and disproportionately in legitimate combat. Even by the flawed official count, they lost nearly half the killed, more than half the missing and 43 percent of the wounded in the 9th Army Corps. Colonel Sigfried listed 781 casualties for his brigade, including 32 officers; Colonel Thomas reported a total of 913. With almost seventeen hundred casualties, they sustained about 43 percent of Burnside's overall losses and 38.5 percent of all Union casualties.[31]

As already noted, Confederates captured and spared some of the 658 black soldiers listed as missing. An apologetic 9th Alabama officer wrote, "I must say we took some of the negroes prisoners. But we will not be held culpable for this when it is considered the numbers we had already slain." More specifically, still another Alabama officer reported Mahone's men captured 432 whites but only 29 blacks in their first attack. In the final rush into the crater, he said that they took 131 black prisoners. In consideration of these numbers, a Richmond *Dispatch* tabulation was probably as near correct a figure as will ever appear. That newspaper reported 150 black prisoners.[32]

Confederate losses were less than half the Federal toll. While no comprehensive official Confederate returns exist, the losses are known by other means. Subordinate officers sent lists of the killed and wounded to newspapers, as was the custom of the day. Collating and compiling losses from one partial report, newspaper casualty lists and private accounts shows that Confederate sustained about seventeen hundred to eighteen hundred casualties.[33]

The dramatic victory boosted Southern spirits and the extermination of so many black Yankees satisfied the need for order and discipline. Racial hatred motivated only a few warped individuals in Southern society. Even as they murdered former slaves at the front, Confederate soldiers continued to send warm greetings to the chattels at home. With wry humor, one wrote, "Howdy to the cause of all our woes." No glaring dichotomy existed for white Southerners: they felt benevolent toward good servants and betrayed by the bad, treacherous ones who deserved and got death.[34]

Colonel William J. Pegram, the young artillery officer, thought that wholesale killing most beneficial. He told his sister, "This was perfectly right, as a matter of policy. . . . It seems cruel to murder them in cold blood, but I think the men who did it had very good cause." The good cause, Pegram explained, was that the blacks had dared to fight them. He added, "I have always said that I wished the enemy would bring some negroes against this army. I am convinced . . . that it has [had] a splendid effect on our men." In North Carolina, plantation mistress Catherine Ann Edmondston believed the "immense slaughter" was only fitting and proper. Citing the blacks' cry of "No Quarter! Remember Fort Pillow!," she considered it only right that their "old masters . . . granted to the full what they so earnestly clamored for."[35]

 The Mine assault's frenzied killing was the most atrocious during the war, "Fort Pillow not excepted," as one Confederate said. But since most Federal witnesses to the butchery were either dead or prisoners, Union authorities never officially learned of it. However, some witnesses to the first stages of the massacre returned to Union lines but neither army nor Congressional investigators pursued the matter. Accordingly, Washington never accused Richmond of murdering black soldiers during the battle and Confederate leaders never had to defend or deny the bloodletting.[36]

13

Mercy and Murder

FOR SOUTHERNERS, THE MASSACRES were not homicidal bloodbaths because they considered blacks less than human. So there was not the same moral, ethical, or psychological impact consequent upon murdering white soldiers. Yet Confederates occasionally spared black Federals, contrary to normal practice. Some survived the Mine assault, for instance, when Confederates said they sickened or tired of the slaughter and Mahone finally ordered them to stop it. Still, at first glance, it was perplexing when a few months later they ruthlessly killed one set of wounded and surrendered blacks while another group went unharmed into captivity. However, for these and other exceptions to the no-quarter rule, there is an explanation, even if speculative.[1]

Shortly after the Mine assault, Private Franklin A. Setzer, 49th North Carolina, wrote home, "I think the yanks is getting tired of it Since they

tride to blo up Peters burg and was so badly disapointed." Although not
tired of the fight, the Yankees were indeed disappointed, angry, and
chagrined. Handiest and easiest to blame were the black troops. Angrily,
a Connecticut artillery officer charged that it "was all the fault of the
nigger troops." Agreeing, a 57th Massachusetts lieutenant wounded at
the crater added, "This war must be fought *out* by *white men*." Nothing
loath, black soldiers also went scapegoating. A 27th U.S. Colored Infantry
sergeant said that he and his comrades could have taken Petersburg had
white troops come to their assistance. "But," he complained, "prejudice
against colored troops prevented them." He charged that they were sent
to slaughter and that falling into Confederate hands "was the equivalent
of death, for no mercy is shown to them when captured." But the 28th
U.S. Colored Infantry's chaplain argued, "None of the troops, white or
colored, are responsible for the actions of the Generals."[2]

Some blamed Grant on the basis of a rumor that he had played cards
miles away while the scheme unraveled. Meade, who suddenly saw the
plan as "one of the most brilliant opportunities," named Burnside the
chief villain. Meade quickly stacked a court of inquiry with his support-
ers, and they readily identified Burnside as the primary culprit. But a
joint committee of Congress held extensive hearings and unequivocally
held Meade responsible. Their scathing report roundly condemned him
for his interference, lack of support, and negativism. While Meade lost
in the larger arena, he succeeded in ousting Burnside from the Army
of the Potomac. Ledlie resigned under pressure but Ferrero and other
censured officers stayed and prospered.[3]

While jubilant that they had balked the Yankees, one aspect of the
crater fight disturbed many Confederates. They knew as an article of faith
that blacks were their inferiors and no match for them. Yet many black
soldiers had stood up to their best. Artillery chief Alexander admitted,
"The fighting of the Negro troops seems to have been about as good
as that of most of the white troops." Those who fought in the trenches
sometimes conceded as much, declaring the blacks had fought "like
bulldogs" or "with an obstinacy that was really surprising." Jerome B.
Yates, the 16th Mississippi sergeant, reported, "The men . . . say that the
Negros fought better than the whites. So it is all stuff about them not
making soldiers."[4]

To explain the anomaly, some resorted to the reassuring, reliable veri-
ties. John Wise, the brigadier's son, acknowledged that black troops had
advanced farther than white Yankees but said they lacked the Anglo-

Saxon's mettle and endurance. With others, a staff officer explained that the "negroes who as usual, [were] primed with whiskey, had been pushed to the front and put into the breach." When a black Federal had lunged at him with a bayonet, Major Haskell, the mortar officer, compared the action to that of a cornered rat.[5]

Good soldiers or bad, the blacks remained an intolerable affront. When they began to man frontline trenches after the mine assault, those sectors blazed day and night. That activity initially puzzled many, including Grant. Hearing what sounded like a brisk battle, Grant telegraphed to ask, "What is the meaning of the heavy firing going on?" With some asperity, Major General Edward O. C. Ord answered, "I suppose it means the same this morning as yesterday and the day before. Previous to the first the rebels . . . called out to our men that they were going to shell Burnsides niggers and they must not mind it—they have shelled us every morning since." When a Pennsylvania regiment relieved black troops in the trenches, they came under incessant fire. Averse to such dangerous nonsense, the Yankees put a stop to it. One of them explained, "Our boys went out on picket last evening and they holard over to the Johnnys that the 2nd Pa was back again and they did not fire a shot. They hate a niger worse than . . . a coperhead snake."[6]

Northern civilians also became more aware of the private war that summer. Thomas M. Chester, a black correspondent for the mainstream Philadelphia *Press*, reported, "Between the negroes and the enemy it is war to the death. . . . Those here have not the least idea of living after they fall into the hands of the enemy, and the rebels act very much as if they entertained similar sentiments." As noted earlier, Confederates were convinced that falling into the hands of black troops meant death. That amused some Federals, while others, particularly officers of black regiments, expressed a wry satisfaction in the unconcealed fear of Southerners who fled across the lines and inadvertently surrendered to black troops.[7]

Though sorely aggrieved by the bungled mine assault, which, if successful, could have considerably shortened the war, Grant tirelessly sought to cut Lee's supply lines on the south and to threaten Richmond on the north. Memorable for black troops were the attacks north of the James River from September 28 to September 30, collectively known as the New Market Heights battles. For this exercise, Butler, their commander, decided to sacrifice some black troops to show that they would fight. Since they had proved it repeatedly and recently, it was an unnecessary, costly, and redundant demonstration really designed to ennoble Benjamin F. Butler. Elements of his Army of the James, almost twenty thousand strong, began a two-pronged thrust toward Richmond's defenses at night-fall on September 28. One wing quickly captured Fort Harrison, a key strongpoint, rendering some of the other New Market redoubts useless. Nevertheless, another wing pushed toward them. Commanded by Major General David S. Birney, that force included Charles J. Paine's black 3rd Division of about three thousand men and a separate black brigade of at least fifteen hundred men in five regiments, led by Brigadier General William Birney. He was the older but markedly less competent brother of the corps commander.[8]

Paine's troops gritted their teeth and rushed the Confederate's formidable first trench line, faltered, and failed. But they succeeded in their second assault, although they suffered severe casualties, some regiments losing three-fifths of their strength. After the second charge, a 5th U.S. Colored Infantry officer said that he was deeply thankful to be alive, considering that just 200 men remained of his regiment's 520 men. Sergeant Joseph O. Cross, 29th Connecticut Infantry (Colored), said that "the Balles did whistle aroun our heads dreadfully" and that "wee all expected it was our last time." In summary, another black soldier simply wrote, "We . . . got used up."[9]

They soon learned that Confederates had been busy between the first and the second attacks. One officer recalled, "Many of our wounded and all of our dead . . . were left in the hands of the rebels." Since they controlled the battlefield between attacks, Confederates had seized the opportunity to plunder the dead and dispatch the wounded. One Federal officer found his color sergeant with legs shattered but still alive. He had dragged himself away and hidden when he saw that Southern soldiers were making short work of any black man still breathing. Another officer, captured and exchanged by mistake ten days later, reported that he also saw Confederates killing the wounded.[10]

Confederates saw the gory harvest from a different perspective. Among the defenders were men of Hood's old Texas brigade, and a 1st Texas soldier cheerfully reported, "We killed in our front about a million dollars worth of niggers, at current prices." His speculation about the motive for the senseless attack was partially correct, but he had the wrong instigator. He thought that perhaps Grant sought to humiliate them while giving some glory to black troops. He declared, "Whatever his purpose . . . it was like flaunting a red flag before a mad bull. No man in our old

Brigade would have retreated from, or surrendered to Niggers. When they charged . . . the fun began." Another 1st Texas veteran recalled that "the word was passed along the line that they were negroes and to give them lead. Every fellow shot . . . as if they were at a shooting match." Supporting their boasts, a 17th Georgia officer wrote that "the Texans . . . killed niggers galore."[11]

Corporal Dick Stars at Fort Gilmer

Meanwhile, William Birney, the black brigade's leader, directed Colonel James Shaw, 7th U.S. Colored Infantry, to take Fort Gilmer, an earthwork almost half a mile distant. Then he countermanded that order, instructing Shaw to use just four companies. Stunned, at first Shaw thought some ridiculous misunderstanding had occurred. But the aide who brought the revised order replied sharply, "Well, *now* the General directs you to send four companies deployed as skirmishers to take the fort." Shaw felt bound to obey, even though Gilmer's defenders, veteran Alabama, Georgia, and Texas infantry, backed by artillery, had already repelled a much larger force. Shaw dutifully ordered Captain Julius A. Weiss to capture the place with four understrength companies. Weiss, chosen because he was the senior captain, exclaimed, "What! take a fort with a skirmish line? . . . I will try, but it can't be done."[12]

So Weiss and his black soldiers went forth on their suicidal mission, never looking back. About 170 officers and men quick stepped from cover and onto the flat plain stretching to Gilmer, perhaps 700 yards away. Weiss said that the dead-level surface offered no shelter or concealment. They immediately came under brisk artillery fire and a Confederate gunner recalled that "the way those negroes fell . . . was very gratifying." When within accurate rifle range, Weiss ordered the men to charge at a run. He thought about 120 men reached the deep, wide ditch or moat surrounding the fort. During their rush forward, two officers were seriously wounded, and forty or fifty enlisted men killed or wounded. Those who reached the ditch found an obstacle six or seven feet deep at the front, much higher against the fort's walls and ten to twelve feet wide. Lieutenant Robert M. Spinney recalled that "there was no wavering, but every man jumped into the trap."[13]

However, hesitation was scarcely an option. They could neither go back nor pause without becoming easy targets. But the moat proved almost as dangerous. Lieutenant Spinney remembered, "Upon looking about . . . we found there was but one face where the enemy could not touch us, so all the survivors rallied at that [inner] face." Then Weiss, brave or foolhardy beyond measure, tried to obey his orders to take the fort. He instructed pairs of men to hoist a comrade to their shoulders and brace themselves to heave the armed third man over the parapet. When they were ready, he gave the signal and he and his forty-man storming party were catapulted up to the parapet. Confederates inside the fort instantly sent them tumbling back into the ditch, shooting many point-blank through head or chest.[14]

Unknown to the Federals, their attack had not only excited the usual fury but their presence in the moat had ignited a competitive spirit among nearby Confederates. Alexander, the artillery brigadier, wrote, "News spread along the line . . . that Negro troops were corralled in [the] Fort Gilmer ditch, & many of the Texans & Georgians, who had never met them before, came running into the fort & asking for 'a chance to shoot a nigger.'" A Texan recounted, "Every fellow with his rifle [was] trying to exterminate the whole of them on the spot if possible." They saw it as akin to a pop-up target shooting gallery. Men raced from one angle of the fort to another, so that, as one Confederate said, "the musket ball would meet each nappy head as it appeared over the wall."[15]

Undeterred by the instant and lethal repulse, the black soldiers again formed human catapult platforms to sling comrades into the fort. Incredibly, they tried it again and yet again and the same thing happened each time. A 20th Georgia sergeant said that "not a head appeared but that it was quickly perforated with one or more balls," and a 1st Texas soldier echoed his words. Weiss and a lieutenant suffered only slight head wounds, but forty to fifty of their men lay dead or wounded in the moat. Finally, the Federals accepted reality: they could do no more. Weiss conceded that it was "impolitic" to make a fourth attempt to leapfrog into the fort. They could neither advance nor retreat, they could not stay where they were, and no rescue force would come. Gilmer's artillerymen hastened the inevitable when they rolled lit shells into the crowded moat. Even then, some tried to throw out the improvised bombs before they exploded in their faces. Bereft of hope, Weiss and his officers agreed they must surrender.

That was easier said than done. Gilmer's defenders had developed a grudging but wary respect for their black opponents. Lieutenant Spinney vainly waved a white handkerchief on the point of his sword. He recalled that "the rebels, fearing it was only done to gain a foothold, would not take notice of it, but called upon me to come in, which I did." At once,

Confederates swarmed around him, not to murder him, but to pluck him clean of anything valuable. That over, Spinney said his men had thrown down their arms and were ready to yield. "Still they would not believe me," he recalled. They made him mount the parapet first; then they ordered the survivors into the fort.[16]

About eighty enlisted men and seven officers, many of them wounded, entered Gilmer as captives. During the confusion, three men bolted for Union lines. Two fell instantly under a fusillade of bullets. G. W. Breckinridge, a seventeen-year-old captain in a Virginia Reserve battalion, recalled that "the third, a big copper-colored nigger, with a thousand bullets—two from my own pistol—whizzing after him, made his escape. What a sprinter he was!" He was also the only one to return unhurt, although nineteen men wounded earlier during the advance crawled back to safety.[17]

Strikingly, the captives reported they suffered no harm or mistreatment, except some verbal abuse from civilians and rear echelon troops they met on their way to the rear. Conflicting emotions plainly pulled at Confederates once the black Federals fell into their hands. One 5th Texas soldier recalled that "it was the only time during the war that I felt like shooting prisoners." Yet he did not and neither did any other of Gilmer's defenders. H. H. Perry, the Georgia brigade's adjutant, said, "I don't think any of the wounded were butchered or any of the negro prisoners were harmed after surrendering." All had witnessed the black soldiers' startling courage in a way that could not be denied. Consequently, the Southern soldiers apparently could not or would not bring themselves to slaughter those who had shown such bravery at such a cost. One called it a "daring attempt," and others said the black soldiers had proved doughty fighters, behaving "much better than the white troops." Forthrightly, one Texan declared that nothing had stopped them. Another Texan reported they had advanced "valorously" to their doom.[18]

Their audacious attack created a store of campfire tales for both armies, but mostly for Confederates. One of Gilmer's artillerymen related, "One negro, who was either drunk or crazy, crawled through a culvert which ran from inside of the fort into the ditch and was shot on the inside." Another recalled that an officer shouted, "Surrender, you black scoundrels!" In response, a stentorian voice replied, "S'rendah yo'seff, sah!" Probably the legend of Corporal Dick enjoyed the widest circulation and soon became army lore. Alexander, the 1st Corps artillery chief, relayed the primary version: "A large Negro helped by his comrades . . . mounted the exterior slope. He was shot & fell back in the ditch, & his comrades were heard to exclaim, 'Dar now! Dey done kill Corporal Dick! Corporal Dick was best man in de rigiment.'" Private O. T. Hanks, 1st Texas, repeated a variant: "One fellow . . . heard them say, 'Say, hand me up another one dar, Corporal Dick, day's done killed dis one'" In most versions, however, it was Corporal Dick who fell, dead with a bullet through his forehead. For his epitaph, a Virginia artilleryman wrote that "Dick was a game kind of a nigger." Alexander added, "After that all colored troops were known in our corps as the 'Corporal Dicks.'"[19]

Often their accounts conveyed a sense of wonderment about the intrepid black soldiers. Then, more than ever, they needed to reconcile indisputable black valor with undeniable black inferiority. So, some relied upon popular and reassuring wisdom. Most favored was the false courage rationale: the black Yankees were "half crazed with whiskey" or just "gloriously drunk." They had gone into battle with canteens filled with a mixture of whiskey and gunpowder, the last to give an extra edge of fearlessness. Others conjured up an imaginary phalanx of white troops behind the blacks, prodding them forward with fixed bayonets. Nevertheless, while shielding themselves with these explanations, Gilmer's defenders apparently bowed to black pluck when they refrained from killing the survivors.[20]

Their treatment was a radical departure from what had happened elsewhere that day. As noted previously, Confederates slew wounded blacks earlier at other New Market clashes and afterward killed some of the few taken prisoner. Youthful and idealistic, Virginia artilleryman Andrew J. Andrews labeled these last killings "a very disgraceful occurrence." He told about a Texan who, seeking to avenge a brother killed that morning, began shooting black prisoners. Andrews added, "He succeeded in killing four before he was checked. The fifth man made good his escape, although volleys were fired at this yellow-faced Ohio negro." While Andrews wrote long after the war, as did others, he still was one of the few Southerners who, at any time, condemned the killings as deliberate murder.[21]

Seldom was respect so hard won as that earned by the Gilmer attack force. Lieutenant Colonel George M. Dennett, 9th U.S. Colored Infantry, called Gilmer that "terrible and disastrous assault." So it was. The assault group's loss was just fractionally shy of 100 percent. 1st Lieutenant George R. Sherman, who entered the fort as a prisoner, reported, "All engaged in the assault, except one, were either killed, wounded, or captured." He said that 62 of the 170 suffered death wounds in the advance or in the moat. The number killed in that ditch is uncertain, but it was probably between thirty-five and forty. Ordinarily, Confederates would not bury fallen blacks. However, their own welfare required it during such static trench warfare. But they found an easy way to get rid of about half the black corpses. Quickly and unceremoniously, they dropped them into an old well, filling it to the brim.

For a time, the Gilmer prisoners lived and worked under tolerable conditions while they labored on Confederate fortifications. Then Butler became aware of their situation. Considering himself the black man's best friend, Butler protested that they worked while exposed to artillery and rifle fire and placed Confederate prisoners in a similar environment. His intervention resulted in the black prisoners going to prison camps, where more than two-thirds slowly expired. Lieutenant Sherman examined the muster rolls after the war and reported, "Fifty-five of the seventy-nine men captured died in prison within six months, either from wounds or privations." Just twenty-three men survived captivity. One man, reclaimed by a former owner, was reenslaved but returned in good condition at the war's end.[22]

In another foray north of the James River in late October, Confederate cavalry slew 1st U.S. Colored Infantry soldiers caught in the open. While the 37th U.S. Colored Infantry formed a hollow square to repel the horse soldiers, the 1st and 22nd U.S. Colored infantries charged Southern infantry. Ill disciplined and led by incompetent officers, the 22nd quickly broke and fled, just as it had a month earlier at New Market. Although that defection left them unsupported, the 1st U.S. Colored Infantry continued across an open field, capturing enemy trenches and two artillery pieces, just as two enemy cavalry regiments neared. Wisely, the 1st's commander decided it was high time to abandon an untenable position. However, one of his officers and fifteen men tarried, trying to haul away the cannons. It was a fatal miscalculation of time and distance. Before they could move, the cavalry rode them down and put them to the sword. Confederates counted thirty-three dead black soldiers. That number accounts for those reported killed in combat and the fifteen men with the captured artillery. Since they had disappeared, even if forever, their officers listed them as captured or missing, a common and misleading practice.[23]

"The Work of Death" Reigns on the Frontier

In the West, just before the Fort Gilmer drama, Confederate cavalry overwhelmed and murdered 1st Kansas Colored soldiers trapped on the open prairie in Indian Territory. The Confederates were the 1st Indian Brigade of eight hundred Cherokees, Creeks, and Seminoles, led by Stand Watie, a slave owner, three-quarter Cherokee, and the South's only Indian general, and a Texas cavalry brigade of twelve hundred men commanded by Richard M. Gano, a Kentucky medical school graduate who had fought Indians in Texas before the war. They were tracking a large Federal wagon train when they chanced upon the Federals in the late afternoon of September 17.

More than fifty black soldiers worked at the hay station about fifteen miles west of Fort Gibson, while sixty to seventy 2nd Kansas Cavalry troopers served as guards. Captain Edgar A. Barker, a Kansas cavalryman who commanded, reported he had 125 effectives. How he defined *effective* is unknown, and his official report, an enviable example of creative military writing, offers no clue. In fact, at least 160 men busied themselves at the hay station. Some were civilian workers or teamsters, and some may have been recruits or unmustered men belonging to the 1st Kansas Colored. Their camp was on a shallow stream that formed ponds up to 150 feet long with narrow connecting ribbons of water.[24]

The 1st Kansas Colored soldiers had already met some of the approaching enemy. They had helped rout Watie's Indians at Cabin Creek about a year earlier, and they had bloodied Gano's 29th Texas at Honey Springs in July 1863. For that affront, the Texans had exacted savage revenge at Poison Spring. When the enemy host attacked the little camp, Barker decided his position was precarious. In his report, he said he ordered the black soldiers and dismounted whites to flee on foot over the open prairie to timber a mile away. If he did pause long enough to give that order, the trapped men ignored his suicidal instructions and continued fighting from cover. Barker, meanwhile, assembled about sixty mounted men and raced toward a gap between Indian units. Grandly, he asserted, "I made at them with a rush they could not withstand and succeeded in cutting my way through." They withstood his rush well enough to kill, wound, or capture forty-odd troopers, two-thirds of his breakout force. Barker and fifteen of his men escaped and galloped madly for Fort Gibson. As they fled, the Texans and Indians overran the hay station.[25]

As Gano said, they immediately "commenced the work of death in earnest," though Watie asserted, "I am not a murderer." Perhaps not—but he and Gano allowed murder to flourish. One of Gano's men recalled, "Here we spread death and destruction in a few minutes." Wiley Britton, the Federal soldier-historian, called it "simply a massacre." Gano hinted that the slaughter occurred because the Federals fired upon a truce flag he had sent forward to demand surrender. However, no one else on either side mentions that, and it does not explain why they butchered blacks but spared whites. Knowing that they could expect no quarter, the black soldiers fought until they ran out of ammunition, and then tried to thwart death by flight or by hiding. Captain George W. Grayson, 2nd Creek, said the camp at first appeared deserted. He recalled, "Presently however, some one of our men discovered a negro hiding in the high weeds . . . and shot and killed him." They found another and then still another, instantly shooting them when flushed from cover. Watie's men suspected more were concealed nearby. Accordingly, Grayson said that "our men proceeded to hunting and shooting them much as sportsmen do quails."[26]

Some black soldiers submerged themselves in the shallow pools, sinking into the murky water. One man lay on his back underneath the bank's overhanging willows, his nose just above the surface, and so escaped detection by the sharp-eyed hunters. Another immersed himself, covered his face with the broad leaves of water lily plants, and also avoided discovery. Soon the hunters became aware of the water evasion technique and thrashed along the stream looking for waterlogged quarry. Private Jefferson P. Baze, 30th Texas, recalled, "The negroes were nearly all killed in a little creek into which they had jumped[.]. . . The water was red with the blood of the dead negroes." He said the Indians dragged their lifeless prey from the water and stripped the bodies of anything they thought worthwhile.

Some black soldiers, fearing discovery was but a step or an instant away, revealed themselves and begged for their lives. Grayson, who later became principal chief of the Creek Nation, declared, "But the men were in no mood for sparing . . . and shot them down as fast as they found them regardless of their pitiful pleading for mercy." He said it was most revolting to him, but his men had become wild beasts and he could do nothing to stop the butchery. If it was repugnant to Grayson, he was an exception among the vengeful Confederates. Private W. T. Sheppard, 5th Texas Partisan Rangers, unabashedly crowed, "The Federals were short a company of negro troops and after the battle they were all 'good' negroes."[27]

Sheppard erred—not all were dead. As many as eight black soldiers became prisoners, joining more than eighty white captives. Phraseology used by Grayson suggests that Indians were the generous victors. He wrote, "Some of our people in other parts of the field had captured six or eight, but in the immediate vicinity of where I was, no negro was taken prisoner." If not reenslaved, they went to a Texas prison camp, where conditions were much better than in camps east of the Mississippi. At least five survived captivity and returned to their regiment by late 1865. In addition, ten escaped despite the relentless hunting and killing. George W. Duval, determined to live, burrowed into a drift in the creek bank and huddled there until nightfall. Then he crawled between two sentries and escaped across the prairie, taking his gun with him. Submarine concealment also worked for at least two others who later walked to safety. Confederates knew a few had escaped but were unconcerned about witnesses to the slaughter. Quite possibly they hoped frightened survivors would serve as a warning to other blacks.

Casualty tabulations vary, but Britton's appears most reliable because he talked to men who lived through the massacre. He wrote, "About 40 colored soldiers were killed, eight captured and ten escaped." Gano reported, "Seventy-three Federals, mostly negroes, lay dead upon the field." He added that they had carried away eighty-five prisoners and had left behind five badly wounded Federals. Differing tallies for black casualties resulted from confusion or indifference to their status. Southerners felt just as angry and betrayed whether black men donned a uniform or aided the Federal cause as civilian workers. No confusion existed about Confederate casualties—they were minimal. Texans counted three wounded and Watie's losses undoubtedly also were light, although he did not report his.[28]

14

Saltville

IN THE FALL OF 1864, Confederates captured hundreds of black Yankees in the West when Federal posts surrendered with or without a fight. Contrary to previous experience, all but a few lived to be reenslaved. Yet at the same time in the East, another slaughter of black soldiers occurred at Saltville, Virginia. However contradictory these events appear at first glace, no inconsistency existed. Nothing had changed—always black soldiers were recovered property and "not considered prisoners of war." The rights of ownership allowed Confederates to do as they pleased with repossessed chattels. They could reenslave or destroy that property, just as they thought best. When large numbers surrendered under circumstances that allowed their captors to herd them south to work on fortifications, officers then restrained their men from wholesale killing and the Confederacy recovered urgently needed labor.[1]

During that period, a transient but important consideration also probably worked to spare many black soldiers. Confederate authorities undoubtedly wished to avoid a public massacre of black soldiers. Richmond—and even Lincoln—believed that a war-weary North might refuse to return Lincoln to a second term. Many in the South pinned their hopes on a negotiated peace, which would not happen with Lincoln. To avoid strengthening his hand, it was advisable for Confederates not to offend the North and the world with another Fort Pillow. There is no trail of verbal or written instructions from Richmond to that effect, so it is a speculative conclusion. Still, Forrest, for one, controlled his men so that no killing sprees took place, even when black troops resisted his usual surrender-or-die ultimatums and inflicted casualties on his men.

Large captures began when Major General Joseph Wheeler and Forrest went raiding and when General John B. Hood embarked upon his meandering march toward Tennessee. Sherman knew Confederates would strike at his rear but was determined not to permit the threat to interfere with his offensive plans. In any event, he knew he could not block their forays. He wrote, "It will be a physical impossibility to protect the roads, now that Hood, Forrest, Wheeler, and the whole batch of devils, are turned loose." He detached some troops as rear guards, ordered Major General George H. Thomas and his Army of the Cumberland back to Nashville to watch over Tennessee, and let it go at that.[2]

Wheeler Fizzles in Georgia

Wheeler's efforts at devilry caused no great harm. He threatened the Federal post at Dalton, Georgia, demanding immediate and unconditional surrender. His ultimatums rejected, he assaulted the much smaller garrison and was repulsed. However, Wheeler scored one victory in mid-August when he detached about 160 men from two cavalry regiments to attack a logging operation near Decatur, Tennessee. His men had the advantage of surprise and quickly overwhelmed about three hundred white and black troops, capturing about two hundred prisoners. Lieutenant Colonel James H. Lewis, 1st Tennessee Cavalry, recalled, "These were the first negro soldiers our men had met in the Federal uniform with arms in their hands. It was with great difficulty that the men could be restrained from shooting them all." Rather than executing the black soldiers, Lewis and other officers chose to parole them, a most unusual move. However, that was the only other option as they could not take them along while operating behind enemy lines.[3]

Forrest Roils Alabama and Tennessee

Forrest accomplished much more on his railroad raid. With forty-five hundred men, he disrupted rail traffic along the Alabama-Tennessee border. Besides any damage he could do, his mere appearance caused turmoil. His reputation and tactics, including the threat of another Fort Pillow, frightened many Federals in his path. Moving rapidly, on September 24, Forrest captured 447 officers and men of three black regiments and the strong post at Athens, Georgia, after he warned that "no lives would be spared" if he had to storm the place. On the next day, Forrest met spirited resistance at the fort guarding the Sulphur Branch trestle bridge, though he threatened again to exterminate the garrison of nine hundred, including four hundred black soldiers, if he had to take the post by force. When almost out of ammunition, the garrison surrendered, though acutely aware of Fort Pillow. Despite their lively defense, Forrest paroled the officers and spared the enlisted men, including the black soldiers.[4]

He continued his sweep for another week, tearing up railroad tracks, destroying bridges, rolling stock and locomotives, cutting telegraph wires, burning or plundering supplies, and overrunning Federal posts. Some commanders of small black garrisons trembled and fled with their men before Forrest even appeared, running away in the dead of the night. As well, several posts manned solely by white soldiers swiftly and meekly surrendered. One stubborn officer, however, resisted until the raiders gave up in disgust and went away. Still, Forrest's raid momentarily lifted Southern morale, though the foray had little impact upon Northern operations.[5]

Federals quickly mobilized in the region and Forrest knew it was time to quit. He marched about two thousand captives southward, including more than nine hundred black soldiers. When his men took the "unbleached" Yankees prisoner, it was not that their rage against them had suddenly evaporated. So, rather than redounding to Forrest's credit, the live captures strengthen the case for his culpability in the earlier killing sprees. Since Southern soldiers felt no differently toward former slaves fighting them, it showed he could control his men if he wished. The restraint displayed on the railroad raid reinforces the conviction that Forrest condoned, if he did not order, the slaughter at Fort Pillow and Brice's Cross Roads. Further, while the lust for vengeance against black Federals had not abated, discipline among Forrest's troops had ebbed with a recent influx of transfers and recruits. Yet Forrest kept a firm grip on his men. That suggests he could have done so even more easily when he led more-disciplined soldiers earlier in the year.[6]

Although alive and well, the hundreds of black captives still caused trouble for Forrest. He had to deplete his fighting strength by assigning troops to guard them on their twelve-day trek to Mobile, Alabama. Furthermore, many never arrived there. Some probably escaped en route or were shot, and former owners may have reclaimed a few. But these losses would not account for all those missing. Annoyed, Forrest wrote Lieutenant General Richard Taylor, the department commander, "I captured . . . upward of 1,000 negroes. I understand only about 800 have reached you." Forrest rightly suspected that guards kept some as servants and sold a number for cash. Neither was an uncommon practice.[7]

Hood Threatens Black Federals

After Forrest came General John B. Hood, a splendid brigade or division commander but an officer without the brains to lead a corps or an army. Driven from Atlanta, which had fallen to Sherman on September 1, Hood wandered uncertainly with his Army of Tennessee. Then he appeared before Dalton in northern Georgia on October 13 and issued a surrender-or-die ultimatum to the mixed Federal garrison. Colonel Lewis Johnson, the post commander, had just 751 men, of whom 626 belonged to his own 44th U.S. Colored Infantry, and he knew he could not hope to withstand an army. Hood promised that all white officers and men would be paroled after surrender but added that no prisoners would be taken if forced to attack. Johnson believed Hood meant every word of it, especially after he met the general in person. He recalled that "when I protested against the barbarous measures which he threatened in his summons, he said that he could not restrain his men and would not if he could; that I could choose between surrender and death." Hood added that he would return former slaves to their owners.

Johnson surrendered with the understanding that all would receive humane treatment. His decision was made easier when he realized that Hood's men ached for the chance to kill black Yankees. His interpretation of their mood was correct. As one Confederate said, they wanted to "kill every damn one of them."[8]

Instead of shooting all, they had to settle for treating them roughly, taking their clothing, and killing just a few. Artilleryman Philip D. Stephenson wrote, "They were disarmed, marched out in a field, strung out in a single line. Most probably had been told that they would be shot and that now their time had come." Right then, however, Confederates wanted only their shoes and not their lives. Next, they marched their prisoners to the railroad and ordered them to tear up the track. "One smart negro," as a 16th Tennessee soldier described him, refused to help wreck his own army's lifeline. That stubborn man, a 44th U.S. Colored Infantry sergeant, was shot dead on the spot. A 1st Arkansas soldier recalled that after that sobering example, "the rest tore up the road readily and rapidly." On the march from Dalton, guards also shot at least five sick blacks who could not keep up with the column.[9]

Although some black prisoners were free men from Ohio and Indiana, Confederates forced all into slavery. On the march to Corinth, Mississippi, citizens and soldiers along the way said they had discovered long-lost runaway slaves among the prisoners and reclaimed them. About 350 reached Corinth to work on the railroad there. Private William E. Bevens, the 1st Arkansas soldier, commented, "This was better than killing them." But a wrathful Colonel Johnson thought neither was acceptable. Upon his return to Dalton on October 15, he urged his superiors to retaliate for the murder and enslavement of his men. He wasted his breath and ink, for his pleas went unanswered. However, while the dead never returned, scores escaped and rejoined the 44th U.S. Colored Infantry, so that Johnson had most of his men back within two months.[10]

Within that same period, Hood managed to lead the Army of Tennessee to destruction in his "Mad Tennessee Campaign," as one of his colonels called it. He broke its back at Franklin on November 30 and delivered the coup de grâce at Nashville in mid-December. With the passing of that once proud army, Southerners despaired. Speaking for many, Captain James L. Cooper, 20th Tennessee, confessed, "I now felt that the Confederacy was indeed gone up, that we were a ruined people." More colorfully, a dejected survivor of Hood's irrational leadership exclaimed, "Ain't we in a hell of a fix, a one-eyed president, a one-legged general and a one-horse confederacy." Many men, convinced it was futile and pointless to continue, quit the struggle. Those who stayed fought with greater desperation as the seemingly endless Northern legions pressed the fight harder and deeper into their homeland.[11]

Federals Denounce Murders Near Nashville

Even as disaster struck, however, some of Forrest's men found an opportunity to execute three officers of black regiments. Harvey's Scouts, a unit under Forrest's command, captured them about December 20, not far from Nashville, and three days later took them aside and shot them. Lieutenant George W. Fitch, 12th U.S. Colored Infantry, survived a bullet to the head, but the others were killed. Federal troops soon rescued him, and he submitted a report that generated anger, protests, and threats from Nashville to Virginia. The 12th U.S. Colored Infantry's colonel charged that his officers were shot by a savage enemy while Colonel Johnson, 44th U.S. Colored Infantry, called it cold-blooded murder and asked superiors to retaliate. Thomas told Hood, "I will not consent that my soldiers shall be thus brutally murdered whenever the fortunes of war place them defenseless within your power." He warned, "Should my troops, exasperated by a repetition of such acts, take no prisoners of war at all in future, I shall in no manner interfere in this exercise of their just vengeance . . . and you will please remember that it is your army and not mine who is responsible for the inauguration of the dreadful policy of extermination."

Grant received a copy of Fitch's report at his headquarters in Virginia. He then politely requested Lee "to have those barbarous practices prohibited as far as they can be controlled." In sterner tones, he referred to Milliken's Bend and said he was convinced that Confederates executed the white officers captured there. Grant concluded, "I believe it has been the practice with many officers and men in the Confederate Army to kill all such officers as may fall into their hands." He let it go at that, apparently satisfied he had done his duty with a pro forma protest. Always Grant seemed somewhat apologetic when he complained to Confederates about their murderous ways with black troops and their white officers. Moreover, he attempted to distinguish between policy and practice when no valid distinction existed. In any event, again Northern authorities declined to take any action whatsoever.[12]

Massacre at Saltville

Earlier, as both Forrest and Hood captured posts in Georgia and Tennessee, Federals sent an expedition to take Saltville in mountainous western Virginia. It was a prize fiercely defended by the South and repeatedly attacked by the North, though its only value lay in the salt produced by the privately owned mines. But plain old salt, that unobtrusive crystalline compound, was in woefully short supply in the South. Yet it was essential for preserving meat, fish, and other foods; for tanning shoe and harness leather; and for the health of man and beast. Although he exaggerated, one former Confederate officer told Northerners that the South lost "Because you had salt."[13]

While it was not quite that vital, salt was so important that the Confederate Congress established the permanent watchdog Committee on Salt Supply. Salt's scarcity or availability and its cost affected people throughout the Confederacy. Theoretically, the South had enough salt sources to satisfy its needs. Scattered here and there were salt mines, springs, and wells, while a lengthy coastline provided a bountiful supply through ocean water evaporation. But Southerners had never fully developed their salt resources, and, in any event, they lacked an efficient distribution system. Moreover, Federal land and naval forces destroyed any vulnerable saltworks at every opportunity and the blockade cut imports.[14]

Geography, topography, and the region's demographics served as natural defenses for the Saltville mines. Steep mountains and twisting valleys barred the way and protected the site in Virginia's remote southwestern corner. Ardent Southern sympathizers who inhabited the sparsely populated area warned Confederate authorities and bushwhacked approaching Federals. A 15th Pennsylvania Cavalry officer said they met bushwhackers at every turn during one tortuous march toward Saltville. He added that the natives were the "most profoundly ignorant and squalidly poor" that he had yet met in the South. Still, however drenched in ignorance, they served as a most effective early warning system for Confederates. Even with reliable guides and good horses, it proved all but impossible for raiders to approach the mines undetected.[15]

Brigadier General Stephen G. Burbridge led the Federal column of about forty-five hundred mounted men to take Saltville, a task for which neither training nor experience had prepared him. His force consisted of Kentucky, Michigan, and Ohio cavalry units and six hundred or more black soldiers, mainly men of the 5th U.S. Colored Cavalry, a regiment still recruiting in Kentucky. Colonel James S. Brisbin, an antislavery orator, had commanded the 5th when it existed only on paper six months earlier. He made the regiment a reality as he gathered officers, recruits, and horses. However, during the march and the subsequent fight, Brisbin stayed with Burbridge and Colonel James F. Wade commanded the black troops. Wade was a Regular Army officer named to lead the embryonic 6th U.S. Colored Cavalry.[16]

They arrived before the Confederate defenses on the cold cloudy morning of October 2, 1864. Of the six hundred black soldiers, one hundred had dropped out during the march from Kentucky, because either they or their horses had become sick or injured. When the remaining five hundred dismounted to fight, one hundred men stayed behind as horse holders. When Brisbin reported that "There were 400 black soldiers engaged in the battle," it is very likely he did not know exactly how many took part. Also, he did not say "400 5th U.S. Colored Cavalry soldiers." He used a generic description because some men were 6th Colored Cavalry recruits, and possibly a third of the original six-hundred-man force came from the 116th Colored Infantry. That regiment had formed in July at Camp Nelson in Kentucky, the same place where the 5th was still organizing. The insertion of as many as two hundred men from the 116th was overlooked, ignored, or unknown to many observers then and since. Their presence, however, raises more questions about the already-uncertain battle statistics, as will become apparent.[17]

Major General John C. Breckinridge, the former senator and vice president of the United States, led the defense with the few troops available. Quite by chance, he got more help when elements of several cavalry brigades, cut off and unable to rejoin Wheeler, rode toward Saltville, reaching the neighborhood just as Federals neared the place. With those reinforcements, Breckinridge had about twenty-eight hundred men. But he did not need superiority or even parity in numbers to defend the mines. Saltville was a natural fortress. Steep slopes with artillery emplacements ringed the site, and defending infantry fired from trenches and rifle pits. Without surprise or overwhelming force, it would always be a hard nut to crack. No chance of surprise existed; Federals lacked overwhelming numbers; and Burbridge divided his troops, thus weakening his main thrust.[18]

The 5th Colored Cavalry, 12th Ohio, and 11th Michigan attacked up a steep slope on the Federal left, with the black soldiers at the end of the line. They struggled upward, fighting at close range, until they neared the crest and open ground before the enemy trenches. Right then, a Confederate officer recalled, "The cry was raised that we were fighting negroes." Fuming with rage, dismounted Tennessee cavalrymen eagerly awaited the blacks. Colonel Wade, leading the 5th, ordered his men to charge, and they rushed forward with a yell. Some 8th Tennessee Cavalry soldiers, men of Forrest's old brigade, leaped from their trenches with pistols in hands and ran to meet the former slaves. In short order, the black soldiers killed a lieutenant and wounded his brother and the others, thus abruptly ending the Confederates' impulsive rush.[19]

After a bitter fight for the crest, Confederates finally repelled the Yankee attack. Black soldiers won plaudits for their conduct, including praise from a Federal Kentucky soldier who wrote home that he "never saw troops fight like they did . . . never thought they would fight." Their bravery came at a cost. Burbridge's chief medical officer listed twenty-two black soldiers killed in the fight, twice as many as the 11th Michigan's eleven dead, and more than the remaining ten regiments combined. Most of the nine Kentucky regiments on the center and right had few casualties, lending support to the contention that they did little.[20]

As night drew near, Burbridge's men found themselves almost out of ammunition and isolated in a hostile mountain fastness while Confederates received reinforcements. They knew they were in trouble. Captain Frank H. Mason, 12th Ohio, said that "there was not even a muleteer . . . who did not know as early as four o'clock on that October afternoon that the best result we could possibly hope for was to escape capture." Given that sobering reality, Burbridge and his officers agreed that they should get out while they could. Leaving the black troops to hold the advanced positions, the rest silently withdrew. After two hours, the blacks also stole back to their horses and began a hurried night retreat over hazardous trails. Among them on that jolting flight were some badly wounded men. Colonel Brisbin said that they "preferred present suffering to being murdered at the hands of a cruel enemy."[21]

Brisbin also asserted, "Nearly all the wounded were brought off." Whether referring only to his black soldiers or to the whole command, either way he was wrong. Most wounded blacks and many whites were left behind. Private George D. Mosgrove, 4th Kentucky (CSA) said the Federals abandoned many slightly wounded black soldiers who were quite able to travel. He charged, "The poor, unfortunate negroes . . . found that they had been deserted by their comrades and left to be massacred—a fate that Burbridge must have known would befall them should they fall into Confederate hands." He was correct—Burbridge, a Kentucky native, surely knew. While Unionist and Southern loyalist Kentuckians nursed a fierce animosity toward each other, that hostility paled beside the murderous rage stirred in Confederates by black soldiers. Though pleased they had killed many of the "poor deluded wretches" during the battle, that did not quench their bloodlust.[22]

Early the next day, Confederates scoured the battlefield, searching for blacks to kill. Murder it was, done in the cool of the morning, many hours removed from the heat and adrenaline rush of battle. Yet Mosgrove related that as they found and dispatched abandoned black Federals, they became "mad and excited to the highest degree . . . they were so

exasperated that they could not be deterred from their murderous work."
He first realized something unusual was afoot soon after he awakened
at dawn to find a dense fog cloaking the valley and the mountains. He
recalled, "Presently I heard a shot, then another and another until the
volume swelled . . . [like] a skirmish line." Puzzled, he mounted his
horse and rode in the fog toward the firing. He understood the cause
when he arrived before the brigades commanded by Brigadier General
Felix H. Robertson and Colonel George G. Dibrell. "They were shooting every wounded negro they could find," Mosgrove reported. "They
were all killed—a multitude of them." Captain Edwin O. Guerrant, a
Kentucky brigade's adjutant, also heard the gunfire. He confirmed that
the constant shooting "sung the death knell of many a poor negro who
was unfortunate enough not to be killed yesterday. Our men took no
negro prisoners."

Mosgrove observed that some black soldiers "were so slightly wounded
that they could even run, but when they ran from the muzzle of one
pistol it was only to be confronted by another. It was bang, bang, bang,
all over the field—negroes dropping everywhere." No place was safe.
Federal Surgeon William H. Gardner worked in a field hospital that
morning when several Confederates entered and seized five wounded
black soldiers. Gardner and an assistant surgeon were outraged but helpless to stop the intruders who took the five from the hospital and shot
them. About the same time, Mosgrove entered a small log cabin and
found seven or eight lightly wounded black soldiers standing with their
backs against the walls. Mosgrove related, "I had scarcely been there a
minute when a pistol-shot from the door caused me to turn." Standing
there was a boy, not older than sixteen, brandishing a pistol in each hand.
Mosgrove told him to hold off until he could get out of the way. When
he did so, the youth shot them all.[23]

Lieutenant George W. Cutler, 11th Michigan, was one of many wounded left on the battlefield. From his position and limited view, he saw eight
or nine black soldiers executed. Two 12th Ohio captains also remained
there under the care of their assistant surgeon and both witnessed the
butchery. Captain Orange Sells reported that he saw "a good many"
blacks killed, all of them soldiers and all wounded but one. He added,
"I heard firing all over the place; it was like a skirmish."[24]

About midway through the murder spree, the shooting momentarily
subsided when Generals Breckinridge and Basil W. Duke emerged from
the mists. An angry Breckinridge ordered an immediate halt to the shoot-

ing. Mosgrove recalled that soon after Breckinridge and Duke left, a youthful Confederate approached a "bright-looking mulatto boy . . . who seemed to think he was in no danger." As the Confederate leveled his pistol, the black boy cried out that General Duke had ordered him to remain there until he returned. Mosgrove related, "It was of no use. In another moment the little mulatto was a corpse."[25]

Sometime during that morning, probably early rather than late, a lone homicidal psychopath began stalking the wounded. He was Champ Ferguson, a guerrilla leader who held a captain's commission in the Confederate army. He often served with regular troops, took orders, and reported to superiors. But almost everyone in the region, civilian or soldier, had long known about and deplored his addiction to killing. In January 1862, a Confederate cavalryman shuddered when he saw Ferguson methodically slay three men in two separate incidents. Six months later, Basil W. Duke, then a colonel, had warned Ferguson that he could not execute prisoners while with regular forces. At that time, Ferguson admitted to killing thirty-two men. About a month before the Saltville fight, Confederate Sergeant John C. Williamson rode through upper middle Tennessee and noted, "Champ Ferguson has operated in this vicinity. All are Southern but opposed to Champ."[26]

Like a spectral ghost, Ferguson had materialized on the Saltville battlefield. There he wandered about, murdering helpless Federals, white and black, and no one stayed his hand. Harry Shocker, a 12th Ohio soldier, saw Ferguson kill five men and watched as he shot others, though he could not determine whether they lived or died. Shocker and a comrade lay wounded on the field when he first glimpsed Ferguson prowling about. Shocker said, "I saw him pointing his pistol down at prisoners lying on the ground, and heard the reports of the pistol and the screams of the men." When the killer moved toward them, Shocker crawled away about forty feet and hugged the ground. Ferguson stood over the other 12th Ohio soldier and asked him what he was doing there and why he came "to fight with the damned niggers." Without waiting for a reply, Ferguson raised his revolver and asked, "Where will you have it, in the back or in the face?" In vain, the Federal cried out, "For God's sake, don't kill me, soldier." The next sound was a pistol shot that ended pleas and life. Somehow Ferguson missed seeing Shocker and went to one of several log cabins surgeons were using as field hospitals. There he extracted two black soldiers, walked them about one hundred yards away, and shot them. Then he returned and took two more black Federals on a short death march. At a minimum, Federal authorities calculated that Ferguson murdered twelve Federals that morning, probably including a second white 12th Ohio man.[27]

While Ferguson killed indiscriminately, others concentrated on blacks. Mosgrove, the 4th Kentucky soldier, thought Tennessee men responsible for most of the killing but conceded that some Kentuckians may have taken part. He argued, however, that they had not met the blacks in battle, so they "had not the same provocation as the Tennesseans." That was a specious argument, since the only incentive required for any Southerner was the sight of armed and uniformed blacks. An aide to Breckinridge wrote home that "it was a great pleasure . . . to go over the field & see so many . . . of the African descent lying mangled & bleeding."[28]

However, Breckinridge became angry when he learned that one of his generals had a role in the atrocities. Just two days later, Breckinridge informed General Robert E. Lee of the crimes committed and apparently named Felix H. Robertson of Texas as the guilty officer. In reply, Lee also condemned such treatment of black prisoners and said that the guilty general had his "unqualified reprobation." He ordered Breckinridge to prefer charges and bring the officer to trial. Robertson, balky and insubordinate, refused to cooperate. He took his small brigade to Georgia to join Wheeler's cavalry and never faced charges or stood trial. Although very willing to relate his exploits in other battles, Robertson afterward carefully avoided talking about Saltville.[29]

Somehow, a few wounded black soldiers, overlooked or captured elsewhere, escaped execution and became prisoners. After the battle, the wounded of both sides, including black Federals, were moved to nearby Emory and Henry College, converted into an army hospital. On the night of October 7, armed men burst into the place, climbed to upper floors, and shot to death two black soldiers in their hospital beds. On the next day, Champ Ferguson forced his way past guards and searched for Federal Lieutenant Elza C. Smith, 13th Kentucky Cavalry. According to witnesses, Ferguson said he harbored a grudge of unspecified nature against Smith and two other Federal officers. Smith he knew by sight but not the others. Finding the wounded lieutenant in his bed, he made sure the officer recognized him, and then killed him with a single bullet to the head. The other two officers eluded Ferguson through the intervention of the hospital's chief surgeon and his staff.[30]

Ferguson then disappeared. But the hospital murders were too much for everyone. Both sides now wanted Ferguson brought to justice. Confederates acted first, arresting and jailing him in early February of 1865. They released him on April 5, citing the difficulty of obtaining witnesses for trial. Federal authorities remained unforgiving. Burbridge called Lieutenant Smith's murder most diabolical and warned Confederates that when he caught Ferguson or his men, they would get short shrift. Thomas E. Bramlette, Kentucky's Union governor, also angrily denounced Ferguson. He protested, "Surely our government should make an official demand upon Confederates to surrender up this man." Bramlette said he knew of more than thirty whites slain by Ferguson. Almost as an aside, he added, "Most of the others murdered were colored troops."[31]

Meanwhile, Burbridge and his troops successfully retreated through the mountains, avoiding Confederates efforts to trap them. In another impressive example of creative military writing, he announced, "We whipped the rebels in every engagement. In the evening our ammunition gave out, and . . . I withdrew the command in excellent order and spirits."

Almost everyone knew just the opposite was true. Confederates hailed Saltville as a victory, and Federal soldiers bemoaned their defeat. Lee called it a handsome success for Confederate arms, while a Richmond official described it as a bloody repulse for the Yankees. Captain Mason, the 12th Ohio historian, unhesitatingly labeled the expedition a costly failure. Men of the 116th Colored Infantry described it as "that disastrous campaign." Pennsylvania cavalrymen passed the retreating troops seven days after the battle and one commented, "They are in a deplorable plight. A great many are without shoes and marching barefoot, having lost their horses. . . . Many have lost arms and everything."[32]

Burbridge reported 350 casualties among the 2,500 men engaged. His chief surgeon counted 54 killed, 190 wounded, and 104 missing, for a total of 348. However, the surgeon warned, "It is impossible for me to give a correct list of the killed and wounded at present, because the recording surgeons were left on the field with the wounded." He promised a correct tally when possible, but that never happened. For one thing, no one knew exactly how many black soldiers took part, despite Colonel Brisbin placing their strength at six hundred men. They came from three separate embryonic or newly formed units. Most belonged to the 5th U.S. Colored Cavalry, a regiment that would not complete organization until October 30, a month after the battle. An unknown but small number came from a 6th Colored Cavalry nucleus, a unit that formally began organizing November 1 and did not complete it until June 21, 1865. Finally, officers of the 116th Colored Infantry, officially mustered on July 12, 1864, said

they contributed as many as two hundred soldiers in fifty-man detachments from each of four companies.[33]

Men in these fledgling units were strangers to one another and to their
officers. Even a lowly 5th Cavalry sergeant confessed that he did not know
the names of his men when they went to Saltville. Further, some recruits
probably were not yet mustered or entered on the rolls. Accordingly, they
did not have to be listed as casualties if they were not on rosters in the
first place. After the expedition, officers also may have resurrected some
dead men by installing ringers in their places. That substitution, it will
be recalled, was effected by assigning the names of dead or missing men
to recruits. Compulsory enlistments helped fill the ranks, and officers in
Kentucky energetically engaged in the practice. In one egregious case,
an angry Lincoln interceded and ordered an overzealous recruiter to stop
torturing prospects to force them to enlist.[34]

Official casualty figures for the black troops were almost certainly
too conservative. James G. Hatchitt, Burbridge's chief surgeon, listed
22 killed, 37 wounded, and 53 missing from the 5th Colored Cavalry,
for a total of 112. Two weeks later, Colonel Brisbin simply reported 118
casualties for 400 black soldiers engaged in the fight. He provided no
breakdown. The accuracy of these early reports is problematic. After
a thorough examination of the 5th's records in the National Archives,
historian Thomas D. Mays established that a few reported missing turned
up, and that the army tried and convicted a couple of them for desertion.
Still, Mays found that at least forty-six men remained missing well after
the war and concluded that Confederates had killed them.[35]

Another historian, however, labeled the massacre a myth, branded
many witnesses as liars, and argued that most missing black soldiers
simply fled from the fight. William Marvel wrote that "the butchering of scores of black prisoners is pure exaggeration. No more than an
even dozen could have been murdered on October 3, and quite possibly
only the five witnessed by Surgeon Gardner." Some historians, perhaps
unaware of Mays's work, accepted Marvel's conclusions. Subsequently,
three researchers went to the National Archives to examine the pertinent
records and learned that the evidence more than supported Mays' contention that Confederates slew at least forty-six black soldiers.[36]

No official reports mention the 116th Colored Infantry at Saltville.
Unfortunately, complete regimental records for that period are nonexis-
tent. Unofficial rosters show only one 116th soldier's death that probably
resulted from the Saltville expedition. But that is an unlikely minimal

toll. Further, no reports deal with casualties, if any, for the 6th Colored Cavalry. Historian Mays's tally of at least forty-six victims is but a good starting point. Given the unreliability of unit records, the possible presence of unlisted, nameless recruits and the substitution of live men for dead or missing enrolled soldiers and the lack of reports for the 6th U.S. Colored Calvary and the 116th U.S. Colored Infantry, only an informed estimate is possible. Loss experience for black troops, participants' testimony, and probability suggest that the murder toll was probably more than fifty. Though that conclusion can be disputed, still no one knew the precise toll then and no one knows it now.[37]

Saltville became the war's last large-scale slaughter of black soldiers, not for lack of will or rage, but because the proper conditions never obtained again. One recurring common denominator in the massacres was at least temporary control of the battlefield for Confederates and, of course, black soldiers to murder. In other battles and clashes, Confederates could and did concentrate their fire upon black troops. For instance, they did just that at Nashville in mid-December, so that the black regiments bore a disproportionate share of Federal casualties.[38]

Before and after Saltville, however, regular Confederate forces and guerrillas continued to murder solitary black soldiers or small groups of them. Many of these incidents were incompletely or never officially reported. Private letters or diaries, memoirs, and postwar testimony exposed murders unknown or ignored by Federal authorities. For example, some 118th U.S. Colored Infantry soldiers became murder victims in early September 1864 at Owensborough, Kentucky. Two weeks later, their commander finally reported that guerrillas had murdered three soldiers after they had surrendered. But the guerrillas were regular Confederate cavalry and one of them later wrote that they "made a charge . . . capturing 13 negro soldiers killed all of them." Sometimes an official report suggests an obvious but missing conclusion. For instance, an 84th U.S. Colored Infantry picket post was attacked in late November near Morganza, Louisiana. Officers reported six killed and wounded and fourteen missing. Perhaps a few missing men escaped, but Confederates probably killed most. In late January of 1865, guerrillas attacked forty men of the 5th U.S. Colored Cavalry, killed nineteen, and wounded at least seventeen. Near the war's end, a 44th U.S. Colored Infantry officer at Chattanooga related that he lost twelve soldiers to Confederates, including one man who escaped, was recaptured, and then executed.[39]

15

Murder in the East

SOUTHERNERS BELIEVED THAT emancipation incited slave revolt, black soldiers undermined white superiority, and both menaced home, family, honor, and just about everything else they held dear. But the North's evolving hard war brought tangible destruction in 1864. Then the threat doubled and became even more personal as Yankee armies laid waste to Southern lands, plundering and burning; invading homes; and mistreating defenseless women, children, and old men. Without giving it much thought, enraged Southerners soon responded in their time-honored way with violence, killing captured white Federals who raided, pillaged, or burned.

During the first three years of the war, Confederates made a sharp distinction between shooting black and white captives. As recounted previously, they believed killing former slaves amounted to exterminating once-valuable livestock gone astray; dispatching ordinary white prisoners was wrong and dishonorable. That distinction dissolved when they decided white Yankees behaved like lawless brigands or pirates, Vandal or Hun hordes. The common denominator in the atrocities, the refusal of quarter to white or black Federals, was the personal challenge and the threat to honor and manhood, home and hearth, law and order. So it was, as one Kentucky Confederate said, that they began "killing scores of his land pirates and house-burners."

In early summer of 1864, Colonel Josiah Gorgas, the Confederate ordnance chief often consulted by President Davis, wrote, "Would that we could hear of no more captures. The war has now assumed that phase in which no mercy can be shown to the enemy. He burns, robs, murders and ravishes, and this is to be met only by killing all." Horatio N. Taft, a Federal government worker in Washington, predicted that shift in March 1864. In his diary, he wrote that "the Rebels are . . . desperate. It [the war] is without doubt assuming a more relentless and cruel character as it progresses, on both sides, but the rebel 'papers' are getting furious and call loudly for vengeance even on the prisoners in their hands, but as we hold many more of theirs than they do of ours they will have to take it out in raving."[1]

Taft erred on two counts. First, most Southerners knew perfectly well that the North enjoyed a significant numerical superiority and increased that advantage with shiploads of "hireling serfs" constantly coming from Europe. So, many complained or boasted that they were fighting the world. They believed, however, that their warrior superiority compensated for the shortfall in numbers. Regardless of numbers, many Southerners also considered the Yankees an effete lot that lacked the backbone, nerve, or stomach for a war of extermination, a black-flag conflict, and would quickly sue for peace. Secondly, Southerners soon added action to the ranting and raving. Word and deed became one.[2]

Northern leaders adopted the hard-war strategy in the spring when they decided that the war's successful prosecution required the destruction of everything that enabled the South to fight. They must crush not only Confederate armies but also the South's morale and resources. That meant seizing or destroying crops, livestock, food stores, slaves, public buildings, transportation facilities, grain mills, saltworks, lead mines, tanneries, factories and machinery, and anything else that even remotely helped the South fight. As Federal armies began tramping across the Southern landscape, they executed the new policy.[3]

As the invading columns left ashes and woe in their wake, Southerners viewed the burning and plundering as criminal acts. In anger and frustration, they held the Yankees to account under Southern customs and codes. Conflating peacetime offenses and wartime acts, Confederates believed the proper punishment for raiders and house burners was death and soon added pillaging and foraging to the list of capital offenses. They rejected the reality that war had changed from a chivalrous knightly clash of arms on isolated battlefields to an all-inclusive struggle. Many remained addicted to an ideal of personal combat, despite firsthand knowledge that fighting had become an impersonal business, that death or wounds usually came from unseen and unknown hands. Most important, they firmly believed their lands and folks at home should be immune from war's wrath.

Aside from the Confederate practice of murdering black soldiers, prior to mid-1864 both sides had largely adhered to the rules of civilized warfare. While neither North nor South showed much mercy to guerrillas, they generally treated captured white soldiers properly. To be sure, a few isolated incidents had marred that record. Southerners protested the Palmyra Massacre in 1862, when Federals executed ten men after a Unionist citizen, presumably murdered, disappeared from that Missouri town. By 1864, reports of random actual and rumored atrocities increased. Northerners condemned the slaying of white soldiers at Fort Pillow, and Federal troops had vowed vengeance after the Nickajack Trace massacre in early 1864, when Confederates executed wounded and captured Illinois infantrymen in Georgia. Then, for some reason, the battle for Nashville in December 1864 produced several instances of Yankees attacking helpless prisoners.[4]

But for the first three years, most Southerners flatly rejected the idea of indiscriminately killing prisoners and turning the struggle into a black-flag war. As a Christian people imbued from an early age with ideals of Southern honor and chivalry, they felt such a course violated core beliefs. When soldiers killed white prisoners, compatriots often disavowed the acts and voiced their contempt for the killers. After one such incident, a hospital matron angrily wrote, "Such men . . . bring dishonor on a brave people, and deserve punishment. . . . He has been guilty of murder, and of the most cowardly kind." Fearing no-quarter warfare, a Georgia soldier's wife begged him never to fight under the black flag. He promised he would not if he could avoid it. Also concerned, a Mississippi infantryman wrote, "I am willing to defend our rights under a Civilized banner but I am very much opposed to the Black Flag. But if the Yankees raises it first I will fight it but if our men raises it first then I am done."[5]

Their heritage of violence and a firm belief in their superiority as warriors led some Southerners to advocate a most sanguinary no-quarter war right from the beginning, arguing that it was the sure and necessary way to victory. Probably the closest any Northerner came to such Draconian proposals was an Ohio state legislator's call for Southern scalps—literally. Immediately after the attack on Fort Sumter, Assemblyman Samuel E. Brown announced, "We propose an appropriation of *one million dollars* to pay for the *scalps of rebels.*" His proposal failed while the black flag gradually became more appealing in the South. In early 1861, Thomas J. (Stonewall) Jackson had preached the fiercest resistance to Yankee invaders, "even to taking no prisoners." In mid-1862, General Beauregard publicly declared, "We will yet have to come to proclaiming this a war to the knife, when no quarter will be asked or granted." Describing himself in 1863 as monomaniac on the subject, a Texas infantry captain wrote, "I have long prayed and petitioned . . . for the black flag. The authorities and the masses were against me." In early 1864, a Georgia lieutenant urged, "War to the knife and the knife to the hilt." Later that year, a soldier in the Shenandoah Valley asserted that "It is a pity we could not surround and kill, not capture or wound, every scoundrel of them." Expressing the underlying belief that Yankees lacked the fortitude for such fighting, a 1st Alabama corporal wrote, "I sincerely believe that if the Black Flag is hoisted there would be Peace in less than six Mos."[6]

As Federals pushed deeper into the South, the demand for retribution increased. An infuriated gentleman soldier in Virginia argued, "If our government had half the nerve it ought to have we should long ago have put a stop to all this marauding by hanging up all the villains so caught to the nearest limb." But President Davis and his cabinet shied away from no-quarter measures, except for the de facto policy aimed at black Federals. They unanimously agreed that retaliation was a hazardous business, one they should reserve for the direst circumstances. Although Secretary of the Navy Stephen R. Mallory waffled about it, he finally concluded that "we must do everything consistent with honor and safety to stave off a war of retaliation." Even when they learned that Federal raiders intended to burn Richmond and kill Davis and his cabinet in February 1864, Davis forbade shooting any of the captured would-be assassins. Lee also advised against extreme measures, despite the provocation.[7]

With each passing month, though, a growing apprehension permeated Southern society. Many knew or sensed that their cause neared collapse. In one last-ditch effort, Davis sent secret missions to Europe to promise slavery's abolishment in return for recognition. But the time for that had passed and the missions failed. New, expanded, and strictly enforced conscription laws mobilized males aged seventeen to fifty, and soon the army began taking even younger boys and older men. They looked for legions from the Trans-Mississippi and earlier hoped for great results from secret weapons, such as the submarine *Hunley* or a steam-powered, bomb-dropping "artificial bird." Yet the phantom legions never came, the *Hunley* sank after its first successful mission in February, and the artificial bird never flew. As hope waned, men and women clung to prayer and the Almighty, and multitudes began to believe that their best chance lay in divine intercession. Young John Wise confirmed that thousands, pale and gaunt, firmly believed that the Deity would finally intercede. Then, absent any other source of manpower, the Confederacy voted to make soldiers of their slaves, an irony of ironies. Although favored by Lee and many ordinary soldiers and citizens, the slaveholding aristocracy fiercely opposed and delayed the move until it was too late to do any good.[8]

Desperate times require desperate remedies, which prompted Southerners to reconsider their conduct of the war. Infuriated citizens, soldiers, and newspaper editors began to call for vengeance against the northern vandals. Several camps emerged, differing only in degree. Some wanted *lex talionis* adopted, the old rule of law allowing a nation to punish enemies who engaged in banned acts. Davis apparently approved that limited response because he was pleased when he heard that no prisoners were taken from a Federal raiding party. Others pressed for black-flag warfare, granting no quarter to any captured, wounded, or surrendered Federals, white or black. War Department clerk John B. Jones reported, "Mr. Seddon . . . intimates the idea that this government is prepared to sanction the most sanguinary remedy; and I understand several members of the cabinet to always have been in favor of fighting—that is, having others fight—under the black flag." Some wanted a war to the knife without pause or remorse, a model that included taking no prisoners but that also meant applying fire and sword to as much of Yankeedom as possible.

"By this doing," asserted a Georgia soldier, "we could conquer a peace in forty days."[9]

Reprisals Escalate in the Shenandoah

First, the Yankees carried fire and sword to Virginia's Shenandoah Valley and Southerners would soon wish for an implacable Stonewall Jackson, black flag hoisted high, driving out the frightened survivors. But Jackson was dead, and now the Yankees were just as implacable. In late May, Grant ordered Major General David Hunter to advance to Lynchburg, destroying railroads, canals, and factories along the way. Hunter enlarged upon those orders considerably, proving himself a journeyman arsonist but an incompetent general. He torched, pillaged, bombarded, ruined, and punished in a manner perceived as sometimes random but always vindictive. Besides burning legitimate targets, his troops torched many private dwellings. He also executed two respected citizens, one for killing a drunken Federal soldier who attacked the citizen in his home, and the other for shooting a collaborator. Hunter made instant martyrs of the pair while earning Southerners enduring scorn, hatred, and loathing. John D. Imboden, Confederate general and Shenandoah Valley native, charged that Hunter's actions matched the "barbarism and implacable personal animosities . . . [of] The Dark Ages."[10]

After Federals burned one woman's house, the enraged owner wrote Hunter, calling him hyenalike and a monster who owned "the relentless heart of a wild beast, the face of a fiend" and declaring that heaven's angels would send his foul name spinning downward for the demons to claim. Valley people, angered by the summary executions of the two citizens, made their cries for redress heard in Richmond. There Davis thought it too late for effective retaliation, and, in any event, he still wanted to "discriminate between robbers and soldiers." Lee shrank from making innocent men suffer for the crimes of others. However, he concluded, "I can see no remedy except in refusing to make prisoners of any soldiers belonging to commands in which these outrages are perpetrated."[11]

Some Federals cringed at the wanton destruction that marked their passage. A surgeon confessed, "I am ashamed to belong to such an army under such a tyrant." An infantryman confided, "The deeds of pillaging, cruelty and robbing done by this army can't be described." But in the beginning, many apparently failed to grasp that their misdeeds had aroused a lethal rage. Rather quickly, however, they understood. That awareness caused one Federal to discard a stolen woman's shirt, fearing immediate execution if captured with it. Yet others continued to loot, and Hunter persisted in arson work even as he began a long retreat from Lynchburg. There Lieutenant General Jubal Early, sent to the valley by Lee, had decisively defeated Hunter.[12]

Grant praised Hunter's efforts in one breath and, in the next, ordered Major General Philip H. Sheridan to relieve him. Grant had wearied of half measures. He told Sheridan to follow the enemy to the death and to lay waste to the valley. Specifically, he instructed that "it is desirable that nothing should be left to invite the enemy to return. Take all provisions, forage and stock wanted . . . such as cannot be consumed, destroy." But he stipulated that buildings should be protected, an injunction that Sheridan partially ignored. He burned hundreds of barns, mills, shops, and other structures, but, unlike Hunter, he largely spared dwellings. Sheridan efficiently razed the valley, causing such havoc as to stun inhabitants and defenders. From early August 1864 to March 1865, Sheridan's troops marched up and down the valley, though the seesaw formal fighting largely ended in October when they defeated Early at Cedar Creek. During the long campaign, his cavalry conducted destructive forays that desolated the region. Brigadier General Wesley Merritt, a cavalry commander, argued, "It was a severe measure . . . but it was necessary as a measure of war." Sheridan could accurately report that "the Valley . . . will have but little in it for man or beast."[13]

On this, all agreed. By October, a Confederate surgeon reported, "The enemy has desolated this country burnt nearly all the ground + barns. It is horrible. . . . We cant subsist in this Valley this winter." That, of course, was precisely the Federal goal, one that Confederates fiercely denounced as underhanded, despicable, unlawful, and cowardly. They indignantly charged that Grant aimed to starve the men he could not beat in the field. Rejecting the legitimacy of such warfare, they saw only criminal ruin inflicted upon innocent noncombatants. Stephen D. Ramseur, a major general at age twenty-seven, voiced the common sentiment when he declared that "these miserable Yankees" had placed themselves beyond the pale by such an uncivilized campaign. Federals countered that the valley had furnished Confederates foodstuffs and men; a raiding and invasion highway for regular Confederate forces; and a shelter for bushwhackers, guerrillas, and partisans.[14]

Shenandoah's defenders reacted aggressively to the North's hard war, waylaying and killing stray Yankees and refusing quarter to small units.

On several occasions, citizens tried to lynch ordinary prisoners captured by regular troops. Partisan Rangers, semiautonomous units that might or might not be part of the regular forces, took some prisoners but dispatched others. At first Southern cavalrymen refused quarter only to those Federals detailed as arson squads, especially the house burners. Then they added to the proscribed list those they considered robbers and pillagers, the rampaging Federals who took anything they needed or fancied from anyone.[15]

Few Federals felt safe in that bitterly hostile territory. Southerners wished them gone or dead, preferably the latter. Knowing this, a Federal surgeon lamented, "Woe unto us if we fall into their hands." Another surgeon noted, "Guerrilla warfare was a favorite resort of the rebels . . . and many of our men were murdered by the cowardly villains who lurked about our camps by day as harmless farmers, and murdered our men at night dressed in Confederate uniforms." In reality, citizens, bushwhackers, and guerrillas struck at any time, and so did the partisans who often switched between citizens' garb and the uniforms of both armies. These irregulars, whether opportunistic citizens or dedicated partisans, easily blended into the area's normal activity and made it extremely difficult to identify those actively hostile. Wesley Merritt, the Federal cavalry general, declared, "The country was . . . the paradise of bushwhackers and guerrillas."[16]

Most effective were the Partisan Ranger units, much more disciplined than the shifting guerrilla bands. Well-mounted and elusive, they avoided pitched battles but were masters of swiftly executed surprise attacks, after which they quickly vanished into the woods and mountains. Some partisan bands were regularly enrolled Confederate army units, while others operated as irregulars. Most well known among the legitimate partisans was Colonel John S. Mosby, who led his 43rd Virginia Cavalry Battalion in the Shenandoah Valley and reigned over Mosby's Confederacy. Although he operated independently, he still answered to General Robert E. Lee, commanding the Army of Northern Virginia. However, no matter what the legal or military status of Partisan Ranger units, friend and foe alike looked upon them askance. Sheridan regarded all as murderous, thieving outlaw guerrillas; Lee thought they often wrought more injury than benefit to the cause.[17]

Neither irregular nor regular Southern forces could halt Sheridan's work of destruction. So they resorted to their own brand of terror. In no time at all, an expanding whirlwind of death enveloped both sides. One veteran Confederate recalled, "Our cavalry followed close after the burners and dealt out vengeance with a vengeful hand. Whenever they caught a party burning, they would take no prisoners, but shoot them down." A well-documented example of such an action occurred in mid-August, when Mosby's men found about thirty Federals torching homes. By one account, the 5th Michigan Cavalry troopers there were retaliating for the murder of one of their sentries the night before.

When the Partisans charged, their leader yelled, "No quarter! No quarter! Take no prisoners!" His orders were unnecessary. One Confederate recalled, "Worked up to madness by this scene . . . the Rangers closed in on the enemy and neither asked nor gave quarter." A *New York Times* war correspondent described it as a massacre and wrote that Federals were killed after they had surrendered. The Partisans said they killed almost every Federal, while Mosby reported that "about twenty-five of them were shot to death for their villainy." One Federal who lived, although shot in the face, said that Mosby's men executed ten men in a ditch. Given that the irregulars exterminated the thirty-man party, save for two or three badly wounded survivors, the *Times* correspondent correctly called it a massacre.[18]

The summary executions triggered a harsh response. Referring to Mosby's men, Grant ordered, "When any of them are caught with nothing to designate what they are hang them without trial." By that, he meant captives must prove they belonged to a regular unit or face immediate death. Within twenty-four hours Sheridan reported that he had "hanged one and shot six" of Mosby's men and soon added that he was "quietly disposing of a number" of the annoying guerrillas. Secretary of War Edwin M. Stanton then made sub-rosa executions the official policy. Calling the irregulars robbers and murderers, Stanton said the proper course was to "deal with them as their crimes merit, without making any report upon the subject."[19]

Ordinary soldiers, furious at the murder of comrades, took matters into their own hands. A Pennsylvania soldier wrote, "We had the pleasure of bering [burying] Mosbeys first liutenant . . . one of our Boys shot him on last Monday throu the hart he was the sunofabitch that cut so many of ower mens throats so he is gon up the spout at last[.]" When a Federal officer learned a captive belonged to Mosby's band, he told the guard, "You must not take any of them prisoners of war." So saying, he drew his revolver and shot the partisan dead. If uncertain about which person had committed a hostile act, they executed all suspects. When a shot from a house killed a soldier, Federals arrested two men on the premises. Unable to determine guilt, an officer ordered both shot. He explained that he did not take them to camp for interrogation because "I was afraid that if I did so I would be reprimanded for so doing." To simplify matters, soldiers would report they had to shoot prisoners when they attempted to escape.[20]

As partisan attacks continued, Grant urged Sheridan to capture the families of Mosby's men to ensure their good conduct. He also suggested a cavalry sweep through Loudoun County, a hotbed of irregular activity, to carry off "crops, animals, negroes, and all men under fifty years of age . . . you will get many of Mosby's men." He argued that males younger than fifty should be held as prisoners of war, not as citizen prisoners, because Confederates would inevitably force them into their army. Insulting Southern sensibilities, Federals held six prominent citizens hostage for a like number of blacks carried away by Confederate raiders. When irregulars began derailing and attacking railroad trains, Federals placed prominent Southern sympathizers or captured guerrillas on the cars, making sure they were exposed to fire. When saboteurs interfered with the Manassas Gap Railroad, Stanton ordered every nearby house torched and every civilian found within five miles of the tracks treated as a bushwhacker. Proactively, Federals organized special antiguerrilla units to hunt down the irregulars in "Mosby's Confederacy." But they could never eliminate them, mainly because the elusive enemy had the support of the populace.[21]

Invariably, retaliation produced counterretaliation, resulting in an expanding, self- sustaining cycle of violence. One such cycle began with the death of Lieutenant Charles McMaster, 2nd U. S. Cavalry, a white Regular Army regiment. McMaster traveled with a wagon train on September 24, 1864, when Mosby's men attacked near Front Royal. They fired into an ambulance, mortally wounding McMaster. With dying breath, he said Mosby's men shot him after he had surrendered. Two women who lived nearby, Southern sympathizers both, said partisans told the same story. But Confederates publicly denied it, and Mosby, who was not present, disingenuously argued, "Lieutenant McMasters was never a prisoner—no prisoners were taken." He said his men shot him in passing. However, in an unpublished account, Mosby later wrote that even if McMaster had surrendered, his men might not have realized it or, in fact, gave no quarter.[22]

Federals captured six of the irregulars and escorted them to Front Royal. Meanwhile, the story of McMaster's killing spread like wildfire and a lust for revenge gripped the troops. They also remembered the Michigan cavalrymen executed by Mosby's men and other murders. Although some uncertainty clouds the matter, apparently Brigadier General Alfred T. A. Torbert, the cavalry corps commander, ordered swift vengeance. Without trial or formality and in full view of horrified townspeople, Federals hanged or shot the six captives. One was a seventeen-year-old youth who lived in Front Royal. Longing for adventure, he had borrowed a horse and ridden off to join the attack. Returned to his home in fetters and with his mother as a spectator, he fell to an executioner's bullet, ending his boyish dreams of glory.[23]

Troops who witnessed the executions cheered the prompt retribution, with some exceptions. Colonel Charles Russell Lowell, a brigade commander, regretted his troops' role in the drama and commented, "I believe some punishment was deserved,—but I hardly think we were within the laws of war, and any violation of them opens the door to all sorts of barbarity." Lowell ignored reality. In the Shenandoah, the laws of war had already foundered. Official reports described McMaster's death but omitted the immediate reprisals. Brigadier General William H. Powell asserted it was "painful and repugnant to my own feelings," yet he never hesitated to kill captives, guilty or innocent. On October 13, Powell heard about a soldier murdered by two men, identified by name as Mosby's men. He promptly hanged a luckless prisoner from Mosby's command and pinned a placard on the corpse, explaining that the execution was a reprisal. Powell also warned that if a two-to-one retaliation for murder was insufficient, "I will increase it to twenty-two-to-one."[24]

Mosby wanted to strike back but first sought approval from Lee. Without mentioning McMaster, he wrote that Brigadier General George A. Custer had ordered the six partisans executed at Front Royal and that Powell had hanged a seventh man. He also complained that Federals placed hostages on trains and had classified him and his men as guerrillas, subject to the death penalty if captured. Mosby told Lee, "As my command has done nothing contrary to the usages of war . . . some attempt at least ought to be made to prevent a repetition of such barbarities. . . . It is my purpose to hang an equal number of Custer's men." Lee said he did not know what could be done about the train hostages but authorized Mosby to retaliate for the executions. Secretary of War Seddon also approved and added that he knew what to do about the hostages. He advised killing the conductors and Federal officers on hostage trains.

Mosby quickly ordered twenty-seven prisoners, most from Custer's regiments, to take part in a death lottery. Seven of them would die—six for those executed at Front Royal and one for the man hanged by Powell. After the highly charged drawing on November 6, 1864, guards marched the seven losers toward Winchester and their doom. One Federal saved himself by appealing to a fellow Mason among partisans they met on the way, and he was traded for one of their prisoners. Soon after, two separately escaped, and another pair, though shot twice each, survived the ordeal. Nothing, however, saved the last three. A note pinned to one corpse proclaimed that they had paid the price for Custer's actions at Front Royal and concluded, "Measure for measure."[25]

Mosby notified Sheridan that it was retaliation but later insisted that it was a "judicial sentence," imposed to save the lives of Federals and Confederates alike. As additional justification, Mosby argued, "No further acts of barbarity were committed on my men." It was true that no more public death spectacles took place. Yet the killing and reprisals never ceased. One of Mosby's men complained about their portrayal as a black-flag gang of thuggish robbers, recalling, "Prisoners . . . expressed surprise that they were taken alive, unless it were our purpose to reserve them for some worse fate than a speedy death." He also noted that regular Southern soldiers often shared that view. It was true enough that the partisans scarcely murdered every prisoner. They took hundreds alive and sent them off to prisoner-of-war camps. Yet the many killings formed the basis for their dark reputation, and uncertainty about their behavior strengthened it. Voicing that common perception, a wary 5th Michigan Cavalry officer observed that "it was no good time to be taken prisoner."[26]

When Sheridan finished with the Shenandoah Valley, the once-lush region had largely become a stricken wasteland. So barren and blackened was much of the countryside that Federals stopped their destructive visits. A Front Royal youth recalled, "They had cleaned up the country so thoroughly that it was hardly necessary to return; for they could not find enough food for the men and horses." By the end of the year, with deep snow covering the bluegrass, the irregulars and their mounts grew weak from hunger. For the want of sustenance, some partisans thought it sensible to disband. Confronting harsh reality, one partisan sighed that the "starry cross was being enveloped in the gloom of annihilation."[27]

By then, most soldiers and some civilians had realized their cause neared collapse. In a poignant letter to his wife, a Georgia soldier confessed, "I am whipped. Sallie, we are a ruined people. There is no chance for us . . . we have done all we can." In early December, an Alabama infantryman wrote, "The boys are generally very much out of heart and say it is no use to fight any longer." Yet they stayed, cold, hungry, and desperate, sick or shell shocked, heeding the call of duty, country, honor, or comrades. Sweet reason and cold logic were no match for those powerful feelings, which helps explain the continued resistance by soldiers, guerrillas, and citizens. Desperation surely drove them to murder Federal soldiers for little gain but at great cost. Still, they must have known that fearful, swift punishment would follow, unlike the pain-less verbal abuse and studied inaction that ensued when they massacred black Federals.[28]

Brutal Murders Mark Weldon March

Southern citizens felt that wrath in early December near Petersburg while Confederate Major General Wade Hampton's cavalry got away with mur-der. Federal Major General Gouverneur Warren's reinforced 5th Army Corps, about twenty-five thousand strong, had marched southward on December 7 to destroy a stretch of the Weldon railroad. Dark skies and severe inclement weather clouded their march across the eerily deserted landscape beyond Sussex Courthouse. They saw few men, and many houses were empty or occupied only by women and children. They met very little opposition but found much applejack along the way. It was so plentiful that the troops irreverently called the expedition the "apple jack raid." That liquor, coupled with the bad weather and a hard night march, caused considerable straggling.[29]

Even on the outward-bound trip, Federals had a foretaste of what lay in store for those who ignored march discipline. Colonel Charles S. Wainwright, an artilleryman, watched as Confederate horsemen suddenly dashed across the road between Federal infantry and cavalry. Left by the roadside was a soldier, "so drunk that he could not stand." Wainwright related that "the squad of rebs . . . tried to take him along but could not, so one of them shot him through the brain with his pistol while the oth-ers pulled off his boots, and left the body. The whole thing was done in a minute."[30]

They reached the Weldon on December 9 and tore up twenty miles of track in two days. Then a fierce storm broke, bringing sleet, snow, bitter cold, and misery to men and animals. Their goal achieved, the troops started back. While they had seen scarcely any male citizens, they soon saw grisly proof of hidden enemies. Along and off the road, they began to find many stripped and mutilated frozen bodies of fellow soldiers. Among the many dead were men detailed to protect householders from pillaging. Private John Haley, 17th Maine, said the discoveries were "calculated to set our bile in motion and to keep us on the march." Unwary men, stragglers, home safeguards, and besotted soldiers were the victims. Battle-hardened Private Charles R. Cox, 1st Maryland, confided, "I never saw anything that harrowed my feelings so before. . . . None but devils could do such deeds." Still shaken days later, Corporal Smith McDonald, 110th Pennsylvania, told about four comrades who had had their throats cut or who were clubbed to death.[31]

More and more stiff, frozen bodies turned up as they marched along. Colonel Robert McAllister, a brigade commander, said they had not gone far when he learned that six or seven dead soldiers lay together in the woods not far from the road. He told his wife, "It was a sad sight. From appearances they had been stripped of all their clothing and, when in the act of kneeling in a circle, they were shot in the head—murdered in coldblood by the would-be 'Chivalry of the South.'" They also found bodies in the small village at Sussex Courthouse and just beyond. Sergeant George Fowle, 39th Massachusetts, reported that "gurillers killed three of our stragglers near the courthouse." Angry Federals also uncovered several murdered men, identified as fellow Yankees, freshly buried in a cellar. Just beyond the courthouse, they found another naked corpse they recognized as a comrade.[32]

Citizens along the route had no immediate cause for mayhem and murder. The Yankees had not raped, plundered, or destroyed. Chaplain Lorenzo Barber, 2nd U.S. Sharpshooters, declared, "Until these outrages were discovered but little destruction of private property had occurred." Blind fury gripped the troops after they found the brutalized bodies, and they promptly fell to avenging the murdered men. With or without orders, up and down the long column, the troops began putting every structure, deserted or inhabited, to the torch. Cox, the 1st Maryland soldier, reported that "orders were issued to burn everything for five miles on each side of the road. It was done with a vengeance. It was a track of fire day and night. . . . The cavalry burnt the houses in our rear while we marched along." Undoubtedly it was done with a vengeance, but Brigadier General Joshua L. Chamberlain, a hero of Gettysburg, reported the torching extended only to a half mile on either side of his brigade's line of march, a more reasonable swath of destruction for foot soldiers.[33]

Colonel Wainwright related, "Scores of men . . . fired every building in sight. None escaped . . . all were burnt, with barely time for the people themselves to get out, saving nothing." He thought it a pitiable sight to see women and children turned adrift in the arctic cold and snow of the winter night. For the record, Warren insisted, "Every effort was made by the officers to stop this incendiarism (which most likely punished only the innocent), and with partial success." But a division's official report related that "nearly every building . . . for miles, was given to the flames." An artillery officer explained, "Coming back, we made clean work of the buildings on the route in retaliation for some of our men who were . . . murdered and mutilated." Their fiery retribution lit the dark winter sky and left mounds of ash and naked chimneys in a swath for twenty miles along the road, making a "sublime sight," according to one soldier.

They knew the best response was to punish the guilty. But almost all the men had fled, so they could catch only a few suspects. While burying the naked corpse found just beyond the courthouse, a black man pointed out the house where the killer hid under corn shucks in the garret. Searchers found him there and there they left him. They fired the house, consuming killer and dwelling. After they found other bodies and some wounded survivors around the small village, they acted swiftly. Private Haley reported, "Some of the residents were seized, and not being able to prove an alibi or explain certain suspicious circumstances, they were hung in the Court House yard." After unearthing the three soldiers freshly buried in the cellar, they arrested the householder. Whether he was accessory, accomplice, murderer, or entirely innocent was of no moment. It was his house, his cellar. Corporal Cox wrote, "The owner of the house was hung without judge or jury." For good measure, they also looted stores and burned the courthouse.[34]

If body counts were the measure, Southerners won the contest. They quietly and efficiently murdered scores, while the Yankees hanged just a few. Federal infantry counted but a handful of casualties from the few clashes with Confederate cavalry. One division commander noted that they "were not at any time during the expedition engaged with the enemy," and yet he had to report fifty-eight men as missing. Confusing and incomplete reports showed 5 killed, 3 wounded, and 136 missing, although a 5th Corps surgeon counted 40 wounded in a cavalry hospital at Sussex Courthouse. Probably some missing men turned up later, but officers thought most had fallen prey to Southern citizens or cavalry. Wade Hampton, the Confederate cavalry leader, probably exaggerated when he reported capturing from 250 to 300 prisoners, and he certainly did so when he made it sound as if his horsemen had repulsed the railroad-wrecking expedition. Once again, the exact number of victims and legitimate casualties will remain unknown.[35]

Those responsible for the atrocious killings brought death and destruction to the very people and land they sought to defend. Yet such efforts persisted to the end. On April 5, just four days before Lee surrendered, Private Haley reported that some irregulars thought they could slow the Federal march to Appomattox. With his sprightly gallows humor, he related that "a few of our men went to check the poultry interests of this section. They were beset by guerrillas who served them as they had served the hens: cut their throats and plucked their clothing."[36]

16

Murder in the West

HISTORIANS SOMETIMES DEBATE when and to what extent, or even if, Southern citizens and soldiers realized they fought a losing fight. Most agree, however, that many Confederate soldiers gradually realized they could not win. One recent study includes the "Diagram of Confederate Expectations and Victory" that shows already low hopes plummeting when Federal armies invaded the Southern heartland in 1864. So it was that the war in the West changed as Sherman's troops pushed a bow wave of fear and anguish before them, generating simmering rage and much desperation. As in the East, weaker Confederates eventually reacted by killing prisoners they considered outlaws rather than honorable soldiers. While it made no sense to execute captives and thus invite retaliation from the numerically superior forces of the Yankee enemy, Southerners swayed to their own cultural drumbeat. Extreme violence was ever the solution when friend or enemy threatened or affronted their values. So it was as much redemption as punishment when they cut a Federal's throat for burning or plundering a Southern home under the North's hard-war policy.

Sherman started his Atlanta campaign on May 7 and steadily pushed southward. Fighting larger and better equipped Federal forces, Confederates steadily gave way, and many began to feel the Northern armies were unstoppable. Private M. J. Bigbie, 33rd Alabama, wrote home, "It is all most un crettibul to tell how wee have kild and slaurterd the yanks and still their seems to be fight in them." With a brave front, he added, "I believe that wee air bound to whip them in this fight though wee have fell back and lost a good deal of ground." More analytical, Minnesota artilleryman Thomas D. Christie in early August wrote, "The desperate offensive fighting of the Enemy . . . show that they know the end is nigh. . . . Everything shows that they are desperate—that is, the Leaders, as for the men, they wish the thing ended."[1]

Both sides generally observed the proprieties when Sherman began his drive to Atlanta, although there were some exceptions to that decorum. When an overzealous or excited Confederate shot a Federal during a truce, his officers acted to repair the breach of faith. Without hesitation, they sent the guilty man across the lines for suitable punishment. A New York artillery corporal acknowledged, "There is honor in them when they agree not to shoot." While the Yankees appreciated the gesture, they sent the soldier back, saying they could not shoot him in cold blood. However, cracks soon appeared in that correct, polite facade. In late April, Confederates shot the wounded and prisoners from the 92nd Illinois Mounted Infantry at Nickajack Trace, Georgia, An angry Federal wrote, "The 92nd have always been very kind to prisoners but after this there will be very few taken by us." In late July, Southerners slew survivors of a trapped raiding force led by Major General George Stoneman. Colonel Horace Capron, a brigade commander, reported, "It is impossible to give the number of killed and wounded, and the fate of many will always be unknown. The men . . . were pursued by both Confederate soldiers and citizens, and undoubtedly a large number were murdered by them even after they surrendered."[2]

The battle for Atlanta and its occupation insulted Southern sensibilities when Federal artillery pounded the city, compelling beleaguered citizens to dig bombproofs in their backyards. Then exploding munitions and raging fires ruined whole districts. Southerners blamed the Yankees for the destruction, although Confederates had also blown up ammunition trains and contributed to the damage. An even-greater outcry roiled the heavens when Sherman ordered all citizens to leave Atlanta after its fall in September 1. They could go north or south, but go they must. He said he did not want to be bothered with or by civilians. Later he said the expulsion decree sent a double message to the South. It was that "one . . . we were in earnest; and . . . if they were sincere in their common and popular clamor 'to die in the last ditch,' that the opportunity would soon come."[3]

Sherman thought that people might "raise a howl against my barbarity and cruelty," and he was right. He replied that war was war, and, anyway, he was not engaged in a popularity contest. Actually, the evacuation order's impact was limited. While Atlanta's population had reached a wartime high of twenty-two thousand before the siege, a voluntary exodus had taken place during the fighting, and probably only about three thousand people remained when the order came. Nevertheless, to many Southerners, Sherman had reached heights of brutality remarkable even for a Yankee. One Confederate officer described him as *the fiend in human form.* President Davis characterized the order as inhuman. In an angry exchange with Sherman, Hood called it "barbarous cruelty." He vowed that "we will fight you to the death. Better die a thousand deaths than submit to live under you or your Government and your negro allies."[4]

Federals Fear Short Shrift in Georgia

With his troops rested and reinforced, Sherman left Atlanta in mid-November to lead his great march to the sea. He told Grant that "if the North can march an army right through the South, it is proof positive that the North can prevail in this contest." He also wrote, "Until we can repopulate Georgia, it is useless to occupy it, but the utter destruction of its roads, houses, and people will cripple their military resources." Sherman ordered his troops to forage liberally, and so they stripped the land of livestock, slaves, and provisions. Captain David P. Conyngham, a volunteer aide and *New York Herald* correspondent, charged that the foraging orders "were soon converted into licenses for indiscriminate plunder . . . without any order or discipline, [foragers] pounced like harpies on the unfortunate inhabitants, stripping them of all provisions, jewelry, and valuables." When foragers descended upon her plantation, one woman calculated that in a few hours they caused a $30,000 loss, a very large sum in those days. Advancing on a broad front, the Federal columns burned railroad depots, mills, factories, cotton, and any other property deemed useful to the Confederacy. Villages, towns, and homes also went up in flames, frequently after a thorough sacking. Contrary to popular belief, however, they did not indiscriminately torch private homes—that came later in South Carolina. Still, a Massachusetts infantry officer reported that they left the countryside a "howling waste."[5]

Southerners soon viewed Sherman's armies as a Vandal horde bent on wanton destruction. A 47th Alabama soldier wrote that "it seems as if their whole intention is to burn and destroy every thing where ever they go." That assessment, even if not strictly true, showed the effectiveness of Sherman's effort to demoralize and terrorize, even causing some Federals to sympathize with Southern civilians. Early on, a 10th Indiana officer wrote, "Can you imagine how these southerners feel seeing their homes and families destroyed? Even though they started this rebellion their wives and children don't deserve to starve." Writing home, a Wisconsin soldier confessed, "I feel so sorry for the poor women, of whom so many were forced to become bad." Many condemned the looting and some condoned Confederate countermeasures. Denouncing the looters, a 2nd Massachusetts Infantry captain noted that pillagers "often fell to the tender mercies of Wheeler's cavalry, and were never heard of again, earning a fate richly deserved."[6]

Sherman's men quickly grasped the peril and realized they could expect little mercy from an infuriated enemy. Shortly after leaving Atlanta, Sergeant William B. Miller, 75th Indiana Infantry, wrote in his diary, "Some Bush Whackers attacted our foragers. . . . They hung some that they Captured which shows that it will not be good for us to fall into their hands." When an infantry major could not stop rowdy soldiers from burning a village near Atlanta, he declared, "If we are to continue our devastation as we began today I don't want to be captured on this trip, for I expect every man of us the rebels capture will get a 'stout rope and a short shrift.'" Just ten days into the march, a staff officer decided that *"we must not be taken prisoners.* I confess that I don't expect any mercy if captured: and the worst of it is that the 'foraging' or pillaging of our men is bound to bring this about. It is all wrong." Always, men moving alone or in small groups took a big risk, and foraging remained a dangerous business. Near the end in North Carolina, an Iowa sergeant wrote, "The Enemy killed all of our men that they caught foraging. You had better believe *that this childe kept close to the road.*"[7]

Murderous actions by Confederates had concerned Sherman's men even before they stepped off on the great march. A firing squad execution particularly caught their attention. On November 2, some Federal troops marched in a steady rain north of Atlanta. That wet curtain enabled watching Confederates to draw close and snap up four soldiers. Captain Charles W. Wills, 103rd Illinois Infantry, reported that they were captured "by 30 rebels and taken eight or ten miles, then formed in line and ordered to about face and fired upon; two fell dead and the other two ran away."[8]

Usually, Major General Joseph Wheeler's cavalrymen served as the executioners. Wheeler, a West Point graduate, commanded Confederate cavalry during Sherman's march across Georgia. With a small force of about three thousand mounted men, Wheeler could only harass the much larger Federal columns. Possibly he hoped the constant attacks upon foragers would deprive Federals of food, thus compelling Sherman to reverse course. A simple desire for vengeance spurred his men. One of them related, "It was silently determined . . . to revenge themselves on the barbarous acts of the foragers of the foe." They shadowed Federal columns and, as one Confederate said, when they found Federals "burning up the country as well as robbing it . . . we did not give them any quarter but shot them down as we overtook them." To illustrate, he said that once they captured forty Federals guilty of "more than the usual devilment." They lined up the prisoners in a lane, told them to run, and then killed every one.[9]

Some units specialized in hunting and killing foragers. Foremost among them were Shannon's Scouts, a roving band of forty-five men detached from Terry's Texas Rangers, the 8th Texas Cavalry. In every way, they operated as an officially sanctioned execution squad. Besides gaining information, their purpose was "punishing marauders wherever found engaged in their nefarious business of robbing and burning homes." In even plainer language, an 6th Texas officer said that "they became quite efficient in killing Yankees without capturing any they found burning houses or insulting women." To that end, Private Enoch O. John, one of Shannon's Scouts, reported they liquidated almost one hundred prisoners in two weeks. In one instance, after capturing fifty-six Federals, John wrote, "We then armed some of the citizens with their guns and let the citizens send them off."[10]

If certain reports appear improbable or embroidered, perhaps they are. But many similar accounts have emerged from a broad spectrum of observers, so that the whole is credible. At the time, Confederates often reacted to baseless horror stories. While ordinary foraging, vandalism, and thievery by Yankees sufficed to push them to murder, reports of rape made them wild and truly homicidal. As the terrible rumors had it, Federal soldiers overnight transformed into manic rapists, sexually assaulting maid and matron. Just a week after Sherman left Atlanta, the frightful stories had already gained currency. Although Federals stoutly denied the charges and some Southerners attested that they knew of no "personal outrages," a euphemism for rape, the dark tales were endlessly repeated among Southern soldiers and civilians. Soon the spurious accusations were enshrined in the region's lore and officially adopted by Confederate leaders. Lieutenant General Wade Hampton, who led Confederate cavalry in the Carolinas after transferring from Virginia, gave his imprimatur to the charges. He asserted that Federals were more savage than Indians, who at least "always respected the persons of . . . female captives." In essence, the rape indictments served as an even more potent inducement and justification for summary executions.[11]

Apparently, many women accepted the rape stories at face value. When Confederate troops passed through sections recently traversed by Federal columns, women urged them to "kill all the wretches." To what extent Confederate soldiers believed or merely professed to believe the rape reports is uncertain. Nevertheless, they acted upon it. Soldiers who executed some foragers explained that "the enemy killed were a party going from house to house ravishing women." They did not, however, offer any evidence of a crime that cried out for such punishment. In another dark tale of criminal lust and swift vengeance, some of Wheeler's men reported they found a woman raving that seven Federal stragglers had tied her up and then, before her eyes, had their will upon her daughter, raping her to death. Mounting their horses, they chased the alleged gang rapists, caught them, and cut their throats.[12]

If Sherman "almost disembowlled the rebellion," as one of his officers said, Confederates almost decapitated many captured Federals. Whether an expression of rage or a desire to inflict special punishment, the cutting of throats from ear to ear became a popular way for Confederates to kill prisoners. Although throat cutting has the ring of an atrocity fable and is obviously a messy, inefficient way to dispatch captives, accounts by many on both sides leave no doubt that such gruesome executions occurred. Sherman's men reported these mutilation deaths throughout, from near Atlanta to North Carolina. Near the end at Raleigh, North Carolina, an

Ohio infantryman wrote home, "We are well aware that they did not carry on a sival warfair before, for we have found here of late many of our men tied up to trees with there throats cut."[13]

That want of "sival warfair" did not mean that no quarter was the absolute rule. Confederates captured and spared many Federals, especially those taken in regular battles. Even then, however, they had to place extra guards around prisoners to protect them from angry soldiers. One officer frankly admitted, "Our men can scarcely be restrained from killing them even after they surrender, and I have no doubt that several have been cruelly murdered." But many captured Federals never reached a prisoner-of-war pen. During a Federal raid to destroy a railway bridge in late November, the 4th Tennessee Cavalry captured four raiders. 1st Lieutenant George B. Guild said a higher-ranking officer ordered the prisoners executed. Although he protested, his objections went unheeded. Guild watched his own soldiers shoot the Federals who tumbled over into high sage. He condemned the act, declaring that "nothing can excuse the killing of prisoners." But, at that juncture, his was a lonely voice.[14]

Confederates raised the stakes considerably when they executed Federals captured in conventional battles. On November 22, for instance, a Confederate force of mostly raw militiamen attacked an infantry brigade holding a strong defensive position at Griswoldville. Before the main fight began, Wheeler's men captured eighteen troopers of the 9th Pennsylvania Cavalry and, during the battle, two Federal infantrymen went missing. Federal Colonel Charles H. Howard reported that most of the prisoners were murdered, some by slashing their throats. They learned this, Howard related, from one or two men who were left for dead but survived because their throats were cut too high up, missing vital blood vessels.[15]

This was too much for Brigadier General Hugh J. Kilpatrick, the Federal cavalry commander. He angrily reported his men were killed after they had surrendered, and he urged prompt reprisals. Impatiently, he wrote Sherman again, repeating the charge and the need for retribution. Sherman replied, "As regards *retaliation*, you must be very careful as to the correctness of any information . . . about the enemy *murdering or mutilating* our men." He gave Kilpatrick permission to retain captured Confederates as hostages, to tell Wheeler about the murders, and to advise him that retaliation loomed. Sherman concluded, "When our men are found, and you are fully convinced the enemy have killed them after surrender . . . or have mutilated their bodies after being killed in fair battle, you may hang and mutilate man for man without regard to rank."[16]

Sherman adopted a cautious approach for several reasons. He worried that some atrocity reports were exaggerated or unfounded. Perhaps he also thought the gruesome deaths were isolated events that did not represent a real shift in Confederate policy. Possibly he hoped that threats of retaliation alone would halt atrocities. Certainly he wanted to avoid precipitating escalating rounds of reprisals. There is no official record of immediate retaliation by Kilpatrick, although also unrecorded are many summary executions by Confederates. For example, there is no mention of a cavalry patrol's slaughter about that time, though the 14th Corps' commander visited the ambush site and saw the bodies. Often matters were discussed verbally and never entered into the written record, so perhaps the freewheeling Kilpatrick retaliated without making written reports.[17]

Sherman's generals banned straggling, strengthened foraging parties, and drove away lurking enemy horsemen, but these defensive measures could reduce but never stop the murders. In late November, for instance, an infantry brigade commander drove off hovering enemy cavalry only after they had murdered three of his men the previous night. By the time they reached Savannah, Georgia, in December, most soldiers knew that surrender or capture might mean death, long a near certainty for black troops. Thereupon the war became a personal matter and ordinary soldiers believed retaliation was necessary. More restrained than most, a Swedish American from Minnesota related that Confederates "mistreated and killed their prisoners. To hear how ruthless they were causes my blood to boil in my veins." Still, he tempered his vengeful thoughts with the belief that the Lord should judge such miscreants. Even so, he added that "punishments can be of some good, for we chastise those we love."[18]

Many men thought the march to Savannah a walk in the park, "an agreeable journey, full of interest," as one officer said. It was not a pleasant stroll for all. Though no major battles occurred, frequent skirmishes resulted in casualties. From November 15 to Sherman's arrival before Savannah on December 10, Federals counted 136 killed, 673 wounded, and 280 missing. Included among the dead were some murdered men, but many no-quarter victims were never found and listed as missing. But some counted as missing survived capture and went to prisoner-of-war camps. As noted, the official reports do not list all those murdered, and some duplication occurred in the unofficial accounts. So, the number of Federals executed after capture again eludes an accurate count. A conservative estimate is that Confederates probably executed 150 or more captives during the march to the sea.[19]

Vengeance Sears the Carolinas

As Sherman prepared to march northward through the Carolinas, his troops planned severe punishment for South Carolina. In their view, that state had instigated the war. So they determined to square accounts with the hotbed of rebellion and to torch everything flammable. Captain David P. Conyngham, still doubling as a war correspondent, had returned from Nashville and wrote, "In Georgia few houses were burned; here few escaped." First, they stripped the country bare, "like so many locusts." What they could not carry off or did not want, they destroyed. A Wisconsin officer explained that it was "the general practice of most of the troops to set every unoccupied house on fire." If the home was occupied, soldiers often made it vacant by ejecting its occupants and then burning it down. Dismayed, a Confederate officer recalled, "We could observe the approach of Sherman's army by the smoke of burning houses and barns."[20]

That destruction accelerated mercy's flight from Southern hearts. Near Robertsville in early February 1865, three Indiana infantrymen left their column and went to a nearby farmhouse to ask for food. Soon they saw sixteen of Wheeler's men approaching. They implored the householder not to give them away and then ran for nearby woods. When the cavalrymen arrived, the elderly farmer pointed toward the woods. Wheeler's men quickly tracked down the three Federals and killed them. "They each had been shot two to four times," a Wisconsin soldier reported. Before that discovery, the farmer had brazenly asked for a guard to protect his home. It was then that a black man, a witness to the whole thing, told what he knew. An angry Brigadier General John W. Geary arrested the farmer as an accessory to murder and ordered farmhouse and outbuildings burned to the ground.[21]

Much more often than in Georgia, Federals burned villages and towns in South Carolina. First they plundered and then burned in whole or part places like Grahamsville, Rarysburg, or Gillisonville, and larger places like Robertsville and Cheraw. Much of Columbia, a city overflowing with refugees, became a charred ruin overnight on February 17, 1865. While the responsibility for Columbia's fire is disputed, the inhabitants blamed Sherman's men. Emma LeConte, who watched the city burn, heard that the bodies of Federal soldiers were found in smoldering ruins. She exclaimed, "How I rejoice . . . if only the whole army could have been roasted alive." LeConte added, "Before they came here, I thought I hated them as much as was possible—now I know there are no limits to the feeling of hatred." When the troops left, a few stragglers became prisoners, and one guard wondered what to do with his captive. "Kill him," cried a young woman, a doctor's daughter who had lost all pity.[22]

Murders increased after Columbia, although perhaps that was mere coincidence. From the right wing, Major Thomas W. Osborn reported on February 22, "Two of our men were found today with their brains beat out, and from all appearances had been captured and murdered." From the left with Sherman's staff, Captain George W. Nichols wrote on February 24:

> Within the last week the Rebel cavalry have committed atrocities upon our foragers. . . . In one instance, a courier was found hanged on the roadside, with a paper attached to his person bearing the words, 'Death to all foragers.' In another instance, three men were found shot, with a similar notice upon their persons. Yesterday, our cavalry . . . found twenty-one of our infantry soldiers lying dead, with their throats cut. . . . All of us understand that the reason assigned for these butcheries is a cruel farce, and that any one of us will meet the same fate if we fall into their bloody hands. There is but one course . . . retaliation, and that fourfold.[23]

Kilpatrick apparently referred to these deaths when he wrote Wheeler on February 22. He said his troopers had found a murdered artillery sergeant and then eight infantrymen, their bodies mutilated and with a note reading "Death to foragers." He charged that the 8th Texas Cavalry, armed with captured repeating rifles, was responsible. Kilpatrick added, "Nine of my cavalrymen were also found murdered yesterday. . . . This makes in all eighteen Federal soldiers murdered yesterday by your people." Kilpatrick said he would shoot the same number of Wheeler's men he held as prisoners unless he received a prompt and satisfactory explanation. Furthermore, he vowed fearful revenge, including burning every house he could reach, if any more murders occurred.

Wheeler denied all. "Much shocked" by the allegations, he believed Kilpatrick mistaken but promised to investigate. However, he declared that neither of his two Texas regiments had repeating rifles or had either taken part in any engagements on the day in question. True, Shannon's Scouts were detached from the 8th Texas, but they certainly remained under Wheeler's command. They used captured Spencer repeaters, and they undoubtedly had murdered the infantrymen. Furthermore, if Wheeler had not known of their atrocities, he learned it from Confederates freed in a field prisoner exchange. They angrily complained that the Scouts' homicidal ways had almost put them before Federal firing squads. Yet Wheeler warned that if Kilpatrick executed his men, he would regard that as murder and act accordingly. In turn, Kilpatrick said he was satisfied with Wheeler's reply and would not shoot any captives. But he warned that if the murders persisted—and he thought they would—he would encourage his troops to retaliate, death for death, man for man.[24]

So many men murdered in one day caused Sherman to decide enough was enough. On February 23, he issued categorical orders to subordinates: "If any of your foragers are murdered, take life for life." To Kilpatrick went the imperative, "You must retaliate man for man. . . . Let it be done at once." Further, Sherman ordered that each corpse bear a label stating that the body represented one-for-one retaliation. Sherman declared that Southerners must realize that they could not dictate the laws of war or peace. Then he wrote Lieutenant General Wade Hampton, the new Confederate cavalry commander. Citing the recent murders, Sherman said he had ordered a similar number of captives executed. He warned, "I hold about 1,000 prisoners . . . and can stand it as long as you." Defending his right to forage, Sherman conceded that it sometimes led to misbehavior. But again he insisted, "I cannot permit an enemy to judge or punish with wholesale murder."

Hampton, whom Sherman derided as a boastful, self-proclaimed champion of South Carolina, quickly replied with a torrent of accusations, denunciations, and counterthreats. He denied that his men killed prisoners "except under circumstances . . . [when] it was perfectly legitimate and proper." In his view, that condition obtained when Federals fired the dwellings of citizens they had just robbed. To stop that, Hampton wrote, "I have directed my men to shoot down all of your men who are caught burning houses." He also said he did not question the right to forage but warned that Federals did so at their own peril. That risk, he asserted, stemmed from an older and more inalienable prerogative—the right of every man to defend his home and protect his dependents. Finally, he declared that "from my heart I wish that every old man and boy . . . would shoot down, as he would a wild beast, the men who are desolating their land, burning their homes, and insulting their women."[25]

Hampton certainly expressed Southern sentiments about Yankee foragers. However, he and they applied a double standard. As recently as July 1864, Confederates had foraged, pillaged, and burned on the way to Washington. After obeying orders to burn Chambersburg, Pennsylvania,

Confederate Brigadier General Bradley T. Johnson condemned the conduct of Southern soldiers. He declared, "Every crime in the catalogue of infamy has been committed, I believe, except murder and rape." Fighting on their own soil but needing supplies their government could not provide, Confederate soldiers robbed fellow Southerners. "Our Brig behaved shamefully all the way around from Tupelo Miss to Raleigh N. C.," wrote a Texas infantryman. Major General Jacob D. Cox, a corps commander under Sherman, reported that "leading [Southern] newspapers demanded the cashiering and shooting of colonels . . . called their conduct worse than the enemy's." As usual, cavalrymen, many of them Wheeler's troopers, were the worst offenders. Indeed, a Confederate artillery officer referred to them as "Wheeler's drunken, plundering Cavalry."[26]

For most Southerners, there was no visible double standard. It just depended upon whose ox was being gored. On February 25, just after Sherman issued his reprisal orders, Confederate cavalrymen killed two 15th Corps foragers. John E. Smith, their division commander, reported, "Two of our men were brutally murdered, in plain view of our skirmishers, after having surrendered, in retaliation for which I ordered two of their men, who were taken in our uniform, to be shot, which was done on the spot." A week later, a similar case excited sympathy for both the dead Federal and the hapless Confederate shot in retaliation. On March 1, a 30th Illinois forager was found beaten to death. In obedience to Sherman's order to take life for a life, the 17th Army Corps commander ordered his provost marshal to select a prisoner and deliver him for execution. That officer avoided the unsettling responsibility by compelling prisoners to play a death lottery. "They were made to draw chits to see who would dye," related one Federal. Losing the draw was a forty-five-year-old father of six children, and some Federals felt sorry for him.[27]

Although a few Confederates mention Sherman's threat to retaliate, it is uncertain how many of them knew about it at the time. Moreover, some who knew dismissed the threat as a bluff. Retaliatory vows and actions had no chance of success unless widely circulated and believed. Sherman did order explanatory placards placed on the bodies of executed men, and Confederates affixed their "Death to Foragers" notes. But both sides ignored those messages and the spiraling violence became fully self-sustaining.[28]

Killing prisoners had no effect on the campaign's course. Sherman slashed through South Carolina without difficulty and left ruin behind. In North Carolina, however, Federal commanders forbade indiscriminate burning because many Unionist people lived in that state, the last to secede. That order was not always obeyed, and one soldier admitted, "Quite a few houses were burned in North Carolina also." When they saw cavalry approaching Fayetteville, North Carolina, a young girl remembered, "It was like the knell of doom." Even as doom neared, murder and retribution continued. Confederates shot one Federal as he lay wounded in bed and another as he stood with fellow prisoners. When Kilpatrick's men entered the open city of Raleigh, North Carolina, a Confederate cavalry officer recklessly emptied his revolver at the advancing Federals. According to a woman who vividly recalled the incident, the Yankees quickly captured and hanged the rash young man.[29]

For Sherman's troops, the war had already ended. They fought their final battle at Bentonville, North Carolina, on March 19. Then Sherman advanced to Goldsboro, where he assembled eighty thousand troops to overwhelm remaining Confederate forces. General Joseph E. Johnston, reinstated to command in the war's last weeks, knew that Lee had already given up and that the cause was lost. He asked for an armistice on April 14 and surrendered on April 26, 1865.[30]

Casualties were light for the Carolinas campaign, considering the 425 miles traversed through hostile territory, the constant skirmishing, and the several battles fought in North Carolina. For the three-month-long campaign, including clashes at Kinston, Averasboro, and Bentonville, Federal troops sustained about thirty-eight hundred casualties. They listed 450 killed, 2,043 wounded, and 1,301 captured or missing. Dead and missing lists included soldiers murdered or refused quarter, so again their numbers cannot be determined. Probably at least fifty Federals were killed after surrendering in the Carolinas. Though the toll was small compared to the overall loss, those deaths had a disproportionate effect on Sherman's men. Most knew that they had balanced on the edge of an abyss, a descent into no-quarter savagery. Not only did they shudder at the fearsome prospect, but they also thought it barbaric.[31]

17

Mobile and Selma

APRIL 1865 BECAME THE WORST and the best month for the North and the cruelest time of all for the South. At last the Confederacy collapsed, the war ended, the sundered nation came together again, a fanatic assassinated Lincoln, while Davis took to futile flight. But even as the war and the South convulsed in dying spasms, men fought and fell, and there still remained time for Forrest and for black soldiers to commit their last atrocities. In his final ignoble victory, Forrest and his escort massacred sleeping or groggy white Yankees near Selma and black troops slaughtered surrendered Rebels at Mobile, both in Alabama. At the time, however, North and South soon forgot about these concluding examples of no-quarter warfare. Events surrounding the war's abrupt end overwhelmed civilians and soldiers alike.

Just three weeks earlier, a black regiment's colonel wrote, "I do not see how our Southern brethren are to stand another season, it seems to me their game is nearly up. How they hold on is a mystery, for endurance they certainly deserve great credit. I wish they had less of it." Starving, freezing, and devoid of hope, Confederates endured, although they knew they could not hold on for long. 1st Sergeant James E. Whitehorne, 12th Virginia Infantry, mournfully confided, "I have fought, suffered, bled and almost died for nearly four years, but I fear the end is very near." Some rejected such talk, at least for home consumption. Colonel William R. J. Pegram, Lee's bright young artillery officer, insisted in mid-March that Confederate prospects were "growing brighter each day," and he scorned the "croakers & cowards" in Richmond. Confronting their dire situation head-on, one of Lee's tattered regiments adopted a pragmatic proposal: "Resolved, that in case our army is overwhelmed and broken up, we will bushwhack them; that is, some of us will."[1]

But the war was not over yet, although some clashes lacked purpose or necessity. In early March, for instance, Brigadier General John Newton decided to advance into Western Florida, for no specific reason and with shifting objectives. His nine hundred men of the 2nd and 99th U.S. Colored Infantry regiments, including a few 2nd Florida Cavalry (U.S.) troopers, made an amphibious landing and marched inland. Newton quickly suffered a resounding defeat at Natural Bridge, about eighteen miles from Tallahassee. Newton's pointless incursion resulted in twenty-nine dead; eighty-one wounded, including several mortally wounded; and thirty-eight men missing. Confederates shot two captured white 2nd Florida Cavalry men as deserters from their army and probably dispatched several wounded blacks. However, about thirty black soldiers survived capture and became prisoners of war.[2]

Forrest Slays Sleeping Federals

On March 22, Brigadier General James H. Wilson started off with fourteen thousand cavalry to Selma, Alabama, a manufacturing and munitions center of the fast-expiring Confederacy. His brigades moved in three columns to mask his objective. Confederates knew that Selma was the likely target, and Forrest developed a plan of "brilliant conception" to smite the Federal cavalry front, rear, and flanks. However sparkling his grand plan, almost everything went wrong. Brigadier General James R. Chalmers's troops and others failed to appear as scheduled, and, worse, unknown to Forrest, Federals captured dispatches that revealed his plans.

Wilson used that intelligence to advantage, meeting only light opposition in a rapid movement toward Selma.[3]

Forrest had won promotion to lieutenant general, his army's second-highest grade, on February 28. That promotion served as a morale booster, underscoring his dramatic raids while other generals met defeat. Unknown or ignored by Richmond authorities was the war's toll on Forrest. Whether caused by mounting stress or by an innate instability, his towering rages had intensified and a tendency to despotism had increased. On the march to intercept Wilson, for instance, he had two citizens, a youth and an older man, wrongly executed as deserters and ordered their bodies left by the roadside, with placards attached naming their alleged crime, as an object lesson for the passing troops. His men, usually his most ardent loyalists, demurred. One called it a black spot on Forrest's reputation; another said that "with the rank and file, it met with pronounced condemnation." John A. Wyeth, Forrest's largely uncritical biographer, described it as an unfortunate incident.[4]

Forrest found Selma ringed by a formidable three-mile-long trench system, but he lacked the troops to man such extensive defenses. So he ordered every male citizen to the trenches and thus added two thousand men to his own fifteen hundred regulars. Wilson soon appeared before Selma with nine thousand veteran cavalrymen. When he attacked, the militia ran. Forrest could not plug the gap opened in his center, and Federals poured over the works. With that, Forrest told his men to mount and fly. Organized resistance collapsed, though Wilson said that some desultory street fighting occurred. By the end of the day, April 2, Federals had captured Selma and rounded up twenty-seven hundred prisoners.[5]

One of those prisoners was Lieutenant Colonel Frank A. Montgomery, 1st Mississippi Cavalry. After surrendering, a Federal soldier raised his gun to shoot him. Montgomery's captor, a sergeant, pushed away the fellow's carbine and berated him as a cowardly scoundrel for trying to murder a prisoner. Then Montgomery learned that other Yankees also felt they should take no prisoners because they had heard that Forrest's troopers had allegedly refused quarter to some of Wilson's men. Montgomery insisted, "It was of course not true, but I make no doubt it cost some of our men their lives that day."[6]

Forrest and his escort traveled northward but soon collided with a body of Federal cavalry. During the ensuing fight, Forrest shot the thirtieth man he had personally killed during the war. After the brief clash, the fleeing Confederates quickly rode off into the pitch-black darkness.

As they moved along an unfamiliar road, they heard a commotion to the side. Lieutenant George L. Cowan recalled that they heard women screaming in the stillness of the night. Those present said Forrest and a few men galloped to the source of the piteous shrieks, a house just off the road. There they reported finding four Federals who had looted the place and then sought to rape the women, hence the commotion. Confederates reported, "Summary was the fate of these wretches." While the accounts are vague in some details, still it appears that the attempted rape charge arose after Forrest and his men executed the hapless soldiers.

Excited by the incident, Forrest's party met a number of Wilson's men, alone or in small groups, moving on the same road. Because the Confederates traveled northward from Selma, the Federals probably thought them friendly troops and made no effort to avoid them. As Forrest and his men encountered Federals, they killed them where they stood or walked, afterward describing them all as pillagers, weighted with plunder.

By then, Forrest rode at the front, and presently they captured a picket post of a Federal unit encamped nearby. One picket identified himself as belonging to the 4th U.S. Cavalry, a Regular Army regiment. On hearing this, Confederates assumed the pickets guarded a 4th Regular bivouac. Although mistaken, that belief influenced their subsequent actions. Joseph G. Vale, a 7th Pennsylvania Cavalry officer, had fought with the 4th and explained that the regulars had bested some of Forrest's troops. Afterward, Confederates said that a 4th Cavalry officer had murdered one of their own after he had surrendered. Vale called it a falsehood but added, "The report was, however, assiduously circulated and generally believed in Forrest's command. . . . *Forrest would not take any of the Fourth United States Cavalry prisoners.*" He overlooked another possible cause for Forrest to seek vengeance. That was the belief that a 4th Regular soldier had fired the shot that killed Forrest's favorite younger brother, Colonel Jeffrey Forrest.[7]

Though risky, Confederates decided to attack the camp. Contemporary accounts of the action derive only from Federal sources, as no similar Confederate accounts have yet emerged. Southern descriptions were written years after the war and warrant profound skepticism. For instance, John W. Wyeth, who was in a Northern prisoner-of-war camp at the time, maintained that a lowly lieutenant made the decision to attack. Clearly, Wyeth sought to insulate Forrest from what followed. Further, all insisted Forrest took no part in the melee. They declared his caring men insisted he stay behind with the horse holders or they would refuse to fall upon the enemy. They supposedly argued that "in a night attack he would be exposed to danger which they were altogether unwilling he should incur." Whatever else might be said about Forrest, he had never avoided danger. But, according to his former soldiers, Forrest docilely acceded and for the first time stayed in the rear of a fight, letting his men face an enemy without him. Removed from the scene, he was therefore not responsible for anything that happened.

Postwar Southern chroniclers described Forrest's men as creeping silently up to the camp they thought harbored 4th U.S. Cavalry soldiers. Instead, the fifty sleeping men belonged to a provisional scouting detachment. Lieutenant Martin J. Miller, 18th Indiana Light Artillery Battery, and a Lieutenant Royce, 4th Cavalry, led the detachment of men seconded to the detachment from different units. Wyeth suggested that many Federals were awake around their campfires, while others said they lay wrapped in their blankets. Probably most were asleep on the ground, while the two officers sheltered in a nearby house. Confederates divided into two groups for front and rear attacks.

Then one Federal heard or saw their stealthy approach. He rose from his bedroll and fired his pistol, wounding Lieutenant Cowan. With that, the Confederates began firing, shooting men in their blankets, or killing them as they staggered to their feet. Both officers were shot as they dashed from the nearby house. Royce, hit in a vital spot, fell dead in his tracks; Miller, mortally wounded, died about twelve hours later. In his version of the slaughter, Cowan asserted, "They made a strong fight. . . . [They] resisted to the last." Wyeth more accurately described it as "a brief and sanguinary encounter." Bloody it was but only for the unsuspecting Federals. Most were shot dead. Confederates said they killed or wounded thirty-five and captured five, while Lieutenant Cowan was their sole casualty. Several Federals escaped, darting into the darkness, running barefoot into the night.[8]

Northerners cried murder and massacre. A surgeon apparently heard Lieutenant Miller's deathbed statement and wrote, "Forrest escaped with his escort of 100 men and . . . came across a party of Federals asleep. . . . He charged on them in their sleep, and refusing to listen to their cries of surrender, killed or wounded the entire party." Another lengthier account by a member of Lieutenant Miller's battery is so detailed that the author likely got his information from one or more of the survivors. William O. Crouse wrote in his journal that "Lieut Miller of our Batt detailed at Divis Headquarters as Chief of Scouts, had with his scout of

50 in number, been surrounded in the night . . . and murdered, but two escaping. This fiendish act had been perpetrated by Gen Forrest and his bodyguard." Captain Lewis M. Hosea, serving on Wilson's staff, wrote home that Forrest had surprised the scouts, killing an officer and thirty-eight men in "cold-blooded and dastardly" style.[9]

After the inevitable Northern outcry, Forrest and his men flatly denied any misconduct. They said it was part of a sustained effort to discredit them and to demonize Forrest. They took particular offense when Yankees asserted that "Forrest fell upon the party with the ferocity of a wild Indian, and killed every man of it." Again, they said Forrest was not present for the bloodbath but meekly remained behind with the horses. Lieutenant Cowan, the only man hurt when, as he said, the Federals made a strong fight, deplored the accusations. He declared, "Not a single man was killed after he surrendered, and any statements to this effect are wholly untrue." Perhaps that was factually correct: Confederates may have shot and killed most of the scouts before they were awake enough to surrender.[10]

That particular aspect exacerbated Northern outrage. When war came in 1861, citizen-soldiers of both sides still clung to some notions today regarded as quaint. Initially, they thought taking cover from enemy fire was cowardly. Throughout, they regarded land mines as underhanded weapons, wire entanglements as unfair, shooting solitary sentries wrong, fighting on the Sabbath wicked, and killing sleeping men as uncivilized and craven. That is why Southerners described the scouts as so awake and alert that they offered stiff resistance. Wilson, for one, scorned Forrest's protestations of innocence. After meeting him a few days after the Selma battle, Wilson said he thought Forrest had killed every last one in the attack on the sleeping Federals. He concluded, "Such incidents as this were far too frequent with Forrest. He appears to have had a ruthless temper which impelled him on every occasion where he had a clear advantage to push his success to a bloody end, and yet he always seemed not only to resent but to have a plausible excuse for the cruel excesses which were charged against him."[11]

Blacks Take No Prisoners at Mobile

During that period in late March and early April, Major General Edward R. S. Canby, commanding at New Orleans, had belatedly invested Mobile's defensive forts. In mid-January, Grant had directed him to march against the port city, an order Canby ignored. As the weeks passed, Grant confessed that he despaired of getting Canby to act. When he finally arrived there on March 27, Grant snorted, "The war was practically over . . . if left alone, it would within a few days have fallen into our hands without any bloodshed whatever."[12]

Canby led one force against Spanish Fort, while Major General Frederick Steele would assault Fort Blakely. Steele, who had led the ill-fated Camden expedition, arrived before Blakely on April 1 with thirteen thousand troops, including a five-thousand-man black division under Brigadier General John P. Hawkins. Of Hawkins's nine regiments, forming three brigades, five had combat experience of some sort but four had yet to meet the enemy. They learned that the fort, about ten miles from Mobile, formed a semicircle three miles in length, with both ends anchored on the east bank of the Blakely River. Forty cannons in nine redoubts protected the main line, while outside rifle pits served as a first defense against attack. About thirty-five hundred troops, a mixture of veterans and new levies, manned the fortifications, all commanded by Brigadier General St. John R. Liddell. Steele began a siege, digging trenches to move troops ever closer while subjecting defenders to artillery and sniper fire.[13]

Those siege operations ended abruptly and unexpectedly on April 9. Spanish Fort had fallen the day before, so Steele ordered strong skirmish lines forward. In one sector, some black soldiers became isolated and pinned down. They worried that Confederates might send a superior force against them, and they expected no quarter if captured. So they attacked. They drove outlying enemy sharpshooters back to the fort's main line and popped into the newly vacated holes. Meanwhile, white troops on their left had gained designated but limited objectives. They then turned the fight into what is called a soldier's battle, an action when common soldiers take the initiative. Without orders, they assaulted the main fort on their own. When a black brigade's commander saw the impetuous movement, he also did not wait for orders. He sent his men forward, and the other two brigades advanced almost simultaneously. Walter A. Chapman, a 2nd lieutenant with the 51st U.S. Colored Infantry, related, "The whole charge was an accident; there were no orders for anything of the kind." Shouting and whooping and cheering, the black soldiers rushed for Blakely.

That sudden onslaught rattled Confederates. Captain Henry M. Crydenwise, 73rd U.S. Colored Infantry, related, "The rebs in their rifle pits . . . became frightened and leaving their pits started at full speed for their main works." Immobilized with a leg wound, a 97th Illinois captain watched the black soldier attack. He recalled that "I could distinctly hear their yell 'Fort Pillow, Fort Pillow.' . . . It is said that the yell made the stoutest hearts quail . . . for that meant no quarter." Lieutenant Chapman reported, "As soon as our niggers caught sight of the retreating figures of the rebs the very devil could not hold them their eyes glittered like serpents and with yells & howls like hungry wolves, they rushed for the rebel works." In between yells, some heard a Confederate officer shout that the "damned niggers are coming."[14]

The assaulting troops, white or black, paid in blood for every yard traversed. As they raced for the fort, one Federal officer said the field was black with Hawkins's men. Probably because they bunched up, just one land mine explosion killed or wounded thirteen men of the 51st U.S. Colored Infantry. Ignoring their losses, the black soldiers struggled through abatis and entered the fort. When they leaped into Blakely's trenches, they trembled with a ferocious bloodlust. One witness reported, "The excitement among the Negroes . . . was *fierce and revengeful.*" Commanding officers glossed over or omitted the ensuing butchery in their reports, but other firsthand accounts described a massacre. There with his men, Lieutenant Chapman said that "the niggers did not take a prisoner, they killed all they took to a man."[15]

Officers tried to restrain the frenzied men, often unsuccessfully. When two 67th U.S. Colored Infantry officers tried to stop the killing, soldiers angrily turned upon them and reportedly shot both. In another fratricidal incident, a Confederate, corralled with other prisoners, said that black soldiers "continued to shoot our men down, shooting between or over the heads of the guards." When he became a target, he appealed to a Federal officer. Quickly, the officer hit the murder-bent black soldier on the head with his revolver and then shot him when he ran away. Then the officer confided that he had found it necessary to so discipline three others who had "bothered" prisoners.

Even with the best will, officers could not possibly be everywhere to restrain the berserk men. What saved many Confederates was head-long flight. They ran from onrushing blacks to the white troops pouring into the fort. Brigadier General Hawkins conceded that his black troops captured only a few prisoners. He said that was so because many Con-federates feared the behavior of his troops and ran to white Federals. Lieutenant Chapman more bluntly said that they fled "to save being butchered by our niggers." Afterward, one Confederate declared that

"Had it not been for the white Federal troops and the white officers of the negro regiments," the blacks would have murdered him.[16]

Blakely fell almost in the blink of an eye. Once started, the assault had breached the defenses and overwhelmed the occupants in less than twenty minutes. As defenders said, very likely more of them were killed or wounded after Federal troops poured into the fort than while trying to repel the attack. Liddell, Blakely's commander, reported, "Some of my men were shot from the rear, while at their guns firing to the front. Thus Blakely fell at the point of the bayonet." Almost as quickly as Federals overran the fort, they rounded up prisoners, officers brought excited black soldiers under control, and the shooting stopped. Given the strictures of time and opportunity, black soldiers probably slew no more than fifty or so unresisting men. Whatever the actual count, Confederates believed that black soldiers had run amok at Blakely and massacred scores of their comrades. They needed no convincing when black soldiers jeered that if they had captured them, they would have been dead men. Later, a Confederate survivor charged, "Blakely was the Yankee Fort Pillow."[17]

Peace Caps the Downward Spiral

Meanwhile, on April 2, the day Selma fell, Lee's Petersburg front collapsed. With 63,000 troops from five army corps, black troops among them, Federals pierced defense lines held by just 18,500 Confederates. Nowhere, however, was the offensive easy or painless. Lee's men stubbornly resisted and probably inflicted more casualties than they took. But Lee knew that he could no longer hold and warned President Davis that the government must abandon Richmond. Lee pinned the Confederacy's rapidly dwindling prospects on joining Johnston in North Carolina. His troops marched toward Amelia Courthouse, where he expected to find supplies and railroad transportation. Close on their heels were Grant's infantrymen, and swinging around and ahead to block their retreat was Sheridan's Cavalry Corps. When Lee's hungry, weary men neared Appomattox, they found no supplies and Sheridan had cut the railroad. Bereft of space, time, and hope, Lee surrendered on April 9, 1865.[18]

Great tumult and uncertainty, euphoria and sadness, excitement and stress, marked those days. On April 14, just five days after Lee surrendered, John Wilkes Booth burst into Lincoln's box at the Ford Theater in Washington and shot the president in the head. Mary Todd Lincoln, seated at his side, told a confidant that her husband never even quivered when the assassin's bullet crashed into his brain. Early on April 15, Lincoln died, plunging the North into grief and anger. Black Americans felt a particularly wrenching sense of loss. Somberly, a 111th U.S. Colored Infantry soldier said, "Uncle Sam is dead." Southerners experienced mixed reactions over Lincoln's assassination, some rejoicing but others regretting both act and loss. Self-interest prompted some of the dismay, as when Mary Chestnut wrote that she knew that "this foul murder will bring down worse miseries on us."[19]

Andrew Johnson, the nation's new leader, issued a proclamation charging that Jefferson Davis and other Confederates had arranged Lincoln's murder and the other assassination plots. Although Booth and his cohorts possibly acted alone, the accusations inflamed Northerners, stoking no-quarter thinking. From near Petersburg, Major Edward W. Bacon, 117th U.S. Colored Infantry, wrote home, "When we get into another fight, there will be no quarter. So every body swears." Also in Virginia, a Maine infantryman advised, "Revenge is the cry in the army & by all." Sherman told his troops that the war had taken a new turn and warned that "woe unto the people who seek to expend their wild passions in such a manner, for there is but one dread result." Major General Jacob D. Cox, one of Sherman's corps commanders, thought that "if active operations were to commence again it would be impossible to restrain the troops from great outrages."[20]

Passions subsided somewhat as Confederate generals surrendered their armies one by one. Last to yield on May 26 was General Edmund Kirby Smith, commanding in the Trans-Mississippi. Formal hostilities had ended, but pockets of resistance continued to annoy the victors. Grant then took a very hard line. He issued a general order, decreeing that "any and all persons found in arms against the United States, or who may commit acts of hostility against it east of the Mississippi River, will be regarded as guerrillas and punished with death." He demanded strict enforcement of his order, effective June 1. Even before his order, subordinate commanders had already adopted a policy of no-quarter treatment for diehards.[21]

Soldiers of both sides were glad when the guns fell silent and they could go home. They knew, as no civilian could, the war's misery and death and rejoiced to leave it all behind. Many also felt thankful for another reason: They feared that the conflict inexorably drifted closer and closer, faster and faster, to a war without mercy. Voicing a not uncommon sentiment, a Confederate cavalryman declared, "I was glad when the war was over because we were getting almost to the black flag which meant

no quarter." Worrying about this in early 1865, a Pennsylvania cavalryman wrote, "This war would soon assume the no quarter system—and
I am not so sure but it will yet." Looking at it from another perspective,
Sherman thought Stonewall Jackson's ideas about taking no prisoners
might have a salutary effect. Sherman said, "Perhaps he was right. It
seems cruel; but if there were no quarter given, most men would keep
out of war." With some exceptions, most soldiers dreaded the prospect,
shrinking from the notion. They thought raising the black flag wrong, a
terrible violation of ethics and morality and an affront to their heartfelt
Christianity. Yet general and private alike saw black flags waving on
the not-so-distant horizon, an inevitable development beyond anyone's
control. Given that terrible reality, they knew that they would respond
in kind, speeding a descent into the savagery they rejected. A 4th Minnesota soldier explained, "The rebels are ruthless. . . . They have killed
some of our men they have caught as prisoners. We have had to pay
them back with the same punishment. But this is so hideous." Deplore
it they might, but they were up to it, hideous or not. Whether wearing
blue or gray, the citizen-soldiers had already demonstrated a capacity
for such warfare.[22]

Epilogue

THEN AND NOW, the war's cost has eluded exact calculation. On both sides, more than six hundred thousand men died—killed in action or mortally wounded, dead from disease or accidents. That tally does not include the irregulars and civilians killed or executed. Consequently, many historians believe the official count errs on the low side.

For one thing, official tabulations report almost 180,000 black soldiers in service, beginning with the war's second half, and about 37,000 died, including 2,751 killed in action. But not one of these figures is correct. Joseph T. Wilson, a black veteran and postwar historian, thought 220,000 was nearer the correct number of black soldiers who served. Even more striking, the National Park Service in the late 1990s compiled a database of 235,000 named black soldiers, although the tabulators later reduced

that base to about 209,000 because they thought name duplication indicated error. Combat deaths were assuredly much higher because of
the hundreds listed as missing who were really dead men; the many
unreported deaths; and, again, because of the practice of substituting live
recruits for those killed. For some of the same reasons, the statisticians
probably undercounted deaths from disease.[1]

Black soldiers became very unwelcome in the occupied South. President Andrew Johnson particularly wanted them banished from Tennessee, his home state. Impoverished and uneducated as a youth, he simmered with poor white prejudices, denouncing black soldiers as insolent,
undisciplined, domineering, depredatory, and disorderly. Further, he said
that they were likely to aid black insurrections and that they drove white
people away. Moreover, he found it "humiliating in the extreme" that
they had taken over his house in Greenville and turned it into a "common negro brothel . . . a sink of pollution." Johnson fumed, "It was bad
enough [when] . . . converted into a rebel hospital, but a negro whore
house is infinitely worse."[2]

Ordered to Texas, black troops feared treachery. They credited a rumor
that when no longer needed, the government would sell them on the
Cuban slave market. Just as bad was the tale that they were bound for
slavery in Texas cotton fields to pay off the war debt. No matter what,
they suspected a one-way trip awaited them. Others became unruly when
the army abruptly and secretly stopped issuing rations to their families.
When herded aboard troop transports in May and June, mutinies erupted.
With strong shows of force, including arrests, confinements, and summary executions, officers quelled the uprisings.[3]

The concept of war crimes and war criminals was in an incipient
stage in 1865 and not yet codified. People and authorities easily recognized a crime when committed during the war but lacked appropriate
comprehensive statutes. In essence, however, Federal authorities branded
some Confederates as war criminals, including prison camp officials.
Swiss-born Henry Wirz, Andersonville's commandant, easily became
the premier miscreant, though he bore little responsibility for the camp's
horrific conditions. After a show trial, Wirz went to the hangman on
November 10, 1865. Robert Ould, Confederate prisoner-exchange agent,
paced a cell for eight weeks before he was cleared of misappropriating
prisoners' funds. Warders and officers of other prisons also faced various
charges. All were cleared, except Private James Duncan of Andersonville's

staff. He was convicted of manslaughter for kicking a prisoner to death. Sentenced to fifteen years imprisonment on June 8, 1866, he escaped thirteen months later.[4]

In a spate of manhunts and prosecutions, Federals pursued a few low-ranking Confederate soldiers and many notorious irregulars. They caught Champ Ferguson, "Sue" Mundy, William C. Quantrill, and other homicidal sociopaths. Ferguson had particularly outraged sensibilities when he murdered that wounded Federal officer in his hospital bed near Saltville, Virginia. Mainly, he was tried and convicted on that charge, although he was also accused of murdering some unnamed black soldiers. After a trial, Ferguson went to the gallows in the early autumn of 1865. Federal troops mortally wounded Quantrill in an ambush, and he died on June 6, 1865.[5]

Northern leaders understood that high-ranking Confederates bore command responsibility for atrocities, but other concerns overrode any desire for either justice or vengeance. Gratified with victory and knowing the nation's war weariness, many leaders were reluctant to open fresh wounds. They hoped to cap the war's passions and move forward once again as a united nation. Grant, influential and popular, expressed that sentiment when he wrote, "Mr. Lincoln, I believe, wanted Mr. Davis to escape, because he did not wish to deal with the matter of his punishment. . . . He thought blood enough had already been spilled." Grant concurred and intervened to spare Confederate military leaders from prosecution. He and others wanted the war's strife and divisiveness over with and done.[6]

Northern people were of two minds about retribution. Opposing currents buffeted them about the massacre of black soldiers. They knew it was wrong when Confederates murdered their former slaves, but they also felt an aversion to executing the responsible whites. As for white Federals murdered in the West, the Shenandoah, or elsewhere, many were unaware of those atrocities. They had fervently sung the wartime ditty about hanging Jeff Davis from a sour apple tree but no groundswell arose for such revenge. Apparently the hanging of Wirz and the capture and imprisonment of Davis satisfied most. So, not one ranking Confederate was tried for ordering or condoning no-quarter treatment for white and black Federals or for the murder of prisoners.

President Johnson pardoned thousands of Confederates, although some remained proscribed even after the second amnesty proclamation of September 1867. His leniency enraged Radical Republicans in Congress. Some ordinary men, particularly soldiers, also believed Southerners should pay for their misdeeds. A New England corporal complained that "the President is fast yielding inch by inch all that we have gained. . . . I think my self it is best to be magnanimous to our conquered foe. But not so much so." Angrily, a Wisconsin soldier charged that "Congress may yet restore Forrest to Citizenship & give him a gold medal bearing the mottoe Ft. Pillow! May God who has sustained us so long save us now from Disgrace."[7]

If any Southerner deserved a speedy trial and swift punishment, it was Nathan B. Forrest. To him belonged the command responsibility for the slaughter of scores of black and white Federals. On his shoulders also rested the deaths of many soldiers of both sides who fell because of Fort Pillow's baleful legacy. Yet he always insisted that he had always acted "in strict accordance with the most humanizing military usages." He remained proscribed even after Johnson's second amnesty proclamation of September 1867, but no war crimes charges ever troubled his postwar existence. Although a grand jury had indicted him for treason in 1864, nothing ever came of it.

Still, Forrest could never shed Fort Pillow's dark shadow. As well, he never recovered his prewar fortune, so that his postwar life was a never-ending struggle to regain financial health. Nevertheless, he found the time to help establish the Ku Klux Klan and became that organization's first leader in the early postwar period. Again, he led murderous followers, which would further darken his name for many Northerners and African Americans. In the end, a sick, emaciated fifty-five-year-old Forrest had experienced a conversion to religion when he died in 1877.[8]

Unlike Forrest, Colonel John S. Mosby always accepted responsibility for his wartime actions and, furthermore, said he would do the same thing all over again. Initially, he resisted surrendering, and Federal authorities posted a $5,000 reward for his capture. Through the intervention of Lee and with Grant's help, he resolved his immediate postwar tribulations and prospered as an attorney. But then he actively supported Grant's bid for a second presidential term, alienating fellow Southerners. He lost his law practice, faced duel challenges, and left the country to serve as American consul in Hong Kong. Upon his return in 1885, he accepted a position, arranged by the dying Grant, with the Southern Pacific Railroad. Mosby died unrepentant in 1916 at the age of eighty-two.[9]

Federal troops caught Major General Joseph Wheeler near Atlanta on May 11, 1865, as he traveled westward under an alias and with forged papers. Although his cavalrymen had murdered many of Sherman's men during the closing campaigns, Wheeler soon gained release from prison and went to Nashville. There, two Federal officers sought vigilante justice, attacking him with club and pistol on August 21, 1865. Wheeler broke free, escaping with his life and a bruised head. After that little bother, all went well. He won eight terms in Congress and served as a major general in the Spanish-American War.[10]

Lieutenant General Wade Hampton, who had admitted ordering the summary execution of Sherman's foragers, hoped to continue the fight in Texas. Such schemes soon collapsed, whereupon Hampton simply went home to his blighted lands in South Carolina. Except for his exclusion from postwar amnesty, he lived unvexed by the government. Hampton helped overcome carpetbagger rule in his state, served as governor, and then became a U.S. senator.[11]

Major General Robert F. Hoke, who commanded during the Plymouth slaughter, went home, prospered in business, and lived for almost fifty years. Colonel William J. Pegram, age twenty-four, who thought butchering black Federals during the Crater fight was right and proper, never returned to his Virginia home. He fell in the war's last days at Five Forks. Federal Colonel Delavan Bates, also twenty-four, wounded while leading the 30th U.S. Colored Infantry at the crater, then would not have bet five dollars on drawing breath another half hour but survived and received a Medal of Honor for his conduct during that assault. Sergeant Decatur Dorsey, 39th U.S. Colored Infantry, also survived and also won a Medal of Honor, the only black soldier to receive one for bravery at the Crater fight.[12]

As the victors, the North had no war criminals. Had the war gone the other way or had an impartial body sat in judgment, many Federals would have squirmed in the dock. Among them would be Major General David Hunter, the Shenandoah Valley's arsonist and executioner, and Colonel William Hoffman, commissary general of prisoners, whose vindictive rule killed many captives by denying them adequate rations. Colonel Fielding Hurst, 6th Tennessee Cavalry (U.S.), charged with robbery, extortion, torture, and murder in Tennessee, belonged with them, as did Colonel William L. McMillen, the incompetent drunk who sabered a defenseless prisoner at Nashville. A victorious South would not have tried Brigadier General Jefferson C. Davis, though he was scorned by his own men for stranding a "dense mass" of black refugees during Sherman's march to the sea, leaving them to face merciless pursuing Confederates.[13]

In such a hypothetical trial, black soldiers and some of their officers would have packed many courtrooms. They killed a large but unknown number of wounded, surrendered, or captured Confederates. Though their lawyers might contend that the defendants only gave as good as they got, that argument would not have saved them.

Black emancipation greatly pained Southern whites who viewed it as a social evil and an economic disaster. One ex-Confederate asserted, "After the negroes got their freedom it made awful fools out of them. That is what brought the Ku Klux into existence." One historian observed that whites reacted "in the time honored Southern way—with violence." Formed to regain home rule and to keep blacks subservient, the Klan used force, including murder. Led by Forrest, Klansmen terrorized carpetbaggers, white Republicans, and blacks. Klansmen and the newly enacted Black Codes proved effective, and Southerners soon restored much of the old ways, at least on the local level.[14]

Overnight, mythmaking became a growth industry in the South. Able spinners devoted much creative effort to explaining the conflict's origins and why the grand struggle became the Lost Cause. Almost all agreed that they fought not for slavery but for self-determination through independence in the War Between the States. Pride, hitched to an unwavering belief in Southern superiority and warrior invincibility, and a tendency to unblushing gasconade, all moved Southerners to sidestep reality. Soon they embraced the welcome dictum that they were not defeated, though clearly they had lost. Most settled upon one pleasing version of that sophistry. A former army hospital matron explained, "They [Yankees] could not with equal numbers and fair fighting succeed over us[;] . . . we were not whipped, but overpowered." An 8th Texas Cavalry officer offered the comprehensive short version when he declared, "Overwhelming numbers with inexhaustible supplies had triumphed."[15]

Northern mythicizers also fell to work but without the sense of urgency or need that spurred their Southern counterparts. Their creations, albeit slow to blossom, proved just as enduring. Schoolchildren learned that Union soldiers fought and died to free the slaves and that they always treated blacks with respect and kindness. *Andersonville* became a freighted word, summoning instant images of medieval Southern cruelty and sadism, while the names of equally atrocious Northern prisons never entered the lexicon.

Secretary of War Edwin M. Stanton ordered ground set aside at Fort Pillow for a monument to commemorate the murdered dead. Now that area is a Tennessee state park, the site of a state prison, and a rewarding ground for archeological digging and discovery. Restoration work enables visitors to gain some idea of how it was in April 1864. But they can no longer envision the gunboats offshore—the Mississippi River has shifted course and now flows a mile and a half away.

The crater itself, where the greatest single slaughter of black soldiers occurred, is part of the Petersburg National Military Park. Probably part of the mine tunnel remains intact, although it is now sealed. Most of the hundreds who fell there on July 30, 1864, and went into mass graves, long ago were exhumed and reburied in a proper cemetery.[16]

Finally, over the years, the Civil War acquired a lily-white complexion, and the black soldiers' role faded from the collective memory. As well, the great struggle was remembered as a fair and square fight, with never an atrocity to sully the national self-image.

ABBREVIATIONS

NOTES

BIBLIOGRAPHY

INDEX

ABBREVIATIONS USED IN NOTES AND BIBLIOGRAPHY

AAS—American Antiquarian Society

ADAH—Alabama Department of Archives and History

AG—Adjutant General

AGO—Adjutant General's Office

AHQ—Arkansas Historical Quarterly

AI—Annals of Iowa

AlHC—Alabama Historical Commission

AlHQ—Alabama Historical Quarterly

ASU—Stephen S. Austin State University

AU—Auburn University

B&L—Battles and Leaders

CCHS—Carroll County Historical Society, McKenzie, Tenn.

CHA—Catawba Historical Association, Newton, N.C.

CHS—Chicago Historical Society

CMSR—Compiled Military Service Record

ConnHS—Connecticut Historical Society

CSCT—Chronicles of Smith County, Tex.

CU—Cornell University

CV—Confederate Veteran

CWH—Civil War History

CW&M—College of William and Mary

CWMC—Civil War Miscellaneous Collection

CWP—*Civil War Papers*

CWT—*Civil War Times*

CWTI—*Civil War Times Illustrated*

ETRC—East Texas Research Center

DU—Duke University

EU—Emory University

FHQ—*Florida Historical Quarterly*

FSA—Florida State Archives

FSU—Florida State University

GC—Gettysburg College

GDAH—Georgia Department of Archives and History

GHQ—*Georgia Historical Quarterly*

GHS—Georgia Historical Society

GNS—*Glimpses of the Nation's Struggle*

HEH—Henry E. Huntington Library

HNOC—Historic New Orleans Collection

HSWC—Historical Society of Washington County, N.C.

HU—Harvard University

IHS—Indiana Historical Society

IJH—*Iowa Journal of History*

IMH—*Indiana Magazine of History*

ISHL—Illinois State Historical Library

ISL—Indiana State Library

IU—Indiana University

JAG—Judge Advocate General

JNH—*Journal of Negro History*

KHS—Kentucky Historical Society

KSHS—Kansas State Historical Society

LC—Library of Congress

LH—*Louisiana History*

LHQ—*Louisiana Historical Quarterly*

LSU—Louisiana State University

MAH—Magazine of American History

MaHS—Massachusetts Historical Society

MaR—Massachusetts Review

MC—Museum of the Confederacy

ME&R—Military Essays and Recollections

MHS—Minnesota Historical Society

MoHS—Missouri Historical Society

MOLLUS—Military Order of the Loyal Legion of the United States

NA—National Archives

NHHS—New Hampshire Historical Society

NCA&R—North Carolina State Archives & Records

NCHR—North Carolina Historical Review

NEHGS—New England Historic Genealogical Society

NHHS—New Hampshire Historical Society

NPS—National Park Service

NYCPL—New York City Public Library

NYHS—New-York Historical Society

NYHSQ—New-York Historical Society Quarterly

NYSL—New York State Library

OC—Oberlin College

OHS—Ohio Historical Society

OR—Official Records

ORN—Official Records of the Union and Confederate Navies

PMHS—Papers of the Military Historical Society of Massachusetts

PN—Personal Narratives

PNB—Petersburg National Battlefield Library

RG—Record Group, National Archives

RISSHS—Rhode Island Soldiers and Sailors Historical Society

RU—Rutgers University

SC—Smith College

SHC—Southern Historical Collection

SHQ—Southwestern Historical Quarterly

SHSP—Southern Historical Society Papers
SHSW—State Historical Society of Wisconsin
THQ—Tennessee Historical Quarterly
TSLA—Tennessee State Library and Archives
TU—Tulane University
UDC—United Daughters of the Confederacy
UA—University of Arkansas, Fayetteville
UF—University of Florida
UG—University of Georgia
UI—University of Iowa
UM—University of Michigan
UNC—University of North Carolina
UO—University of Oklahoma
USAMHI—United States Army Military History Institute
USC—University of South Carolina
UT—University of Texas
UV—University of Virginia
UW—University of Wisconsin
VHS—Virginia Historical Society
VMH&B—Virginia Magazine of History and Biography
VMI—Virginia Military Institute
VSLA—Virginia State Library and Archives
VTU—Virginia Polytechnic Institute and State University
WP—War Papers
WPA—Works Progress Administration
WRHS—Western Reserve Historical Society
WSI—War Sketches and Incidents
WTHSP—West Tennessee Historical Society Papers
WVUL—West Virginia University Libraries
YU—Yale University

NOTES

Introduction

1. Grimsley, *Hard Hand*, 120–41. See also Royster, *Destructive War*.

2. Rice, *Reminiscences*, 187–89.

3. For white-for-white reprisals, see George Kryder to Wife, Aug. 4, 1862, Bowling Green State University, Ohio; ORN 26:745–46, 762; and *Official Records of the Union and Confederate Armies*, 44:685–86, 601. *Official Records* (OR) citations are from series 1 unless otherwise noted and indicate volume, part, and page, in that order, using Arabic numerals, rather than the original Roman numerals, for volume and part.

4. Randall, *Civil War*, 506–7; Wiley, *Southern Negroes*, 328, and *Johnny Reb*, 314; Jordan, "Was There a Massacre?" 99–133.

5. Quarles, *Negro in Civil War*, 206, 267; Cornish, *Sable Arm*, 158–80; McPherson, *Negro's Civil War*, 216, and *Marching Toward Freedom*, 81; Franklin, *From Slavery to Freedom*, 292, 284.

6. Tarbell, *Life of Lincoln*; Wilson, *History of American People*, vol. 4; Paludan, *People's Contest*, 213–14; Mitchell, *Civil War Soldiers*, 175–76.

7. Glatthaar, *Forged in Battle*, 155–56; Trudeau, *Like Men of War*, 61.

8. Hollandsworth, "Execution of White Officers," 475–89.

9. Smith, *Black Soldiers*; for white soldier deaths, see Glatthaar, *March to the Sea*, 127–28, cited in Urwin, *Black Flag*, 7.

10. Jimerson, *Private War*, 111–15.

11. Urwin, *Black Flag*, 7, 101, 147, 231; Mitchell, *Civil War Soldiers*, 175; Trudeau, *Like Men of War*, 273; Wiley, *Johnny Reb*, 314; Rawick, *American Slave*, 18:259.

12. Tarbell, *Life of Lincoln*, 3:122, 126; Franklin, *From Slavery to Freedom*, 262, 288; Jimerson, *Private War*, 41, 43, 92; Cornish, *Sable Arm*, 84; Paludan, *People's Contest*, 200, 229, 381.

13. Leech, *Reveille in Washington*, 272; Hattaway and Jones, *How the North Won*, 270–72; Mitchell, *Civil War Soldiers*, 195–97; Linderman, *Embattled Courage*, 247–48.

14. On nationalism, see Faust, *Confederate Nationalism*; Jones, *Command and Strategy*, 238; and Gallagher, *Confederate War*, 81; on class and slavery, see Hattaway and Jones, *How the North Won*, 85–86; for dejected soldier, see Clark, *Stars and Bars*, 155.

15. Faust, *Confederate Nationalism*, 59; Jones, *Command and Strategy*, 238. On Southern violence, see Franklin, *Militant South*; Bruce, *Violence and Culture*; and Nisbett and Cohen, *Culture of Honor*.

16. For massacre of about twenty-five white Federals and *New York Times* reference, see Williamson, *Mosby's Rangers*, 213–15.

17. For quaint ideas, see Silas W. Browning to Sarah, June 22, 1863, Silas W. Browning Papers, http://www.intac.com/~blenderm/53rd_Mass_f/browning1.html (accessed Apr. 28, 2001); Nichols, *Great March*, 86, 91.

18. Basler, *Collected Works*, 2:250; McPherson, *What They Fought For*, 50.

19. Thomas R. Roulhac to Mother, Mar. 13, 1864, UNC.

20. White, *Prison Life*, 52.

21. Hastings, *Armageddon*.

1. Emancipation and Black Soldiers

1. Basler, *Collected Works*, 5:388–89.

2. Grant, *Letters*, 69, 85.

3. Cavins, *Civil War Letters*, 90; Brewster, *This Cruel War*, 57, 64.

4. *OR* 3:466–67, 469–70, 485–86; Nicolay and Hay, *Complete Works*, 4:416–20.

5. *OR* 14:341; Nichols, *Perry's Saints*, 104–5; Buchanan, "The Negro," 81n18; Du Pont, *Civil War Letters*, 2:44–45; *OR* ser. 3, 2:42–43.

6. Diggins, "Recollections," script, NYCPL; for sailor prejudice, see Oviatt, *Civil War Marine*, 69; *OR* 6:176–77, 248, 257, 263–64; *OR* ser. 3, 1:609–10, 626, 2:29–30, 31, 292; Higginson, *Army Life*, 214; MacGregor and Natly, *Blacks in Armed Forces*, 2:183, 185, Docs. 56 and 60; *Statutes at Large*, 2:271–77 (1845), 12:592, and 12:599 (1862); War Department, *Regulations for the Army*, 1857, par. 1299; Nicolay and Hay, *Complete Works*, 6:441–42.

7. *OR* 14:363; *OR* ser. 3, 2:147–48, 196–98, 292; Nicolay and Hay, *Complete Works*, 6:443–44; Chase, *Lincoln's Cabinet*, 99–100.

8. *OR* ser. 3, 2:346, 152, 695, 3:20; *OR* 14:375, 377; Higginson, *Army Life*, 214; Nicolay and Hay, *Complete Works*, 6:444–45; Ross, *Tabular Analysis*, 21.

9. *OR* 15:543, 548–49, 552–53, 555–57, 559; Butler, *Autobiography*, 491–93; Ross, *Tabular Analysis*, 24; AGO, List of Officers, 1st Regiment Louisiana Native Guards (Free Colored), Sept. 26, 1862, and Lists of Officers, 2nd and 3rd Regiment[s] Louisiana Native Guards (Free Colored), October 1862, RG 94, NA.

10. Cory, "Sixth Kansas Cavalry," 7; Charles R. Jennison to Gov. Charles Robinson, Aug. 22, 1862, KSHS; *OR* ser. 3, 1:280–81, 2:294–95, 311, 314, 445, 479; James M. Williams, "Historical Sketch of the First Kansas Colored Volunteers," 1–2, Mss. Col. #545, KSHS.

11. Tarbell, *Life of Lincoln*, 3:95–101, 110–116; for typical adverse opinion, see Fisk, *Hard Marching*, 29.

12. Basler, *Collected Works*, 5:336–37; Chase, *Lincoln's Cabinet*, 99–100; Thomas and Hyman, *Stanton*, 238–40; Welles, *Diary*, 1:70–71; Nicolay and Hay, *Complete Works*, 6:127.

13. Chase, *Lincoln's Cabinet*, 149–52; Basler, *Collected Works*, 5:433–36.

14. "Address to the President," Sept. 24, 1862, Charles and Sara Robinson Papers, KSHS; Basler, *Collected Works*, 5:436–37; Mahlon D. Manson to Wife, Jan. 26, 1863, ISL; Sherman, *Recollections*, 1:330; Logan, *Reminiscences*, 76, 79–80; Stampp, *Indiana Politics*, 148, 156; Thomas and Hyman, *Stanton*, 247.

15. Daly, *Diary*, 177; Lee, *Wartime Washington*, 186, 187n5; George Starbird to Marianne Starbird, Oct. 10, 1862, Schoff Coll., UM; Cavins, *Civil War Letters*, 98.

16. Riddle, *Reminiscences*, 204; Fowle, *Letters to Eliza*, 17, 19; McAllister, *Civil War Letters*, 212; Weinberg, *John Elliott Cairnes*, 144–45.

17. Basler, *Collected Works*, 5:530–37; Welles, "History of Emancipation," 249–50; Bates, *Diary*, 262–64; Chase, "Letters," 55.

18. Tarbell, *Life of Lincoln*, 3:123–26; Basler, *Collected Works*, 6:28–30; Riddle, *Reminiscences*, 208.

19. Hay, *Lincoln*, 50n2, 125; Bates, *Diary*, 292; Williams, *Lincoln and His Generals*, 170–78; Sherman, *Home Letters*, 252; Grant, *Papers*, 9:196.

20. Hayes, *Diary and Letters*, 2:377, 388; Garfield, *Wild Life*, 207, 211; Sievers, *Benjamin Harrison*, 1:179–80, 275.

21. Douglass, *Life and Times*, 354, 352; Redkey, *Grand Army*, 24, Hezekiah Ford Douglas.

22. Basler, *Collected Works*, 6:408–9; Cogley, *Seventh Indiana Cavalry*, 164; Schofield, *Forty-Six Years*, 74; Gray and Ropes, *War Letters*, 72.

23. Heymann, *American Aristocracy*, 122; Hiram F. Covey to Friends, Nov. 29, 1862, Ness Coll., UM; Barber, *Civil War Letters*, 116; Geer, *Diary*, 55.

24. John Pierson to Daughter, Mar. 15, 1863, Schoff Coll., UM; Weld, *War Diary*, 147; Potter, "Lincoln's Policies," 360–64; Luther Short to Father, May 10, 1863, ISL; Cort, *Dear Friends*, 61–62; William M. Heyser, diary, Jan. 1, 1863, UV electronic; Edwin O'Harron to Mother, Feb. 28, 1863, UM.

25. John Vliet to Mr. Boge, Feb. 2, 1863, Thomas W. Sweeny Papers, HEH; Sam Pile to George M. Miller, Jan. 10, 1863, UV electronic; Wainwright, *Diary of Battle*, 74; Thomas S. Howland to Mother, Dec. 4, [1862], MaHS.

26. Cross, "Yankee Soldier," 135; Marion Munson to Friends, Feb. 19, 1863, Joshua Van Hoosen Coll., UM; Hugh B. Roden to Family, Feb. 16, 1863, Schoff Coll., UM; Boyd, *Civil War Diary*, 133–34.

27. Shank, *One Flag*, 59; James R. French to Parents, Apr. 2, 1863, Albert Wilder Papers, UM; William C. H. Reeder to Brother, May 4, 1863, USAMHI; W. W. Phelps to Cousin, Jan. 4, 1863, Jesse Phelps Papers, UM; Spiegel, *Your True Marcus*, 226–27.

28. OR 24, 3:157; Ripley, *Vermont General*, 153; Grant, *Papers*, 8:94; David P. Craig to Wife, Jan. 25, 1863, ISL; Mary E. Clark to Emily, Feb. 9, 1863, Ross-Kidwell Papers, IHS; Fremantle, *Diary*, 70, May 10, 1863; Wildes, *One Hundred and Sixteenth Ohio*, 44–45. See also Simmons, "Confederate Letters," 31; Goodloe, *Confederate Echoes*, 207.

29. Cochrane, *American Civil War*, 4–12; Hamlin, *Life and Times*, 429, 430–31, 438–39; Chase, *Lincoln's Cabinet*, 99–100, July 22, 1862; Thomas E. Dawson to Father, Jan. 26, 1862, ISL; Silber and Sievens, *Yankee Correspondence*, 92, Justus F. Gale.

30. Eaton, *Grant, Lincoln*, 53; *OR* ser. 3, 3:695–96.

31. Chetlain, *Recollections*, 106–7; Sherman, *Home Letters*, 252; Lyman, *Meade's Headquarters*, 102; M. W. Rodman to Rep. James A. Cravens, Mar. 1, 1863, James Addison Cravens Papers, IU.

32. Abbott, "The Negro," 373; Andrew J. McGarrah to Parents, Mar. 8, 1863, IHS; Felix Brannigan to Sister, July 16, 1862, LC; Kircher, *A German*, 92.

33. For June 30, 1863, letter where Keeler thought slaves' "spirit & self-respect had been crushed," see Keeler, *Aboard the USS Florida*, 60; Carter, "Fourteen Months'," 159; McGarrah to Parents, Mar. 8, 1863, IHS; Basler, *Collected Works*, 5:423, 6:149–50.

34. Sherman, *Home Letters*, 253, Apr. 17, 1863; Lyman, *Meade's Headquarters*, 102, May 7, 1864.

35. Horatio N. Taft, diary, Feb. 18, 1863, LC electronic; George H. Cadman to Wife, May 9, 1863, UNC; Connolly, *Three Years*, 58, 146.

36. Thomas S. Howland to Mother, Dec. 4, [1862], MaHS; Freyburger, *Gold Rush*, 40; David S. Morgan to Dear Companion, Mar. 14, 1863, David S. Morgan Papers, http://www.kiva.net/~bjohnson/DSMorgan911.htm (accessed Mar. 23, 2001); James T. Miller to Sister, Feb. 6, 1863, Schoff Coll., UM; Browne, *Four Years in Secessia*, 437–38.

37. Francis G. Barnes to Wife, from Port Hudson, La., June 23, 1863, NYSL; Supervisory Committee for Recruiting Colored Regiments, *Free Military School*, 1–12; Berlin et al., *Free at Last*, 67–68; Boyd, *Civil War Diary*, 118–19; James T. Miller to Siblings, Apr. 25, 1864, Schoff Coll., UM; Ripley, *Vermont General*, 153. See also White, "White Papers," 265.

38. For "Sambo's Right to Be Kilt," see Miller, *Photographic History*, 9:176, 178; Haley, *Rebel Yell*, 204; August V. Kautz to Mrs. Savage, Mar. 29, 1865, ISHL.

2. The Southern Perspective

1. Bates, *Texas Cavalry*, 119–20; Medford, "Diary," 220.

2. Dawson, *Diary*, 330, Nov. 9, 1862; DeLeon, *Four Years*, 219; Thom, *My Dear Brother*, 68; Griffin, *Gentleman and Officer*, 278n6; Ravenel, *Private Journal*, 159; Fleet, *Green Mount*, 174; Bettersworth and Silver, *Mississippi*, 2:279.

3. On Peace Democrats, see Brooks, *Washington in Lincoln's Time*, 104.

4. Chestnut, *Civil War*, 146; Bacot, *Confederate Nurse*, 51; Myers, *Children of Pride*, 296; Dawson, *Diary*, 146, June 30, 1862; Clark, *Stars and Bars*, 203.

5. Bettersworth and Silver, *Mississippi*, 2:235; Elmore, *Heritage of Woe*, 83; Jones, "Negro Slaves," 168.

6. Rawick, *American Slave*, 19:215; Chestnut, *Civil War*, 113–4; Harrison, *Recollections Grave and Gay*, 142; Lane, *Dear Mother*, 338.

7. Chestnut, *Civil War*, 211, 153; Heyward, *Confederate Lady*, 67, 80; Clark, *Stars and Bars*, 148; Rawick, *American Slave*, 3:170, 6:3, 7:27–28, 147–48, 337–38; Grimball, "Journal," Aug. 4, 1863, UNC electronic; Preston, *Private War*, 73; Putnam, *Richmond*, 177–180, 262–66.

8. Simpson, *Far, Far from Home*, 99, 256; Harry St. John Dixon, diary, "Poor Dick" entry, Jan. 29, 1864, UNC; Rawick, *American Slave*, 6:3–4.

9. Nugent, *Dear Nellie*, 129, 132; Olmstead, *Memoirs*, 76; Moore, *Rebellion Record*, "Diary," 8:36.

10. Jackson, *Three Rebels*, 79; Moore, *Rebellion Record*, 8:51; Duke, *Reminiscences*, 228.

11. Pollard, *Southern History*, 2:472; Akin, *Letters*, 33; Sheeran, *Confederate Chaplain*, 72–73; Chestnut, *Civil War*, 464.

12. Brandt, *Mr. Tubbs' Civil War*, 72–73; Rawick, *American Slave*, 16:34, and see also 7:49, 18:2, and 19:216; Jerome Bussey to Robert Crouse, July 4, 1862, Crouse Coll., UM; Cavins, *Civil War Letters*, 81.

13. Patterson, *Yankee Rebel*, 130; John H. Bills, diary, July 11, 1864, UNC; Mrs. James G. Ramsay to James, Nov. 18, 1864, UNC.

14. Andrews, *War-Time Journal*, 11; Randall, *Civil War*, 60–81.

15. Small, *Road to Richmond*, 279; Olmsted, *Cotton Kingdom*, 557–63; Hepworth, *Whip, Hoe and Sword*, 109; Logan, *Volunteer Soldier*, 396.

16. Dyer and Moore, *Tennessee Veterans*, where most respondents report social stratification; Pember, *Southern Woman's Story*, 38–41; Trueheart and Trueheart, *Rebel Brothers*, 103; Chamberlayne, *Virginian*, 280.

17. John C. Birdwell to Wife, Oct. 27, 1862, Whitaker-Fenley Papers, ASU; John W. Reese to Wife, Mar. 26, May 26, 1863, DU.

18. Fewell, *Dear Martha*, 121; Dekle, "Peter Dekle's Letters," 16.

19. Montgomery, *Johnny Cobb*, 60; Harrison, "Civil War Journal," 137, 139; Elmore, *Heritage of Woe*, 110–11.

20. Duke, *Reminiscences*, 223; Fisk University, *Unwritten History of Slavery*, 298, 129; Johns, *Forty-Ninth Massachusetts*, 295. For horse trading over a legacy of slaves, see Mills, "Letters," 294, 295–96.

21. Candler, "Watch on the Chattahoochee," 428; Medford, "Diary," 220, Apr. 8, 1864; Sherman, *Memoirs*, 2:123; Houghton and Houghton, *Two Boys*, 80–81.

22. Ford, *Origins of Southern Radicalism*, 369; Elias Davis to Mother, Dec. [18?], 1863, UNC; Cate, *Two Soldiers*, 70.

23. Fleet, *Green Mount*, 349; Chestnut, *Civil War*, 88, 238, 246, July 4, Nov. 17, Nov. 27, 1861; Smedes, *Memorials*, 179; Fox, *Northern Woman*, 139, 146.

24. Gordon, *Reminiscences*, 19; Chestnut, *Civil War*, 153, Aug. 18, 1861.

25. Gray and Ropes, *War Letters*, 247.

26. Duke, *Reminiscences*, 469.

27. Olmsted, *Cotton Kingdom*, 555; Blackburn, *Reminiscences*, 102–3; Morgan, *Recollections*, 192.

28. Dinkins, *1861 to 1865*, 155; Rawick, *American Slave*, 6:3, 18:259.

29. Warner, *Generals in Gray*, 322, 332; Morton, *Artillery*, 101–4; Cochran, *Noted American Duels*, 4–15, and chap. 11, "Dueling in Dixie"; Thomas C. [Cochoran] to John, Sept. 29, 1862, Jefferson C. Davis file, IHS; Warner, *Generals in Blue*, 343–44.

30. Henry C. Carpenter to Sister, Dec. 12, 1862, VTU electronic; Reagan, *Memoirs*, 164–65; Garrett, *Civil War Letters*, 53; List of U.S. Soldiers Executed, AGO, RG 153, NA.

31. Olmstead, *Memoirs*, 17; Lyman, *Meade's Headquarters*, 99, May 17, 1864; Shotwell, *Papers*, 1:487; Simmons, "Letters," 44; Anderson, *Campaigning*, 150.

32. OR 32, 1:605; Ridley, *Battles*, 195; Oates, *The War*, 466.

33. Strong, *Diary*, 283; Gabriel P. Sherrill to Cosin [sic], Mar. 24, 1864, George M. Wilkinson Papers, CHA; OR 32, 1:600.

34. Sparks, *War Between the States*, 70; Taylor and Taylor, *Cruel War*, 133; Yearns and Barrett, *North Carolina*, 258; Moore, *Rebellion Record*, "Diary," 8:22.

35. Jerome B. Yates to Mother, Aug. 10, 1863, Heartman Coll., UT; Jerome B. Yates CMSR, RG 94, AGO, NA; Graham, *Papers*, 183; Park, "Diary," 371; Early, *Memoirs*, 291.

36. OR 14:599; OR ser. 2, 5:795–97.

37. Urwin, *Black Flag*, 140 and 150n36, citing the *Washington* (Ark.) *Telegraph*, June 8, 1864; Bates, *Texas Cavalry*, 270.

38. OR 13:727.

39. Bean, "House Divided," 410; Henry L. Stone to Father, Feb. 13, 1863, KHS; Anderson, *Campaigning*, 136.

3. First Encounters

1. William M. Parkinson to Wife, May 17, 1863, EU; Francis G. Barnes to Wife, June 23, 1863, NYSL; Bates, *Texas Cavalry*, 270.

2. McPherson, *Battle Cry*, 510; Cornish, *Sable Arm*, 84, 87; Berlin et al., *Freedom*, 2:548–49.

3. OR 53:455–57; Williams, "Historical Sketch," 3, KSHS; Burke, *Military History*, 408; Elkanah Huddleston to F. G. Adams, Dec. 3, 1882, "Battle of Island Mound," KSHS; Kansas AG, *Report*, 585; Stearns, "First Kansas Colored Inf't"; Muster Rolls, Companies A-E & G, 79th U.S. Colored Infantry (New), "Record of Events Sections, Returns for November–December 1862," RG 94, NA. When the army redesignated many black regiments, the 1st Kansas Colored became the 79th U.S. Colored Infantry.

4. OR 53:457; Huddleston, "Battle of Island Mound"; Burke, *Military History*, 582.

5. Huddleston, "Battle of Island Mound"; "Record of Events," 79th U.S. Colored Infantry, "A" Co., RG 94, NA; Williams, "Historical Sketch," 3, KSHS; House Committee on War Claims, "First Kansas Colored," 1.

6. OR 14:189; Forten, *Journals*, 428, Jan. 1, 1863.

7. OR 14:190–94.

8. OR ser. 2, 4:945–46, 954; for St. Catherine's Island, see *Atlas to Accompany the Official Records* (reprint, New York, 1958), plate 135A; Berlin et al., *Freedom*, 2:570–71.

9. On Hunter and Phelps, see OR 14:599, General Order 60, Aug. 21, 1862.

10. OR ser. 2, 5:795–97, Davis proclamation, Dec. 24, 1862.

11. Sherman, *Memoirs*, 2:13; Early, *Memoirs*, 291.

12. Higginson, *Army Life*, 1–2, 5, 46–49, 55–59; OR 14:195–97; Dancy, "Reminiscences," 70; Towne, *Letters and Diary*, 101, Feb. 2, 1863; Seth Rogers, journal letter of Feb. 5, 1863, USAMHI. Higginson's unreported missing men may be an early instance of assigning the names of missing or dead soldiers to new recruits, for which see Wilson, *Black Phalanx*, 123.

13. Higginson, *Army Life*, 55–59, 74–76; Chamberlain, "Letter," 85–95.

14. Higginson, "Reoccupation," 467; Higginson, *Army Life*, 75.

15. OR 14:226–27, 232–33, 237–39; Higginson, *Army Life*, 81–82, 84, 87–90, 95, 97; James S. Rogers, journal letter, Mar. 18, [1863], Sophia Smith Coll., SC; Stephens and Stephens, "Rouges," 81; James Montgomery to Mrs. George L. Stearns, Apr. 25, 1863, KSHS; Higginson, "Reoccupation," 474.

16. Higginson, *Army Life*, 96–97; Cadwell, *Sixth Regiment*, 60; Martin and Schafer, *Jacksonville's Ordeal*, 161–62.

17. Rogers letter, Mar. 18, [1863], SC; Orra B. Bailey to Wife, Mar. 13, 1863, LC; OR 14:435–36, Lincoln to Hunter, Apr. 1, 1863.

18. Stephens and Stephens, "Rouges," 81; OR 28, 2:11–13, Beauregard to Quincy A. Gillmore.

19. Williams, "Historical Sketch," 3–5, KSHS; OR 22, 1:321–22; Burke, *Military History*, 409–10; Berlin et al., *Freedom*, 2:574–78.

20. AG, *Official Army Register*, 8:246, 248, 250; Ross, *Tabular Analysis*, 24; AGO, List of Officers, 1st and 2nd Regiments Louisiana Native Guards (Free Colored), and Mustering Officer Return [listing officers] for 3d Regiment Louisiana Native Guards (Free Colored), RG 94, NA; OR 26, 1:9–13.

21. Flinn, *Campaigning with Banks*, 115, 187; Hoffman, *Camp, Court*, 97; OR 26, 1:44, 508–9; Magee, "Confederate Letters," 210; Irwin, *Nineteenth Army Corps*, 166–69; Grant, *Papers*, 8:92–93.

22. "Opposing Forces at Port Hudson, La.," in Johnson and Buel, *Battles and Leaders*, 3:598–99; Wilson, *Black Phalanx*, 525; OR 26, 1:172–73; Defenders of Port Hudson, "Fortification and Siege," 321; W. B. Shelby, "Report" (unpaginated), Aug. [8], 1863, [5], TU; Taylor, "Extraordinary Perseverance," 333.

23. William Dwight to Mother, May 26, 1863, Dwight Family Papers, MaHS; Defenders of Port Hudson, "Fortification and Siege," 321–22; Wright, *Port Hudson*, 35–36.

24. OR 26, 1:68; Wilson, *Black Phalanx*, 526; Frederick Y. Dabney, "Report" (unpaginated), Aug. 24, 1863, [10], TU; Shelby, "Report," [5], TU.

25. OR 26, 1:70; Henry M. Crydenwise to Parents, June 5, 1863, EU; Cross, "Yankee Soldier," 147; Wilson, *Black Phalanx*, 123, 214, 217; Smith, *Company K*, 65–66.

26. For "it was a battle," see Defenders of Port Hudson, "Fortification and Siege," 321; Howard C. Wright to Mother, July 16, 1863, NYHS; Robert F. Wilkinson to Father, June 3, 1863, NYHS; Flinn, *Campaigning with Banks*, 74; Kingman, *Tramping Out*, 208; George R. Sanders to Mr. Burnham, July 15, 1863, Burnham File, YU.

27. OR 26, 1:47, 554–55; Kendall, "Recollections," 1134; Smith, *Company K*, 76–77; James Grimsley to Anna, July 11, 1863, IHS.

28. OR 26, 1:66; George L. Andrews to Wife, July 8, July 12, 1863, LSU.

29. OR 15:716–17; OR 26, 1:539; OR ser. 3, 3:46; Ullmann, "Organization of Colored Troops," 2; Gardner, "Yankee in Louisiana," 276.

30. Babcock, *Selections from Letters*, 74n22; Johns, *49th Massachusetts*, 285.

31. OR 26, 1:68, 70; Moore, *Rebellion Record*, 7:210; OR ser. 2, 6:631, 924–25.

32. E. R. Manson to Friend John, Oct. 19, 1864, DU.

4. Milliken's Bend

1. *OR* ser. 2, 5:795–97; Henry G. Marshall to Folks at Home, May 3, 1863, Schoff Coll., UM; William M. Parkinson to Brother James and to Wife, May 20, May 25, 1863, EU.

2. On black soldiers, see again Jerome B. Yates to Mother, Aug. 10, 1863, UT.

3. Calvin Shedd to Wife and Children, Aug. 12, 1863, South Caroliniana Library, USC; Romeyn, "Colored Troops," 13–15; Rickard, "Services with Colored Troops," 5; *OR* ser. 2, 6:115.

4. *OR* 24, 2:457–59; Taylor, *Destruction and Reconstruction*, 137–38; Paludan, *Presidency of Lincoln*, 207–8; Greene, *The Mississippi*, 2; Ward, *Civil War*, 127; Ballard, *Vicksburg*, 25; Jones, *Command and Strategy*, 162–63.

5. *OR* 24, 2:467, 447; Sears, "Milliken's Bend," 7–8; Grant, *Memoirs*, 1:545.

6. *OR* 24, 2:448, 458, 467; *OR* ser. 3, 3:453; Sears, "Milliken's Bend," 9, 11, 14, 18–19; Cornwell, "Dan Caverno," typescript, USAMHI, 137–38, 141.

7. Blessington, *Texas Division*, 97; Cornwell, "Dan Caverno," 133–34, 138–40; Furness, "Negro as Soldier," 476.

8. Cornwell, "Dan Caverno," USAMHI, 133–34, 138–40; Sears, "Milliken's Bend," 9–11, 15–17.

9. *OR* 24, 2:464, 469; Blessington, *Texas Division*, 100, 102–3; Sears, "Milliken's Bend," 14; Cade, *Texas Surgeon*, 58.

10. Sears, "Milliken's Bend," 14; Smith, *Life and Letters*, 70; *OR* 24, 2:453; Ankeny, *Kiss Josey*, 163; McGregor, *Dearest Susie*, 53; Moore, *Rebellion Record*, 7:12–15.

11. *OR* 24, 2:468–69, 466, 459.

12. *OR* ser. 2, 6:21–22, 115.

13. Knox, *Camp-fire and Cotton-Field*, 315; *OR* 24, 3:425–26.

14. Smith, *Life and Letters*, 309–13; *OR* 24, 3:444, 469.

15. Cornwell, "Dan Caverno," USAMHI, 121–22, 135, 137, 140; *OR* 24, 2:468–69; B. Marshall Mills to Parents, June 7, 1864, Caleb Mills Papers, IHS; AG, *Official Register*, 8:152, 222.

16. Cade, *Texas Surgeon*, 58; Sears, "Milliken's Bend," 15. Cade's estimate of seventy to eighty prisoners accords with other reports, for which see *OR* 24, 2:468–69; Blessington, *Texas Division*, 99–100; and Cornwell, "Dan Caverno," USAMHI, 136.

17. Cade, *Texas Surgeon*, 58; Blessington, *Texas Division*, 97; *OR* 24, 2:467; E. P. Becton to Mary, June 13, July 1, 1863, UT; Ingram and Ingram, *Civil War Letters*, 54; Holmes, *Brokenburn*, 219.

18. Knox, *Camp-Fire and Cotton-Field*, 315–17; Taylor, *Destruction and Reconstruction*, 181; *OR* 24, 2:457, 105, 425; Becton to Mary, July 1, 1863, UT; S. W. Farrow to Josephine, July 4, 1863, UT.

19. Becton to Mary, July 1, 1863, UT; Bragg, *Letters*, 142–43; Ingram and Ingram, *Letters*, 55–56; *OR* 24, 2:466; Bailey, "Texas Cavalry Raid," 144–46; Anderson, *Campaigning*, 112; Blessington, *Texas Division*, 114.

20. Anderson, *Campaigning*, 112; Crandall and Newell, *Ram Fleet*, 311; Simmons, "Letters," 34; Bragg, *Letters*, 144; *OR* 24, 3:590, L. Kent to John A. Rawlins, Sept. 24, 1863; Hollandsworth, "Execution of White Officers," 479–80.

21. *OR* 24, 2:466; Becton to Mary, July 1, 1863, UT.

22. McGuire, *Diary*, 229; Edmondston, *Journal*, 426–28.

23. Anderson, *Memoirs*, 361; James B. Rounsaville to Family, July 9, 1863, CWMC, USAMHI; Wagner, *Letters*, 63.

24. Skinner and Skinner, *Death of a Confederate*, intro., xxx; Reagan, *Memoirs*, 161; Watson, *East Texas*, 16.

25. *OR* 26, 1:238–39, 240; Garcia, *Celine*, 127.

26. *OR* 26, 1:239, 240; Garcia, *Celine*, 127–29; Pascoe, "Confederate Cavalry," 95.

27. Garcia, *Celine*, 131–32; *OR* ser. 2, 6:924.

28. *OR* ser. 2, 6:177–78, 189, 244; *OR* 26, 1:240.

29. *OR* ser. 2, 6:244, 258, 631, 924–25.

5. Fort Wagner

1. Bernstein, *Draft Riots*; McPherson, *Battle Cry*, 686, 646; Emilio, *Fifty-Fourth Regiment*, 31–33, 36–37; *OR* 14:462.

2. Shaw, *Blue-Eyed*, 339, 342–43; Emilio, *Fifty-Fourth Regiment*, 40–43; James, "Assault on Fort Wagner," 14; Gooding, *Altar*, 10.

3. Shaw, *Blue-Eyed*, 343; Bowditch, "War Letters," 436; Gooding, *Altar*, 31; Evans, *Intrepid Warrior*, 222 and 222n2.

4. Shaw, *Blue-Eyed*, 285, 366, 368–69, 367n4; *OR* ser. 3, 3:252, 419–20; Riddle, *Reminiscences*, 252; Steiner, *Life of Reverdy Johnson*, 77; James Montgomery to Sen. Henry S. Wilson, Jan. 22, 1864, KSHS; William H. Simons to Sister, [c. June 1864], in Cross, "Civil War Letters," 234; Lewis H. Douglass to R. G. Hinton, May 1, 1895, KSHS.

5. Emilio, *Fifty-Fourth Regiment*, 49, 51–53; Gillmore, "Before Charleston," *B&L* 5:55–57.

6. Shaw, *Blue-Eyed*, 379–81; *OR* 28, 1:12, 414–15; Johnson, *Defense of Charleston*, 97; Emilio, *Fifty-Fourth Regiment*, 53, 55–61; Redkey, *Grand Army*, 33–34, 1st Sgt. R. J. Simmons; Ellsworth D. S. Goodyear, diary, July 16, 1864, Goodyear Family Papers, YU.

7. Shaw, *Blue-Eyed*, 385; Emilio, *Fifty-Fourth Regiment*, 57–63, 392; Stephens, *Voice of Thunder*, 244.

8. Pressley, "Extracts from Diary," 59; *OR* 28, 1:75; Shaw, *Blue-Eyed*, 387n5; Emilio, *Fifty-Fourth Regiment*, 62; Lane, *Dear Mother*, 253.

9. Shaw, *Blue-Eyed*, 385; Appleton, "That Night," 11; Emilio, *Fifty-Fourth Regiment*, 62.

10. Emilio, *Fifty-Fourth Regiment*, 49, 72–75; Hallowell, "Negro as a Soldier," 13; Nathaniel Paige, in *Negro in Military Service*, 2585–87, RG 94, NA; Shaw, *Blue-Eyed*, 350–51.

11. Emilio, *Fifty-Fourth Regiment*, 72–75, 79–80; [Richard] H. L. Jewett to [illegible], July 19, 1863, Boston Athenaeum; Appleton, "That Night," 13; Lewis Douglass to Amelia, July 20, 1863, Carter Woodson Papers, LC; Gooding, *Altar*, 38–39, 40n10.

12. Emilio, *Fifty-Fourth Regiment*, 81–83; Pinckney, "Diary," 42, typescript, MC; James W. Grace to R. A. Pierce, July 22, 1863, New Bedford (Mass.) Free

Public Library; Stephen A. Swail[e]s, "Statement of S. A. Swailes," Aug. 12, 1863, Cabot G. Russell Papers, NYCPL; Appleton, "That Night," 13–15.

13. *OR* 28, 1:16, 77, 418–19; Little, *Seventh Regiment New Hampshire*, 119; Edrington, "True Glory," 45; Calvin Shedd to Wife and Children, July 29, 1863, USC.

14. Emilio, *Fifty-Fourth Regiment*, 392, 402, 431; AG, *American Decorations*, 16; Calvin Shedd to Wife, Aug. 3, 1863, USC; Fox, *Losses*, 54, 423, 441.

15. A. A. McKethan, "Fifty-First Regiment," in Clark, *Histories of Several Regiments*, 3:208–9; Johnson, *Defense of Charleston*, 104; Hayne, "Defense of Wagner," 605; George P. Harrison to Dr. Burt G. Wilder, Mar. 16, 1915, B. G. Wilder Papers, CU; David B. Harris to Wife, July 29, 1863, DU; Taylor, *Lee's Adjutant*, 266–67n99; Holmes, *Diary*, 287.

16. Hayne, "Defense of Wagner," 606; Cobb, "Service of Tar Heels," 216; Pinckney, "Diary," 41, MC; Harrison to Wilder, Mar. 16, 1915, CU; Emilio, *Fifty-Fourth Regiment*, 98–99, 102–3; A. S. Fisher to Afflicted Captin [sic], July 31, 1863, GC.

17. *OR* ser. 2, 6:134; Roman, *Beauregard*, 1:137–38; Hagood, *Memoirs*, 184; Emilio, *Fifty-Fourth Regiment*, 100–1.

18. *OR* ser. 2, 6:123, 125, 134, 171, 190, 138–39; Emilio, *Fifty-Fourth Regiment*, 403–6; *OR* 14:199–204; *OR* ser. 5:708, 823–27.

19. *OR* ser. 2, 5:940–41, Joint Resolutions, Confederate Congress, April 30–May 1, 1863.

20. *OR* ser. 2, 6:193, 194; 7:673, 703–4; Emilio, *Fifty-Fourth Regiment*, 405–6, 405–8; Westwood, *Black Troops*, 93.

21. *OR* ser. 2, 6:163, Lincoln's edict, issued as General Order No. 252, July 31, 1863.

22. Donaghy, *Army Experience*, 183–84.

23. Grant, "Under Fire," 356–57; Hitchcock, *Fifty Years*, 447, 457.

24. Grant, "Under Fire," 357, 356; *OR* ser. 2, 7:1206; Emilio, *Fifty-Fourth Regiment*, 410–11, 419, 422–24.

6. Olustee

1. Calvin Shedd to Wife, Aug. 3, 1863, USC; George W. Scott to Bettie, Mar. 9, 1864, George Washington Scott Papers, FSA; *OR* ser. 3, 3:1111–15; *OR* 26, 1:684.

2. Dawson, *Diary*, 146; Fred Smith to Father, Apr. 1, Apr. 7, 1864, CWTI Coll., USAMHI; Fleet, *Green Mount*, 329; Fay, *Infernal War*, 296, 302.

3. *OR* 29, 1:910–11, 911–17; Moore, *Rebellion Record*, 8:297–301; *OR* ser. 2, 6:1127–30, 877–78.

4. *OR* 33:253–56.

5. Liddell, *Liddell's Record*, 191; Edmondston, *Journal*, 589–90.

6. Strother, *Virginia Yankee*, 259; Hawks, *Woman Doctor's War*, 61; for Johnson's hanging, not included in JAG, " Soldiers Executed," see *Harper's Weekly*, July 9, 1864, and Library of Congress negative LC—B8171—783.

7. Lowry, *Stories*, 123–31; JAG, "Soldiers Executed."

8. *OR* 35, 1:291, 321, 324, 331, 341; Olmstead, *Memoirs*, 140.

9. Basler, *Collected Works*, 7:53–56, 126; Chase, *Lincoln's Cabinet*, 190; *OR* 35, 1:278–83; Nicolay and Hay, *Complete Works*, 9:283; Alfred F. Sears to Thomas S. Brooks, Feb. 6, 1864, Thomas S. Brooks Papers, FSA; Thayer, *John Hay*, 1:163.

10. *OR* 35, 1:284–86, 277; Hawley, "Comments," *B&L* 4:79; John W. M. Appleton, "Journal," 157, WVUL; Hay, *Lincoln*, 164. On Seymour's "extreme" prejudices, see also Du Pont, *Civil War Letters*, 2:321–22.

11. *OR* 35, 1:288, 290, 301–3; Cory, "Friel Letters," 21; Redkey, *Grand Army*, 41, Rufus S. Jones; Andrew F. Ely to Aaron K. Peckham, Feb. 27, 1864, RU; Crowninshield, *First Regiment*, 263.

12. *OR* 35, 1:289, 315, 298; Palmer, *Forty-Eighth Regiment*, 133; James C. Beecher to [Frances B. Johnson], Mar. 11, 1864, Radcliffe Institute, HU.

13. *OR* 35, 1:289; James F. Hall to Dear Ones, Feb. 23, 1864, UF electronic; Ferdinand Davis, "Personal Recollections" [unpaginated, 1904], UM; William F. Penniman, "Reminiscences," 57, typescript copy, UNC; Emilio, *Fifty-Fourth Regiment*, 170, 174–75; Appleton to Wife, Feb. 24, 1864, WVUL; Duren, "Occupation," 276; A. S. Fisher to Dear Friend, Mar. 14, 1865, GC.

14. *OR* 35, 1:289, 298, 300, 332–33; Hall to Dear Ones, Feb. 23, 1864, UF electronic; Woodford, "Connecticut Yankee," 251; Moore, *Rebellion Record*, 8:416, Surgeon A. P. Aeichhold [Heichhold].

15. Egan, "Florida Campaign," 8–11; Stephens, *Voice of Thunder*, 197; Duren, "Occupation," 285; Moore, *Rebellion Record*, 8:416; Emilio, *Fifty-Fourth Regiment*, 183; *OR* ser. 2, 7:876.

16. Lawrence Jackson, "As I Saw and Remembered the Battle of Olustee," [2], typescript, Jan. 17, 1929, Edward C. Sanchez Papers, UF; Mills, "Letters," 297.

17. Returned Prisoner, *Voice from Rebel Prisons*, 4.

18. Penniman, "Reminiscences," 60–61. See also "H. W. B." to Editor, Athens *Southern Banner*, Mar. 9, 1864, UF electronic.

19. Charles C. Jones to Wife, Feb. 27, 1864, Charles Colcock Jones Family Papers, Ms. 215, UG; Henry Shackelford to Mother, Feb. 20, 1864, Atlanta *Daily Intelligencer*, Mar. 2, 1864; James M. Jordan to Louisa, Feb. 21, 1864, "Letters from Confederate Soldiers, 1860–1865," 2:480, typescript, GDAH; Joab Roach to Fannie E. Rouse, Mar. 5, 1864, GHS; Winston Stephens to Wife, Feb. 21, 1864, UF; Edwin D. Tuttle to Parents, May 7, 1864, EU.

20. Thomas W. Houston to J. W. Baggs, Mar. 20, 1864, 5th Georgia Calvary electronic; Stephens to Wife, Feb. 21, 1864, UF; Tuttle to Parents, Mar. 7, 1864, EU.

21. *OR* 35, 1:298, 328, 2:330; *OR* ser. 2, 7:174, 986–88, 991; Appleton to Wife, Feb. 24, 1864, WVUL; Emilio, *Fifty-Fourth Regiment*, 424–25, 426; White, *Prison Life*, 46; Crowninshield, *First Regiment*, 263; Charles C. Jones to Wife, Feb. 27, 1864, UG.

22. Ransom, *Diary*, 86; Emilio, *Fifty-Fourth Regiment*, 29–30; Richardson, *Secret Service*, 416; McElroy, *Andersonville*, 163; Sneden, *Eye of the Storm*, 225; Sprague, *Lights and Shadows*, 129; Gooding, *Altar*, intro., xxxi.

23. White, *Prison Life*, 46; McElroy, *Andersonville*, 162; Emilio, *Fifty-Fourth Regiment*, 428; Goss, *Soldier's Story*, 160–61; *OR* ser. 2, 7:198–99.

24. Lyman, *Meade's Headquarters*, 79; Henry Bradford letter from Johnson's Island, Mar. 20, 1864, FSU; House, *Violent Rebel*, 109–10; S. W. Holladay to Parents, Mar. 9, 1864, CCHS; *OR* ser. 4, 3:324.

25. Emilio, *Fifty-Fourth Regiment*, 177; Little, *Seventh Regiment New Hampshire*, 227, 224; *OR* 35, 1:33, 290–92; Westervelt, *Civil War Story*, 117; Moore, *Rebellion Record*, 8:409, 413–15; Stephens, *Voice of Thunder*, 297; Appleton to Wife, Feb. 24, 1864, WVUL; Wilson, *Black Phalanx*, 270.

26. *OR* ser. 2, 7:876.

7. The Yazoo to Suffolk

1. Welles, *Diary*, 1:218, Jan. 10, 1863; Basler, *Collected Works*, 6:149–50; Ross, *Tabular Analysis*, 3–4; Adams, *Autobiography*, 166; Bowditch, "War Letters," 469.

2. Dunham and Dunham, *Through the South*, 112; on favoritism shown black troops, see Dudley Gale, letter, Nov. 5, 1864, Dave Zullo Catalog #58, Mar. 1992.

3. Ross, *Tabular Analysis*, 19; Wilson, *Black Phalanx*, 465.

4. For the 3rd's history, see Main, *Story of Marches*; Lucien P. Waters to Brother Lemuel, Feb. 22, 1865, NYHS.

5. Jones, *Command and Strategy*, 185–86; *OR* 32, 1:178, 183, 316–17, 320; Wood, *Ninety-Fifth Regiment*, 92–93.

6. *OR* 32, 1:322–23; Main, *Story of Marches*, 112–13, 274, 289; unsigned letter from 1st Texas Legion camp, Mar. 12, 1864, Demetria Ann Hill Papers, UT; Crabb, *All Afire to Fight*, 205; Keen, "War Experiences," 63; Rose, *Ross' Brigade*, 105.

7. *OR* 32, 1:390, 323, 327; Main, *Story of Marches*, 115.

8. Barron, *Lone Star*, 181–83; Griscom, *Fighting with Ross*, 112–13; Rose, *Ross' Brigade*, 105n; *OR* 32, 1:831; Main, *Story of Marches*, 115. See also Ross, *Personal Letters*, 61–62.

9. *OR* 32, 1:326–27, 831.

10. *OR* 1:324–29, 383–85, 390–91; Main, *Story of Marches*, 117, 289–90; Barron, *Lone Star*, 182; Logwood, "Fifteenth Tennessee," in Lindsley, *Military Annals*, 727–28; Griscom, *Fighting with Ross*, 113–14; Barron, *Lone Star*, 182–83.

11. Main, *Story of Marches*, 120, 275, 290–91; Wood, *Ninety-Fifth Regiment*, 95; *OR* 32, 1:387; Barron, *Lone Star*, 183; Logwood, "Fifteenth Tennessee," in Lindsley, *Military Annals*, 729–30.

12. *OR* 32, 1:194, 387; Main, *Story of Marches*, 128.

13. *OR* 32, 1:194; unsigned letter, Mar. 12, 1864, Demetria Ann Hill Papers, UT.

14. Moore, *Rebellion Record*, 8:6, "Rumors and Incidents"; Houghton and Houghton, *Two Boys*, 73; Patterson, "Irrepressible Optimism," 350; Petty, *Journey*, 215; Elias Davis to Mother, Dec. [18], 1863, UNC.

15. Barron, *Lone Star*, 185–86; Griscom, *Fighting with Ross*, 115; *OR* 32, 1:653; Dyer, *Compendium*, 786; Smith, *Black Soldiers*, 293, citing Regimental Returns, Co. G, and Record of Events, both 3rd U. S. Colored Cavalry, RG 94, NA.

16. John J. Peck on Suffolk in August V. Kautz, "Operations south of the James," *B&L* 4:533n; *OR* 33:238–9; Ross, *Tabular Analysis*, 19.

17. Unknown Confederate, "Gen. Ransom's Expedition," Charlotte (N.C.) *Bulletin*, Mar. 18, 1864; Thomas R. Roulhac to Mother, Mar. 13, 1864, Ruffin Papers, UNC; Gabriel P. Sherrill to Cosin [sic], Mar. 17, 1864, CHA; Chambers, *Diary*, 183; Robert D. Graham, "Fifty-Sixth Regiment," in Clark, *Histories of Several Regiments*, 3:337.

18. Unknown, "Ransom's Expedition," Charlotte (N.C.) *Daily Bulletin*, Mar. 1864; Edmondston, *Journal*, 547; Roulhac to Mother, Mar. 13, 1864, UNC.

19. OR 33:239; Unknown, "Ransom's Expedition," Charlotte (N.C.) *Daily Bulletin*, Mar. 1864; Berlin et al., *Freedom*, 2:548–49; on black burials, see Eli Peal to Wife, May 1, 1864, NCA&R, and Elliott S. Welch to Mother, Oct. 30, 1864, Elliott Stephen Welch Papers, DU.

20. OR 33:237–39.

21. Grant, *Memoirs*, 2:115, 118, 120, 129–32; OR 32, 3:245–46, 585–86.

22. Brown, *University Greys*, 54, Willis M. Lea; "Memphis," in Atlanta *Memphis Daily Appeal*, May 2, 1864; Smedes, *Memorials*, 179; Morton, *Artillery*, 13; Oates, *The War*, 466; Dixon, diary, Nov. 18, Dec. 23, 1864, UNC; Bevens, *Reminiscences*, 225–27.

23. Grant, *Memoirs*, 2:346; OR 39, 3:659, 2:121; OR 32, 3:411.

24. Snider, "Reminiscences," 240–41; OR 32, 1:543; Sherman, *Memoirs*, 2:12–13; Moore, *Rebellion Record*, 8:56; Morgan, "Reminiscences," 31; McGee, *72nd Indiana*, 274.

25. OR 32, 1:611, 1:542–46, 3:157; Hancock, *Diary*, 338, 339–41; Witherspoon, *Reminiscences*, in Henry, *Forrest*, 101–2; Hawkins, "West Tennessee Unionists," 35–42; Report of the Joint Committee, *Fort Pillow*, 71.

26. OR 32, 1:547; Hancock, *Diary*, 340–43; J. V. Greif, "Civil War Recollections," comp. Mrs. D. G. Murrell (1905–8), set 2, 6, McCracken County Public Library, Paducah, Ky.; Jennie Fyfe to [Netie], Apr. 6, 1864, Fyfe Family Coll., UM.

27. OR 32, 1:547–48; ORN 26:202; Hubert Saunders to Mother from USS *Peosta*, Mar. 28 [1864], DU; Hancock, *Diary*, 341–42; Moore, *Rebellion Record*, 8:500, 502; George, *History*, 76; Head, *Sixteenth Tennessee*, 436.

28. OR 32, 1:548, 607; Fyfe to Sisters, Mar. 20, 1864, UM; Gorgas, *Diary*, 89.

29. OR 32, 1:607, 549; Hancock, *Diary*, 343, Mar. 25, 1864; Fyfe to Dear Ones, Mar. 31, 1864, UM; Saunders to Mother, Apr. 25, 1864, DU; Moore, *Rebellion Record*, 8:501.

30. Greif, "Recollections," set 1, 33, 35; Hager, "Second Tennessee Cavalry," in Lindsley, *Military Annals*, 616; Moore, *Rebellion Record*, 503, "Another Account"; OR 32, 1:610.

8. Fort Pillow

1. In recent years, African American activists have sought to remove statues and to rename schools and parks honoring Forrest, for examples of which see *New York Times*, Jan. 1, 1998; Memphis *Commercial-Appeal*, July 30, Aug. 2, Aug. 3, Aug. 4, 2005; *Los Angeles Times*, Aug. 5, 2005.

2. Sleeth, "Fort Pillow," 72, 77–78, 82–83, 87–88; Report of Joint Committee, *Fort Pillow*, 67, 41; OR 32, 1:179, 556, 2:311, 318, 556; Tennessee Civil War Centennial Commission, *Tennesseans*, 353–54.

3. *OR* 32, 1:559, 609; Anderson, "True Story," 322; Hollis, "Diary," 96; Mainfort, *Archaeological Investigations*, 3, 7, 9, 11, 13, 29. Morning twilight time is by courtesy of U.S. Naval Observatory, Washington, D.C.

4. Lionel F. Booth CMSR, RG 94, AGO, NA; Report of Joint Committee, *Fort Pillow*, 65, 38, 86; *OR* 32, 1:539, 568; Monthly Return, Bradford's Battalion, Apr. 8, 1864, AGO, RG 94, NA; Cimprich and Mainfort, "Fort Pillow Revisited," 294n2; *ORN* 26:219; *New Era* log, Apr. 12, 1864, Logs of U.S. Naval Ships, RG 24, NA; Charles Robinson to Folks at Home, Apr. 17, 1864, Mortimer Robinson and Family Papers, MHS. Erroneous strength figures are at *OR* 32, 1:556.

5. Anderson, "True Story," 322–23; *OR* 32, 1:528, 535, 559; Booth CMSR; Robinson to Folks, Apr. 17, 1864, MHS; Cimprich and Mainfort, "Fort Pillow Revisited," 298n17; Tennessee Civil War Centennial Commission, *Tennesseans*, 353–54; Report of Joint Committee, *Fort Pillow*, 67; Hancock, *Diary*, 357.

6. Anderson, "True Story," 322; Wyeth, *Forrest*, 342–43; Fitch, "Dr. Fitch's Report," 27, 31; *OR* 32, 1:560–61, 594, 596, 614; Hancock, *Diary*, 358–59; *New Era* log, Apr. 12, 1864, NA.

7. Hancock, *Diary*, 366–68; Head, *Sixteenth Tennessee*, 436; Witherspoon, *Reminiscences*, in Henry, *Forrest*, 103, 108.

8. Hancock, *Diary*, 359; Anderson, "True Story," 323; Achilles V. Clark to Sisters, Apr. 14, 1864, Confederate Coll., TSLA; *OR* 32, 1:615, 559–61; Report of Joint Committee, *Fort Pillow*, 82.

9. *OR* 32, 1:566; *ORN* 26:220; Fitch, "Dr. Fitch's Report," 31, 36; Report of Joint Committee, *Fort Pillow*, 42, 39, 92, 86; *New Era* log, Apr. 12, 1864, NA.

10. Clark to Sisters, Apr. 14, 1864, TSLA.

11. Samuel H. Caldwell to Wife, Apr. 15, 1864, WPA, Civil War Letters, 4:61, TSLA; "Marion," in Mobile (Ala.) *Advertiser and Register*, Apr. 26, 1864.

12. "Vidette," in Mobile (Ala.) *Advertiser and Register*, Apr. 17, 1864; "Memphis," in Atlanta *Memphis Daily Appeal*, May 2, 1864. The *Appeal* published in several different Southern cities during the war.

13. Report of Joint Committee, *Fort Pillow*, 32, 39, 42, 43.

14. Robinson to Folks, Apr. 17, 1864, MHS; Report of Joint Committee, *Fort Pillow*, 36, 33, 121; Fitch, "Dr. Fitch's Report," 36; *OR* 32, 1:537.

15. "Memphis," in Atlanta *Memphis Daily Appeal*, May 2, 1864; *OR* 32, 1:610.

16. Carroll, *Autobiography*, 28; Report of Joint Committee, *Fort Pillow*, 13, 19, 21, 22, 25, 39, 52, 55, 94; Fitch, "Dr. Fitch's Report," 36.

17. Report of Joint Committee, *Fort Pillow*, 13, 20–21, 25–26, 47, 51, 58–59, 85, 90, 107, 75; *OR* 32, 1:525, 537; Fitch, "Capture of Fort Pillow," 440–41.

18. Carroll, *Autobiography*, 28, UNC; Report of Joint Committee, *Fort Pillow*, 13, 19, 21, 22, 25, 39, 52, 55, 94; Fitch, "Dr. Fitch's Report," 36.

19. Report of Joint Committee, *Fort Pillow*, 13, 20–21, 25–26, 47, 51, 58–59, 85, 90, 107, 75; *OR* 32, 1:525, 537; Fitch, "Capture of Fort Pillow," 440–41.

20. Bryan McAlister, "Forrest on Fort Pillow," in Moore, *Rebellion Record*, 8:55–56; Wyeth, *Forrest*, 381; Atlanta *Memphis Daily Appeal*, June 14, 1864.

21. Report of Joint Committee, *Fort Pillow*, 39–40; *OR* 32, 1:616; Anderson,

"True Story," 324; W. R. Dyer, Diaries 1863–1864, Apr. 12, 1864, Confederate Coll., TSLA.

22. Anderson, "True Story," 324; Head, *Sixteenth Tennessee*, 440; Swift, "Letters," 54; ORN 26:222; Hancock, *Diary*, 364; Report of Joint Committee, *Fort Pillow*, 39–40, 45, 34, and see also 43, 85.

23. Report of Joint Committee, *Fort Pillow*, 47, 30, 31, 34, 35, 40, 42, 44, 58, 90–92.

24. Anderson, "True Story," 324; OR 32, 1:598–99; Hancock, *Diary*, 364; ORN 26:222–24, 224–26; Satterlee, *The Journal*, 233; Report of Joint Committee, *Fort Pillow*, 91, 91–92, 50–51, 107–9, 100–1.

25. Anderson, "True Story," 325; Report of Joint Committee, *Fort Pillow*, 89, William B. Purdy; OR 32, 1:558, 565; Satterlee, *The Journal*, 234.

26. OR 32, 1:598, 609, 622; Caldwell to Wife, Apr. 15, 1864, TSLA; "Vidette," in *Mobile* (Ala.) *Advertiser and Register*, Apr. 17, 1864; Clark to Sisters, Apr. 14, 1864, TSLA; Alfred T. Fielder, diaries, Vol. 3, Confederate Coll., TSLA, Apr. 15, 1864.

27. OR 32, 1:555–56, 562, 568–70; ORN 26:224; Monthly Returns, Bradford's Battalion, Apr. 8, 1864, AGO Records, and 11th U.S. Colored Infantry, May 10, 1864, AGO Records [the unit that absorbed the 6th Colored Heavy Artillery survivors], RG 94, NA; Fitch, "Dr. Fitch's Report," 29–30; List of Prisoners, Confederate Records, RG 109, NA. See also Cimprich, *Slavery's End*, 94, table 6.

28. OR 32, 1:599, 609, 610, 612, 615, 616; Report of Joint Committee, *Fort Pillow*, 90, 100; ORN 26:222, 224; "Vidette," in *Mobile* (Ala.) *Advertiser and Register*, Apr. 17, 1864; "Memphis," in Atlanta *Memphis Daily Appeal*, May 2, 1864.

9. The Camden Expedition

1. Report of Joint Committee, *Fort Pillow*, 101–2; OR 32, 1:589, 592; Head, *Sixteenth Tennessee*, 440; Hancock, *Diary*, 362; Jordan and Pryor, *Campaigns*, 455.

2. OR ser. 2, 6:163; Moore, *Rebellion Record*, 8:418–19; for reprisal threat, see CMSR Pvt. Wilson Wood, 6th U.S. Colored Heavy Artillery, AGO, RG 94, NA; Rice, *Reminiscences*, 188–89. For General Order 100, Apr. 21, 1863, see OR ser. 2, 5:671–82.

3. Basler, *Collected Works*, 7:301–3, 328–29; Nicolay and Hay, *Complete Works*, 6:481–84; Thomas and Hyman, *Stanton*, 372–74; Bates, *Diary*, 365, 369; Welles, *Diary*, 2:23–25; Bancroft, *William H. Seward*, 2:328–29, 333–35.

4. Nicolay and Hay, *Complete Works*, 6:484; Basler, *Collected Works*, 7:345–46.

5. OR 32, 3:362, 364, 366–67, 373, 464; Chetlain, *Recollections*, 101.

6. Berlin et al., *Freedom*, ser. 2, 587–88; Holzer, *Dear Mr. Lincoln*, 346–47; Steiner, *Reverdy Johnson*, 83; Sunderland, *Five Days to Glory*, 156; Lucius P. Mox to Jennie, Apr. 27, 1864, UV electronic; *Harper's Weekly*, Apr. 30, 1864; Samuel Evans to Father, June 11–12, 1864, OHS; Hough, *Soldier in the West*, 188; Sherman and Sherman, *Letters*, 234.

7. Report of Joint Committee, *Fort Pillow*, 4, 1; OR 32, 1:601; Welles, *Diary*, 2:24, May 5, 1864.

8. Daniel Densmore to Friends, June 3–5, 1864, Benjamin Densmore and Family Papers, MHS; Goulding, "Colored Troops," 153; Bouton, *Events*, 80–81; Strong, *Diary*, 463–64.

9. *OR* 32, 1:586–87; Rickard, "Services with Colored Troops," 36; Connolly, *Three Years*, 191–92.

10. John Garibaldi to Wife, Apr. 22, 1864, VMI electronic; Richard White to Cousin, Apr. 23, 1864, Ross Family Papers, VSLA; House, *Violent Rebel*, 130; Edmondston, *Journal*, 549–50.

11. *OR* 32, 1:607, 613–17, 595, 604–5.

12. Wyeth, *Forrest*, 337, 592.

13. Chestnut, *Civil War*, 596; Eldred Simkins to Eliza Trescott, Aug. 8, 1864, HEH.

14. Randall, *Civil War*, 592; Nicolay and Hay, *Complete Works*, 8:285–89, 9:289, 296, 300; Sherman, *Memoirs*, 1:386, 388, 397; Grant, *Memoirs*, 2:139; *OR* 34, 1:657–59, 661, 824–25; Anderson, "Southern Arkansas," 242; White, "Bluecoat's Account," 82–84.

15. Irwin, "Red River Campaign," *B&L* 345–62; Sherman, *Home Letters*, 289, 291; Hubbard, "Letters," 316; G. B. Crain to R. D. Orton, May 8, 1864, Orton Family Papers, ETRC, ASU; Frank D. Harding to Father, May 28, 1864, UW; Andrews, *North Reports*, 515–17.

16. *OR* 34, 1:661–63, 676, 679–80; Earle, "Roll, Accounts and History of the 1st Kansas Colored Volunteer Regiment," "Note" leaf after p. 27, NEHGS; Stinson, "Yankees in Camden," in Jones, *Heroines of Dixie*, 278, 280, 283.

17. *OR* 34, 1:680, 743; Pearson, "War Diary," 5:437–38; Williams, "Historical Sketch," 9, KSHS; Earle, "1st Kansas," 24, NEHGS.

18. *OR* 34, 1:743–46, 748–49, 754, 781, 818–19, 825–26, 828, 844, 848–49; Avera, "Extracts," 102–3; Williams, "Historical Sketch," 9–11, KSHS; Earle, "1st Kansas," 25, NEHGS; Lothrop, *First Regiment Iowa Cavalry*, 180–81.

19. *OR* 34, 1:746, 754, 756; Earle, "1st Kansas," 25, and "Note" leaf after 26, NEHGS; Kerby, *Kirby Smith's Confederacy*, 312; [Alfred G. Hearn] to Sallie, Apr. 20, 1864, Solomon Spence Family Papers, Old State House Museum, Little Rock, Ark.; William M. Stafford, "Battery Journal," April 18, 1864, M. D. Hutcheson Papers, Camden, Ark., quoted in Urwin's "We Cannot Treat Negroes," in his *Black Flag*, 135; Britton, *On the Border*, 2:291.

20. Anderson, "Southern Arkansas," 242–43; Avera, "Extracts," 107; Fay, *Infernal War*, 298, 391.

21. [Hearn] to Sallie, Apr. 20, 1864; Harrell, "Arkansas," in Evans, *Confederate Military History*, 10:250; Wesley W. Bradly to Wife, Apr. 21, 1864, Wesley W. Bradley Papers; *OR* 34, 1:692.

22. *OR* 34, 1:746, 756; Williams, "Historical Sketch," 11, KSHS; Sperry, *33d Iowa*, 81; Crawford, *Kansas*, 117.

23. Crawford, *Kansas*, 117; *OR* 34, 1:746, 792, 820, 844; Fox, *Losses*, 24, 515. A higher black casualty count is at Earle, "1st Kansas," 25, NEHGS.

24. Sperry, *33d Iowa*, 81; Earle, "1st Kansas," 25, NEHGS; *OR* 34, 1:668, 676, 680, 712–13, 763; Drake, "General Steele," 66, 68; Pearson, "War Diary," 5:439.

25. OR 34, 1:713–14, 788–89, 793–94, 835–36; Atkinson, "Battle of Marks Mill," 382; Anderson, "Southern Arkansas," 243; Avera, "Extracts," 103–4; Drake, "General Steele," 68–70.

26. Edwards, *Shelby*, 279; Fleming, "Personal Reminiscences of Military Prison Life," Fulton-Lenz Papers, USAMHI; Pearson, "War Diary," 5:441; OR 34, 1:714–15.

27. OR 34, 1:665, 714, 787; Bradly to Wife, May 12, 1864, electronic; Dyer, *Compendium*, 683; Britton, *On the Border*, 2:295.

28. Long, "Jenkin's Ferry," 2–4; Nicholson, "Jenkin's Ferry," 505; OR 34, 1:668–69, 677, 680; Sperry, *33d Iowa*, 88–89.

29. OR 34, 1:782, 799–800, 757–58; William M. McPheeters, diary, Apr. 30, 1864, MoHS; Bragg, *Letters*, 226; Earle, "1st Kansas," 27, NEHGS; Crawford, *Kansas*, 119–20.

30. OR 34, 1:758, 782; White, "Bluecoat's Account," 88; Joseph Hotz to Wife, May 5, May 9, 1864, trans. from the German, IHS; Crawford, *Kansas*, 121, 123–24. See also Musser, *Soldier Boy*, 124.

31. OR 34, 1:697, 758, 813; Crawford, *Kansas*, 124–29; Sperry, *33d Iowa*, 92; Reuben F. Playford, "An Outrageous Lie," Carbondale (Kans.) *Astonisher & Paralyzer*, Feb. 12, 1887; White, "Bluecoat's Account," 87–88; John R. Graton to Wife, May 6, 1864, KSHS; Edwards, *Shelby*, 295, 297; Fay, *Infernal War*, 395.

32. Nicholson, "Jenkin's Ferry," 511; Milton P. Chambers to Brother, May 6, 1864, UA; Yeary, *Boys in Gray*, 437.

33. Yeary, *Boys in Gray*, 799, 437, Williams and Jones; Bragg, *Letters*, 230; Cade, *Texas Surgeon*, 99; Crawford, *Kansas*, 124. For Confederate Brig. Gen. T. N. Waul on "mutilation and murder, which the barbarity of the enemy had inflicted," see OR 34, 1:817.

34. OR 34, 1:670; Burke, *Military History*, 430; Nicholson, "Jenkin's Ferry," 512, 514–15.

35. OR 34, 1:668, 672, 783; McPheeters diary, Apr. 30, 1864, MoHS; Anderson, "Southern Arkansas," 243; J. G. Graham to R. D. Orton, May 8, 1864, Orton Family Papers, ETRC, ASU; Musser, *Soldier Boy*, 125; Wilson, *Black Phalanx*, 241.

36. White, "Bluecoat's Account," 89; Julius Schlaich to Dear [illegible], May 5, 1864, German script, trans. by Ingrid Wollank, SHSW; OR 34, 1:689, 671.

37. William Blain to Wife, May 17, 1864, quoted in Urwin, *Black Flag*, 145.

10. The Plymouth Pogrom

1. Porter, *Campaigning with Grant*, 125.

2. Hawkins, "Early Coast Operations," B&L 1:632–59; Poor, "Yankee Soldier," 130; Chauncey B. Welton to Parents, Sept. 15, 1863, UNC; Edmondston, *Journal*, 551, 458, 466–67.

3. Dowdey, *Experiment in Rebellion*, 338; OR 33:92–99, 865–70; Paris, "Hangings at Kinston," in Yearns and Barrett, *North Carolina*, 58–59; U.S. Congress, House, *Murder of Union Soldiers*.

4. OR 51, 2:292, 857–58, 946–47; Dowdey and Manarin, *Lee*, Docs. 648, 653, 655, 660, and 663; Beauregard, "Drewry's Bluff," 4:195; Grant, *Memoirs*, 2:138.

5. *OR* 51, 2:857–58; Barrow, "Civil War Letters," 80; Elliott, "First Battle," *B&L* 4:626.

6. *OR* 33:296–98; Kellogg, *Life and Death*, 25, 27; Smith, "Capture of Plymouth," 324–25, 327–28, 333; Fiske, *War Letters*, 54; Nate Lanpheur, "Fall of Plymouth, North Carolina," 3–4, 7, script, DU; Stephen T. Andrews to Maggie, Feb. 23, 1864, Stephen T. Andrews Papers; Cooper, *Rebel Prisons*, 14; Blakeslee, *Sixteenth Connecticut*, 55.

7. *OR* 33:298–99, 301–3; *ORN* 9:637, 639, 640–45; Harrill, *Reminiscences*, 16–17; Lanpheur, "Plymouth," 15, DU; John W. Wynne to Father, Apr. 24, 1864, VHS; Lynch, "Action at Plymouth," in Yearns and Barrett, *North Carolina*, 61; Lee, "Diary,"14; Goss, *Soldier's Story*, 59; Blakeslee, *Sixteenth Connecticut*, 58; Donaghy, *Army Experiences*, 151, 158; John A. Hedrick to Brother, May 8, Apr. 25, 1864, Benjamin Sherwood Hedrick Papers, DU.

8. Ludwig, "8th Regiment," and Graham, "Capture of Plymouth," in Clark's *Histories of Several Regiments*, 1:400; 5:183–90; *OR* 33:299; Blakeslee, *Sixteenth Connecticut*, 58–59; Waddell, *Last Year*, 13; George W. Love to Sister, Apr. 24, 1864, Matthew N. Love Papers, DU; Henry T. Guion, journal, [92], W. A. Hoke Papers, UNC; Goss, *Soldier's Story*, 59; Cooper, *Rebel Prisons*, 30; Unnamed civilian, "The Plymouth Battles," Raleigh (N.C.) *Daily Confederate*, May 3, 1864, and for no-quarter advocacy, see also "The Fall of Plymouth—A Specimen of Yankee Lying," Raleigh (N.C.) *Daily Confederate*, May 2, 1864; Edwin C. Peirson to Parents, Apr. 21, 1864 (microfilm only), EU.

9. Smith, "Capture of Plymouth," 339–41; William Beavans, diary, Apr. 20, 1864, UNC; Donaghy, *Army Experience*, 161–62; Billingsley, *Flag to Cross*, 68; Cooper, *Rebel Prisons*, 33. Note that Jordan and Thomas, "Massacre at Plymouth," question the hospital steward story because they could not identify him as belonging to any unit there. However, he might have been there on detached service. In any event, the tale matches events, though it does seem odd that a Louisiana deserter was recognized in North Carolina.

10. McNary, "Rebel Prisons," 25–27; Stein, *Thirty-Seventh Regt.*, 39.

11. Kellogg, *Life and Death*, 40; Goss, *Soldier's Story*, 62; Mosher, *Civil War*, 206; Donaghy, *Army Experience*, 156; Morgan, *Personal Reminiscences*, 189.

12. *OR* 33:301, 870; Smith, "Capture of Plymouth," 324; for 10th U.S. Colored Infantry detachment, see Dyer, *Compendium*, 1725; John W. Darden, "Story of Washington County," [8], typescript, NC Coll., UNC; *OR* ser. 2, 7:459–60; Billingsley, *Flag to Cross*, 69; Jimerson, *Private War*, 115 and 115n49, citing letter from Rebecca P. Davis to Burwell Davis, May 9, 1864, typescript, in private possession; Goss, *Soldier's Story*, 61. Jordan and Thomas, "Massacre at Plymouth," question Sgt. Johnson's existence and suspect that Butler fabricated the account. However, the truth does not hinge upon Johnson's testimony.

13. Merrill, *24th Independent Battery*, 217; Donaghy, *Army Experience*, 155; Cooper, *Rebel Prisons*, 34; *OR* ser. 2, 7:459–60; Goss, *Soldier's Story*, 61. See also Robbins, "Some Recollections of a Private," 31, ConnHS.

14. Frank P. O'Brien, in Bossie O'Brien Baer, "With the Passing Years," 27–28, undated typescript, HSWC; William I. Clopton to Mother, Apr. 24, 1864, DU; Cooper, *Rebel Prison*, 33; Morgan, *Personal Reminiscences*, 189; Mosher, *Civil*

War, 205. See also "The Plymouth Battles," Raleigh (N.C.) *Daily Confederate*, May 3, 1864.

15. Billingsley, *Flag to Cross*, 69; Charles A. Wills to Wife, Apr. 22, Apr. 24, 1864, CW&M; "The Plymouth Battles," Raleigh (N.C.) *Daily Confederate*, May 3, 1864; Blakeslee, *Sixteenth Connecticut*, 60; O'Brien, in Baer, "Passing Years," 27–28; Darden, "Washington County," [8–9].

16. Reed, *101st Pennsylvania*, 135; Durrill, *War of Another Kind*, 207; ORN 9:641; Goss, *Soldier's Story*, 57, 61–62; OR 51, 2:870; OR ser. 2, 7:78.

17. OR 33:305, 321, 298, 300, 303; OR 51, 2:870; Kean, *Inside the Government*, 144; Chestnut, *Civil War*, 596; Roman, *Beauregard*, 2:544; Williams, "Fifty-Fourth Regiment," in Clark, *Histories of Several Regiments*, 3:274; for unit losses, see Raleigh (N.C.) *Daily Confederate*, Apr. 30, May 2, May 5, 1864; Phisterer, *Statistical Record*, 216; Dyer, *Compendium*, 823.

18. OR 33:279; Hay, *Lincoln*, 172; Welles, *Diary*, 2:16–17; Bates, *Diary*, 361.

19. For New York *Tribune*, Philadelphia *Inquirer*, and New York *Herald* of Apr. 26, 1864, see Blakeslee, *Sixteenth Connecticut*, 68, 71, 72; *New York Times*, Apr. 22–23, Apr. 25–26, 1864.

20. OR ser. 2, 7:468; "The Fall of Plymouth—A Specimen of Yankee Lying," Raleigh (N.C.) *Daily Confederate*, May 2, 1864. For swift, harsh retaliation, see ORN 26:745–46, 762.

21. Reed, *101st Pennsylvania*, 136–38; Dickey, *103d Pennsylvania*, 268–70. Here these regimental histories are verbatim matches. Dickey collaborated with Reed on the first and listed himself as chief author of the second.

22. William A. Biggs to Sister, May 3, 1864, Asa Biggs Papers, DU; Eli Peal to Wife, May 1, 1864, NCA&R; OR 33:1320–21, 1331–32; OR 51, 2:882–84; Roman, *Beauregard*, 2:199, 547; Beauregard, "Drewry's Bluff," 4:195.

23. OR 36, 1:216, 990–91; Byrd C. Willis, diary, May 7, May 8, 1864, and Rawleigh Dunaway to Sister, May 12, 1864, VSLA; Grimes, *Extracts of Letters*, 50.

24. Giles W. Shurtleff to Mary Burton, May 17, 1864, OC; Washington, *Eagles on Their Buttons*, 41, 97n29; Robert G. Fitzgerald, diary, May 16, 1864, Microfilm #4177, SHC, UNC.

25. Henry Pippitt to Mother, June 20, 1864, UM; Butler, *Autobiography*, 669; Means, "Sixty-Third Regiment (Fifth Cav.)," in Clark, *Histories of Several Regiments*, 3:604–6; ORN 10:87, 90–91; OR 36, 2:269–71; Simonton, "James River," 482–84, 486–87; Carter, "Fourteen Months'," 161; Gill, *Courier for Lee*, 49.

26. Simonton, "James River," 487; Redkey, *Grand Army*, 98; Hay, *Lincoln*, 240–41; Booth, *Maryland Soldier*, 116.

27. Grant, *Memoirs*, 2:293–94; OR 40, 1:704; Samuel J. Hopkins, journal, June 18, 1864, RU; Rhodes, *All for the Union*, 163; Carlos P. Lyman to Dear Ones, June 19, 1864, WRHS; Alexander, *Fighting*, 419; Leslie, *Leslie's Illustrated*, 438.

28. Holland, "From Slavery to Freedom," 15; Christian A. Fleetwood, diary, June 15, 1864, LC; Carter, "Fourteen Months'," 165, 167; Redkey, *Grand Army*, 102, William H. Hunter. See also Robert G. Fitzgerald, diary, June 15, 1864, UNC.

29. Fitzgerald, diary, June 15, 1864, UNC; Hall, "Mine Run," 236–39; Dayton E. Flint to Father, June 20, 1864, USAMHI; Clarke, *Back Home*, 142; Fisk, *Hard Marching*, 231.

30. Ford, *Adams Letters*, 2:153–54; Thompson, *My Country*, 109.

31. Brown, *Diary*, 56; Edward W. Bacon to Kate, Sept. 26–27, 1864, Edward Woolsey Bacon Papers, AAS; Furness, "Negro as Soldier," 480.

11. Brice's Cross Roads

1. Rice, *Reminiscences*, 187; Porter, *Campaigning with Grant*, 126.

2. B. W. H. Pasron to A. A. Shafer, Mar. 24, 1863, *CWTI* Coll., USAMHI; Lee, *Wartime Washington*, 237; Wash Vosburgh to Ella, Aug. 22, 1864, Ness Coll., UM; Brewster, *Cruel War*, 316.

3. John Slaver to Rosanna, Aug. 17, 1864, Ness Coll., UM; Lemuel Jones to Brother, Feb. 12, 1864, Miscl. Civil War Letters, Filson Club Historical Society; Parks, *Letters*, 41; Abbott, "The Negro," 373; Cox, "Letters," 1:64, 2:187; Francis G. Barnes to Wife, Jan. 8, 1865, NYSL; O'Hagan, "Diary," 408.

4. Redkey, *Grand Army*, 258–62, B. W., and "Private," 43rd U.S. Colored Infantry.

5. Breckinridge, *Lucy Breckinridge*, 194; Currey, "Fear in North Carolina," 43, Apr. 13, 1865.

6. Lonn, *Desertion*, 22–24; Power, *Lee's Miserables*, 182–83; Robert N. Verplanck to Mother, Oct. 18, 1864, Adriance Memorial Library, Poughkeepsie, N.Y.; J. T. Kern to Mother, Apr. 2, 1864, J. T. Kern Papers (#2526), UNC, also electronic.

7. Howard, "Wilson's Raid in Georgia," in News and Courier, *Our Women*, 187; Strother, *Virginia Yankee*, 255; Edmondston, *Journal*, 463; Baylor, "The Army Negro," 365–69.

8. Smith, *Soldier's Friend*, 132; Patterson, *Yankee Rebel*, 128; Ward, *My Country*, 101.

9. *ORN* 15:441–54; *OR* 35, 1:397, 2:123; *OR* ser. 2, 7:198–99; Perkins, "Two Years," 536.

10. For sailor executions, see *ORN* 12:651, 13:83, 15:152–61, and 26:418–18; as prisoners, see Bosson, *Forty-Second Regiment*, 418, and Ramold, *Slaves, Sailors, Citizens*, 132–37; Durkin, *Stephen R. Mallory*, 319–20; Welles, *Diary*, 2:168–72.

11. Cowden, *Fifty-Ninth Regiment*, 92; Densmore to Friends, June 4, 1864, MHS; *OR* 32, 1:586–87.

12. John A. Crutchfield to Wife, May 22, 1864, CCHS; Sherman, *Memoirs*, 2:52; *OR* 39, 1:148, 217–18, 221–23, 153–56; Hanson, "Defeat of Sturgis," 4:420.

13. *OR* 39, 1:172, 176, 179, 181–82, 186, 197–98, 213, 216, 223; Hancock, *Diary*, 282; Henry M. Austin to Toledo *Blade*, Apr. 7, 1879, http://www.iowa-counties.com/civilwar/2nd-infantry-Austin.htm (accessed July 29, 1999; entry later discontinued); Cowden, *Fifty-Ninth Regiment*, 92, 94–98, 110–11, 115, 118, 120–22; Wood, *Ninety-Fifth Regiment*, 111–12; Scott, *Cavalry Regiment*, 242, 246–47; John Merrilies, diary, typescript, CHS, 2:66, June 10, 1864; William H. Stewart, diary, June 10, 1864, typescript, UNC.

14. John A. Crutchfield to Wife, June 13, 1864, CCHS; H. A. Tyler to Edmund W. Rucker, June 22, 1864, Edmund Winchester Rucker Papers, Birmingham Public Library; Witherspoon, *Tishomingo Creek*, in Henry, *Forrest*, 124.

15. *OR* 32, 1:586–87, 587; Witherspoon, *Tishomingo Creek*, 124; Merrilies, diary, CHS, 2:66; Webster Moses to Nancy, June 21, 1864, KSHS; Hord, "Brice's X Roads," 530; Hancock, *Diary*, 390; Hanson, *Minor Incidents*, 74; Morton, *Artillery*, 184. See also Chalmers, "Forrest and His Campaigns," 474.

16. Andrus, *Letters*, 87; Hord, "Brice's X Roads," 530; Agnew, "Battle of Tishomingo Creek," 402.

17. Cogley, *Seventh Indiana Cavalry*, 116; Cowden, *Fifty-Ninth Regiment*, 119; Abbott, "The Negro," 380; Bouton, *Events*, 81; *OR* 32, 1:587; Reed, "Guntown and Tupelo," 308.

18. Wilson, *Black Phalanx*, 349; Witherspoon, *Tishomingo Creek*, 134; Head, *Sixteenth Tennessee*, 444–45; Agnew, "Battle of Tishomingo Creek," 402; Yeary, *Boys in Gray*, 236, R. J. Fort; Dyer and Moore, *Tennessee Veterans*, 1:375, Solomon N. Brantley.

19. Hancock, *Diary*, 400, June 12, 1864; Witherspoon, *Tishomingo Creek*, 134; *OR* 39, 1:127; Wilson, *Black Phalanx*, 349; Kellogg, *Life and Death*, 143, 145.

20. *OR* 39, 1:174, 214, 224; Merrilies, diary, CHS 2:66; Abbott, "The Negro," 379–80; MacDonald, "Brice's Cross Roads,"457.

21. Witherspoon, *Tishomingo Creek*, 134; Morton, *Artillery*, 197.

22. *OR* 39, 1:125, 127; Fox, *Losses*, 22, 547; Dyer, *Compendium*, 787.

23. Agnew, "Battle of Tishomingo Creek," 402; Head, *Sixteenth Tennessee*, 445; Hancock, *Diary*, 399; *OR* 32, 1:586, 590.

24. McPherson, *Battle Cry*, 748; *OR* 39, 1:95, 159–60, 2:123–24; Henry M. Newhall to Siblings, June 15, 1864, ISHL; Satterlee, *The Journal*, 251, 254; Samuel Evans to Father, June 11, June 12, 1864, OHS; Austin to Toledo *Blade*, Apr. 7, 1879.

25. *OR* 35, 1:14, 120–22, 124; Fox, *Record of Service*, 29–31; Califf, *Seventh Regiment*, 28–29; Johnson, *Defense of Charleston*, 214–15; Andrews, *Footprints*, 140.

26. Andrews, *Footprints*, 141–43.

27. Hollandsworth, "Execution of White Officers," 488–89.

28. Andrews, *Footprints*, 143–44; *OR* 35, 1:16, 85, 264, 267.

12. The Petersburg Mine

1. Jones, *Command and Strategy*, 203; Shaver, *Sixtieth Alabama*, 63–65; Giles Shurtleff to Mary, July 21, 1864, OC; Bosbyshell, *48th in the War*, 164–66.

2. Meade and Meade, *Life and Letters*, 2:217, 218; *OR* 40, 1:59, 556–68; Report of Joint Committee, *Attack on Petersburg*, 14–15, 126–28; Bosbyshell, *48th in the War*, 166–69.

3. Grant, *Memoirs*, 2:310; Report of Joint Committee, *Attack on Petersburg*, 119, 123, 125; *OR* 40, 1:177, 280; Thomas, "Colored Troops," *B&L* 4:563–64.

4. Grant, *Papers*, 11:303, 305–7, 312–13, 320–23; Meade and Meade, *Life and Letters*, 2:217–18; *OR* 40, 1:46, 132–34; Report of Joint Committee, *Attack on Petersburg*, 16–17, 42, 102, 125.

5. Newberry, "The Petersburg Mine," 121; Grant, *Memoirs*, 2:313; Report of Joint Committee, *Attack on Petersburg*, 124.

6. Meade, *Life and Letters*, 2:217; *OR* 40, 1:103–4, 118–19, 557–8, 563, 788; Weld, *War Diary*, 353, July 30, 1864; Conrad Noll, diaries, July 30, 1864, UM;

Hugh L. Kerrick to Sister, Aug. 30, 1864, PNB; Powell, "Petersburg Crater," *B&L* 4:551; William Taylor to Wife, July 31, 1864, CW&M; Byron M. Cutcheon, "Personal Recollections," chap. "The Battle of the Crater," 14, UM; Porter, *Campaigning with Grant*, 264.

7. Kilmer, "Dash into the Crater," 774–76; *OR* 40, 1:108; Dowdey and Manarin, *Lee*, Doc. 843; Bernard, *War Talks*, 151, 177–78n, 213–14.

8. Report of Joint Committee, *Attack on Petersburg*, 21, 34, 105, 122; *OR* 40, 1:166, 103–4, 118–19; Thomas, "Colored Troops," *B&L* 4:564; Porter, "Petersburg Mine," 231; *OR* 40, 1:104, 106, 124–25, 596–97; Bowley, "Petersburg Mine," 7–10; Hall, "Mine Run," 223–24; Thomas, "Colored Troops," *B&L* 4:564–65. See also Albert Rogall, diary, July 30, 1864, OHS.

9. *OR* 40, 1:596; Bowley, "Petersburg Mine," 9–10; Hall, "Mine Run," 224, 233, 235, 237, 238–39; William Baird, "Reminiscences," 20, UM.

10. *OR* 40, 1:105, 598; Thomas, "Colored Troops," *B&L* 4:565; Bowley, "Petersburg Mine," 10–11; Delavan Bates to Parents, July 30, 1865, Delavan Bates letters, electronic; Bernard, *War Talks*, 183.

11. Bowley, "Petersburg Mine," 11; Allen, *Fourth R.I.*, 289; Christian A. Fleetwood, diary, July 30, 1864, LC; Report of Joint Committee, *Attack on Petersburg*, 135; Isaac L. Brown, diary, July 30, 1864, NCA&R; George E. Barton to Mother, July 31, 1864, AAS.

12. Taylor, *Lee's Adjutant*, 178–79; Henry Van Leuvenigh Bird to Wife, Aug. 5, 1864, VHS; Chambers, *Diary*, 210; Andrews, *South Reports*, 410n74.

13. Phillips, "Wilcox's Alabamians," 490; Featherston, "Graphic Account," 364; Alexander, *Fighting*, 462.

14. William J. Pegram to Jenny, Aug. 1, 1864, Pegram-Johnson-McIntosh Papers, VHS; Allen, *Fourth R.I.*, 289–90; Mickley, *Forty-Third Regiment*, 75; Etheredge, "Another Story," 204–5; Bernard, *War Talks*, 156, 159.

15. Bernard, *War Talks*, 215–16, 320, 160; *OR* 40, 1:792; Stewart, *Pair of Blankets*, 156–59; Hudson, *Sketches*, 57; Wise, *End of an Era*, 363.

16. Haskell, *Memoirs*, 76–77; Day, *Company I*, 84; Kerrick to Sister, Aug. 30, 1864, PNB; Bernard, *War Talks*, 316–317.

17. Dorsey M. Binion to Sister, Aug. 1, 1864, Michael Musick Coll., USAMHI; Haskell, *Memoirs*, 78; Alexander, *Fighting*, 462; Pegram to Jenny, Aug. 1, 1864, VHS; Jerome Yates to Marie, Aug. 3, 1864, UT; Weld, *War Diary*, 356–57.

18. Bowley, "Petersburg Mine," 12–13; Jackman, *Sixth New Hampshire*, 320; William H. Randall, "Incidents of the Battle," in his "Reminiscences" [unpaginated], UM; Committee of the Regimental Association, *Thirty-Fifth Massachusetts*, 271–72.

19. For Mahone's no-prisoner order, see Phillips, "Wilcox's Alabamians," 490, and Bird to Wife, Aug.5, 1864, VHS; Bernard, *War Talks*, 216; Haskell, *Memoirs*, 77; Matthew N. Love to Mother, Aug. 6, 1864, PNB; Wise, *End of an Era*, 366; John W. Love to Sister, Aug. 2, 1864, Matthew N. Love Papers, DU. See also Stewart, "Carnage at the 'Crater,'" 42.

20. Bird to Wife, Aug. 5, 1864, VHS; Kenfield, "Captured," 233; Herbert, "Eighth Alabama," 150; Haskell, *Memoirs*, 77; Freeman, *Letters*, 50.

21. Kilmer, "Dash into the Crater," 775–76; Bowley, "Petersburg Mine," 14;

Houghton and Houghton, *Two Boys*, 133; Haskell, *Memoirs*, 78. See also Hudson, *Sketches*, 59.

22. Haskell, *Memoirs*, 77; Herbert, "Eighth Alabama," 150; Yeary, *Boys in Gray*, 84, 24; Stewart, "Charge," 82, 85; Rickard, "Services with Colored Troops," 30.

23. Yates to Marie, Aug. 3, 1864, UT; Yates CMSR, RG 94, AGO, NA; Holt, *Mississippi Rebel*, 289; Stewart, "Carnage at the 'Crater'," 41; Kenfield, "Captured," 233.

24. Bernard, *War Talks*, 216–17; *OR* 40, 1:792; Stewart, "Charge," 85; Harrill, *Reminiscences*, 29; Trueheart and Trueheart, *Rebel Brothers*, 114.

25. Bowley, "Petersburg Mine," 15; Grant, *Papers*, 12:326n, Francis J. D'Avignon letter, Oct. 13, 1864; Haskell, *Memoirs*, 79–80.

26. Shearman, "Battle of the Crater," 16; Palfrey, *Bartlett*, 119; Grant, *Papers*, 12:326n.

27. Owen, *In Camp and Battle*, 345; Rickard, "Services with Colored Troops," 29; Bowley, "Petersburg Mine," 16.

28. Bowley, "Petersburg Mine," 16; Shearman, "Battle of the Crater," 16–17; Beecham, *As If Glory*, 192; David W. Pipes, journal, 37, HNOC; Kenfield, "Captured," 233.

29. Baird, "Reminiscences," 20, UM; Alexander, *Fighting*, 462; Wise, *End of an Era*, 368–71.

30. Houghton, *Seventeenth Maine*, 221; Chamberlayne, *Virginian*, 249; *OR* 40, 1:167, 246–250, 598, 753; Dowdey and Manarin, *Lee*, Doc. 843; NPS, "Poplar Grove National Cemetery," 3; Grant, *Papers*, 11:361.

31. *OR* 40, 1:598; Thomas, "Colored Troops," *B&L* 4:567.

32. Alexander, *Fighting*, 462; Jerome Yates to Marie, Aug. 3, 1864, UT; Featherston, "Graphic Account," 373, 369; Herbert, "Eighth Alabama," 148, 150.

33. *OR* 40, 1:788, 793; Bernard, *War Talks*, 165–66, 186, 209, 217, 320, 324–33; McMaster, "Battle of the Crater," 123; Hudson, *Sketches*, 60; Featherston, "Graphic Account," 362, 373; for letter listing casualties, including Maj. Bagby's younger brother, see John R. Bagby to Brother, letter fragment, c. Aug. 1864, VHS.

34. Bird, *Granite Farm*, 217.

35. Pegram to Jenny, Aug. 1, 1864, VHS; Edmondston, *Journal*, 600.

36. Bernard, *War Talks*, 165.

13. Mercy and Murder

1. On orders to stop the killing, see Phillips, "Wilcox's Alabamians," 490; Bird to Wife, Aug. 5, 1864, VHS; Hanks, *Benton's Company*, 35.

2. Franklin A. Setzer to Wife, Aug. 7, 1864, UV; Ford, *Adams Letters*, 2:172; Clark S. Wortley, diary, July 31, 1864, EU; Charles W. Smith to Emma, Aug. 1, 1864, Lewis Leigh Coll., USAMHI; George E. Barton to Mother, Aug. 3, 1864, AAS; Redkey, *Grand Army*, 114, 112.

3. Brown, *Diary*, 108; Vautier, *88th Pennsylvania*, 196; Meade and Meade, *Life and Letters*, 2:218; *OR* 40, 1:172–74, 42–43, 531, 128–29; Report of Joint Committee, *Attack on Petersburg*, 8, 10.

4. Alexander, *Fighting*, 462; Bird to Wife, Aug. 5, 1864, VHS; Trueheart and Trueheart, *Rebel Brothers*, 115; Yates to Marie, Aug. 3, 1864, UT.

5. Wise, *End of an Era,* 366; Sorrel, *Recollections,* 258–59; Haskell, *Memoirs,* 77.

6. Grant, *Papers,* 12:54; Henry Pippitt to Mother, Dec. 5, 1864, UM. See also Chisholm, *Civil War Notebook,* 33; Warfield, *Memoirs,* 185.

7. Chester, *Black Correspondent,* 109; Day, *Company I,* 83; Edward W. Bacon to Kate, Sept. 26–27, 1864, AAS.

8. OR 42, 1:132, 134, 136, 144, 161, 793–95; Grant, *Memoirs,* 2:333–34; Butler, *Autobiography,* 742.

9. OR 42, 1:819–20; Samuel A. Duncan to Miss Julia, Oct. 22, 1864, Duncan-Jones Papers, NHHS; Goulding, "Colored Troops," 149–50; Elliott F. Grabill to Anna, Sept. 30, 1864, OC; James H. Wickes to Father, Oct. 4, 1864, Boston Public Library; Cross, "Civil War Letters," Cross to Wife, Oct. 4, [1864]; Christian A. Fleetwood, diary, Sept. 29, 1864, LC.

10. Grabill to Anna, Sept. 30, 1864, OC; Goulding, "Colored Troops," 150–51; Chester, *Black Correspondent,* 147.

11. Hamilton, *Company M,* 61–62; Hanks, *Benton's Company,* 36–37; Martin, "Assault Upon Fort Gilmer," 269; Austin, *Georgia Boys,* 70.

12. OR 42, 1:772; Califf, *Seventh Regiment,* 41–42; Sherman, "Assault on Gilmer," 6–7; Perry, "Assault," 413–14.

13. Califf, *Seventh Regiment,* 42–43, 44; Sherman, "Assault on Gilmer," 11; Johnston, "Attack," 441; Moore, *Cannoneer,* 264.

14. Califf, *Seventh Regiment,* 43–44; Johnston, "Attack," 441; Hanks, *Benton's Company,* 37; Cole, *Huntsville to Appomattox,* 182–87.

15. Alexander, *Fighting,* 478; Hanks, *Benton's Company,* 37; Lott, "Two Boys," 417; Breckinridge, "Boy Captain," 416. See also Cole, *Huntsville to Appomattox,* 182–87.

16. Califf, *Seventh Regiment,* 43–44; Granberry, "That Fort Gilmer Fight," 413; Hanks, *Benton's Company,* 37; Cole, *Huntsville to Appomattox,* 184; Perry, "Assault," 415; Sherman, "Assault on Gilmer," 20.

17. Califf, *Seventh Regiment,* 43; Sherman, "Assault on Gilmer," 11; Breckinridge, "Boy Captain," 416.

18. Lott, "Two Boys," 416; Perry, "Assault," 413, 415; Sherman, "Assault on Gilmer," 25–27; Califf, *Seventh Regiment,* 44–45; Corbin, *Letters,* 80; Hanks, *Benton's Company,* 37; Polley, *Hood's Texas Brigade,* 252, 256.

19. Henry Marshall to Folks at Home, Oct. 2, 1864, Schoff Coll., UM; Johnston, "Attack," 441; Polley, *Hood's Texas Brigade,* 256; Hanks, *Benton's Company,* 37–38; Andrews, *Sketch,* 49; Alexander, *Fighting,* 478. See also Moore, *Cannoneer,* 264.

20. Sorrel, *Recollections,* 253; Cole, *Huntsville to Appomattox,* 184.

21. Andrews, *Sketch,* 47; Goulding, "Colored Troops," 150–51; Chester, *Black Correspondent,* 147, dispatch Oct. 9, 1864.

22. Dennett, *Ninth U.S.C. Troops,* 15; Sherman, "Assault on Gilmer," 10–13; Granberry, "That Fort Gilmer Fight," 415; Andrews, *Sketch,* 49.

23. OR 42, 1:151, 814–17; Edward W. Bacon to Kate, Oct. 31, 1864, AAS; Welch, *Hampton Legion,* 30, 64–65.

24. Britton, *On the Border,* 2:244–47; Watie, "Some Letters," 31; OR 41, 1:771,

785, 788–89; Crawford, "Saline Guard," 84; Williams, "Historical Sketch," 12, KSHS; Bradly to Nanna, Sept. 30, 1864, electronic.

25. *OR* 41, 1:771–72, 785; Britton, *On the Border,* 2:291.

26. Watie, "Some Letters," 47; *OR* 41, 1:776, 789; Yeary, *Boys in Gray,* 684; Britton, *On the Border,* 2:246; George W. Grayson, "Red Paths and White," 115–17, typescript, E. E. Dale Coll., UO.

27. Britton, *On the Border,* 2:246–47; Yeary, *Boys in Gray,* 45–46, 684, 352–53, 643, 812, 830–31; Grayson, "Red Paths and White," 117, UO.

28. Grayson, "Red Paths and White," 117, UO; Britton, *On the Border,* 2:246; *OR* 41, 1:785, 789; for five named men who returned from captivity, see Kansas AG, *Report,* 594–96, under Co. K "Remarks."

14. Saltville

1. Col. William P. Hardeman to Lt. Col. Hubert A. McCaleb, July 30, 1864, with CMSR Pvt. Wilson Wood, 6th U.S. Colored Heavy Artillery, AGO, RG 94, NA; *OR* 39, 1:721–23; Confederate States, *Exchange of free colored troops.*

2. Sherman, *Memoirs,* 2:130, 144, 152.

3. *OR* 38, 1:23, 162, 323–24; Morgan, "Reminiscences," 28–30; Peter Steketee to Brother, Oct. 24 1864, UM; Lewis, "First Tennessee Cavalry," in Lindsley, *Military Annals,* 891.

4. Hubbard, *Notes of a Private,* 155; *OR* 39, 1:514, 518–20, 521–23, 533–34, 543–45; Morton, *Artillery,* 224–26, 233–36; Duncan, *Recollections,* 163; Young, *Seventh Tennessee Cavalry,* 104–5; Joseph K. Nelson, "Recollections,"46–47, typescript copy, ed. Josephine Nelson, CWMC, USAMHI; Lyon, "Memoirs, 44.

5. Hollis, "Diary," 110–11, Sept. 25–Oct. 2, 1864; Hancock, *Diary,* 469–70; Sipes, *Seventh Pennsylvania,* 140–43.

6. *OR* 39, 1:548; for "unbleached," see Robert E. Corry to Wife, June 17 1864, AU; Morton, *Artillery,* 232.

7. *OR* 39, 3:816 and ser. 2, 6:1022–23; Berlin et al., *Freedom,* 592–93; Mathes, *Old Guard in Gray,* pt. 2:97–98.

8. Olmstead, *Memoirs,* 148; *OR* 39, 1:717–20; Hood, "Invasion of Tennessee," *B&L* 4:426; Bevens, *Reminiscences,* 199; Worsham, *Old Nineteenth Tennessee,* 135.

9. Williamson, "Diary," 72; *OR* 39, 1:717–23, 803–10; Stephenson, *Memoir,* 255; Carden, "Memories," chap. 9.

10. *OR* 39, 1:720–23; Bevens, *Reminiscences,* 201; Romeyn, "Colored Troops," 23; Stuart Hall to Sister Emma, Nov. 17, 1864, Morris Stuart Hall Papers, UM.

11. Olmstead, *Memoirs,* 159; Watkins, *Co. Aytch,* 209; James A. McCord to Brother, Dec. 3, 1864, EU; *OR* 45, 1:39–40, 343, 505, 507–8, 2:628; Connelly, *Autumn of Glory,* 506–11; Taylor, *Destruction and Reconstruction,* 216; Hood, *Advance and Retreat,* 302–3; Cooper, "Diary," 169, Dec. 17, 1864 [date is incorrect]; Clark, *Stars and Bars,* 155.

12. *OR* 45, 1:748; *OR* 49, 2:1189, T. T. Land; *OR* ser. 2, 8:19–20, 64, 171, 393; Stuart Hall to Sister, Feb. 14, 1865, UM.

13. Lonn, *Salt,* 13–18. On private ownership of salt mine, see White Family Papers, 1794–1921, UV.

14. Lonn, *Salt*, 19–34, 39.

15. For Saltville, see OR *Atlas*, Plate 118-A; Kirk, *Fifteenth Pennsylvania*, 419.

16. Ross, *Tabular Analysis*, 19; OR 39, 1:556–57; James S. Brisbin to Wife, Sept. 20, 1864, UI.

17. OR 39, 1:557; Michigan AGO, *Michigan*, 733; Kireker, *116th Regiment*, 1, 64, 73, 9.

18. OR 39, 1:555, 2:877, 867, 871, 881; Fisher, *They Rode*, 114; Mays, "Price of Freedom," 43, 56n22; Michigan AGO, *Michigan*, 731–32.

19. OR 39, 1:557; Mason, *Twelfth Ohio*, 64–65; Guild, *Fourth Tennessee*, 100; Lindsley, *Military Annals*, 671, Col. Dibrell's account; Tennessee Civil War Centennial Commission, *Tennesseans*, 73.

20. OR 39, 1:557, 553; Thomas J. Hoge to Tillie, Nov. 4, 1864, Wise-Clark Family Papers, UI.

21. OR 39, 1:552 557; Mason, *Twelfth Ohio*, 57–68; Michigan AGO, *Michigan*, 732.

22. OR 39, 1:557; Mosgrove, *Kentucky Cavaliers*, 207; Mortimer H. Johnson to Wife, c. late October 1862, VMI electronic; Ward, *My Country*, 101.

23. Mosgrove, *Kentucky Cavaliers*, 206–8; Guerrant, diary, Oct. 3, 1864, UNC; OR 39, 1:564 and 555n.

24. Mason; *Twelfth Ohio*, 70; Sensing, *Champ Ferguson*, 183. Note that Sensing misspelled Cutler's name, listing it as *Carter*.

25. Mosgrove, *Kentucky Cavaliers*, 207.

26. Sensing, *Champ Ferguson*, 40–42; Weathered, "Diary," January 1863; Duke, *Reminiscences*, 123–24; Williamson, "Diary," 65, Aug. 28, 1863.

27. Sensing, *Champ Ferguson*, 185–86, 176; Mays, "Price of Freedom," 75–76.

28. Mosgrove, *Kentucky Cavaliers*, 206, 208; Davis, *Breckinridge*, 458.

29. Mosgrove, *Kentucky Cavaliers*, 207; OR ser. 2, 7:1020; OR 39, 1:565; Baldwin, "Felix Robertson," 177–78. Historian William C. Davis identified Robertson as the culprit, for which see Davis, *Breckinridge*, 460n8.

30. OR 39, 1:554; Sensing, *Champ Ferguson*, 178–87; Mason, *Twelfth Ohio*, 68–70; Ridley, *Battles*, 527–30.

31. Sensing, *Champ Ferguson*, 212, 210; OR 49, 1:765; Grant, *Papers*, 14:463–64.

32. OR ser. 2, 7:1020; A. C. Dicken, diary, Oct. 3–5, 1864, KHS; Jones, *Rebel Clerk's Diary*, 2:299–300; Mason, *Twelfth Ohio*, 67–68; Kireker, *116th Regiment*, 64; Wilson, *Column South*, 201.

33. OR 39, 1:552, 553, 557; Ross, *Tabular Analysis*, 19, 26; Mays, "Price of Freedom," 87; Kireker, *116th Regiment*, 1, 64, 73, 95.

34. Sgt. Samuel Walker, undated affidavit in George Turner's pension file, 5th U.S. Colored Calvary, Civil War Pension Files, RG 15, NA; OR 49, 1:668.

35. OR 39, 1:553, 557; Mays, "Price of Freedom," 88–90.

36. Marvel, "Battle of Saltville, 10–19, 46–60; Brown et al., "Saltville Massacre Update"; Mays, "Price of Freedom," 88–90.

37. For Pvt. Levi Parker, Co. G, who died at Prestonburg, Ky., and for returns, see Kireker, *116th Regiment*, 102, 64.

38. OR 45, 1:103, 105.

39. OR 39, 1:492; Dyer and Moore, *Tennessee Veterans*, 2:623, Alford L. Dale; OR 41, 1:936; OR 49, 1:9, 582, 589; *Cincinnati Daily Gazette*, Jan. 28, 1865, David Brown site, http://mywebpages.comcast.net/5thuscc/simpson.htm (accessed Sept. 29, 2006); Stuart Hall to Sister, Mar. 16, 1865, UM. For some other incidents, see Samuel D. Barnes, diary, Apr. 24, May 1, 1864, LC; Addeman, "Reminiscences," 22–23.

15. Murder in the East

1. Overley, "Williams's Kentucky Brigade, C.S.A.," 461; Gorgas, *Diary*, 123–24, July 7, 1864; Taft, diary, Mar. 20, 1864, LC.

2. Hanks, *Benton's Company*, 39; Elias Davis to Mother, Dec. [18?], 1863, UNC.

3. For excellent studies of the expanded war, see Grimsley, *Hard Hand*, and Royster, *Destructive War*.

4. OR 22, 1:816–18; OR 32, 1:682; Cort, *Dear Friends*, 136–37; King, *Three Years*, 192–201. For Yankee atrocities at Nashville, see Bir, "Remenecence," 45; Watkins, *Co. Aytch*, 215; Ryan, "Experience of a Confederate," electronic.

5. Unsigned letter, Mar. 12, 1864, Demetria Ann Hill Papers, UT; Cumming, *Journal*, 200, 216; James M. Jordan to Wife, Nov. 10, 1862, "Letters," typescript, GDAH, 2:456; Landers, *Weep Not*, 155.

6. Sam E. Brown to John Sherman, Apr. 14, 1861, John Sherman Papers, LC; Royster, *Destructive War*, 40; for Beauregard, see Moore, *Rebellion Record*, 8:6, "Rumors and Incidents"; Petty, *Journey*, 222, 215; Patterson, "Irrepressible Optimism," 350; Frederick Anspach to Brother Robert, June 23, 1864, UV; Powers, "Report," 585.

7. Shotwell, *Papers*, 1:473; OR ser. 2, 4:946; Durkin, *Stephen R. Mallory*, 249; Reagan, *Memoirs*, 182; OR 33:222–23.

8. Polignac, "Polignac's Mission," 326–34; Evans, *Judah P. Benjamin*, 262–63, 268–69, 278–79; OR ser. 4, 2:995–99, 3:1133; Fitzpatrick, *Letters to Amanda*, 166; Power, *Lee's Miserables*, 264–65; Wise, *End of an Era*, 395, 414; OR 46, 2:1308 and ser. 4, 3:1161–62.

9. Royster, *Destructive War*, 73; Eldred Simkins to Eliza Trescott, Aug. 8, 1864, Simkins Papers, HEH; OR 40, 1:35; Cate, *Two Soldiers*, 165; Gorgas, *Diary*, 138; Adamson, *Sojourns*, 173; Jones, *Rebel Clerk's Diary*, 2:308–9.

10. Grant, *Memoirs*, 2: 251, 303–4; Du Pont, *Campaign of 1864*, 49–51, 68–69; OR 37, 1:145, 528; Fannie Wilson to Papa, June 17, 1864, and Sidney Marlin to Wife, June 14, 1864, both VMI electronic; Crook, *Autobiography*, 114; Moore, "General Hunter's Raid," 183–85, 187–88; Imboden, "Fire, Sword," 169–70.

11. Jones, *Heroines*, 310–11, 307; Vogtsberger, *Dulanys of Welbourne*, 164–65; Wilson to Papa, June 17, 1864, VMI; OR ser. 2, 7:430–32.

12. Neil, *Shenandoah Valley*, 36, 39; James F. Ellis, diary, June 13, 1864, Roy Bird Cook Coll., WVUL; Watson, "Union Soldier," pt. 4, VMI.

13. Grant, *Papers*, 11:251: Grant, *Memoirs*, 2:301, 318–21, 582; Merritt, "Sheridan," *B&L* 4:500–21, 512–13; Napoleon B. Brisbine to Siblings, Sept. 16, Sept. 24, 1864, VMI electronic; Sheridan, *Memoirs*, 2:99–100.

14. Isaac White to Jinnie, Oct. 2, 1864, VTU electronic; McDonald, *Laurel Brigade*, 258; Commager, *Blue and the Gray*, 2:1048.

15. Forsythe, *Guerrilla Warfare*, 28; Reader, *Fifth West Virginia Cavalry*, 284; Watson, "Union Soldier," pt. 1, VMI; Phillips and Hill, *War Stories*, 222–23.

16. Neil, *Shenandoah Valley*, 37; Stevens, *Sixth Corps*, 410; Merritt, "Sheridan," 512.

17. *OR* 43, 1:55–56; Trueheart and Trueheart, *Rebel Brothers*, 132; Sneden, *Eye of the Storm*, 148–49; Sheridan, *Memoirs*, 2:99; Dowdey and Manarin, *Lee*, Doc. 649.

18. Casler, *Stonewall Brigade*, 242; Williamson, *Mosby's Rangers*, 213–15; Munson, *Reminiscences*, 146–47; *OR* 43, 1:634; Avery, *Under Custer's Command*, 105.

19. Grant, *Papers*, 12:13; *OR* 43, 1:822, 841, 2:305; Williamson, *Mosby's Rangers*, 458–59; Stackpole, *Sheridan*, 373.

20. Stackpole, *Sheridan*, 373; Williamson, *Mosby's Rangers*, 458–59; *OR* 43, 1:508, 2:470–71, 820.

21. Grant, *Papers*, 12:13, 15; *OR* 43, 1:43, 55–56, 508, 563, 842, 843–44, 847, 862, 942, 965, 2:11, 348, 565, 639, for arson and removal orders; on hostages, see 1:836, 2:335, 341, 347–48, 388–89.

22. Williamson, *Mosby's Rangers*, 239–40; [Warrenton *Virginian*], "Hanging of Mosby's Men," 108; Wallace, *Memories*, 49; Mosby, "Retaliation," 315–16; Wert, *Mosby's Rangers*, 211–14.

23. Wallace, *Memories*, 50; Avery, *Under Custer's Command*, 109–10; Ashby, *Valley Campaigns*, 292–93; Palmer et al., "Horror of the War," 239–41; Williamson, *Mosby's Rangers*, 240–41.

24. Avery, *Under Custer's Command*, 110; Emerson, *Lowell*, 353; *OR* 43, 1:441, 508–9.

25. *OR* 43, 2:909–10, 566; Mosby, "Retaliation," 319, 321; Palmer et al., "Horror of the War," 241–43; Williamson, *Mosby's Rangers*, 288–91; Munson, *Reminiscences*, 149–51.

26. Mosby, *Memoirs*, 301–3; *OR* 43, 2:290, 412, 414–15, 446–47; Mosby, "Retaliation," 316; Munson, *Reminiscences*, 121–23; Williamson, *Mosby's Rangers*, 295–97; Wallace, *Memories*, 50.

27. William J. Black, diary, Oct. 19, 1864, VMI electronic; Stevens, *Sixth Corps*, 414–28; Ashby, *Valley Campaigns*, 300, 298; Myers, *Comanches*, 353–55.

28. Lane, *Dear Mother*, 340, William Stillwell to Sallie, Jan. 21, 1865; Taylor, *Cruel War*, 310, Grant to Malinda Taylor, Dec. 3, 1864; for "shell shocked" soldier, see John W. Love to Family, Aug. 18, 1864, Matthew N. Love Papers, DU.

29. Alexander Newburger, diary, May 31, 1864, LC; *OR* 42, 1:24, 443–47, 453–54; Vautier, *88th Pennsylvania*, 203.

30. Wainwright, *Diary of Battle*, 488–89.

31. *OR* 42, 1:443–46; Haley, *Rebel Yell*, 227; Lord, *They Fought*, 274; Smith McDonald letter, Dec. 17, 1864, Smith McDonald Papers.

32. McAllister, *Letters*, 558; Fowle, *Letters*, 147; Lord, *They Fought*, 274; Wainwright, *Diary of Battle*, 490.

33. OR 42, 1:356–57; Crowninshield, *First Regiment*, 247; Lord, *They Fought*, 274; Chamberlain, *Through Blood & Fire*, 142–46, letters Dec. 14 and Dec. 19, 1864.

34. Wainwright, *Diary of Battle*, 490, 488; OR 42, 1:446, 357; Benjamin F. Oakes to J. A. Richardson, Dec. 13, 1864, VMI electronic; Haley, *Rebel Yell*, 227; Lord, *They Fought*, 274.

35. For Federal casualty reports, see OR 42, 1:57, 351, 460, 482, 498, 514, 524; for Hampton's report, see OR 42, 1:950–51; Edmondston, *Journal*, 643, Dec. 13, 1864.

36. Haley, *Rebel Yell*, 260.

16. Murder in the West

1. For diagram, see Jones, *Command and Strategy*, 300; M. J. Bigbie to Wife, July 1, 1864, M. J. Bigbie Papers, http://members.aol.com/wwhitby/letter_g.html (accessed Sept. 29, 2006); Thomas D. Christie to Sarah J. Christie, Aug. 5, 1864, James C. Christie Family Papers, MHS, also at http://www.mnhs.org/library/Christie/td_christie.html.

2. Davis, "Atlanta Campaign," 16; OR 32, 1:682–85; Cort, *Dear Friends*, 136–37; OR 38, 2:920, 928.

3. Osborn, *Fiery Trail*, 17; Fredrick Winkler, letter #200, Sept. 5, 1864, 26th Wisconsin Web site; OR 38, 5:837, 839, 794; Sherman, *Memoirs*, 2:111–12.

4. OR 38, 5:794; OR 39, 2:420, 422; Winkler letter #200, Sept. 5, 1864; Isaac Scherck to J. L. Myers, Sept. 9, 1864, American Jewish Archives, electronic; Davis, *Rise and Fall*, 2:564.

5. OR 39, 3:162, 660, 713; Nichols, *Great March*, 57, 61; Conyngham, *Sherman's March*, 243, 245–47, 255, 270, 276–77; Lunt, *Wartime Journal*, 25–26; Osborn, *Fiery Trail*, 52–53; Oakey, "Marching Through Georgia," 4:678.

6. Christopher P. C. McKnight to Martha M. McKnight, Oct. 8, 1864, Christopher P. C. McKnight Papers, http.www.rootsweb.com/~okgenweb/civilwar/letters/mcknight.htm (accessed Sept. 27, 2006); Thomas A. Cobb to Cousin, Aug. 6, 1863, Thomas A. Cobb Papers, http://www.indianainthecivilwar.com/letters/10th/Cobb.htm (accessed Sept. 27, 2006); Ernst Damkoehler to Mathilde, Feb. 21, 1864, 26th Wisconsin site; Oakey, "Marching Through Georgia," 4:678.

7. Miller, "March to the Sea," 220, Nov. 18, 1864; Connolly, *Three Years*, 298; Hitchcock, *Marching with Sherman*, 87, 110; Malcom, "Such Is War," 349.

8. Wills, *Army Life*, 317.

9. Robert H. Peel to Alice, Sept. 7, 1864, Robert H. Peel Papers, http://myweb.cableone.net/4jdurham/peel/lastroll.html (accessed Sept. 24, 2006); DuBose, *Wheeler*, 436; Hemming, "Confederate Odyssey," 79.

10. Graber, *Terry Texas Ranger*, 238; Blackburn, *Reminiscences*, 165; John, "Shannon's Scouts," 26–29.

11. Bird, *Granite Farm*, 223, 224n12; Sherman, *Memoirs*, 2:183; LeConte, *When the World Ended*, 58; OR 47, 2:597.

12. Nugent, *Dear Nellie*, 224; DuBose, *Wheeler*, 436n12; Chestnut, *Civil War*, 745–46.

13. Geary, *Politician Goes to War*, 217; Conyngham, *Sherman's March*, 270–71; Early, *Letters*, 102.

14. Nugent, *Dear Nellie*, 224; Guild, *Fourth Tennessee*, 107–8.

15. Wills, *Army Life*, 323–24; Cox, *Sherman's March*, 30; Hitchcock, *Marching with Sherman*, 98.

16. Hitchcock, *Marching with Sherman*, 87; OR 44:685–86, 601.

17. Brown et al., *Behind the Guns*, 132–33.

18. OR 44:197; Anderson, *Marching Barefoot*, "Anderson to Wife," Dec. 26, 1864.

19. Gage, *Vicksburg to Raleigh*, 261; Winkler letter #229, Dec. 17, 1864, 26th Wisconsin Web site; Dyer, *Compendium*, 721. For some examples of unreported murders, see Boddy, *Civil War Journal*, 109, 111, 170.

20. Rath, *Left for Dixie*, 71; Conyngham, *Sherman's March*, 311; Winkler letter #245, Jan. 31, 1865, 26th Wisconsin Web site; William Howell, "History of the 25th Alabama Infantry," chap. "Nashville," ADAH, http://home.earthlink.net/~sdriskell/25th/25th.htm (accessed Sept. 29, 2006).

21. Reid, *View from Headquarters*, 227–28; OR 47, 1:683, 814, 170.

22. Conyngham, *Sherman's March*, 310; George Elliott, diary, Mar. 5, 1865, George Elliott Papers, http://www.indianainthecivilwar.com/letters/97th/elliott.htm; Osborn, *Fiery Trail*, 127–32, 134–35; LeConte, *When the World Ended*, 55, 60; Royster, *Destructive War*, 33.

23. Osborn, *Fiery Trail*, 143; Nichols, *Great March*, 161.

24. OR 47, 1:533, 860–61; DuBose, *Wheeler*, 437–38; Blackburn, *Reminiscences*, 166.

25. OR 47, 2:537, 544, 546, 596; Sherman, *Memoirs*, 2:287.

26. OR 43, 1:7; William Stanton to Mary Moody, Mar. 30, 1865, UT; Cox, *Sherman's March*, 41, 230–31; Charles C. Jones to Wife, Dec. 21, 1864, Charles Colcock Jones Family Papers, UG.

27. OR 47, 1:327–28, 318–19.

28. Guild, *Fourth Tennessee*, 114; Blackburn, *Reminiscences*, 165–66.

29. Winkler letter #251, Mar. 13, 1865, 26th Wisconsin Web site; Anderson, *Marching Barefoot*, [c. April 1865]; Worth, "Sherman's Raid," 48; Maclean, "Last Raid," 474–75; Nichols, *Great March*, 239; Spencer, *Last Ninety Days*, 160–61.

30. OR 47, 1:1027.

31. Dyer, *Compendium*, 835.

17. Mobile and Selma

1. Robert W. Barnard to Dora, Mar. 19, 1865, Historical Society of Washington, D.C.; Whitehorne, *Diary*, 60; Pegram, "Boy Artillerist," 248; Moore, *Cannoneer*, 271.

2. OR 49, 1:58–64, 67; ORN 17:818–21; OR ser. 2, 8:441–42, 471, 500–1.

3. Wyeth, *Forrest*, 594; OR 49, 2:173–74, 1:350.

4. OR 49, 2:1172; Duncan, *Recollections*, 187; Rainey, *Experiences*, 96; Hubbard, *Notes of a Private*, 184–86; Wyeth, *Forrest*, 589.

5. Vale, *Minty and the Cavalry*, 429–440; Wyeth, *Forrest*, 603–5; Wilson, *Under the Old Flag*, 2:232; OR 49, 1:359–61; George Kryder to Wife, Apr. 26, 1865, Bowling Green State University, electronic; Davidson, *War Was the Place*, 109–11.

6. Montgomery, *Reminiscences*, 242–44.

7. Davidson, *War Was the Place*, 109–11; Jordan and Pryor, *Forrest*, 675–76; Wyeth, *Forrest*, 605–7; Vale, *Minty and the Cavalry*, 146–47, 256–57.

8. Crouse, "Journal of William O. Crouse, 18th Indiana Battery," 34–35, bound vol., IHS; Wyeth, *Forrest*, 607–9; Jordan and Pryor, *Forrest*, 677.

9. Rowell, *Yankee Artillerymen*, 255; OR 49, 1:406; Crouse, "Journal," 34–35, IHS; Hosea, "Some Side Lights," 17–18.

10. Wyeth, *Forrest*, 608–9.

11. OR 49, 1:351; Wilson, *Under the Old Flag*, 2:240–42.

12. Grant, *Memoirs*, 2:408–11, 518–19.

13. Andrews, *Campaign of Mobile*, 95–123; Jackson, *Some of the Boys*, 240–43; James B. Lockney, journal, Mar. 17–26, 1865, SHSW; OR 49, 1:267, 275.

14. Henry M. Crydenwise to Parents, Apr. 10, 1865, EU; Andrews, *Campaign of Mobile*, 194–201; Walter A. Chapman to Parents, Apr. 11, 1865, YU; Frey, *Grandpa's Gone*, 144, citing Carlos W. Colby, "Memoirs of Military Service," ed. Joseph G. Bilby, *Military Images* 3 (September–October 1981), 29.

15. Chapman to Parents, Apr. 11, 1865, YU; Musser, *Soldier Boy*, 201; Henry Ketzle, diary, Apr. 1865, Henry Ketzle Papers, http://www.ketzle.com/diary/rightpane.html (accessed Sept. 27, 2006); Andrews, *Campaign of Mobile*, 200; Samuel Crawford to Unknown, Apr. 12, 1865, typescript, letter fragment, AlHC.

16. Crawford to Unknown, Apr. 12, 1865, AlHC; Andrews, *Campaign of Mobile*, 201; Frey, *Grandpa's Gone*, 149; OR 49, 1:287, 289–90; Chapman to Parents, Apr. 11, 1865, YU.

17. OR 49, 1:99, 283, 287; Marshall, *Eighty-third Ohio*, 165; Liddell, *Liddell's Record*, 196; Chambers, *Journal*, 373–74; Stephenson, *Memoir*, 367–68; Yeary, *Boys in Gray*, 555, W. R. Murphy.

18. Goodyear, diary, Apr. 2, 1865, YU; Gordon, *Reminiscences*, 395–413; Grant, *Memoirs*, 2:436–53; Dowdey and Manarin, *Lee*, Docs. 980–990.

19. Lee, *Wartime Washington*, 499; Taft, diary, Apr. 30, 1865, LC; Shaw, "Our Last Campaign," 31; Nelson, "Recollections," 54, USAMHI; Pryor, *My Day*, UNC electronic ed., 258; Chestnut, *Civil War*, 791.

20. OR 49, 2:566–67; Clay-Copton, *Belle of the Fifties*, UNC electronic ed., 248; Early, *Letters*, 102; Edward W. Bacon to Kate, Apr. 26, 1865, AAS; Edwards, *Dear Friend Anna*, 124; OR 47, 3:238–39, 1:937.

21. OR 48, 1:265–69; OR 46, 3:1134; OR 49, 2:420, 1025–26.

22. Hemming, "Confederate Odyssey," 84; Early, *Letters*, 102, to Wife, Apr. 18, 1865; Royster, *Destructive War*, 42, quoting S. H. M. Byers, "Some Personal Recollections of General Sherman," in *McClure's Magazine* 3 (1894): 218; William W. Pritchard, journal, Feb. 9, 1865, quoted in Grimsley, *Hard Hand*, 202; Anderson, *Marching Barefoot*, [c. April 1865]; Musser, *Soldier Boy*, 127.

Epilogue

1. *OR* ser. 3, 4:1283, 5:114, 138; Dyer, *Compendium*, 12; Wilson, *Black Phalanx*, 123; NPS, "Civil War Soldiers and Sailors."

2. Thomas and Hyman, *Stanton*, 440; *OR* 49, 2:1108, 1110–11.

3. Berlin et al., *Freedom*, 2:721–24; Browne, "Colored Cavalry," 11–13; Newton, *Out of the Briars*, 70.

4. *OR* ser. 2, 8:784–92, 667–68, 957–61, 926–28; Dorris, *Pardon and Amnesty*, 342.

5. *OR* ser. 2, 8:743; Sensing, *Champ Ferguson*, 177, 247–53; Smith, *Journal*, 228–29; for Henry Magruder and Sue Mundy, see Kentucky AG, *Confederate Volunteers*, 2:412–13; Sipes, *Seventh Pennsylvania*, 254; Mason, *Twelfth Ohio*, 52–53; Cogley, *Seventh Indiana Cavalry*, 193–208; McCorkle, *Three Years with Quantrill*, 206–7, 224n5.

6. Grant, *Memoirs*, 2:522; Mosby, *Memoirs*, 383–93.

7. Dorris, *Pardon and Amnesty*, 344; Edwards, *Dear Friend Anna*, 140; Lockney, journal, Apr. 17, 1865, SHSW. See also Stewart, diary, 2:78, May 19, 1865, UNC.

8. Hurst, *Nathan Bedford Forrest*, 271, 328–46, 380–86; Henry, *Forrest*, 343–44; Robuck, *Personal Experience*, 99–136; Toney, *Privations of a Private*, 124–27; Duke, *Reminiscences*, 347–48.

9. *OR* 46, 3:830, 1080; Williamson, *Mosby's Rangers*, 398–99; Mosby, *Memoirs*, 383–99; Ramage, *Gray Ghost*, 302, 262–332, 339–40.

10. Maury, *Recollections*, 221–23; *OR* 49, 2:725–26; *OR* ser. 2, 8:726, 728–29; Warner, *Generals in Gray*, 333.

11. *OR* 47, 2:596, 3:829; Warner, *Generals in Gray*, 122–23.

12. Warner, *Generals in Gray*, 140–41; Bates to Parents, July 30, 1865, Delavan Bates Papers, electronic; *OR* 40, 1:748.

13. Robertson, "Scourge of Elmira," 80–98; *OR* 32, 1:612; 3:117–19, 664–65; Warner, *Generals in Gray*, 284, 392n444; Kerr, "Atlanta to Raleigh," 215–16; Miller, "March to the Sea," 230.

14. Carden, "Memories," 11–12, electronic; Williams, *Ku Klux Klan Trials*, 1.

15. Smith, *Soldier's Friend*, 159; Blackburn, *Reminiscences*, 178.

16. *New York Times*, Dec. 26, 1865; Mainfort, *Archaeological Investigations*, 6–8; Lykes, *Petersburg National Park*, NPS Historical Handbook Ser. No. 13.

BIBLIOGRAPHY

Unpublished Documents and Collections

Adriance Memorial Library, Poughkeepsie, N.Y.—Papers of Robert N. Verplanck

Alabama Department of Archives and History—Papers of Sarah R. Espy, Crenshaw Hall, and William Howell

Alabama Historical Commission, Fort Morgan State Historic Site—Papers of Samuel Crawford

American Antiquarian Society, Worcester, Mass.—Papers of Edward Woolsey Bacon and George E. Barton

American Philosophical Society—Papers of Albert D. Bache

Auburn University—Papers of Robert E. Corry

Birmingham Public Library—Papers of H. A. Tyler

Boston Athenaeum—Papers of Richard H. L. Jewett

Boston Public Library—Papers of James H. Wickes

Carroll County Historical Society, McKenzie, Tenn.—Papers of R. M. Boman, John A. Crutchfield, and S. W. Holladay

Catawba Historical Association, Newton, N.C.—Papers of Gabriel Powell Sherrill

Chicago Historical Society—Papers of John Merrilies

College of William and Mary—Papers of William Taylor and Charles A. Wills

Connecticut Historical Society—Papers of Charles G. Lee, George Robbins, and Edward Willey

Cornell University—Papers of George P. Harrison

Duke University, William R. Perkins Library—Papers of William A. Biggs, William I. Clopton, David B. Harris, Jesse Harrison, John A. Hedrick, William Hoyle, Nate Lanpheur, George Washington Love, John W. Love, Matthew N. Love, Robert C. Love, Joseph F. Maides, E. R. Manson, James O. Moore, John C. Palmer, Uriah N. Parmelee. Alonzo Reed, John W. Reese, Simeon Royse, Hubert Saunders, Henry J. H. Thompson, Elliott Stephen Welch, Alice Williamson, James Wingard, Ella Gertrude Clanton Thomas, and Pinckney Rayburn Young

Emory University, Robert W. Woodruff Library—Papers of Henry M.
    Crydenwise, James A. McCord, William M. Parkinson, Edwin C. Peirson,
    Edwin D. Tuttle, and Clark S. Wortley
Filson Club Historical Society, Louisville, Ky.—Papers of William and
    Benjamin Jones and Lunsford Yandell
Florida State Archives—Papers of James Clark, George W. Scott, and Alfred
    F. Sears
Florida State University—Papers of Henry Bradford
Georgia Department of Archives and History—"Letters from Confederate
    Soldiers, 1860–1865," including James M. Jordan
Georgia Historical Society—Papers of Joab Roach
Gettysburg College—Papers of A. S. Fisher
Harvard University, Radcliffe Institute—Papers of James C. Beecher
Henry E. Huntington Library—Papers of James E. Glazier, Henry W.
    Halleck, Eldred Simkins, Delos Van Deusen, and John Vliet
Historic New Orleans Collection—Papers of Charles Bennett, Michael
    Guinan, and David W. Pipes
Historical Society of Washington County, Plymouth, N.C—Papers of Bossie
    O'Brien Hundley Baer
Historical Society of Washington, D.C.—Papers of Robert W. Barnard
Illinois State Historical Library—Papers of Humphrey Hughes Hood, Henry
    M. Newhall, W. H. Price, and August V. Kautz
Indiana Historical Society—Papers of Thomas W. Botkins, Mary E. Clark,
    William O. Crouse, Jefferson C. Davis, John Dragoo, William Forder,
    James Grimsley, John C. Hackhiser, Charles C. Halls, John P. Hawkins,
    Daniel W. Hilligoss, Joseph Hotz, William A. Ketcham, Andrew J.
    McGarrah, B. Marshall Mills, Thomas Prickett, James S. Thomas, Amos
    C. Weaver, and Vincent Wicker
Indiana State Library—Papers of Jerry J. Barker, Levi Bartholomew, George
    F. Chittenden. Lyman S. Chittenden, David P. Craig, Richard L. Daw-
    son, Mahlon D. Manson, and Luther Short
Indiana University—Papers of James Addison Cravens
Kansas State Historical Society—Papers of James G. Blunt, Lewis Douglass,
    B. L. Dugdale, John Francis, John Graton, Elkanah Huddleston, C. R.
    Jennison, James Montgomery, Webster W. Moses, Charles Robinson,
    Edmund G. Ross, Mary E. Stearns, Benjamin F. Van Horn, and James
    M. Williams
Kentucky Historical Society—Papers of A. C. Dicken and Henry L. Stone
Library of Congress—Papers of Orra B. Bailey, Samuel D. Barnes, R. R.
    Barrow, Felix Brannigan, Samuel E. Brown, Douglas J. Cater, Lewis
    Douglass, Charles Calvin Enslow, Christian A. Fleetwood, George O.
    Jewett, Robert E. Lee, Alexander Newburger, Howard Malcolm Smith,
    and Robert Augustus Toombs
Louisiana State University, Hill Memorial Library—Papers of George L.
    Andrews, Benjamin W. Johnson, and John H. Ransdell

Massachusetts Historical Society—Papers of William Dwight Jr. and Thomas
S. Howland
McCracken County Public Library, Paducah, Ky.—Papers of J. V. Greif
Minnesota Historical Society—Papers of John F. Aiton, Thomas D. Christie,
Daniel Densmore, James Peet, Amasa K. Richards, and Charles Robinson
Missouri Historical Society—Papers of William M. McPheeters and Ethan
Pinnell
Montana Historical Society—Papers of Edward M. Galligan
Museum of the Confederacy, Richmond, Va.—Papers of Thomas Pinckney
New Bedford (Mass.) Free Public Library—Papers of James W. Grace
New England Historic Genealogical Society—Papers of Ethan Earle
New Hampshire Historical Society—Papers of Samuel A. Duncan
New-York Historical Society—Papers of Clifford Thomson, Lucien P. Waters,
Robert F. Wilkinson, and Howard C. Wright
New York City Public Library—Bartholomew Diggins and Stephen A. Swailes
New York State Library, Albany—Papers of Francis G. Barnes and Dealton
Cooper
North Carolina State Archives and Records—Papers of Isaac L. Brown, James
O. A. Kelly, Eli Peal, and Joseph M. Whitehill
Oberlin College—Papers of Elliott Grabill and Giles Shurtleff
Ohio Historical Society—Papers of Samuel Evans, John Wesley Marshall,
Benjamin F. Morris, Albert Rogall, and Benjamin F. Wade
Old State House Museum, Little Rock, Ark.—Papers of Alfred G. Hearn
Petersburg National Battlefield Library—Papers of Hugh L. Kerrick and
Matthew N. Love
Rutgers University—Papers of Andrew Fremont Ely, Samuel J. Hopkins, and
Henry Whitney
Smith College—Papers of James S. Rogers
South Carolina Historical Society—Papers of Charles T. Trowbridge
State Historical Society of Wisconsin—Papers of James B. Lockney and
Julius Schlaich
Stephen S. Austin State University, East Texas Research Center—Papers of
John C. Birdwell, G. B. Crain, Henry T. Curl, J. G. Graham, and Henry
L. Watson
Tennessee State Library and Archives—Papers of Anthony W. Caldwell,
Samuel H. Caldwell, Achilles V. Clark, W. R. Dyer, Alfred T. Fielder, and
James Branch O'Bryan
Tulane University, Howard-Tilton Memorial Library—Papers of Frederick
Y. Dabney, James DeBaun, Paul F. De Gournay, A. J. Lewis, William R.
Miles, W. B. Shelby, Marshall J. Smith, and unknown diarist
U.S. Army Military History Institute—Papers of J. Henry Beatty, Dorsey M.
Binion, Francis Boland, George C. Chandler, Nelson Chapin, David
Cornwell, Nicholas DeGraff, William H. Dunham, John Faller, Robert
H. Fleming, Dayton E. Flint, John Habberton, Henry Henney, James W.
Hildreth, August V. Kautz, Frank McGregor, Joseph Kibler Nelson, B. W.

H. Pasron, William W. Pritchard, William C. Reeder, Seth Rogers, James and Thomas Rounsaville, Joseph J. Scroggs, Jacob Seibert, Charles Smith, Fred Smith, Eben P. Sturges, John W. Sturtevant, and William Woodruff
University of Arkansas, Fayetteville—Papers of Rebecca Ann Campbell and Milton P. Chambers
University of Florida, P. K. Yonge Library—Papers of Lawrence Jackson and Winston Stephens
University of Georgia—Papers of Charles C. Jones
University of Iowa—Papers of James Sanks Brisbin, Thomas Jefferson Hoge, and W. C. Ream
University of Michigan, Ann Arbor—Papers of William Baird, George H. Bates, Henry C. Bates, Adelbert Baughman, Jerome Bussey, Horace Charles, Hiram F. Covey, Byron M. Cutcheon, Ferdinand Davis, James G. Derrickson, James R. French, Jennie Fyfe, Abram E. Garrison, Claudius Grant, Phineas A. Hagar, Morris Stuart Hall, Luther Hemingway, George W. Lawrence, Frederick Lehman, Conrad Noll, Henry G. Marshall, Charles M. Maxim, James T. Miller, James T. Munson. W. Edwin O'Harron, W. W. Phelps, John Pierson, Henry Pippitt, William H. Randall, Hugh B. Roden, John Slaver, George Starbird, Peter Steketee, Oliver Van Valin, and Wash Vosburgh
University of North Carolina, Chapel Hill—Papers of William Beavans, Jessie Bernard, Overton Bernard, John Houston Bills, Braxton Bragg, George H. Cadman, John W. Darden, Elias Davis, Harry St. John Dixon, Robert G. Fitzgerald, Edward Owings Guerrant, Henry T. Guion, Charles W. [T.] Loehr, William Porcher Miles, William F. Penniman, Mrs. James G. Ramsay, Thomas R. Roulhac, Ira B. Sampson, William H. Stewart, Chauncey B. Welton, and Lewis Whitaker
University of Oklahoma—Papers of George W. Grayson
University of South Carolina—Papers of George H. Pettit and Calvin Shedd
University of Texas, Austin—Unsigned letter from 1st Texas Legion camp and papers of E. P. Becton, S. W. Farrow, David M. Ray, William Stanton, and Jerome Yates
University of Virginia, Alderman Library—Papers from Frederick Anspach, Edward Cook Barnes, John Herbert Claiborne, and Franklin Setzer, and White Family Papers, 1794–1921
University of Wisconsin—Papers of Frank D. Harding
Virginia Historical Society—Papers of John R. Bagby, Henry V. L. Bird, John O. Collins, Hodijah Meade, William Johnson Pegram, and John J. Wynne
Virginia Military Institute—Papers of Robert H. Campbell and Abram Fulkerson
Virginia State Library and Archives—Papers of Rawleigh Dunaway, Richard White, and Byrd C. Willis
West Virginia University Libraries—Papers of John W. M. Appleton and James F. Ellis
Western Reserve Historical Society—Papers of Carlos P. Lyman

Yale University Library—Papers of Walter A. Chapman, Ellsworth D. S. Goodyear, Charles G. Merrill, Alonzo Rembaugh, George R. Sanders, and Lewis Weld

Privately Held Papers

Stephen T. Andrews Papers—held by Sally Earnest, Pittsboro, N.C.
M. J. Bigbie Papers, http://www.33rdalabama.org/letters.htm
Wesley W. Bradly Papers—held by Bradly family, Georgetown, Tex.; http:// truittb.home.texas.net/WWBradly.htm
Thomas A. Cobb Papers, http://www.indianainthecivilwar.com/letters/10th/ cobb.htm
George Elliott Papers, http://www.indianainthecivilwar.com/letters/97th/ elliott.htm
Dudley Gale Papers, Dave Zullo Catalog #58
Henry Ketzle Papers, http://www.ketzle.com/diary/rightpane.html
Smith McDonald Papers, Dave Zullo, Gaithersburg, Md.
Christopher P. C. McKnight Papers, http://www.rootsweb.com/~okgenweb/ civilwar/letters/mcknight.htm
David S. Morgan Papers, http://www.kiva.net/~bjohnson/Letters.htm
Robert H. Peel Papers, http://myweb.cableone.net/4jdurham/peel/ltr090764. html
David Warman Papers, http://www.homepages.dsu.edu/jankej/civilwar/ warman.htm

Electronic Sources

American Jewish Archives, Hebrew Union College, www.jewish-history. com/civilwar.htm—Papers of Alexander Hart, Edwin I. Kursheedt, Isaac Scherck, Eleanor Cohen Seixas, and Philip Whitlock
Augustana College of Illinois, http://sparc5.augustana.edu/library/civil. html—Papers of Basil H. Messler
Bowling Green State University, http://www.bgsu.edu/colleges/library/cac/ ms0163a.html—Papers of George Kryder
Delavan Bates letters, transcribed by William S. Saint Jr., http://www.roots-web.com/~necivwar/CW/bates/genbate1.html
5th Georgia Cavalry site, http://www.5thgacavalry.info/5thcavalry/letters/ letters.htm—Papers of Thomas W. Houston
Library of Congress, http://memory.loc.gov/—Civil War photographs and papers of Horatio N. Taft
Silas W. Browning Papers, http://homepage.mac.com/netchemistwb/53rd_ Mass_f/browning1.html
26th Wisconsin site by Russell Scott, http://www.russscott.com/~rscott/ 26thwis—Papers of Ernst Damkoehler and Fredrick Winkler
University of Florida, http://extlab1.entnem.ufl.edu/olustee—Bogle obituary, papers of George E. Eddy, "H. W. B." letter, papers of James F. Hall and Edmond H. Jones

University of North Carolina, http://docsouth.unc.edu/author.html/—Papers
    of Meta M. Grimball, J. T. Kern, Dolly S. Lunt, and Andrew Sproul
University of Virginia, "The Valley of the Shadow—The War Years," digital
    project, http://valley.vcdh.virginia.edu—Papers of William Tell Barnitz,
    L. M. Blackford, William M. Heyser, Sylvester McElheney, Henry C.
    Metzger, Jacob D. Miller, John J. Miller, Lucius P. Mox, and Sam Pile
Virginia Military Institute, http://www.vmi.edu/archives/Manuscripts/
    msguide2.html—Papers of William J. Black, Napoleon B. Brisbine,
    Joseph W. Crowther, Abram Fulkerson, John Garibaldi, J. O. Humphreys,
    Mortimer H. Johnson, Andrew J. McCoy, Sidney Marlin, Benjamin F.
    Oakes, Achilles J. Tynes, William G. Watson, and Fannie Wilson
Virginia Polytechnic Institute and State University, http://spec.lib.vt.edu/
    civwar/—Papers of Archibald Atkinson, Henry C. Carpenter, and Isaac
    White

Public Documents

Adjutant General. *American Decorations: A List of Awards of the Congres-
    sional Medal of Honor, the Distinguished-Service Cross, and the Distin-
    guished-Service Medal, 1862–1926.* Washington, D.C.: GPO, 1927.
———. *Official Army Register of the Volunteer Forces of the United States Army
    for the Years 1861, '62, '63, '64, '65.* 8 pts. Washington, D.C.: GPO, 1867.
Confederate States of America Congress. House of Representatives. *Amend-
    ment to the Title, Joint Resolutions in reference to slaves captured in arms,
    and the exchange of free colored troops of the enemy.* 2d sess., Feb. 15, 1864.
    Richmond, Va.
———.House of Representatives. *Report of the Committee on Salt Supply.*
    Richmond, Va., 1864.
Illinois Adjutant General. *Report of the Adjutant General of the State of
    Illinois.* Vol. 8, *Reports for the Years 1861–66.* Springfield, Ill.: Journal
    Company, 1901.
Kansas Adjutant General. *Report of the Adjutant General of the State of Kan-
    sas, 1861–1865.* Topeka: Kansas State Printing, 1896.
Kentucky Adjutant General. *Confederate Kentucky Volunteers, War 1861—65.*
    2 vols. Frankfort, Ky.: State Journal Company, 1915.
Lykes, Richard Wayne. *Petersburg National Military Park, Virginia.* National
    Park Service Historical Handbook Series No. 13. Washington, D.C.: GPO,
    1951. Reprint, 1961.
Mainfort, Robert C., Jr. *Archaeological Investigations at Fort Pillow State His-
    torical Area: 1976–1978.* Research Series 4. Nashville: Division of Archae-
    ology, Tennessee Department of Conservation, 1980.
Michigan Adjutant General's Office. *Michigan in the War.* Comp. John Rob-
    ertson. Rev. ed. Lansing, Mich.: W. S. George, 1882.
National Park Service. "Civil War Soldiers and Sailors Project." http://www.
    cr./nps.gov/cultural.htm.
[National Park Service]. "Poplar Grove National Cemetery, Petersburg Na-
    tional Battlefield." Brochure. Washington, D.C.: GPO, [1979?]

Official Records of the Union and Confederate Navies in the War of the Rebellion. 31 vols. Washington, D.C.: GPO, 1894–1922.

Ross, Joseph B. *Tabular Analysis of the Records of the U.S. Colored Troops and Their Predecessor Units in the National Archives of the United States.* Special List No. 33. Washington, DC: GPO, 1973, 1985.

Statutes at Large, Treaties and Proclamations of the United States of America, 1789–1873. 15 vols. Boston: Little, Brown, 1789–1873.

Supervisory Committee for Recruiting Colored Regiments. *Free Military School for Applicants for Commands of Colored Troops.* Philadelphia: King & Baird, 1863.

——. *Report of the Supervisory Committee for Recruiting Colored Regiments.* Philadelphia: King & Baird, 1864.

Tennessee Civil War Centennial Commission. *Tennesseans in the Civil War: A Military History of Confederate and Union Units with Available Rosters of Personnel.* Nashville: Centennial Commission, 1964. Reprint, Knoxville: University of Tennessee Press, 1985.

U. S. Congress. House. Committee on War Claims. *Report on Officers and Enlisted Men of First Kansas Colored Volunteers.* Report No. 3157. 51st Cong., 1st sess., Sept. 23, 1890.

——. House. *Murder of Union Soldiers in North Carolina.* Executive Doc. No. 98. 39th Cong., 1st sess., 1866.

——. *Report of the Joint Committee on the Conduct of the War on the Attack on Petersburg on the 30th Day of July, 1864.* 38th Cong., 2d sess., [Feb.?] Rep. Com. 114. 1865.

——. *Report of the Joint Committee on the Conduct of the War on the Fort Pillow Massacre and on Returned Prisoners.* 38th Cong., 1st sess., [May?] Rep. Com. 63 and 68. 1864.

War Department. *Regulations for the Army of the United States, 1857.* New York: Harper & Bros., 1857.

The War of the Rebellion: Atlas to Accompany the Official Records of the Union and Confederate Armies. Washington, D.C.: GPO, 1891–1895. Reprint. *Official Atlas of the Civil War.* New York: Thomas Yoseloff, 1958

The War of the Rebellion: A Compilation of the Official Records of the Union and Confederate Armies. 128 vols. Washington, D.C.: GPO, 1880–1901.

National Archives and Records Administration

Civil War Pension Files. RG 15.

Compiled Military Service Records. RG 94.

List of prisoners captured by Major General Forrest at Fort Pillow, Tenn., Apr. 12, 1864, and other points. War Department. Confederate Records. RG 109.

List of U.S. Soldiers Executed by United States Military Authorities During the Late War. JAG Records, RG 153. Washington, DC. Aug. 1, 1885.

Logs of U.S. Naval Ships. RG 24.

Monthly Return, Bradford's Battalion [13th Tennessee Volunteer Cavalry], Apr. 8, 1864 (filed with muster rolls). AGO Records. RG 94.

Monthly Return, 11th U.S. Colored Infantry, AGO Records, RG 94.

The Negro in the Military Service of the United States, 1639–1886. Microfilm Publication M858. 7 vols. RG 94.

Register of Letters Received, 16th Army Corps (16 A.C., Vol. 9), for Mar. 1864, RG 393.

Primary Books

Adams, Charles Francis, Jr. *Charles Francis Adams, 1835–1915: An Autobiography.* Boston: Houghton Mifflin, 1916.

Adamson, Augustus P. *Sojourns of a Patriot: The Field and Prison Papers of an Unreconstructed Confederate.* Ed. Richard Bender Abell and Fay Adamson Gecik. Murfreesboro, Tenn.: Southern Heritage Press, 1998.

Akin, Warren. *Letters of Warren Akin, Confederate Congressman.* Ed. Bell Irvin Wiley. Athens: UG Press, 1959.

Alexander, Edward Porter. *Fighting for the Confederacy: The Personal Recollections of General Edward Porter Alexander.* Ed. Gary W. Gallagher. Chapel Hill: UNC Press, 1989.

Allen, George H. *Forty-Six Months with the Fourth R. I. Volunteers, in the War of 1861 to 1865.* Providence, R.I.: J. A. & R. A. Reid, 1887.

Anderson, Ephraim M. *Memoirs: Historical and Personal; Including the Campaigns of the First Missouri Confederate Brigade.* St. Louis: Times Printing, 1868. Reprint, Dayton, Ohio: Morningside Bookshop, 1972.

Anderson, John Q., ed. *Campaigning with Parsons' Texas Cavalry Brigade, CSA: The War Journals and Letters of the Four Orr Brothers, 12th Texas Cavalry Regiment.* Hillsboro, Tex.: Hill Junior College Press, 1967.

Anderson, Peter D. *Marching Barefoot: A Collection of Civil War Letters Written by Peter Daniel Anderson to His Wife and Children in Scandia, Minnesota.* Comp. Ralph C. E. Peterson. Trans. from the Swedish. Minneapolis: Bind-a-Book, 1991.

Andrews, Andrew J. *A Sketch of the Boyhood Days of Andrew J. Andrews of Gloucester County, Virginia, and His Experience as a Soldier in the Late War Between the States.* Richmond, Va.: Hermitage Press, 1905.

Andrews, Christopher C. *History of the Campaign of Mobile; Including the Cooperative Operations of Gen. Wilson's Cavalry in Alabama.* New York: D. Van Nostrand, 1867.

Andrews, Eliza F. *The War-Time Journal of a Georgia Girl, 1864–1865.* New York: D. Appleton, 1908.

Andrews, W. H. *Footprints of a Regiment: A Recollection of the 1st Georgia Regulars, 1861–1865.* Atlanta: Long Street Press, 1992.

Andrus, Onley. *The Civil War Letters of Sergeant Onley Andrus.* Ed. Fred Albert Shannon. Urbana: University of Illinois Press, 1947.

Ankeny, Henry G. *Kiss Josey For Me!* Ed. and comp. Florence Ankeny Cox. Santa Ana, Calif.: Friis-Pioneer Press, 1974.

Ashby, Thomas A. *The Valley Campaigns: Being the Reminiscences of a Non-Combatant While Between the Lines in the Shenandoah Valley During the War of the States.* New York: Neale, 1914. UNC electronic ed., 1998, http://docsouth.unc.edu/author/a.html.

Austin, Aurelia, ed. and comp. *Georgia Boys with "Stonewall" Jackson; James Thomas Thompson and the Walton Infantry.* Athens: UG Press, 1967.

Avery, James H. *Under Custer's Command: The Civil War Journal of James Henry Avery.* Comp. Karla Jean Husby. Ed. Eric J. Wittenberg. Washington, D.C.: Brassey's, 2000.

Babcock, Willoughby M., Jr. *Selections from the Letters and Diaries of Brevet Brigadier General Willoughby Babcock of the 75th New York Volunteers.* [Albany]: University of the State of New York, 1922.

Bacot, Ada W. *A Confederate Nurse: The Diary of Ada W. Bacot, 1860–1863.* Ed. Jean V. Berlin. Columbia: USC Press, 1994.

Barber, Charles. *The Civil War Letters of Charles Barber.* Ed. Raymond G. Barber and Gary E. Swinson. Torrance, Calif.: Gary E. Swinson, 1991.

Barron, S. B. *The Lone Star Defenders: A Chronicle of the Third Texas Cavalry, Ross' Brigade.* New York: Neale, 1908. Reprint, Waco, Tex.: W. M. Morrison, 1964.

Basler, Roy P., ed. *The Collected Works of Abraham Lincoln.* 9 vols. New Brunswick, N.J.: RU Press, 1955.

Bates, Edward. *The Diary of Edward Bates.* Ed. Howard K. Beale. New York: Da Capo, 1971. Originally published as Vol. 4, *Annual Report.* Washington, D.C.: American Historical Association, 1930.

Bates, James C. *A Texas Cavalry Officer's Civil War: The Diary and Letters of James C. Bates.* Ed. Richard Lowe. Baton Rouge: LSU Press, 1987.

Beecham, Robert K. *As If It Were Glory: Robert Beecham's Civil War from the Iron Brigade to the Black Regiments.* Ed. Michael E. Stevens. Madison, Wisc.: Madison House, 1998.

Berlin, Ira, Barbara J. Fields, Steven F. Miller, Joseph P. Reidy, and Leslie S. Rowland, eds. *Free at Last: A Documentary History of Slavery, Freedom, and the Civil War.* New York: New Press, 1992.

Berlin, Ira, Joseph P. Reidy, and Leslie S. Rowland, eds. *Freedom: A Documentary History of Emancipation, 1861–1867.* 4 vols. *Series 2: The Black Military Experience.* New York: Cambridge University Press, 1982.

Bernard, George S., ed. and contributor. *War Talks of Confederate Veterans.* Petersburg, Va.: Fenn & Owen, 1892.

Bevens, William E. *Reminiscences of a Private: William E. Bevens of the First Arkansas Infantry, C.S.A.* Ed. Daniel E. Sutherland. Reprint, Fayetteville: UA Press, 1991.

Billingsley, Amos S. *From the Flag to the Cross; or, Scenes and Incidents of Christianity in the War.* Philadelphia: New World Publishing, 1872.

Bird, Edgeworth and Sallie Bird. *The Granite Farm Letters: The Civil War Correspondence of Edgeworth & Sallie Bird.* Ed. John Rozier. Athens: UG Press, 1988.

Blackburn, James K. P. *Reminiscences of the Terry Rangers.* Austin: Littlefield Fund for Southern History, UT, 1919. Reprinted as pt. 2, *Terry Texas Ranger Trilogy.* Austin, Tex.: State House Press, 1996.

Blakeslee, B. F. *History of the Sixteenth Connecticut Volunteers.* Hartford, Conn.: Case, Lockwood and Brainard, 1875.

Blessington, Joseph P. *The Campaigns of Walker's Texas Division.* New York: Lange, Little, 1875. Reprint, Austin, Tex.: Pemberton Press, 1968.

Boddy, William. *Private William Boddy's Civil War Journal: Empty Saddles . . . Empty Sleeves . . .* Ed. Robert E. Berkenes. Altoona, Iowa: TiffCor Publishing, 1996.

Booth, George W. *Personal Reminiscences of a Maryland Soldier in the War Between the States, 1861–1865.* Baltimore: Fleet, McGinley, 1898. Reprint, Gaithersburg, Md.: Butternut Press, 1986.

Bosbyshell, Oliver Christian. *The 48th in the War, Being a Narrative of the Campaigns of the 48th Regiment, Infantry, Pennsylvania Veteran Volunteers.* Philadelphia: Avil Printing, 1895.

Bosson, Charles P. *History of the Forty-Second Regiment Infantry, Massachusetts Volunteers, 1862, 1863, 1864.* Boston: Mills, Knight, 1886.

Bouton, Edward. *Events of the Civil War.* Los Angeles: Kingsley, Moles and Collins, [1906].

Boyd, Cyrus F. *The Civil War Diary of Cyrus F. Boyd, Fifteenth Iowa Infantry, 1861–1863.* Ed. Mildred Thorne. Iowa City: State Historical Society of Iowa, 1953. Reprint, Millwood, N.Y.: Kraus Reprint, 1977.

Bragg, Junius N. *Letters of a Confederate Surgeon, 1861–1865.* Ed. Mrs. T. J. Gaughan. Camden, Ark.: Hurley, 1960.

Brandt, Nat, ed. *Mr. Tubbs' Civil War.* Syracuse, N.Y.: Syracuse University Press, 1996.

Breckinridge, Lucy. *Lucy Breckinridge of Grove Hill: The Journal of a Virginia Girl, 1862–1864.* Ed. Mary D. Robertson. Columbia: USC Press, 1994.

Brewster, Charles H. *When This Cruel War Is Over: The Civil War Letters of Charles Harvey Brewster.* Ed. David W. Blight. Amherst: University of Massachusetts Press, 1992.

Britton, Wiley. *The Civil War on the Border.* 2 vols. New York: G. P. Putnam's Sons, 1890–99.

Brooks, Noah. *Washington in Lincoln's Time.* New York: Century, 1895. Reprint, New York: Rinehart, 1958.

Brown, Augustus C. *The Diary of a Line Officer.* New York: privately printed, [1906].

Brown, Maud M. *The University Greys: Company A, Eleventh Mississippi Regiment, Army of Northern Virginia, 1861–1865.* Richmond, Va.: Garrett & Massie, 1940.

Brown, Thaddeus C. S., Samuel J. Murphy, and William G. Putney. *Behind the Guns: The History of Battery I, 2nd Regiment, Illinois Light Artillery.* Carbondale: Southern Illinois University Press, 1965.

Browne, Junius H. *Four Years in Secessia.* Hartford, Conn.: O. D. Case, 1865.

Burke, William Smith. *Military History of Kansas Regiments During the War for the Suppression of the Great Rebellion.* Leavenworth, Kans.: W. S. Burke, 1870.

Butler, Benjamin Franklin. *Autobiography and Personal Reminiscences of Major-General Benj. F. Butler: Butler's Book.* Boston: A. M. Thayer, 1892.

———. *The Private and Official Correspondence of General Benjamin F. Butler During the Period of the Civil War.* 5 vols. Norwood, Mass.: Plimpton, 1917.

Cade, Edward W. *A Texas Surgeon in the C.S.A.* Ed. John Q. Anderson. Confederate Centennial Studies 6. Tuscaloosa, Ala.: Confederate Publishing, 1957.

Cadwell, Charles K. *The Old Sixth Regiment, Its War Record, 1861–5.* New Haven, Conn.: Tuttle, Morehouse & Taylor, 1875.

Califf, Joseph M. *Record of the Services of the Seventh Regiment, U.S. Colored Troops.* Providence, R.I.: E. L. Freeman, 1878. Reprint, Freeport, N.Y.: Books for Libraries, 1971.

Carroll, John W. *Autobiography and Reminiscences of John W. Carroll.* Henderson, Tenn.: n.p., 1898. UNC electronic ed., 1996, http://docsouth.unc.edu/carroll/carroll.html.

Casler, John O. *Four Years in the Stonewall Brigade.* 4th ed. Guthrie, Okla.: State Capital Printing, 1893. Reprint, Dayton, Ohio: Morningside Bookshop, 1971.

Cate, Wirt Armistead, ed. *Two Soldiers: The Campaign Diaries of Thomas J. Key, C.S.A., and Robert J. Campbell, U.S.A.* Chapel Hill: UNC Press, 1938.

Cater, Douglas J. *As It Was: Reminiscences of a Soldier of the Third Texas Cavalry and the Nineteenth Louisiana Infantry.* [Austin, Tex.]: privately printed, 1981. Reprint, Austin, Tex.: State House Press, 1990.

Cavins, Elijah H. C. *The Civil War Letters of Col. Elijah H. C. Cavins, 14th Indiana.* Owensboro, Ky.: Cook-McDowell, 1981.

Chamberlain, Joshua L. *Through Blood & Fire: Selected Civil War Papers of Major General Joshua Chamberlain.* Ed. Mark Nesbit. Mechanicsburg, Pa.: Stackpoole Books, 1996.

Chamberlayne, John H. *Ham Chamberlayne—Virginian; Letters and Papers of an Artillery Officer in the War for Southern Independence, 1861–1865.* Ed. C. G. Chamberlayne. Richmond, Va.: Dietz, 1932.

Chambers, Henry A. *Diary of Captain Henry A. Chambers.* Ed. T. H. Pearce. Wendell, N.C.: Broadfoot's Bookmark, 1983.

Chambers, William Pitt. *Journal of William Pitt Chambers, 1862–1865.* Mississippi Historical Society Centenary Series 5. Jackson: Mississippi Historical Society, 1925.

Chase, Salmon P. *Inside Lincoln's Cabinet: The Civil War Diaries of Salmon P. Chase.* Ed. David Donald. New York: Longmans, Green, 1954.

Chester, Thomas Morris. *Thomas Morris Chester, Black Civil War Correspondent; His Dispatches from the Virginia Front.* Ed. R. J. M. Blackett. Baton Rouge: LSU Press, 1989.

Chestnut, Mary Boykin. *Mary Chestnut's Civil War.* Ed. C. Vann Woodward. Originally published as *A Diary from Dixie.* New York: D. Appleton, 1905. Rev. ed., New Haven, Conn.: YU Press, 1981.

Chetlain, Augustus L. *Recollections of Seventy Years.* Galena, Ill.: Gazette Publishing, 1899.

Chisholm, Daniel. *The Civil War Notebook of Daniel Chisholm*. Ed. W.
    Springer Menge and J. August Shimrak. New York: Orion Books, 1989.
Clark, Walter, ed. *Histories of the Several Regiments and Battalions from
    North Carolina in the Great War 1861–65*. 5 vols. Raleigh, N.C.: State of
    North Carolina, 1901.
Clark, Walter A. *Under the Stars and Bars; or, Memories of Four Years Service
    with the Oglethorpes of Augusta, Georgia*. Augusta, Ga.: Chronicle Print-
    ing, 1900. Reprint, Jonesboro, Ga.: Freedom Hill Press, 1987.
Clarke, Hermon. *Back Home in Oneida: Hermon Clarke and His Letters*. Ed.
    Harry F. Jackson and Thomas F. O'Donnell. Syracuse, N.Y.: Syracuse
    University Press, 1965.
Clay-Copton, Virginia. *A Belle of the Fifties: Memoirs of Mrs. Clay, of Ala-
    bama, Covering Social and Political Life in Washington and the South,
    1853–66*. New York: Doubleday, Page, 1905. UNC electronic ed., 1998,
    http://docsouth.unc.edu/author/c.html.
Cochrane, John. *American Civil War: Memories of Incidents . . . Including the
    Proposition Made in a Speech . . . in November, 1861*. New York: Rogers &
    Sherwood, 1879.
Cogley, Thomas S. *History of the Seventh Indiana Cavalry Volunteers*.
    LaPorte, Ind.: Herald, 1876. Reprint, Dayton, Ohio: Morningside House,
    1991.
Cole, Robert T. *From Huntsville to Appomattox: R. T. Cole's History of 4th
    Regiment, Alabama Volunteer Infantry, C.S.A., Army of Northern Virginia*.
    Ed. Jeffrey D. Stocker. Knoxville: University of Tennessee Press, 1996.
Commager, Henry S., ed. *The Blue and the Gray: The Story of the Civil War
    as Told by the Participants*. 2 vols. Indianapolis: Bobbs-Merrill, 1950.
Committee of the Regimental Association. *History of the Thirty-Fifth Regi-
    ment Massachusetts Volunteers, 1862–1865*. Boston: Mills, Knight, 1884.
Connolly, James Austin. *Three Years in the Army of the Cumberland: The Let-
    ters and Diary of Major James A. Connolly*. Ed. Paul M. Angle. Blooming-
    ton: IU Press, 1959.
Conyngham, David P. *Sherman's March Through the South. With Sketches
    and Incidents of the Campaign*. New York: Sheldon, 1865.
Cooper, Alonzo. *In and Out of Rebel Prisons*. Oswego, N.Y.: R. J. Oliphant,
    1888. Reprint, Alexandria, Va.: Time-Life Books, 1983.
Corbin, Richard W. *Letters of a Confederate Officer to His Family in Europe,
    During the Last Year of the War of Secession*. Paris: Neal's English Library,
    [1902]. Reprint, Baltimore: Butternut and Blue, 1993.
Cort, Charles E. *Dear Friends: The Civil War Letters and Diary of Charles
    Edwin Cort*. Comp. and ed. Helyn W. Tomlinson. N.p.: Helyn Tomlinson,
    1962.
Cowden, Robert. *A Brief Sketch of the Organization and Services of the Fifty-
    Ninth Regiment of United States Colored Infantry*. Dayton, Ohio: United
    Brethren, 1883.
Cox, Jacob D. *Sherman's March to the Sea; Hood's Tennessee Campaign &
    the Carolina Campaigns of 1865*. New York: Da Capo, 1994. Originally

published as *The March to the Sea: Franklin and Nashville*. New York: Charles Scribner's Sons, 1882.

Crawford, Samuel J. *Kansas in the Sixties*. Chicago: A. C. McClurg, 1911.

Crandall, Warren D., and Isaac D. Newell. *History of the Ram Fleet and the Mississippi Marine Brigade . . . the Ellets and their Men*. St. Louis: Buschart Bros., 1907.

Crook, George. *General George Crook: His Autobiography*. Ed. Martin F. Schmitt. 2d ed. Norman: UO Press, 1960.

Crowninshield, Benjamin W. *A History of the First Regiment of Massachusetts Cavalry Volunteers*. Boston: Houghton Mifflin, 1891.

Cumming, Kate. *Kate: The Journal of a Confederate Nurse*. Ed. Richard B. Harwell. Baton Rouge: LSU Press, 1959. Originally published as *A Journal of Hospital Life in the Confederate Army of Tennessee from the Battle of Shiloh to the End of the War*. Louisville, Ky.: John P. Morton, 1866.

Daly, Maria L. *Diary of a Union Lady*. Ed. Harold E. Hammond. New York: Funk & Wagnalls, 1962.

Davidson, William H., ed. *War Was the Place*. Old Oakbowery, Ala.: Chattahoochee Valley Historical Society, 1961.

Davis, Jefferson. *The Rise and Fall of the Confederate Government*. 2 vols. New York: D. Appleton, 1881. Reprint, New York: Thomas Yoseloff, 1958.

Dawson, Sarah Morgan. *A Confederate Girl's Diary*. Ed. James I. Robertson Jr. Boston: Houghton Mifflin, 1913. Reprint, Bloomington: IU Press, 1960.

Day, William A. *A True History of Company I, 49th Regiment North Carolina Troops, in the Great Civil War Between the North and South*. Newton, N.C.: Enterprise Job Office, 1893.

DeLeon, Thomas Cooper. *Four Years in Rebel Capitals; An Inside View of Life in the Southern Confederacy, from Birth to Death*. Mobile, Ala.: Gossip Printing, 1890. Reprint, Alexandria, Va.: Time-Life Books, 1983.

Dennett, George M. *History of the Ninth U.S.C. troops, from its Organization till muster out, with list of names of all officers and enlisted men, who have ever belonged to the regiment*. Philadelphia: King & Baird, 1866.

Dickey, Luther S. *History of the 103d Regiment Pennsylvania Veteran Volunteer Infantry, 1861–1865*. Chicago: L. S. Dickey, 1910.

Dinkins, James. *1861 to 1865: Personal Recollections and Experiences in the Confederate Army by an "Old Johnnie."* Cincinnati: Robert Clark, 1897. Reprint, Dayton, Ohio: Morningside Bookshop, 1975.

Donaghy, John. *Army Experience of Capt. John Donaghy, 103d Penn'a Vols., 1861–1864*. De Land, Fla.: E. O. Painter, [1926].

Douglass, Frederick. *Life and Times of Frederick Douglass*. Reprint, New York: Bonanza, 1962.

Dowdey, Clifford, and Louis H. Manarin, eds. *The Wartime Papers of R. E. Lee*. Boston: Little, Brown, 1961.

Duke, Basil W. *Reminiscences of General Basil W. Duke*. Garden City, N.Y.: Doubleday, Page, 1911. Reprint, Freeport, N.Y.: Books for Libraries, 1969.

Duncan, Thomas D. *Recollections of Thomas D. Duncan, Confederate Soldier*. Nashville: McQuiddy Printing, 1922.

Dunham, Alburtus A., and Charles L. Dunham. *Through the South with a Union Soldier.* Ed. Arthur H. DeRosier Jr. Johnson City: East Tennessee State University, 1969.

Du Pont, Henry A. *The Campaign of 1864 in the Valley of Virginia and the Expedition to Lynchburg.* New York: National Americana Society, 1925.

Du Pont, Samuel F. *Samuel Francis Du Pont: A Selection from His Civil War Letters.* 3 vols. Ed. John D. Hayes. Ithaca, N.Y.: Eleutherian Mills Historical Library, Cornell University Press, 1969.

Dyer, Gustavus W., and John Trotwood Moore, comps. *The Tennessee Civil War Veterans Questionnaires.* 5 vols. Easley, S.C.: Southern Historical Press, 1985.

Early, Jacob. *Letters Home: The Personal Side of the American Civil War.* Comp. and ed. Robert A. Driver and Gloria S. Driver. Rev. ed. Roseburg, Ore.: Robert A. and Gloria S. Driver, 1993.

Early, Jubal A. *War Memoirs: Autobiographical Sketch and Narrative of the War Between the States.* Philadelphia: J. B. Lippincott, 1912. Reprint, Bloomington: IU Press, 1960.

Early, Jubal A., J. William Jones, Robert A. Brock, James P. Smith, Hamilton J. Ekenrode, Douglas Southall Freeman, and Frank E. Vandiver, eds. *Southern Historical Society Papers.* 52 vols. Richmond, Va.: Southern Historical Society, 1876–1910.

Eaton, John. *Grant, Lincoln and the Freedmen.* New York: Longmans, Green, 1907. Reprint, New York: Negro Universities Press, 1969.

Edmondston, Catherine. *Journal of a Secesh Lady: The Diary of Catherine Ann Devereux Edmondston, 1860–1866.* Ed. Beth G. Crabtree and James W. Patton. Raleigh, N.C.: Division of Archives and History, State of North Carolina, 1979.

Edwards, Abial H. *Dear Friend Anna: The Civil War Letters of a Common Soldier from Maine.* Ed. Beverly Hayes Kallgren and James L. Crouthamel. Orono: University of Maine Press, 1992.

Edwards, John N. *Shelby and His Men: or, the War in the West.* Cincinnati: Miami Printing, 1867.

Elmore, Grace B. *Heritage of Woe: The Civil War Diary of Grace Brown Elmore, 1861–1868.* Athens: UG Press, 1997.

Emilio, Luis F. *A Brave Black Regiment: History of the Fifty-Fourth Regiment of Massachusetts Volunteer Infantry, 1863–1865.* 2d ed. Boston: Boston Book, 1894.

Evans, Clement A., ed. *Confederate Military History.* 12 vols. Atlanta: Confederate Publishing, 1899.

——. *Intrepid Warrior, Clement Anselm Evans, Confederate General from Georgia.* Ed. and comp. Robert Grier Stephens Jr. Dayton, Ohio: Morningside House, 1992.

Fay, Edwin H. *This Infernal War: The Confederate Letters of Sgt. Edwin H. Fay.* Ed. Bell Irvin Wiley and Lucy E. Fay. Austin: UT Press, 1958.

Fewell, Alexander F. *Dear Martha . . .: The Confederate War Letters of a*

South Carolina Soldier, Alexander Faulkner Fewell. Comp. and ed. Robert H. Macintosh Jr. Columbia, S.C.: R. H. Macintosh, 1976.

Fisk, Wilbur. *Hard Marching Every Day.* Ed. Emil and Ruth Rosenblatt. Lawrence: University Press of Kansas, 1992. Originally published as *Anti-rebel: The Civil War Letters of Wilbur Fisk.* Croton-on-Hudson, N.Y.: Rosenblatt, 1983.

Fisk University, Social Science Institute. *The Unwritten History of Slavery: Autobiographical Accounts of Negro Ex-Slaves.* Comp. Ophelia Settle Egypt. Nashville, Tenn.: Fisk University, 1945.

Fiske, Joseph E. *War Letters of Capt. Joseph E. Fiske (Harvard, '61), written to his parents during the War of the Rebellion . . .* Wellesley, Mass.: Maugus Press, [19—?].

Fitzpatrick, Marion H. *Letters to Amanda from Sergeant Major Marion Hill Fitzpatrick, Company K, 45th Georgia Regiment . . . 1862–1865.* Ed. Mansel Hammock. Culloden, Ga.: Mansell Hammock, 1976.

Fleet, Benjamin R. *Green Mount; A Virginia Plantation Family During the Civil War.* Ed. Betsy Fleet and John D. P. Fuller. Lexington: University of Kentucky Press, 1962.

Flinn, Frank M. *Campaigning with Banks in Louisiana, '63 and '64, and with Sheridan in the Shenandoah Valley in '64 and '65.* Lynn, Mass.: Thomas P. Nichols, 1887.

Ford, Worthington Chauncey, ed. *A Cycle of Adams Letters, 1861–1865.* 2 vols. Boston: Houghton Mifflin, 1920.

Forsythe, John W. *Guerrilla Warfare and Life in Libby Prison.* Ed. Melvin Lee Steadman. Algona, Iowa: Republican Steam Print, 1892. Reprint, Annandale, Va.: Turnpike Press, 1967.

Forten, Charlotte L. *The Journals of Charlotte Forten Grimké.* Ed. Brenda Stevenson. New York: Dryden Press, 1955. New ed. New York: Oxford University Press, 1988.

Fowle, George. *Letters to Eliza from a Union Soldier, 1862–1865.* Ed. Margaret Greenleaf. Chicago: Follett, 1970.

Fox, Charles B. *Record of the Service of the Fifty-Fifth Regiment of Massachusetts Volunteer Infantry.* Cambridge, Mass.: John Wilson and Son, 1868.

Fox, Tryphena. *A Northern Woman in the Plantation South: Letters of Tryphena Blanche Holder Fox.* Ed. Wilma King. Columbia: USC Press, 1993.

Freeman, Benjamin H. *The Confederate Letters of Benjamin H. Freeman.* Ed. Stuart T. Wright. Hicksville, N.Y.: Exposition Press, 1974.

Fremantle, Arthur J. L. *The Fremantle Diary, Being the Journal of Lieutenant Colonel Arthur James Lyon Fremantle, Coldstream Guards, on His Three Months in the Southern States.* Ed. Walter Lord. New York: J. Bradburn, 1864. Reprint, Boston: Little, Brown, 1954.

Frey, Jerry, ed. *Grandpa's Gone: The Adventures of Daniel Buchwalter in the Western Army, 1862–1865.* Shippensburg, Pa.: Burd Street, 1998.

Freyburger, Michael. *Gold Rush & Civil War Letters to Ann from Michael Freyburger.* Shelbyville, Ill.: Shelby County Historical and Genealogical Society, 1986.

Gage, Moses D. *From Vicksburg to Raleigh; or, a Complete History of the Twelfth Regiment Indiana Volunteer Infantry, and the Campaigns of Grant and Sherman.* Chicago: Clarke, 1865.

Garcia, Celine Fremaux. *Celine: Remembering Louisiana, 1850–1871.* Ed. Patrick J. Geary. Athens: UG Press, 1987.

Garfield, James A. *The Wild Life of the Army: Civil War Letters of James A. Garfield.* Ed. Frederick D. Williams. East Lansing: Michigan State University Press, 1964.

Garrett, David R. *The Civil War Letters of David R. Garrett, Detailing the Adventures of the 6th Texas Cavalry, 1861–1865.* Ed. Max Lale and Hobart Key Jr. Marshall, Tex.: Port Caddo Press, 1963.

Geary, John W. *A Politician Goes to War: The Civil War Letters of John White Geary.* Ed. William A. Blair. University Park: Pennsylvania State University Press, 1995.

Geer, Allen M. *The Civil War Diary of Allen Morgan Geer, Twentieth Regiment Illinois Volunteers.* Ed. Mary Ann Anderson. Denver, Colo.: Robert C. Appleman, 1977.

George, Henry. *History of the 3d, 7th, 8th and 12th Kentucky C.S.A.* Louisville, Ky.: C. T. Dearing, 1911. Reprint, Melber, Ky.: Simmons Historical Publications, 1987.

Gill, John. *Courier for Lee and Jackson, 1861–1865: Memoirs.* Ed. Walbrook D. Swank. Baltimore: Sun Printing, 1904. Reprint, Shippensburg, Pa.: Burd Street, 1993.

Gooding, James H. *On the Altar of Freedom.* Ed. Virginia M. Adams. Amherst: University of Massachusetts Press, 1991.

Goodloe, Albert Theodore. *Confederate Echoes: A Soldier's Personal Story of Life in the Confederate Army from the Mississippi to the Carolinas.* Nashville: Smith & Lamar, 1907. Reprint, Washington, D.C.: Zenger, 1983.

Gordon, John B. *Reminiscences of the Civil War.* New York: Charles Scribner's Sons, 1904. Reprint, Gettysburg, Pa.: Civil War Times, 1974.

Gorgas, Josiah. *The Civil War Diary of General Josiah Gorgas.* Ed. Frank E. Vandiver. University: University of Alabama Press, 1947.

Goss, Warren Lee. *The Soldier's Story of his Captivity at Andersonville, Belle Isle and Other Rebel Prisons.* Boston: Lee & Shepard, 1866.

Graber, Henry W. *A Terry Texas Ranger: The Life Record of H. W. Graber.* Dallas: Privately printed, with title elements reversed, 1916. Reprint, Austin, Tex.: State House Press, 1987.

Graham, James A. *The James A. Graham Papers, 1861–1884.* Ed. H. M. Wagstaff. The James Sprunt Historic Studies 20, vol. 3. Chapel Hill: UNC Press, 1928.

Grant, Ulysses S. *Letters of Ulysses S. Grant to his Father and his Youngest Sister, 1857–1878.* Ed. Jesse Grant Cramer. New York: G. P. Putnam's Sons, 1912.

——. *The Papers of Ulysses S. Grant.* Ed. John Y. Simon. 20 vols. Carbondale: Southern Illinois University Press, 1967–.

——. *Personal Memoirs of U.S. Grant.* 2 vols. New York: Charles L. Webster, 1885.

Gray, John C., and John C. Ropes. *War Letters, 1862–1865, of John Chipman Gray and John Codman Ropes.* Cambridge: Massachusetts Historical Society, 1927.

Griffin, James B. *A Gentleman and an Officer: A Military and Social History of James B. Griffin's Civil War.* Ed. Judith N. McArthur and Orville V. Burton. New York: Oxford University Press, 1996.

Grimes, Bryan. *Extracts of Letters of Major-General Bryan Grimes to His Wife, Written While in Active Service in the Army of Northern Virginia.* Comp. Pulaski Cowper. Ed. Gary W. Gallagher. Raleigh, N.C.: Edwards, Broughton, 1883. Reprint, Wilmington, N.C.: Broadfoot, 1986.

Griscom, George L. *Fighting with Ross' Texas Cavalry Brigade, C.S.A.: The Diary of George L. Griscom, Adjutant, 9th Texas Cavalry Regiment.* Ed. Homer L. Kerr. Hillsboro, Tex.: Hill Junior College Press, 1976.

Guild, George B. *A Brief Narrative of the Fourth Tennessee Cavalry Regiment, Wheeler's Corps, Army of Tennessee.* Nashville: n.p., 1913.

Hagood, Johnson. *Memoirs of the War of Secession.* Columbia, S.C.: State, 1910.

Haley, John West. *The Rebel Yell & the Yankee Hurrah: The Civil War Journal of a Maine Volunteer.* Ed. Ruth L. Silliker. Camden, Maine: Down East Books, 1985.

Hamilton, D. H. *History of Company M, First Texas Volunteer Infantry, Hood's Brigade, Longstreet's Corps, Army of the Confederate States of America.* Written 1925. Waco, Tex.: W. M. Morrison, 1962.

Hancock, R[ichard] R. *Hancock's Diary: or, a History of the Second Tennessee Confederate Cavalry.* 2 vols. in 1. Nashville: Brandon Printing, 1887.

Hanks, O. T. *History of Captain B. F. Benton's Company, Hood's Texas Brigade, 1861–1865.* Austin, Tex.: Morrison Books, 1984.

Hanson, G. A. *Minor Incidents of the Late War, As Seen and Chronicled by an Eye-Witness.* Bartow, Fla.: Sessions, Bartow & Kilpatrick, 1887.

Harrill, Lawson. *Reminiscences, 1861–1865.* Statesville, N.C.: Brady, 1910.

Harrison, Constance. *Recollections Grave and Gay.* New York: Charles Scribner's Sons, 1911.

Haskell, John C. *The Haskell Memoirs.* Ed. Gilbert E. Govan and James W. Livingood. New York: G. P. Putnam's Sons, 1960.

Hawks, Esther H. *A Woman Doctor's Civil War: Esther Hill Hawks' Diary.* Ed. Gerald Schwartz. Columbia: USC Press, 1984.

Hay, John. *Lincoln and the Civil War in the Diaries and Letters of John Hay.* Ed. Tyler Dennett. New York: Dodd, Mead, 1939.

Hayes, Rutherford B. *Diary and Letters of Rutherford Birchard Hayes, Nineteenth President of the United States.* Columbus, Ohio: Archaeological and Historical Society, 1922. Reprint, New York: Kraus Reprint, 1971.

Head, Thomas A. *Campaigns and Battles of the Sixteenth Regiment Tennessee Volunteers in the War Between the States.* Nashville: Cumberland

Presbyterian Publishing, 1885. Reprint, McMinnville, Tenn.: Womack
    Printing, 1961.

Henry, Robert Selph. *As They Saw Forrest*. Jackson, Tenn.: McCowat-Mercer,
    1956.

Hepworth, George H. *The Whip, Hoe and Sword*. Boston: Walker, Wise,
    1864. Reprint, Freeport, N.Y.: Books for Libraries, 1971.

Heyward, Pauline DeCaradeuc. *A Confederate Lady Comes of Age: The Jour-
    nal of Pauline DeCaradeuc Heyward, 1863–1888*. Columbia: USC Press,
    1992.

Higginson, Thomas Wentworth. *Army Life in a Black Regiment*. Boston:
    1870. Reprint, East Lansing: Michigan State University Press, 1960.

Hitchcock, Ethan A. *Fifty Years in Camp and Field: Diary of Major-Gen-
    eral Ethan Allen Hitchcock, U.S.A*. Ed. W. A. Croffut. New York: G. P.
    Putnam's Sons, 1909. Reprint, Freeport, N.Y.: Books for Libraries, 1971.

Hitchcock, Henry. *Marching with Sherman: Passages from the Letters and
    Campaign Diaries of Henry Hitchcock*. Ed. M. A. DeWolfe Howe. New
    Haven, Conn.: YU Press, 1927.

Hoffman, Wickham. *Camp, Court and Siege; A Narrative of Personal Adven-
    ture and Observation During Two Wars: 1861–1865; 1870–1871*. New York:
    Harper and Brothers, 1877.

Holmes, Emma. *The Diary of Miss Emma Holmes, 1861–1866*. Ed. John F.
    Marszalek. Baton Rouge: LSU Press, 1979.

Holmes, Sarah K. (Stone). *Brokenburn: The Journal of Kate Stone, 1861–1868*.
    Ed. John Q. Anderson. Baton Rouge: LSU Press, 1955.

Holt, David E. *A Mississippi Rebel in the Army of Northern Virginia: The
    Civil War Memoirs of Private David Holt*. Ed. Thomas D. Cockrell and
    Michael B. Ballard. Baton Rouge: LSU Press, 1995.

Holzer, Harold, comp. and ed. *Dear Mr. Lincoln: Letters to the President*.
    Reading, Mass.: Addison-Wesley, 1993.

Hood, John B. *Advance and Retreat: Personal Experiences in the United States
    & Confederate States Armies*. New Orleans: Hood Orphan Memorial
    Fund, 1880. Reprint, Bloomington: IU Press, 1959.

Hough, Alfred L. *Soldier in the West: The Civil War Letters of Alfred Lacey
    Hough*. Ed. Robert G. Athearn. Philadelphia: University of Pennsylvania
    Press, 1957.

Houghton, Edwin B. *The Campaigns of the Seventeenth Maine*. Portland:
    Short & Loring, 1866.

Houghton, W. R., and M. B. Houghton. *Two Boys in the Civil War and After*.
    Montgomery, Ala.: Paragon, 1912.

House, Ellen R. *A Very Violent Rebel: The Civil War Diary of Ellen Renshaw
    House*. Ed. Daniel E. Sutherland. Knoxville: University of Tennessee
    Press, 1996.

Hubbard, John M. *Notes of a Private*. Memphis, Tenn.: E. H. Clarke & Bro.,
    1909. 3rd ed. St. Louis: Nixon-Jones, 1913.

Hudson, Joshua H. *Sketches and Reminiscences*. Columbia, S.C.: State, 1903.

Ingram, George W., and Martha F. Ingram. *Civil War Letters of George W. and Martha F. Ingram, 1861–1865.* Comp. Henry L. Ingram. College Station: Texas A&M Press, 1973.

Irwin, Richard B. *History of the Nineteenth Army Corps.* New York: G. P. Putnam's Sons, 1892.

Jackman, Lyman. *History of the Sixth New Hampshire Regiment in the War for the Union.* Concord, N.H.: Republican Press Association, 1891.

Jackson, Edgar, ed. *Three Rebels Write Home, Including the Letters of Edgar Allan Jackson, James Fenton Bryant, Irvin Cross Wills and Miscellaneous Items.* Franklin, Va.: News Publishing, 1955.

Jackson, Isaac. *Some of the Boys. . .: The Civil War Letters of Isaac Jackson, 1862–1865.* Ed. Joseph Orville Jackson. Carbondale: Southern Illinois University Press, 1960.

Johns, Henry T. *Life with the Forty-Ninth Massachusetts Volunteers.* Pittsfield, Mass.: C. A. Alvord, 1864. Reprint, Washington, D.C.: Ramsey and Bisbee, 1890.

Johnson, John. *The Defense of Charleston Harbor, Including Fort Sumter and the Adjacent Islands, 1863–1865.* Charleston, S.C.: Walker, Evans & Cogswell, 1890.

Johnson, Robert U., and Clarence C. Buel, eds. *Battles and Leaders of the Civil War.* 4 vols. New York: Century, 1884–1888.

Jones, J. B. *A Rebel War Clerk's Diary at the Confederate States Capital.* 2 vols. Ed. Howard Swiggett. Reprint, New York: Old Hickory Bookshop, 1935.

Jones, Katherine M. *Heroines of Dixie: Confederate Women Tell Their Story of the War.* Indianapolis: Bobbs-Merrill, 1955.

Kean, Robert G. H. *Inside the Confederate Government: The Diary of Robert Garlick Hill Kean.* Ed. Edward Younger. New York: Oxford University Press, 1957.

Keeler, William F. *Aboard the USS Florida: 1863–65.* Ed. Robert W. Daly. Annapolis, Md.: U.S. Naval Institute, 1968.

Kellogg, Robert H. *Life and Death in Rebel Prisons: Giving a Complete History of the Inhuman and Barbarous Treatment of Our Brave Soldiers by Rebel Authorities.* Hartford, Conn.: L. Stebbins, 1865.

King, John M. *Three Years with the 92d Illinois: The Civil War Diary of John M. King.* Ed. Claire E. Swedberg. Mechanicsburg, Pa.: Stackpole, 1999.

Kingman, Eugene. *Tramping Out the Vintage, 1861–1864: The Civil War Diaries and Letters of Eugene Kingman.* Almond, N.Y.: Helene C. Phelan, 1983.

Kircher, Henry A. *A German in the Yankee Fatherland: The Civil War Letters of Henry A. Kircher.* Ed. Earl J. Hess. Trans. from the German. Kent, Ohio: Kent State University Press, 1983.

Kireker, Charles. *History of the 116th Regiment U. S. C. Infantry.* Philadelphia: King & Baird, 1866.

Kirk, Charles H., ed. and comp. *History of the Fifteenth Pennsylvania Volunteer Cavalry, Which Was Recruited and Known as the Anderson Cavalry in the Rebellion of 1861–1865.* Philadelphia: n.p., 1906.

Knox, Thomas W. *Camp-fire and Cotton-field: Southern Adventure in Time of War.* New York: Blelock, 1865.

Landers, Eli P. *Weep Not For Me Dear Mother.* Ed. Elizabeth W. Roberson. Gretna, La.: Pelican, 1996.

Lane, Mills, ed. *Dear Mother: Don't grieve about me. If I get killed, I'll only be dead: Letters from Georgia Soldiers in the Civil War.* Savannah, Ga.: Beehive Press, 1977.

LeConte, Emma. *When the World Ended: The Diary of Emma LeConte.* New York: Oxford University Press, 1957.

Lee, Elizabeth Blair. *Wartime Washington: The Civil War Letters of Elizabeth Blair Lee.* Ed. Virginia Jeans Laas. Urbana: University of Illinois Press, 1991.

Liddell, St. John R. *Liddell's Record: St. John Richardson Liddell, Brigadier General, C. S. A. . . .* Ed. Nathaniel C. Hughes. Dayton, Ohio: Morningside House, 1985.

Lindsley, John B., ed. *The Military Annals of Tennessee, Confederate.* Nashville, Tenn.: J. M. Lindsley, 1886.

Little, Henry F. W. *The Seventh Regiment New Hampshire Volunteers in the War of the Rebellion.* Concord: Seventh New Hampshire Veteran Association, 1896.

Logan, John A. *The Volunteer Soldier of America.* Chicago: R. S. Peale, 1887.

Logan, Mary. *Reminiscences of the Civil War and Reconstruction.* Rev. ed. Carbondale: Southern Illinois University Press, 1970. Originally published as *Reminiscences of a Soldier's Wife; An Autobiography, by Mrs. John A. Logan.* New York: C. Scribner's Sons, 1913.

Lothrop, Charles H. *A History of the First Regiment Iowa Cavalry Veteran Volunteers, From Its Organization in 1861 to Its Muster Out of the United States Service in 1866.* Lyons, Iowa: Beers & Eaton, 1890.

Lunt, Dolly Sumner. *A Woman's Wartime Journal: An Account of the Passage over Georgia's Plantation of Sherman's Army on the March to the Sea, as Recorded in the Diary of Solly Sumner Lunt (Mrs. Thomas Burge).* New York: Century, 1918.

Lyman, Theodore. *Meade's Headquarters, 1863–1865: Letters of Colonel Theodore Lyman from the Wilderness to Appomattox.* Ed. George R. Agassiz. Boston: Atlantic Monthly Press, 1922.

MacGregor, Morris J., and Bernard C. Natly, eds. *Blacks in the United States Armed Forces: Basic Documents.* 3 vols. Wilmington, Del.: Scholarly Resources, 1977.

Main, Edwin M. *The Story of the Marches, Battles and Incidents of the Third United States Colored Cavalry, a Fighting Regiment in the War of the Rebellion, 1861–1865.* Louisville, Ky.: Globe Printing, 1908.

Marshall, Thomas B. *History of the Eighty-third Ohio Volunteer Infantry, the Greyhound Regiment.* Cincinnati: Eighty-Third Ohio Volunteer Infantry Association, 1912.

Mason, Frank H. *The Twelfth Ohio Cavalry; A Record of Its Organization and Services in the War of the Rebellion.* Cleveland, Ohio: Nevins' Steam Printing, 1871.

Mathes, J. Harvey. *The Old Guard in Gray. Researches in the Annals of the Confederate Historical Association*. Memphis, Tenn.: S. C. Toof, 1897. Reprint, Memphis, Tenn.: Burke's Book Store, 1975.

Maury, Dabney H. *Recollections of a Virginian in the Mexican, Indian, and Civil Wars*. 3rd ed. New York: Charles Scribner's Sons, 1894.

McAllister, Robert. *The Civil War Letters of General Robert McAllister*. Ed. James I. Robertson. New Brunswick, N.J.: RU Press, 1965.

McCorkle, John. *Three Years with Quantrill. Written by O. S. Barton*. Armstrong, Mo.: Armstrong Herald, 1914. Reprint, Norman: UO Press, 1992.

McDonald, William N. *A History of the Laurel Brigade, Originally the Ashby Cavalry of the Army of Northern Virginia, and Chew's Battery*. Ed. Bushrod C. Johnson. Baltimore: Sun Job Printing, 1907.

McElroy, John. *Andersonville: A Story of Rebel Military Prisons*. Toledo, Ohio: D. R. Locke, 1879.

McGee, Benjamin F. *History of the 72d Indiana Volunteer Infantry of the Mounted Lightning Brigade*. Lafayette, Ind.: S. Vater, 1882.

McGregor, Frank. *Dearest Susie: A Civil War Infantryman's Letters to His Sweetheart*. Ed. Carl E. Hatch. New York: Exposition Press, 1971.

McGuire, Judith W. *Diary of a Southern Refugee During the War*. New York: E. J. Hale, 1867. Reprint, New York: Arno Press, 1972.

Meade, George G., and George G. Meade Jr. *The Life and Letters of George Gordon Meade, Major-General United States Army*. Ed. George G. Meade III. 2 vols. New York: Charles Scribner's Sons, 1913.

Merrill, J. W. *Records of the 24th Independent Battery, N.Y. Light Artillery, U.S.V.* Perry, N.Y.: Ladies' Cemetery Association, 1870.

Mickley, Jeremiah M. *The Forty-Third Regiment United States Colored Troops*. Gettysburg, Pa.: J. E. Wible, 1866.

Montgomery, Frank A. *Reminiscences of a Mississippian in Peace and War*. Cincinnati: Robert Clarke, 1901. UNC electronic ed., 1999, http://docsouth.unc.edu/author.html.

Moore, Edward A. *The Story of a Cannoneer Under Stonewall Jackson*. New York: Neale, 1907. Reprint, Alexandria, Va.: Time-Life Books, 1983.

Moore, Frank. *The Rebellion Record: A Diary of American Events, with Documents, Narratives, Illustrative Incidents, Poetry, etc.* 11 vols. New York: D. Van Nostrand, 1864–1868.

Morgan, James M. *Recollections of a Rebel Reefer*. London: Constable, 1918.

Morgan, William H. *Personal Reminiscences of the War of 1861–5*. Lynchburg, Va.: J. P. Bell, 1911. Reprint, Freeport, N.Y.: Books for Libraries, 1971.

Morton, John Watson. *The Artillery of Nathan Bedford Forrest's Cavalry*. Nashville, Tenn.: M. E. Church, South, 1909.

Mosby, John S. *The Memoirs of Colonel John S. Mosby*. Boston: Little, Brown, 1917.

Mosgrove, George D. *Kentucky Cavaliers in Dixie: Reminiscences of a Confederate Cavalryman*. Louisville, Ky.: Courier-Journal Job Printing, 1895.

Mosher, Charles C. *Charlie Mosher's Civil War: From Fair Oaks to Andersonville with the Plymouth Pilgrims (85th N.Y. Infantry)*. Ed. Wayne Mahood. Hightstown, N.J.: Longstreet House, 1994.

Munson, John W. *Reminiscences of a Mosby Guerrilla*. New York: Moffat, Yard, 1906.

Musser, Charles O. *Soldier Boy: The Civil War Letters of Charles O. Musser, 29th Iowa*. Ed. Barry Popchock. Iowa City: UI Press, 1995.

Myers, Frank M. *The Comanches: A History of the White's Battalion, Virginia Cavalry, Laurel Brig., Hampton Div., A.N.V., C.S.A.* Baltimore: Kelly, Piet, 1871. Reprint, Marietta, Ga.: Continental Book, 1956.

Myers, Robert M., ed. *The Children of Pride: A True Story of Georgia and the Civil War*. Abridged ed. New Haven, Conn.: YU Press, 1984.

Neil, Alexander. *Alexander Neil and the Last Shenandoah Valley Campaign; Letters of an Army Surgeon to his Family, 1864*. Ed. Richard R. Duncan. Shippensburg, Pa.: White Mane, 1996.

News and Courier. *"Our Women in the War."—The Lives They Lived; the Deaths They Died. From the Weekly News and Courier*. Charleston, S.C.: News and Courier, 1885.

Newton, Alexander H. *Out of the Briars: An Autobiography and Sketch of the Twenty-Ninth Regiment Connecticut Volunteers*. Philadelphia: A. M. E. Book Concern, [1910]. Reprint, Miami: Mnemosyne Publishing, 1969.

Nichols, George Ward. *The Story of the Great March. From the Diary of a Staff Officer*. New York: Harper and Bros., 1865.

Nichols, James M. *Perry's Saints or the Fighting Parson's Regiment in the War of the Rebellion*. Boston: D. Lothrop, 1886.

Nicolay, John G., and John Hay, eds. *Complete Works of Abraham Lincoln*. New and enlarged ed. 12 vols. Harrogate, Tenn.: Lincoln Memorial University, 1894.

Nugent, William L. *My Dear Nellie: The Civil War Letters of William L. Nugent to Eleanor Smith Nugent*. Ed. William M. Cash and Lucy Somerville Howorth. Jackson: University Press of Mississippi, 1977.

Oates, William C. *The War Between the Union and the Confederacy and Its Lost Opportunities, with a History of the 15th Alabama Regiment*. New York: Neale, 1905.

Olmstead, Charles H. *The Memoirs of Charles H. Olmstead*. Ed. Lilla M. Hawes. Savannah: Georgia Historical Society, 1974.

Olmsted, Frederick L. *The Cotton Kingdom: A Traveller's Observations on Cotton and Slavery in the American Slave States*. Ed. Arthur M. Schesinger. New York: Mason Brothers, 1861. Reprint, New York: Alfred A. Knopf, 1953.

Osborn, Thomas W. *The Fiery Trail: A Union Officer's Account of Sherman's Last Campaigns*. Ed. Richard Harwell and Philip N. Racine. Knoxville: University of Tennessee, 1986.

Oviatt, Miles M. *A Civil War Marine at Sea: The Diary of Medal of Honor Recipient Miles M. Oviatt*. Ed. Mary P. Livingston. Shippensburg, Pa.: White Mane Books, 1998.

Owen, William M. *In Camp and Battle with the Washington Artillery of New Orleans*. Boston: Ticknor, 1885.

Palmer, Abraham J. *The History of the Forty-Eighth Regiment New York State Volunteers in the War for the Union, 1861–1865.* Brooklyn, N.Y.: Veteran Association of the Regiment, 1885.

Parks, George. *The Civil War Letters of Private George Parks, Company C., 24th New York Cavalry Volunteers.* Ed. Joseph M. Overfield. Buffalo, N.Y.: Gallagher Printing, 1992.

Patterson, Edmund D. *Yankee Rebel: The Civil War Journal of Edmund De-Witt Patterson.* Ed. John G. Barrett. Chapel Hill: UNC Press, 1966.

Pember, Phoebe Yates. *A Southern Woman's Story: Life in Confederate Richmond.* Ed. Bell Irvin Wiley. New York: G. W. Carleton, 1879. New ed., Jackson, Tenn.: McCowat-Mercer, 1959.

Petty, Elijah P. *Journey to Pleasant Hill: The Civil War Letters of Capt. Elijah P. Petty, Walker's Texas Division, CSA.* Ed. Norman D. Brown. San Antonio: Institute of Texan Culture, UT, 1982.

Phillips, David L., and Rebecca L. Hill, eds. *War Stories: Civil War in West Virginia.* Leesburg, Va.: Gauley Mount Press, 1991.

Pollard, Edward A. *Southern History of the War.* 2 vols. in 1. New York: C. B. Richardson, 1866. Reprint, New York: Fairfax, 1990.

Polley, Joseph B. *Hood's Texas Brigade: Its Marches, Its Battles, Its Achievements.* New York: Neale, 1910.

Porter, Horace. *Campaigning with Grant.* New York: Century, 1897. Reprint, Bloomington: IU Press, 1961.

Preston, Madge. *A Private War: Letters and Diaries of Madge Preston, 1862–1867.* Ed. Virginia W. Beauchamp. New Brunswick, N.J.: RU Press, 1987.

Pryor, Sara A. *My Day: Reminiscences of a Long Life.* New York: Macmillan, 1909. UNC electronic ed., 1998, http://docsouth.unc.edu/author.html.

Putnam, Sallie B. *Richmond During the War; Four Years of Personal Observation.* New York: G. W. Carleton, 1867. Reprint, Alexandria, Va.: Time-Life Books, 1983.

Rainey, Isaac N. *Experiences of I. N. Rainey in the Confederate Army.* Columbia, Tenn.: W. F. Rainey, 1965.

Ransom, John L. *John Ransom's Diary.* Auburn, N.Y.: Privately printed as *Andersonville Diary,* 1881. Reprint, New York: Paul S. Ericksson, 1963.

Rath, John. *Left for Dixie: The Civil War Diary of John Rath.* Ed. Kenneth Lyftogt. Parkersburg, Iowa: Mid-Prairie Books, 1991.

Ravenel, Henry W. *The Private Journal of Henry William Ravenel, 1859–1887.* Ed. Arney R. Childs. Columbia: USC Press, 1947.

Rawick, George P., ed. *The American Slave: A Composite Autobiography.* Ser. 1 and 2, 19 vols. Comp. Federal Writers' Project, WPA, 1936–37, published 1941. Reprint, Westport, Conn.: Greenwood, 1972.

———. *The American Slave: A Composite Autobiography.* Supp., Ser. 1. 12 vols. Westport, Conn.: Greenwood, 1977.

Reader, Frank S. *History of the Fifth West Virginia Cavalry, Formerly the Second Virginia Infantry, and of Battery G, 1st West Va. Light Artillery.* New Brighton, Pa.: Daily News, 1890.

Reagan, John H. *Memoirs, with Special Reference to Secession and the Civil War.* Ed. Walter F. McCaleb. New York: Neale, 1906.

Redkey, Edwin S., ed. *A Grand Army of Black Men: Letters from African-American Soldiers in the Union Army, 1861–1865.* New York: Cambridge University Press, 1992.

Reed, John A. *History of the 101st Regiment Pennsylvania Veteran Volunteer Infantry, 1861–1865.* Chicago: L. S. Dickey, 1910.

Reid, Harvey. *The View from Headquarters: Civil War Letters of Harvey Reid.* Ed. Frank L. Byrne. Madison: State Historical Society of Wisconsin, 1965.

Returned Prisoner of War, *A Voice from Rebel Prisons; Giving an Account of Some of the Horrors of the Stockades.* Boston: Geo. C. Rand & Avery, 1865.

Rhodes, Elisha Hunt. *All for the Union: The Civil War Diary and Letters of Elisha Hunt Rhodes.* Ed. Robert Hunt Rhodes. Lincoln, R.I.: Andrew Mobray, 1985. 2d ed. New York: Orion Books, 1991.

Rice, Allen Thorndike. *Reminiscences of Abraham Lincoln, by Distinguished Men of His Time.* New York: North American Review, 1888.

Richardson, Albert D. *The Secret Service, the Field, the Dungeon, and the Escape.* Hartford, Conn.: American Publishing, 1866.

Riddle, Albert G. *Reminiscences of Men and Events in Washington, 1860–1865.* New York: G. P. Putnam's and Sons, 1895.

Ridley, Bromfield L. *Battles and Sketches of the Army of Tennessee.* Mexico, Mo.: Missouri Printing, 1906.

Ripley, Edward H. *Vermont General: The Unusual War Experiences of Edward Hastings Ripley, 1862–1865.* Ed. Otto Eisenschiml. New York: Devin-Adair, 1960.

Robuck, J. E. *My Own Personal Experience and Observation as a Soldier in the Confederate Army During the Civil War, 1861–1865; Also, During the Period of Reconstruction.* N.p.: [1911]. Reprint, Memphis, Tenn.: Burke's Book Store, [1978].

Roman, Alfred. *The Military Operations of General Beauregard in the War Between the States, 1861 to 1865.* 2 vols. New York: Harpers & Brothers, 1884.

Rose, Victor M. *Ross' Texas Brigade, Being a Narrative of Events Connected with Its Service in the Late War Between the States.* Louisville, Ky.: Courier-Journal, 1881. Reprint, Kennesaw, Ga.: Continental Book, 1960.

Ross, Lawrence S. *Personal Civil War Letters of General Lawrence Sullivan Ross, with Other Letters.* Comp. and transcribed by Perry W. Shelton. Ed. Shelly Morrison. Austin, Tex.: Shelly and Richard Morrison, 1994.

Satterlee, John L., comp. and ed. *The Journal & the 114th, 1861–1865.* Springfield, Ill.: Phillips Bros., 1979.

Schofield, John M. *Forty-Six Years in the Army.* New York: Century, 1897.

Scott, William Forse. *The Story of a Cavalry Regiment: The Career of the Fourth Iowa Veteran Volunteers from Kansas to Georgia, 1861–1865.* New York: G. P. Putnam's Sons, 1893.

Shank, John D. *One Flag One Country and Thirteen Greenbacks a Month: Letters from a Civil War Private and His Colonel.* Ed. Edna J. Shank Hunter. San Diego, Calif.: Hunter Publications, 1980.

Shaver, Lewellyn A. *A History of the Sixtieth Alabama Regiment, Gracie's Alabama Brigade*. Montgomery, Ala.: Barrett & Brown, 1867. Reprint, Gaithersburg, Md.: Butternut Press, n.d.

Shaw, Robert G. *Blue-Eyed Child of Fortune: The Civil War Letters of Colonel Robert Gould Shaw*. Ed. Duncan Russell. Athens: UG Press, 1992.

Sheeran, James B. *Confederate Chaplain: A War Journal of Rev. James B. Sheeran, C.ss.R, 14th Louisiana, CSA*. Ed. Joseph T. Durkin. Milwaukee: Bruce, 1960.

Sheridan, Philip H. *Personal Memoirs of P. H. Sheridan*. 2 vols. New York: Charles L. Webster, 1888.

Sherman, John. *John Sherman's Recollections of Forty Years in the House, Senate and Cabinet*. 2 vols. Chicago: Werner, 1895.

Sherman, John, and William T. Sherman. *The Sherman Letters: Correspondence Between General and Senator Sherman from 1837 to 1891*. Ed. Rachel Sherman Thorndike. New York: Charles Scribner's Sons, 1894.

Sherman, William T. *Home Letters of General Sherman*. Ed. M. A. DeWolfe Howe. New York: Charles Scribner's Sons, 1909.

——. *Memoirs of General William T. Sherman*. New York: D. Appleton, 1875. Reprint. 2 vols. in 1, paperback. New York: Da Capo, 1984.

Shotwell, Randolph A. *The Papers of Randolph Abbott Shotwell*. Ed. J. G. de Roulhac and Rebecca Cameron. 2 vols. Raleigh: North Carolina Historical Commission, 1929.

Silber, Nina, and Mary Beth Sievens, eds. *Yankee Correspondence: Civil War Letters between New England Soldiers and the Home Front*. Charlottesville: University Press of Virginia, 1996.

Simpson, Taliaferro N., and Richard W. Simpson. *Far, Far from Home: The Wartime Letters of Dick and Tally Simpson, Third South Carolina Volunteers*. Ed. Guy R. Everson and Edward H. Simpson Jr. New York: Oxford University Press, 1994.

Sipes, William B. *The Seventh Pennsylvania Veteran Volunteer Cavalry: Its Record, Reminiscences and Roster*. Pottsville, Pa.: Miners' Journal, 1905.

Skinner, Arthur N., and James L. Skinner, eds. *The Death of a Confederate: Selections from the Letters of the Archibald Smith Family of Roswell, Georgia, 1864–1956*. Athens: UG Press, 1996.

Small, Abner R. *The Road to Richmond*. Ed. Harold Adams Small. Berkeley: University of California, 1939.

Smedes, Susan Dabney. *Memorials of a Southern Planter*. Ed. Fletcher A. Green. Baltimore: Cushings and Bailey, 1887. Reprint, New York: Alfred A. Knopf, 1965.

Smith, Benjamin T. *Private Smith's Journal*. Ed. Clyde C. Walton. Chicago: Lakeside Press, 1963.

Smith, Daniel P. *Company K, First Alabama Regiment, or Three years in the Confederate Service*. Prattville, Ala.: By the Survivors, 1885.

Smith, S. E. D. *The Soldier's Friend; Being a Thrilling Narrative of Grandma Smith's Four Years' Experience and Observations . . . During the Late Disastrous Conflict in America*. Memphis, Tenn.: Bulletin Publishing, 1867.

Smith, Walter G. *Life and Letters of Thomas Kilby Smith, Brevet Major-General United States Volunteers, 1820–1887.* New York: G. P. Putnam's Sons, 1898.

Sneden, Robert Knox. *Eye of the Storm: A Civil War Odyssey.* Ed. Charles F. Bryan Jr. and Nelson D. Lankford. New York: Free Press, 2000.

Sorrel, Gilbert Moxley. *Recollections of a Confederate Staff Officer.* Ed. Bell Irvin Wiley. New York: Neale, 1905. Reprint, Jackson, Tenn.: McCowat-Mercer, 1958.

Sparks, A. W. *The War Between the States as I Saw It.* Tyler, Tex.: Lee & Burnett, 1901. Reprint, Longview, Tex.: D&D Publishing, 1987.

Spencer, Cornelia P. *The Last Ninety Days of the War in North-Carolina.* New York: Watchman Publishing, 1866. Reprint, Wilmington, N.C.: Broadfoot, 1995.

Sperry, Andrew F. *History of the 33d Iowa Infantry Volunteer Regiment, 1863–1866.* Des Moines, Iowa: Mills, 1866.

Spiegel, Marcus M. *Your True Marcus: The Civil War Letters of a Jewish Colonel.* Ed. Fran L. Byrne and Jean P. Soman. Kent, Ohio: Kent State University Press, 1985.

Sprague, Homer B. *Lights and Shadows in Confederate Prisons; A Personal Experience, 1864–65.* New York: G. P. Putnam's Sons, 1915.

Stein, A. H. *History of the Thirty-Seventh Regt. U.S.C. Infantry.* Philadelphia: King & Baird, 1866. Electronic ed., http://www.rootsweb.com/~ncusct/37uscti.htm.

Stephens, George E. *A Voice of Thunder: The Civil War Letters of George E. Stephens.* Ed. Donald Yacovone. Urbana: University of Illinois Press, 1997.

Stephenson, Philip D. *The Civil War Memoir of Philip Daingerfield Stephenson, D.D.* Ed. Nathaniel C. Hughes. Conway, Ark.: UCA Press, 1995.

Stevens, George T. *Three Years in the Sixth Corps.* Albany, N.Y.: S. R. Gray, 1866. Reprint, Alexandria, Va.: Time-Life Books, 1984.

Stewart, William H. *A Pair of Blankets.* New York: Broadway Publishing, 1911.

Strong, George Templeton. *Diary of the Civil War, 1860–1865.* Ed. Allan Nevins. Reprint, New York: Macmillan, 1962.

Strother, David H. *A Virginia Yankee in the Civil War: The Diaries of David Hunter Strother.* Ed. Cecil D. Eby Jr. Chapel Hill: UNC Press, 1961.

Sunderland, Glenn W. *Five Days to Glory.* Cranbury, N.J.: A. S. Barnes, 1970.

Taylor, Grant, and Malinda Taylor. *This Cruel War: The Civil War Letters of Grant and Malinda Taylor, 1862–1865.* Ed. Ann K. Blomquist and Robert A. Taylor. Macon, Ga.: Mercer University Press, 2000.

Taylor, Richard. *Destruction and Reconstruction.* New York: D. Appleton, 1879.

Taylor, Walter H. *Lee's Adjutant: The Wartime Letters of Colonel Walter Herron Taylor, 1862–1865.* Ed. R. Lockwood Tower, with John S. Belmont. Columbia: USC Press, 1995.

Thom, J. Pembroke. *My Dear Brother: A Confederate Chronicle.* Ed. and comp. Catherine Thom Bartlett. Richmond, Va.: Dietz, 1952.

Thompson, Richard S. *While My Country is in Danger: The Life and Letters of Lieutenant Colonel Richard S. Thompson, Twelfth New Jersey Volunteers.* Ed. Gerry H. Poriss and Ralph G. Poriss. Hamilton, N.Y.: Edmonston Publishing, 1994.

Toney, Marcus B. *The Privations of a Private.* 2d ed. Nashville, Tenn.: M. E. Church, South, 1907.

Towne, Laura M. *Letters and Diary of Laura M. Towne, Written from the Sea Islands of South Carolina, 1862–1864.* Ed. Rupert S. Holland. Cambridge, Mass.: Riverside Press, 1912. Reprint, New York: Negro Universities Press, 1969.

Trueheart, Charles W., and Henry M. Trueheart. *Rebel Brothers: The Civil War Letters of the Truehearts.* Ed. Edward B. Williams. College Station: Texas A&M University Press, 1995.

Vale, Joseph G. *Minty and the Cavalry: A History of Cavalry Campaigns in the Western Armies.* Harrisburg, Pa.: Edwin K. Meyers, 1886.

Vautier, John D. *History of the 88th Pennsylvania Volunteers in the War for the Union, 1861–1865.* Philadelphia: J. B. Lippincott, 1894. Reprint, Gaithersburg, Md.: Butternut Press, 1986.

Vogtsberger, Margaret Ann, ed. *The Dulanys of Welbourne: A Family in Mosby's Confederacy.* Berryville, Va.: Rockbridge, 1995.

Waddell, Alfred M. *The Last Year of the War in North Carolina, including Plymouth, Fort Fisher and Bentonsville: An Address Before the Association Army of Northern Virginia.* Delivered Oct. 28, 1887. Richmond, Va.: William Ellis Jones, 1888.

Wagner, William F. *Letters of William F. Wagner, Confederate Soldier.* Ed. Joe M. Hatley and Linda B. Huffman. Wendell, N.C.: Broadfoot's Bookmark, 1983.

Wainwright, Charles S. *A Diary of Battle: The Personal Journals of Colonel Charles S. Wainwright, 1861–1865.* Ed. Allan Nevins. New York: Harcourt, Brace & World, 1962.

Walkley, Stephen. *History of the Seventh Connecticut Volunteer Infantry, Hawley's Brigade, Terry's Division, Tenth Army Corps, 1861–1865.* Hartford, Conn.: n.p., [1905].

Wallace, Robert C. *A Few Memories of a Long Life.* Ed. John M. Carroll. New ed. Fairfield, Wash.: Ye Galleon Press, 1988.

Ward, William W. *For the Sake of My Country: The Diary of Col. W. W. Ward, 9th Tennessee Cavalry, Morgan's Brigade, C.S.A.* Ed. R. B. Rosenburg. Murfreesboro, Tenn.: Southern Heritage Press, 1992.

Warfield, Edgar. *A Confederate Soldier's Memoirs.* Richmond, Va.: Masonic Home Press, 1936.

Watkins, Samuel R. *"Co. Aytch," Maury Grays, First Tennessee Regiment; or, a Sideshow of the Big Show.* Chattanooga, Tenn.: Times Printing, 1900.

Watson, James M. *Confederate from East Texas: The Civil War Letters of James Monroe Watson.* Ed. Judy Watson McClure. Quanah, Tex.: Nortex Press, 1976.

Welch, Stephen E. *Stephen Elliott Welch of the Hampton Legion.* Ed. John
    M. Priest. Shippensburg, Pa.: White Mane, 1994.
Weld, Stephen Minot. *War Diary and Letters of Stephen Minot Weld,
    1861–1865.* 2d ed. Boston: Massachusetts Historical Society, 1979.
Welles, Gideon. "The History of Emancipation." In *Civil War and Recon-
    struction: Selected Essays.* Ed. and comp. Albert Mordell. New York:
    Twayne Publishers, 1959.
———. *Diary of Gideon Welles.* 3 vols. Boston: Houghton Mifflin, 1911.
Westervelt, John H. *The Civil War Story of John H. Westervelt, Engineer, 1st
    New York Volunteer Engineer Corps.* Ed. Anita Palladino. New York: Ford-
    ham University Press, 1997.
White, Henry S. *Prison Life Among the Rebels: Recollections of a Union
    Chaplain.* Ed. Edward D. Jervey. Kent, Ohio: Kent State University Press,
    1990.
Whitehorne, James E. *Diary of J. E. Whitehorne, 1st Sergt. Co. "F" 12th Va.
    Infantry, A. P. Hill's 3rd Corps, A.N. Va.* Ed. Fletcher L. Elmore Jr. Utica,
    Ky.: McDowell, 1995.
Wildes, Thomas F. *Record of the One Hundred and Sixteenth Regiment Ohio
    Infantry Volunteers in the War of the Rebellion.* Sandusky, Ohio: I. F.
    Mack, 1884.
Williamson, James J. *Mosby's Rangers: A Record of the Operations of the
    Forty-Third Battalion Virginia Cavalry, From Its Organization to the
    Surrender.* New York: Ralph B. Kenyon, 1896. Reprint, Alexandria, Va.:
    Time-Life Books, 1982.
Wills, Charles W. *Army Life of an Illinois Soldier, Including a Day by Day
    Record of Sherman's March to the Sea: Letters and Diaries of the Late
    Charles W. Wills.* Comp. Mary E. Kellogg. Washington, D.C.: Globe
    Printing, 1906.
Wilson, James H. *Under the Old Flag: Recollections of Military Operations
    in the War for the Union, the Spanish War, the Boxer Rebellion, etc.* 2 vols.
    New York: D. Appleton, 1912.
Wilson, Joseph T. *The Black Phalanx; A History of Negro Soldiers of the
    United States in the Wars of 1775–1812, 1861–'65.* Hartford, Conn.: Ameri-
    can Publishing, 1890. Reprint, New York: Arno, 1968.
Wise, John S. *The End of an Era.* 11th imprint. Boston: Houghton Mifflin,
    1902.
Wood, Wales W. *History of the Ninety-Fifth Regiment Illinois Infantry Volun-
    teers, from Its Organization in the Fall of 1862, Until Its Final Discharge
    from the United States Service, in 1865.* Chicago: Tribune Book and Job
    Printing, 1865.
Worsham, W. J. *The Old Nineteenth Tennessee Regiment, CSA.* Knoxville,
    Tenn.: Paragon Printing, 1902.
Worth, Josephine B. "Sherman's Raid." J. E. B. Stuart chapter in *War Days in
    Fayetteville, North Carolina: Reminiscences of 1861 to 1865,* comp. UDC,
    46–56. Fayetteville, N.C.: Judge Printing, 1910.

Wright, Howard C. *Port Hudson: Its History from an Interior Point of View as Sketched from the Diary of an Officer.* Originally published in newspapers in 1863 and 1866; in book form by the St. Francisville (La.) *Democrat* in 1937. Reprint, Baton Rouge, La.: Committee for the Preservation of the Port Hudson Battlefield, 1961.

Yearns, W. Buck, and John G. Barrett, eds. *North Carolina Civil War Documentary.* Chapel Hill: UNC Press, 1980.

Yeary, Mamie, comp. *Reminiscences of the Boys in Gray, 1861–1865.* Dallas: Smith & Lamar, M. E. Church, South, 1912.

Young, J. P. *The Seventh Tennessee Cavalry (Confederate): A History.* Nashville, Tenn.: M. E. Church, South, 1890. Reprint, Dayton, Ohio: Morningside Bookshop, 1976.

Primary Articles

Abbott, Abial R. "The Negro in the War of the Rebellion." *ME&R* 3, MOLLUS–Ill. (1899): 373–84.

Addeman, J. M. "Reminiscences of Two Years with the Colored Troops." *PN,* 2nd ser., 7 RISSHS (1880): 5–38.

Agnew, Samuel A. "Battle of Tishomingo Creek." *CV* 8, no. 9 (Sept. 1900): 401–3.

Anderson, C. T. "Campaigning in Southern Arkansas: A Memoir by C. T. Anderson." Ed. Roman J. Zorn. *AHQ* 8 (Autumn 1949): 240–44.

Anderson, Charles W. "The True Story of Fort Pillow." *CV* 3 (November 1895): 322–26.

Appleton, John W. M.: "That Night at Fort Wagner, by One Who Was There." *Putnam's Magazine,* n.s., 4, no. 19 (July 1869): 9–16.

Atkinson, Edward. "The Battle of Marks Mill." Ed. J. H. Atkinson. *AHQ* 14 (Winter 1955): 381–84.

Avera, William F. "Extracts from the Memoirs of William Franklin Avera." Ed. Henry Cathey. *AHQ* 22 (Summer 1963): 99–116.

Barrow, Henry W. "Civil War Letters of Henry W. Barrow to John W. Fries." Ed. Marian H. Blair. *NCHR* 34, no. 1 (Jan. 1957): 68–85.

Baylor, George. "The Army Negro." *SHSP* 31 (1903): 365–69.

Bean, W. G., ed. "A House Divided: The Civil War Letters of a Virginia Family." *VMH&B* 59 (1951): 397–422.

Beauregard, [Pierre] Gustave T. "The Defense of Drewry's Bluff." *B&L* 4:195–205.

Bir, Louis. "Remenecence of My Army Life." Ed. George P. Clark. *IMH* 101, no. 1 (Mar. 2005): 15–57.

Bowditch, Charles P. "War Letters of Charles P. Bowditch, 1861–1864." *Proceedings* (MaHS) 57 (May 1924): 414–95.

Bowley, Freeman S. "The Petersburg Mine." *WP* 6, MOLLUS–Calif. ([San Francisco], n.p., 1889): 1–17.

Breckinridge, G. W. "Story of a Boy Captain." *CV* 13, no. 9 (Sept. 1905): 415–16.

Browne, Frederick W. "My Service in the U.S. Colored Cavalry." *Sketches of War History* 6, MOLLUS–Ohio (Cincinnati: n.p., 1908): 1–14.

Buchanan, John C. "The Negro as Viewed by a Michigan Civil War Soldier: Letters of John C. Buchanan." Ed. George M. Blackburn. *Michigan History* 47 (Mar. 1963): 75–84.

Candler, Allen D. "Watch on the Chattahoochee: A Civil War Letter." Ed. Elizabeth Hulsey Marshall. *GHQ* 3 (1959): 427–28.

Carden, Robert C. "Civil War Memories of Robert C. Carden." Boone (Iowa) *Independent* (series begins Apr. 1912), http://www2.dmci.net/users/bmacd/default.htm.

Carter, Solon A. "Fourteen Months' Service with Colored Troops." *CWP* 1, MOLLUS–Mass. (Boston: By the Commandery, 1900): 155–79.

Chalmers, James R. "Forrest and His Campaigns." *SHSP* 7, no. 10 (Oct. 1879): 451–86.

Chamberlain, Valentine. "A Letter of Captain V. Chamberlain, 7th Connecticut Volunteers." Ed. T. Frederick Davis. *FHQ* 15 (Oct. 1956): 85–95.

Chase, Charles. "Letters of a Maine Boy." Ed. Norman C. Delaney. *CWH* 5 (Mar. 1959): 45–61.

Cobb, S. J. "Service of the Tar Heels." *CV* 8 (May 1900): 215–16.

Cooper, James L. "The Civil War Diary of Captain James Litton Cooper, September 30, 1861 to January, 1865." Ed. William T. Alderson. *THQ* 15 (June 1956): 141–73.

Cory, David M., ed. "The Friel Civil War Letters." *Journal of Long Island History* 5 (Winter 1965): 18–26.

Cox, Charles H. "The Civil War Letters of Charles Harding Cox." Ed. Lorna Lutes Sylvester. Pts. 1 and 2. *IMH* 68 (Mar., Sept. 1972): 24–78; 181–239.

Crawford, William A. "A Saline Guard: The Civil War Letters of Col. William Ayers Crawford, C.S.A., 1861–1865," *AHQ* 32 (Spring 1973): 71–93.

Cross, Henry M. "A Yankee Soldier Looks at the Negro." Ed. William C. Bryant II. *CWH* 7, no. 2 (June 1961): 133–48.

Cross, Joseph O. "The Civil War Letters of J. O. Cross, 29th Connecticut Volunteer Infantry (Colored)." Ed. Kelly Nolin. *ConnHS Bulletin* 60, 3–4 (Summer–Fall 1995): 211–35.

Currey, Mary E. "Fear in North Carolina: 'What an Awful and Grand Spectacle It Is!'" Ed. Ted Yeatman. *CWT* 22, 9 (Apr. 1984): 41–43.

Dancy, James M. "Reminiscences of the Civil War." *FHQ* 37 (July 1958): 66–89.

Davis, Leander E. "'The Consequences of Grandeur': A Union Soldier Writes of the Atlanta Campaign." Ed. William C. Niesen. *Atlanta History* 33, no. 3 (Fall 1989): 5–19.

Defenders of Port Hudson Association. "Fortification and Siege of Port Hudson." *SHSP* 14 (1886): 305–48

Dekle, Peter. "Peter Dekle's Letters." *CWH* 4, no. 1 (1958): 11–22.

Drake, F. M. "Campaign of General Steele." *WSI* 1, MOLLUS–Iowa (Des Moines, Iowa: P. C. Kenyon, 1893): 60–73.

Duren, C. M. "The Occupation of Jacksonville, February 1864 and the Battle of Olustee." *FHQ* 32, no. 4 (Apr. 1954): 262–87.

Edrington, William E. "True Glory." *Blue & Gray Magazine* 7 (Apr. 1990): 45.

Egan, Patrick. "The Florida Campaign with Light Battery C, Third Rhode Island Heavy Artillery." *PN* 6, no. 10, RISSHS (Providence: By the Society, 1905): 5–25.

Elliott, Gilbert. "The First Battle of the Confederate Ram Albemarle." *B&L* 4:625–27.

Etheredge, William H. "Another Story of the Battle of the Crater." *SHSP* 37 (1909): 203–7.

Featherston, John C. "Graphic Account of Battle of Crater." *SHSP* 33 (1905): 358–74.

Fitch, Charles. "Capture of Fort Pillow—Vindication of General Chalmers." *SHSP* 7 (1879): 440–41.

——. "Dr. Fitch's Report on the Fort Pillow Massacre." Ed. John Cimprich and Robert C. Mainfort. *THQ* 44 (Spring 1985): 27–39.

Furness, William Eliot. "The Negro as a Soldier." *ME&R* 2, MOLLUS–Ill. (Chicago: A. C. McClurg, 1894): 457–87.

Gardner, Henry R. "A Yankee in Louisiana: Selections from the Diary and Correspondence of Henry N. Gardner, 1862–1866." Ed. Kenneth E. Shewmaker and Andrew K. Prinz. *LH* 5, no. 3 (Summer 1964): 271–95.

Gillmore, Quincy A. "The Army Before Charleston in 1863." *B&L* 4:52–71.

Goulding, Joseph H. "The Colored Troops in the War of the Rebellion." *Proceedings of the Reunion Society of Vermont Officers* 2 (read Nov. 3, 1892; Burlington, Vt.: n.p., 1906): 137–54.

Granberry, J. A. H. "That Fort Gilmer Fight." *CV* 13, 9 (Sept. 1905): 413.

Grant, George W. "Under Fire at Charleston While a Prisoner of War." *GNS* 4, MOLLUS–Minn. (St. Paul, Minn.: H. L. Collins, 1898): 351–63.

Hall, H. Seymour. "Mine Run to Petersburg." *War Talks in Kansas*, MOLLUS–Kans. (Kansas City, Mo.: Franklin Hudson, 1906): 206–49.

Hallowell, Norwood P. "The Negro as a Soldier in the War of the Rebellion." *Civil and Mexican Wars*, Military Historical Society of Massachusetts. Read Jan. 5, 1892. Boston: Little, Brown, 1897.

Hanson, E. Hunn. "Forrest's Defeat of Sturgis at Brice's Cross-Roads." *B&L* 4:419–21.

Harrison, Samuel. "The Civil War Journal of Dr. Samuel Harrison." Ed. Charles L. Wagandt. *CWH* 13 (1967): 131–46.

Hawkins, Isaac R. "West Tennessee Unionists in the Civil War: A Hawkins Family Letter." Ed. Harles L. Lufkin. *THQ* 46, no. 1 (Spring 1987): 33–42.

Hawkins, Rush C. "Early Coast Operations in North Carolina." *B&L* 1:632–59.

Hawley, Joseph R. "Comments on General Jones's Paper." *B&L* 4:79–80.

Hayne, Paul H. "The Defense of Fort Wagner." *Southern Bivouac* (Feb. 1886): 599–608.

Hemming, Charles C. "A Confederate Odyssey." *American Heritage* 36, no. 1 (Dec. 1984): 69–84.

Herbert, Hilary A. "Colonel A. Herbert's History of the Eighth Alabama Volunteer Regiment, C.S.A." Ed. Maurice S. Fortin. *AlHQ* 39, nos. 1–4 (1977): 5–321.

Higginson, Thomas Wentworth. "The Reoccupation of Jacksonville in 1863." *CWP* 2, MOLLUS–Mass. (Boston: By the Commandery, 1900): 467–74.

Holland, Milton M. "From Slavery to Freedom." *CWTI* 11 (Nov. 1972): 10–15.

Hollis, Elisha T. "The Diary of Captain Elisha Tompkin Hollis, CSA." Ed. William W. Cheser, *WTHSP* 39 (Dec. 1985): 83–118.

Hood, John B. "The Invasion of Tennessee." *B&L* 4:425–37.

Hord, Henry E. "Brice's X Roads from a Private's View." *CV* 12, no. 11 (Nov. 1904): 529–30.

Hosea, Lewis M. "Some Side Lights of the War for the Union." *Sketches of War History* 9, MOLLUS–Ohio (Cincinnati: By the Commandery, 1912): 1–19.

Hubbard, Lucius F. "Letters of a Union Officer: L. F. Hubbard and the Civil War." Ed. N. B. Martin, *Minnesota History* 35 (1957): 313–19.

Imboden, John D. "Fire, Sword, and the Halter" in *Philadelphia Weekly Times, Annals of the War* (reprint, Gettysburg, Pa.: Civil War Times, 1974): 169–83.

Irwin, Richard B. "The Red River Campaign." *B&L* 4:345–62.

James, Garth W. "The Assault on Fort Wagner." Read Nov. 12, 1880. *WP* 1, MOLLUS–Wisc. (Milwaukee: Burdick, Amitage and Allen, 1891): 9–30.

John, Enoch D. "On the Road to the Sea: Shannon's Scouts." Ed. Paul Scott. *CWTI* 21, no. 9 (Jan. 1983): 26–29.

Johnston, Charles. "Attack on Fort Gilmer, September 29, 1864." *SHSP* 1, no. 6 (June 1876): 438–42.

Jones, C[harles] C., Jr., "Negro Slaves During the Civil War." *MAH* 16, no. 2 (Aug. 1886): 168–75.

Kautz, August U. "Operations South of the James River." *B&L* 4:533–37.

Kendall, John I. "Recollections of a Confederate Officer." Ed. John S. Kendall. *LHQ* 29, no. 4 (Oct. 1946): 1041–1228.

Kenfield, Frank. "Captured by Rebels: A Vermonter at Petersburg, 1864." *Vermont History* 36 (Autumn 1968): 230–35.

Kerr, Charles D. "From Atlanta to Raleigh." *GNS* 1, MOLLUS–Minn. (St. Paul, Minn.: St. Paul Book and Stationery, 1887): 202–23.

Kilmer, George L. "The Dash into the Crater." *Century Illustrated Monthly* 34, n. s. 12 (May–October 1887): 774–76.

Lee, Charles G. "The Diary of Charles G. Lee in the Andersonville and Florence Prison Camps, 1864." Ed. Paul C. Helmreich. ConnHS *Bulletin* 41 (Jan. 1976): 14–15.

Long, John W. "A Union Soldier's Personal Account of the Red River Expedition and the Battle of Jenkin's Ferry." *Grassroots* 8 (July 1988): 2–4 (Grant County Museum, Sheridan, Ark.).

Lott, Jess B. "Two Boys of the Fifth Texas Regiment." *CV* 13, no. 9 (Sept. 1905): 416–17.

Lyon, Hylan B. "Memoirs of Hylan B. Lyon, Brigadier General, C.S.A." Ed. Edward M. Coffman. *THQ* 18 (Mar. 1959): 35–53.

MacDonald, Colin F. "The Battle of Brice's Cross Roads." *GNS* 6, MOLLUS–Minn. (Minneapolis: Aug. Davis, 1909): 443–62.

Maclean, Clara D. "The Last Raid." *SHSP* 13 (1885): 466–76.

Magee, Warren G. "The Confederate Letters of Warren G. Magee." Ed. Bell Irvin Wiley. *Journal of Mississippi History* 5 (Jan.–Oct. 1943): 204–13.

Malcom, Frank. "'Such Is War': The Letters of an Orderly in the 7th Iowa Infantry." Ed. James I. Robertson Jr. *IJH* 58 (Oct. 1960): 321–56.

Martin, John H. "The Assault Upon Fort Gilmer." *CV* 13, no. 6 (June 1905): 269–70.

McMaster, F. W. "The Battle of the Crater, July 30, 1864—Extract from a Speech of Colonel McMaster," *SHSP* 10 (1882):119–23.

McNary, Oliver R. "What I Saw and Did Inside and Outside of Rebel Prisons." Read Dec. 3, 1900. *War Talks*, MOLLUS–Kans. (Kansas City, Mo.: Franklin Hudson, 1906). Reprinted in *War Talks in Kansas* (Wilmington, N.C.: Broadfoot, 1992): 25–44.

Medford, Harvey C. "The Diary of H. C. Medford, Confederate Soldier." Ed. Rebecca W. Smith and Marion Mullins. *SHQ* 34 (July 1930–Apr. 1931): 106–40, 203–30.

Merritt, Wesley. "Sheridan in the Shenandoah Valley." *B&L* 4:500–21.

Miller, William B. "'We have surely done a big work': The Diary of a Hoosier Soldier on Sherman's March to the Sea." Ed. Jeffrey L. Patrick and Robert Willey. *IMH* 94, no. 3 (Sept. 1998): 213–39.

Mills, Luther Rice. "Letters of Luther Rice Mills—A Confederate Soldier." Ed. George D. Harmon. *NCHR* 4, no. 3 (July 1927): 285–310.

Moore, J. Scott. "General Hunter's Raid." *SHSP* 27 (1899): 179–91.

Morgan, Thomas J. "Reminiscences of Service with Colored Troops in the Army of the Cumberland, 1863–1865." *PN* ser. 3, 13, RISSHS (Providence, R.I.: By the Society, 1885): 5–52.

Mosby, John S. "Retaliation." *SHSP* 27 (1899): 314–22.

Newberry, Walter C. "The Petersburg Mine." Read Nov. 13, 1890. *ME&R* 3, MOLLUS–Ill. (Chicago: Dial Press, 1899): 111–24.

Nicholson, William L. "The Engagement at Jenkin's Ferry." *AI* 2 (Oct. 1914): 505–19.

Oakey, Daniel. "Marching Through Georgia and the Carolinas." *B&L* 4:671–79.

O'Hagan, Joseph B. "The Diary of Joseph B. Hagan, S.J., Chaplain of the Excelsior Brigade." Ed. William L. Lucey. *CWH* 6 (1960): 402–9.

Overley, Milford. "Williams's Kentucky Brigade, C. S. A." *CV* 13, 10 (Oct. 1905): 460–62.

Palmer, W. Ben, J. W. Hammond, and Robert M. Harrover. "A Horror of the War: How General Custer Hung Some of Mosby's Men." *SHSP* 25 (1897): 239–44.

Park, Robert E. "Diary of Robert E. Park, Macon, Georgia, Late Captain Twelfth Alabama Regiment, Confederate States Army." *SHSP* 1 (1876): 370–86.

Pascoe, W. H. "Confederate Cavalry Around Port Hudson." *SHSP* 33 (1905): 83–96.

Patterson, Josiah B. "Irrepressible Optimism of a Georgia Confederate in 1864: A Letter." Ed. Martin Abbott. *GHQ* 37 (1953): 348–50.

Pearson, Benjamin F. "Benjamin F. Pearson's War Diary." Pts. 1–6. *AI*, ser. 3, 15 (Oct. 1925–Jan. 1927), pt. 5: 433–64.

Pegram, William R. J. "'The Boy Artillerist': Letters of Colonel William Pegram, C.S.A." Ed. James I. Robertson. *VMH&B* 98 (Apr. 1990): 221–60.

Perkins, Frances B. "Two Years with a Colored Regiment: A Woman's Experience." *New England Magazine* 17 (Jan. 1898): 533–45.

Perry, H. H. "Assault on Fort Gilmer." *CV* 13, no. 9 (Sept. 1905): 413–15.

Phillips, B. F. "Wilcox's Alabamians in Virginia." *CV* 15 (Nov. 1907): 490.

Polignac, Camille J. [Prince]. "Polignac's Mission." *SHSP* 35 (1907): 326–34.

Poor, Walter S. "A Yankee Soldier in a New York Regiment." Ed. James J. Heslin. *NYHSQ* 50, no. 2 (Apr. 1966): 109–49.

Porter, Charles H. "The Petersburg Mine." Read Jan. 12, 1885. *PMHS* 5 (Boston: n.p., 1906): 223–39.

Potter, Henry A. "Lincoln's Policies as Seen by a Michigan Soldier." Ed. Donald W. Disbrow. *Michigan History* 45 (Dec. 1961): 360–64.

Powell, William H. "The Battle of the Petersburg Crater." *B&L* 4:545–60.

Powers, John W. "Report of a Corporal of the Alabama First Infantry on Talk and Fighting Along Mississippi, 1862–63." Ed. John W. Partin. *AIHQ* 20, no. 1 (Spring 1958): 583–94.

Pressley, John G. "Extracts from the Diary of Lieutenant-Colonel John G. Pressley, of the Twenty-Fifth South Carolina Volunteers." *SHSP* 14 (1886): 35–62.

Reed, Joseph R. "Guntown and Tupelo." *WSI* 2, MOLLUS–Iowa (Des Moines, Iowa: Kenyon Press, 1898): 300–24.

Rickard, James H. "Services with Colored Troops in Burnside's Corps." *PN* ser. 5, 1, RISSHS (Providence, R.I.: By the Society, 1894): 5–43.

Rogall, Albert. "The Civil War Diary of Colonel Albert Rogall." Ed. Frank Levstik. *Polish American Studies* 27 (Spring–Autumn 1970): 33–79.

Romeyn, Henry. "With Colored Troops in the Army of the Cumberland." *WP* 51, MOLLUS–Washington, D.C. (Washington, D.C.: n.p., 1904): 3–26.

Ryan, Milton A. "Experience of a Confederate Soldier in Camp and Prison in the Civil War 1861–1865." Memoir written c. 1912. Http://www.izzy. net/~michaelg/ma-ryan.htm (accessed Sept. 28, 2006).

Sears, Cyrus. "The Battle of Milliken's Bend." Read before MOLLUS–Ohio, Oct. 7, 1908. Printed by the author when refused by the Commandery. Columbus, Ohio: F. J. Heer, 1909.

Shaw, James. "Our Last Campaign and Subsequent Service in Texas." *PN* 6, no. 9, RISSHS (Providence, R.I.: By the Society, 1905): 10–52.

Shearman, Sumner U. "Battle of the Crater and Experiences of Prison Life." *PN* 5, no. 8, RISSHS (Providence, R.I.: By the Society, 1898): 1–38.

Sherman, George R. "Assault on Fort Gilmer and Reminiscences of Prison Life." *PN* 5, no. 7, RISSHS (Providence, R.I.: By the Society, 1894): 5–33.

Simmons, John. "The Confederate Letters of John Simmons." Ed. Jon Harrison. *CSCT* 14 (Summer 1975): 25–57.

Simonton, Edward. "The Campaign Up the James River to Petersburg." *GNS* 5, MOLLUS–Minn. (St. Paul, Minn.: Review Publishing, 1903): 481–95.

Sleeth, Addison. "Soldiering at Fort Pillow, 1862–1864: An Excerpt from the Civil War Memoirs of Addison Sleeth." Ed. Robert C. Mainfort Jr. and Patricia E. Coats. *WTHSP* 36 (Oct. 1982): 72–90.

Smith, William M. "The Siege and Capture of Plymouth." *Personal Recollections* 1, MOLLUS–N.Y. (New York: By the Commandery, 1891): 322–43.

Snider, S. P. "Reminiscences of the War." *GNS* 2, MOLLUS–Minn. (St. Paul, Minn.: St. Paul Book and Stationery, 1890): 234–44.

Stearns, J. H. "First Kansas Colored Infantry." Paper read before Montgomery Post, Grand Army of the Republic, and published in the *Linn County* (Kans.) *Republic*, Jan. 1902.

Stephens, Winston and Octavia Stephens. "'Rouges and Black Hearted Scamps': Civil War Letters of Winston and Octavia Stephens, 1862–1863." Ed. Ellen E. Hodges and Stephen Kerber. *FHQ* 57 (July 1978): 54–82.

Stewart, William H. "Carnage at 'The Crater,' Near Petersburg." *CV* 1, no. 2 (Feb. 1893): 41–42.

———. "The Charge of the Crater: A Graphic Account of the Memorable Action." *SHSP* 25 (1897): 77–90.

Swift, John. "Letters from a Sailor on a Tinclad." *CWH* 7, no. 1 (Mar. 1961): 48–62.

Taylor, Thomas J. "An Extraordinary Perseverance': The Journal of Capt. Thomas J. Taylor, C.S.A." Ed. Lillian T. Wall and Robert M. McBride. *THQ* 31 (1972): 328–59.

Thomas, Henry G. "The Colored Troops at Petersburg." *B&L* 4:563–67.

Ullmann, Daniel. "Organization of Colored Troops and the Regeneration of the South." Address before Soldier's and Sailor's Union of the State of New York at Albany, Feb. 5, 1868. Washington, D.C.: Great Republic Office, 1868.

[Warrenton *Virginian*]. "Hanging of Mosby's Men in 1864." *SHSP* 24 (1896): 108–9.

Watie, Stand. "Some Letters of General Stand Watie." Ed. Edward E. Dale. *Chronicles of Oklahoma* 1, no. 1 (Jan. 1921): 30–59.

Watson, William G. "A Union Soldier in the Shenandoah Valley in 1864," pt. 4, VMI, http://www.vmi.edu/archives/Manuscripts/msguide2.html (accessed Mar. 3, 2000).

Weathered, John. "The Wartime Diary of John Weathered," http://www.jackmasters.net/we1863.html (accessed Sept. 12, 1999).

White, Herman L. "The White Papers: Letters (1861–1865) of Pvt. Herman Lorenzo White, 22nd Regiment Massachusetts Volunteers." Ed. Kathleen Kroll and Charles Moran. *MaR* 18 (Summer 1977): 248–70.

White, Lonnie J., ed. "A Bluecoat's Account of the Camden Expedition."
    AHQ 24 (Spring 1965): 82–89.
Williamson, John C. "The Civil War Diary of John Coffee Williamson." Ed.
    J. C. Williamson. *THQ* 15 (1956): 61–74.
Wilson, Fannie. "Letter to Papa." *Rockbridge County* (Va.) *News* (c. 1924),
    VMI, http://www.vmi.edu/archives/Manuscripts/msguide2.html.
Woodford, Milton M. "A Connecticut Yankee Fights at Olustee: Letters from
    the Front." Ed. Vaughn D. Bornet. *FHQ* 27, no. 3 (Jan. 1949): 237–59.

Primary Newspapers and Periodicals

Athens (Ala.) *Southern Banner*; Atlanta *Daily Intelligencer*; *Baltimore American*; Baxter Springs (Kans.) *Daily News*; Boston *Daily Evening Transcript*;
Boston *Herald*; Boston *Journal*; Carbondale (Kans.) *Astonisher & Paralyzer*; Charlotte (N.C.) *Daily Bulletin*; Chicago *Tribune*; Cincinnati *Daily Gazette*; *Confederate Veteran*; Detroit *Free Press*; *Harper's Weekly*; Linn
County (Kans.) *Republic*; Memphis (Tenn.) *Commercial Appeal*; Memphis (Tenn.) *Daily Appeal*; Mobile (Ala.) *Advertiser and Register*; New
York *Times*; Philadelphia *Weekly Times*; Raleigh (N.C.) *Daily Confederate*;
Richmond (Va.) *Enquirer*; *Southern Bivouac*; *Weekly Anglo-African*

Secondary Sources

Alotta, Robert I. *Civil War Justice: Union Army Executions Under Lincoln*.
    Shippensburg, Pa.: White Mane, 1980.
Andrews, J. Cutler. *The North Reports the Civil War*. Pittsburgh: University of
    Pittsburgh Press, 1955.
———. *The South Reports the Civil War*. Princeton, N.J.: Princeton University
    Press, 1970.
Aptheker, Herbert. *A Documentary History of the Negro People in the United
    States*. 2 vols. New York: Citadel Press, 1951.
Bailey, Anne J. "A Texas Cavalry Raid: Reaction to Black Soldiers and Contrabands." *CWH* 35, no. 2 (June 1989): 138–62.
Baldwin, Helen P. "The Life Story of Brig. Gen. Felix Robertson." Ed. James
    H. Colgin. *Texana* 8 (Spring 1970): 154–82.
Ballard, Michael B. *Vicksburg: The Campaign That Opened the Mississippi*.
    Chapel Hill: UNC, 2004.
Bancroft, Frederic. *The Life of William H. Seward*. 2 vols. New York: Harper
    and Bros., 1899. Reprint, Gloucester, Mass.: Peter Smith, 1967.
Barrett, John G. *The Civil War in North Carolina*. Chapel Hill: UNC Press,
    1963.
Belz, Herman. "Law, Politics, and Race in the Struggle for Equal Pay during
    the Civil War." *CWH* 22, no. 3 (Sept. 1976): 197–213.
Bennett, Michael J. *Union Jacks: Yankee Sailors in the Civil War*. Chapel Hill:
    UNC Press, 2004.
Bernstein, Iver. *The New York City Draft Riots*. New York: Oxford University
    Press, 1990.
Bettersworth, John K. and James W. Silver, eds. *Mississippi in the Confedera-*

cy. 2 vols. Jackson, Miss.: Mississippi Department of Archives and History and LSU Press, 1961. Reprint, New York: Kraus Reprint, 1970.

Bonnell, John C., Jr. *Sabers in the Shenandoah: The 21st New York Cavalry, 1863–1866*. Shippensburg, Pa.: Burd Street, 1996.

Brown, David, Phyllis Brown, and Bryce Suderow, "The Saltville Massacre Update," http://members.home.net/5thuscc/massacr.html (accessed Sept. 9, 1999).

Bruce, Dickson D., Jr. *Violence and Culture in the Antebellum South*. Austin: UT Press, 1979.

Carroll, Joseph C. *Slave Insurrections in the United States, 1800–1865*. Boston: Chapman & Grimes, 1938. Reprint, New York: Negro Universities Press, 1968.

Cimprich, John. *Fort Pillow, a Civil War Massacre and Public Memory*. Baton Rouge: LSU Press, 2005.

———. *Slavery's End in Tennessee, 1861–1865*. University: University of Alabama Press, 1985.

Cimprich, John, and Robert C. Mainfort, Jr. "The Fort Pillow Massacre: A Statistical Note." *Journal of American History* 76, no. 3 (Dec. 1989): 830–37.

———. "Fort Pillow Revisited: New Evidence about an Old Controversy." *CWH* 38, no. 4 (1982): 293–306.

Cochran, Hamilton. *Noted American Duels and Hostile Encounters*. Philadelphia: Chilton, 1963.

Coggins, Jack. *Arms and Equipment of the Civil War*. New York: Doubleday, 1962.

Commager, Henry S., ed. *The Blue and the Gray: The Story of the Civil War as Told by the Participants*. 2 vols. Indianapolis: Bobbs-Merrill, 1950.

Connelly, Thomas Lawrence. *Autumn of Glory; The Army of Tennessee, 1862–1865*. Baton Rouge: LSU Press, 1971.

Cornish, Dudley. *The Sable Arm: Negro Troops in the Union Army, 1861–1865*. New York: Longmans, Green, 1956. Paperback reprint, New York: W. W. Norton, 1966.

Cory, Charles E. "The Sixth Kansas Cavalry and its Commander." KSHS (Topeka), 1910.

Crabb, Martha L. *All Afire to Fight: The Untold Tale of the Civil War's Ninth Texas Cavalry*. New York: Avon Books, 2000.

Cunningham, Edward. *The Port Hudson Campaign, 1862–1863*. Baton Rouge: LSU Press, 1863.

Cunningham, Frank. *General Stand Watie's Confederate Indians*. San Antonio, Tex.: Naylor, 1959.

Davis, William C. *Breckinridge: Statesman, Soldier, Symbol*. Baton Rouge: LSU Press, 1974.

Dorris, Jonathan T. *Pardon and Amnesty under Lincoln and Johnson*. Chapel Hill: UNC Press, 1953.

Dowdey, Clifford. *Experiment in Rebellion*. New York: Doubleday, 1940. Reprint, Freeport, N.Y.: Books for Libraries, 1970.

DuBose, John W. *General Joseph Wheeler and the Army of Tennessee*. New York: Neale, 1912.

Durden, Robert F. *The Gray and the Black—The Confederate Debate on Emancipation*. Baton Rouge: LSU Press, 1972.

Durkin, Joseph T. *Stephen R. Mallory: Confederate Navy Chief*. Chapel Hill: UNC Press, 1954.

Durrill, Wayne K. *War of Another Kind: A Southern Community in the Great Rebellion*. New York: Oxford University Press, 1990.

Dyer, Frederick H. *A Compendium of the War of the Rebellion*. Des Moines, Iowa: Dyer Publishing, 1908. Reprint, Dayton, Ohio: Morningside Book-shop, 1978.

Edwards, John N. *Noted Guerrillas; or, The Warfare of the Border*. St. Louis: Bryan, Brand, 1877. Reprint, Dayton, Ohio: Morningside Bookshop, 1976.

Emerson, Edward W. *Life and Letters of Charles Russell Lowell*. Boston: Houghton Mifflin, 1907. Reprint, Port Washington, N.Y.: Kennikat Press, 1971.

Evans, Eli N. *Judah P. Benjamin: The Jewish Confederate*. New York: Free Press, 1988.

Evans, Robert G., ed. and comp. *The 16th Mississippi Infantry: Civil War Letters and Reminiscences*. Jackson: University Press of Mississippi, 2002.

Faust, Drew Gilpin. *The Creation of Confederate Nationalism: Ideology and Identity in the Civil War South*. Baton Rouge: LSU Press, 1989.

Fisher, John E. *They Rode with Forrest and Wheeler: A Chronicle of Five Tennessee Brothers' Service in the Confederate Western Cavalry*. Jefferson, N.C.: McFarland, 1995.

Fitzhugh, George. *Cannibals All! or, Slaves Without Masters*. Richmond, Va.: A. Morris, 1857.

Fleming, Walter L. *Civil War and Reconstruction in Alabama*. New York: Columbia University Press, 1905. Reprint, New York: Peter Smith, 1949.

Foner, Eric. *Forever Free: The Story of Emancipation and Reconstruction*. Picture ed. Joshua Brown. New York: Alfred A. Knopf, 2005.

Ford, Lacy K., Jr. *Origins of Southern Radicalism: The South Carolina Up-country, 1800–1860*. New York: Oxford University Press, 1991.

Fox, William F. *Regimental Losses in the American Civil War*. Albany, N.Y.: Albany Publishing, 1889.

Franklin, John Hope. *From Slavery to Freedom: A History of Negro Americans*. 3d ed. New York: Alfred A. Knopf, 1967.

——. *The Militant South, 1800–1861*. Cambridge: HU Press, 1956. Reprint, Boston: Beacon Press, 1966.

Gallagher, Gary W. *The Confederate War*. Cambridge: HU Press, 1997.

Genovese, Eugene D. *From Rebellion to Revolution: Afro-American Slave Revolts in the Making of the Modern World*. Baton Rouge: LSU Press, 1979.

Glatthaar, Joseph T. *Forged in Battle: The Civil War Alliance of Black Soldiers and White Officers*. New York: Free Press, 1990.

——. *The March to the Sea and Beyond: Sherman's Troops in the Savannah and Carolinas Campaigns*. New York: New York University Press, 1985.

Greene, Francis V. *The Mississippi*. New York: Charles Scribner's Sons, 1883.

Grimsley, Mark. *The Hard Hand of War: Union Military Policy Toward Southern Civilians, 1861–1865*. New York: Cambridge University Press, 1995.

Guthrie, James M. *Camp-Fires of the Afro-American; or The Colored Man as a Patriot, Soldier, Sailor*. Philadelphia: Afro-American Publishing, 1899. Reprint, New York: Johnson Reprint, 1970.

Hamlin, Charles E. *The Life and Times of Hannibal Hamlin*. Cambridge, Mass.: Riverside, 1899.

Hastings, Max. *Armageddon: The Battle for Germany, 1944–1945*. New York: Alfred A. Knopf, 2004

Hattaway, Herman, and Archer Jones. *How the North Won: A Military History of the Civil War*. Urbana: University of Illinois Press, 1983.

Hay, Thomas Robson. "The South and the Arming of the Slaves." *Mississippi Valley Historical Review* 6, no. 1 (June 1919–Mar. 1920): 34–73.

Hewitt, Lawrence L. *Port Hudson, Confederate Bastion on the Mississippi*. Baton Rouge: LSU Press, 1987.

Heymann, C. David. *American Aristocracy: The Lives and Times of James Russell, Amy and Robert Lowell*. New York: Dodd, Mead, 1980.

Hollandsworth, James G., Jr. "The Execution of White Officers from Black Units by Confederate Forces During the Civil War." *LH* 35, no. 3 (Fall 1994): 475–89.

Horn, Stanley F. *The Army of Tennessee*. Indianapolis: Bobbs-Merrill, 1941.

Hurst, Jack. *Nathan Bedford Forrest: A Biography*. New York: Alfred A. Knopf, 1993.

Jimerson, Randall C. *The Private Civil War*. Baton Rouge: LSU Press, 1988.

Jones, Archer. *Civil War Command and Strategy*. New York: The Free Press, 1992.

Jordan, John L. "Was There a Massacre at Fort Pillow?" *THQ* 6 (June 1947), 99–133.

Jordan, Thomas, and J. P. Pryor. *The Campaigns of Lieut.-Gen. N. B. Forrest, and of Forrest's Cavalry*. New Orleans: Blelock, 1868.

Jordan, Weymouth T., Jr., and Gerald W. Thomas. "Massacre at Plymouth: April 20, 1864." *NCHR* 73, no. 2 (Apr. 1995): 126–97.

Kerby, Robert L. *Kirby Smith's Confederacy: The Trans-Mississippi South, 1863–1865*. New York: Columbia University Press, 1972.

Leech, Margaret. *Reveille in Washington, 1860–1865*. New York: Harper & Brothers, 1941.

Leslie, Frank. *Frank Leslie's Illustrated: Famous Leaders and Battle Scenes of the Civil War*. Ed. Louis Shepheard Moat. New York: Mrs. Frank Leslie, 1896.

Levine, Bruce. *Confederate Emancipation: Southern Plans to Free and Arm Slaves during the Civil War*. New York: Oxford University Press, 2006.

Linderman, Gerald F. *Embattled Courage: The Experience of Combat in the American Civil War*. New York: Free Press, 1989.

Livermore, Thomas L. *Numbers and Losses in the Civil War in America, 1861–1865*. Boston: Houghton Mifflin, 1901. Reprint, Dayton, Ohio: Morningside Bookshop, 1986.

Lonn, Ella. *Desertion During the Civil War*. New York: Century, 1928. Reprint, Gloucester, Mass.: Peter Smith, 1966.

——. *Salt as a Factor in the Confederacy*. New York: Walter Neale, 1933.

Lord, Francis A. *They Fought for the Union*. Harrisburg, Pa.: Stackpole, 1960. Reprint, New York: Bonanza, 1960.

Lowry, Thomas P. *The Stories the Soldiers Wouldn't Tell: Sex in the Civil War*. Mechanicsburg, Pa.: Stackpole Books, 1994.

Mainfort, Robert C., Jr. "Fort Pillow Revisited: New Evidence About an Old Controversy." *CWH* 28, no. 4 (1982): 293–306.

Martin, Richard A., and Daniel L. Schafer. *Jacksonville's Ordeal by Fire: A Civil War History*. Ed. James R. Ward. Jacksonville, Fla.: Florida Publishing, 1984.

Marvel, William. "The Battle of Saltville: Massacre or Myth?" *Blue and Gray* 8, no. 6 (Aug. 1991): 10–19, 46–60.

McConnell, Stuart. *Glorious Contentment: The Grand Army of the Republic, 1865–1900*. Chapel Hill: UNC Press, 1996.

McPherson, James M. *Battle Cry of Freedom: The Civil War Era*. New York: Oxford University Press, 1988.

——. *Marching Toward Freedom: Blacks in the Civil War, 1861–1865*. New York: Facts on File, 1994. Originally published in different form. New York: Alfred A. Knopf, 1967.

——. *The Negro's Civil War: How American Negroes Felt and Acted During the War for the Union*. New York: Pantheon, 1965.

——. *What They Fought For 1861–1865*. Baton Rouge: LSU Press, 1994.

Miller, Francis T., ed. *The Photographic History of the Civil War*. 10 vols. New York: Review of Reviews, 1911.

Mitchell, Reid. *Civil War Soldiers*. New York: Viking, 1988. Reprint, New York: Touchstone, 1989.

——. *The Vacant Chair: The Northern Soldier Leaves Home*. New York: Oxford University Press, 1993.

Monaghan, Jay. *Civil War on the Western Border*. Boston: Little, Brown, 1955.

Montgomery, Horace. *Johnny Cobb: Confederate Aristocrat*. University of Georgia Monographs 11. Athens: UG Press, 1964.

Morris, Thomas D. *Southern Slavery and the Law, 1619–1860*. Chapel Hill: UNC Press, 1996.

Nisbett, Richard E., and Dov Cohen. *Culture of Honor: The Psychology of Violence in the South*. Boulder, Colo.: Westview Press, 1996.

Palfrey, Francis W. *Memoir of William Francis Bartlett*. Boston: Houghton, Osgood, 1878.

Paludan, Phillip Shaw. *A People's Contest: The Union and Civil War, 1861–1865*. New York: Harper & Row, 1988.

——. *The Presidency of Abraham Lincoln*. Lawrence: University Press of Kansas, 1994.

——. *Victims: A True Story of the Civil War*. Knoxville: University of Tennessee Press, 1981.

Paradis, James M. *Strike the Blow for Freedom: The 6th United States Colored Infantry in the Civil War.* Shippensburg, Pa.: White Mane, 1993.

Phisterer, Fredrick. *Statistical Record of the Armies of the United States,* New York: Charles Scribner's Sons, 1883, Reprint, New York: Blue & Gray Press, n.d.

Power, J. Tracy. *Lee's Miserables: Life in the Army of Northern Virginia from the Wilderness to Appomattox.* Chapel Hill: UNC Press, 1998.

Preisser, Thomas M. "The Virginia Decision to Use Negro Soldiers in the Civil War, 1864–1865." *VMH&B* 83, no. 1 (Jan. 1975): 98–113.

Quarles, Benjamin. *The Negro in the Civil War.* Boston: Little, Brown, 1953.

Rable, George C. *Civil Wars: Women and the Crisis of Southern Nationalism.* Urbana: University of Illinois Press, 1989.

Ramage, James A. *Gray Ghost: The Life of John Singleton Mosby.* Lexington: University Press of Kentucky, 1999.

Ramold, Steven J. *Slaves, Sailors, Citizens: African Americans in the Union Navy.* DeKalb: Northern Illinois University Press, 2002.

Randall, J. G. *The Civil War and Reconstruction.* Boston: D. C. Heath, 1953.

Robertson, James I., Jr. "The Scourge of Elmira." In *Civil War Prisons,* ed. William B. Hesseltine, 80–97. Kent, Ohio: Kent State University Press, 1962.

Rosnow, Ralph L. *Rumor and Gossip: The Social Psychology of Hearsay.* New York: Elsevier Scientific Publishing, 1976.

Rowell, John W. *Yankee Artillerymen: Through the Civil War with Eli Lily's Indiana Battery.* Knoxville: University of Tennessee Press, 1975.

Royster, Charles. *The Destructive War: William Tecumseh Sherman, Stonewall Jackson, and the Americans.* New York: Alfred A. Knopf, 1991.

Schott, Thomas E. *Alexander H. Stephens of Georgia: A Biography.* Baton Rouge: LSU Press, 1988.

Sensing, Thurman. *Champ Ferguson, Confederate Guerilla.* Nashville, Tenn.: Vanderbilt University Press, 1942.

Shannon, Fred A. "The Federal Government and the Negro Soldier, 1861–1865." *JNH* 11, no. 1 (Jan. 1926): 563–83.

Sievers, Henry J. *Benjamin Harrison.* 3 vols. Chicago: Henry Regnery, 1952.

Simpson, Brooks D. *Let Us Have Peace: Ulysses S. Grant and the Politics of War and Reconstruction, 1861–1868.* Chapel Hill: UNC Press, 1991.

Smith, John D., ed. *Black Soldiers in Blue: African American Troops in the Civil War Era.* Chapel Hill: UNC Press, 2002.

Stackpole, Edward J. *Sheridan in the Shenandoah: Jubal Early's Nemesis.* New York: Bonanza, 1961.

Stampp, Kenneth M. *Indiana Politics During the Civil War.* 2d ed. Bloomington: IU Press and the Indiana Historical Bureau, 1978.

Steiner, Bernard C. *Life of Reverdy Johnson.* Baltimore: Norman, Remington, 1914. Reprint. New York: Russell & Russell, 1970.

Stephenson, Darl L. *Headquarters in the Brush: Blazer's Independent Union Scouts.* Athens: Ohio University Press, 2001.

Stephenson, N. W. "The Question of Arming the Slaves." *American Histori-cal Review* 18, no. 2 (Jan. 1913): 295–308.

Sword, Wiley. *Southern Invincibility: A History of the Confederate Heart*. New York: St. Martin's, 1999.

Tarbell, Ida M. *The Life of Abraham Lincoln*. 4 vols. New York: Doubleday & McClure, 1900. Reprint, New York: Lincoln History Society, 1902.

Tatum, Georgia Lee. *Disloyalty in the Confederacy*. Chapel Hill: UNC Press, 1934. Reprint, New York: AMS Press, 1970.

Thayer, William R. *The Life and Letters of John Hay*. 2 vols. Boston: Hough-ton Mifflin, 1908.

Thomas, Benjamin P., and Harold M. Hyman. *Stanton: The Life and Times of Lincoln's Secretary of War*. New York: Alfred A. Knopf, 1962.

Trudeau, Noah A. *Like Men of War: Black Troops in the Civil War, 1862–1865*. Boston: Little, Brown, 1998.

Tuckerman, Charles K. "President Lincoln and Colonization." *MAH* 16, no. 4 (Oct. 1886): 329–32.

Urwin, Gregory J. W., ed., *Black Flag over Dixie: Racial Atrocities and Repri-sals in the Civil War*. Carbondale: Southern Illinois University Press, 2004.

Ward, Andrew. *River Run Red: The Fort Pillow Massacre in the American Civil War*. New York: Viking, 2005.

Ward, Geoffrey C. *The Civil War: An Illustrated History*. Based on film script by Geoffrey C. Ward, Ric Burns, and Ken Burns. New York: Alfred A. Knopf, 1995.

Warner, Ezra J. *Generals in Blue: Lives of the Union Commanders*. Baton Rouge: LSU Press, 1964.

———. *Generals in Gray: Lives of the Confederate Commanders*. Baton Rouge: LSU Press, 1959.

Washington, Versalle F. *Eagles on Their Buttons: A Black Infantry Regiment in the Civil War*. Columbia: University of Missouri Press, 1999.

Weinberg, Adelaide. *John Elliott Cairnes and the American Civil War: A Study in Anglo-American Relations*. London: Kingswood Press, [1969].

Wert, Jeffry D. *Mosby's Rangers*. New York: Simon and Schuster, 1990.

Westwood, Howard C. *Black Troops, White Commanders and Freedmen Dur-ing the Civil War*. Carbondale: Southern Illinois University Press, 1992.

Wiley, Bell Irvin. "Billy Yank and the Black Folk." *JNH* 36 (Spring 1951): 35–52.

———. *The Life of Johnny Reb, the Common Soldier of the Confederacy*. India-napolis: Bobbs-Merrill, 1943.

———. *Southern Negroes, 1861–1865*. New Haven, Conn.: YU Press, 1938.

Williams, Lou Falkner. *The Great South Carolina Ku Klux Klan Trials, 1871–1872*. Athens: UG Press, 1996.

Williams, T. Harry. *Lincoln and His Generals*. New York: Gramercy Press, 2001.

Wills, Brian Steel. *A Battle from the Start: The Life of Nathan Bedford Forrest*. New York: HarperCollins, 1992.

Wilson, Suzanne C., comp. *Column South with the Fifteenth Pennsylvania Cavalry, from Antietam to the Capture of Jefferson Davis.* Ed. J. Ferrell Colton and Antoinette G. Smith. Flagstaff, Ariz.: J. F. Colton, 1960.

Wilson, Woodrow. *A History of the American People.* 5 vols. New York: Harper & Brothers, 1901–2.

Winters, John D. *The Civil War in Louisiana.* Baton Rouge: LSU Press, 1963.

Wyeth, John Allan. *That Devil Forrest.* Originally published as *The Life of General Nathan Bedford Forrest.* New York: Harper & Bros., 1899. Reprint, New York: Harper & Bros., 1959.

Academic Papers

Bright, Simeon M. "The McNeill Rangers: A Study in Confederate Guerrilla Warfare." Master's thesis, West Virginia University, 1950.

Keen, Newton A. "The Civil War Experiences of Newton Asbury Keen." Ed. William C. Billingsley. Master's thesis, Texas Technological College, Lubbock, 1967.

Martin, N. B. "L. F. Hubbard and the Fifth Minnesota: Letters of a Union Volunteer, 1862–1866." History seminar project, San Francisco State College, 1956.

Mays, Thomas D. "The Price of Freedom: The Battle of Saltville and the Massacre of the Fifth United States Colored Cavalry." Master's thesis, Virginia Polytechnic Institute and State University, 1992.

Spraggins, Tinsley Lee. "Economic Aspects of Negro Colonization During the Civil War." Ph.D. diss., American University, Washington, D.C., 1957.

INDEX

The note "pl" indicates the presence of relevant plates in the gallery following page 134. Maps are indicated by "m" following the page number. The abbreviation "n" indicates a note.

George S. Burkhardt is an independent scholar and writer who lives in Long Beach, California, with his wife, an artist. Once a radio copywriter in Santa Barbara, California, then a daily newspaper reporter, Burkhardt once was the editor and publisher of California's smallest daily, the *Corning Daily Observer*. In the early 1980s, he began researching the ostensibly random atrocity incidents reported during the Civil War and eventually realized that a pattern existed. This book is the result of more than twenty years of that research.